Culture Blooming

Culture Blooming

Nurturing Workplaces Where People Grow

Abi Adamson

Berrett-Koehler
PUBLISHERS

Berrett-Koehler Publishers, Inc.
1333 Broadway, Suite P100
Oakland, CA 94612-1921
(510) 817-2277
bkconnection.com

Ordering Information
Quantity sales. Special discounts are available on quantity purchases by corporations, associations, individuals, and others. For details, please go to bkconnection.com to see our bulk discounts or contact bookorders@bkpub.com for more information.
Textbook exam/desk copies. Please consult the General FAQ at bkconnection.com.
Bookstore orders for trade or textbook use. For print books, please contact Penguin Random House Publisher Services at customerservice@penguinrandomhouse.com. For ebooks, contact your favorite distributor.

Distributed to the US trade and internationally by Penguin Random House Publisher Services.

The authorized representative in the EU for product safety and compliance is
EU Compliance Partner, Pärnu mnt. 139b-14, 11317 Tallinn, Estonia,
www.eucompliancepartner.com, +372 5368 65 02.

Printed in the United States of America

Berrett-Koehler books are printed on long-lasting acid-free paper. When it is available, we choose paper that has been manufactured by environmentally responsible processes. These may include using trees grown in sustainable forests, incorporating recycled paper, minimizing chlorine in bleaching, or recycling the energy produced at the paper mill.

Cataloging-in-Publication Data is on file at the Library of Congress.
Library of Congress Control Number: 2026008145
ISBN 9798890572103 (paperback) | ISBN 9798890572110 (pdf) | ISBN 9798890572127 (epub)

First Edition
35 34 33 32 31 30 29 28 27 26 10 9 8 7 6 5 4 3 2 1

Book production: Happenstance Type-O-Rama
Cover design: Ashley Ingram
Cover photograph: Allec Gomes

For my granny Comfort Iyabode,
who has loved me the way sunflowers love the sun:
completely, warmly, and without condition.
And for everyone who has ever wilted in the wrong soil.

CONTENTS

INTRODUCTION: Why Good People Can't Bloom 1

1. Soil: The Dirt in Your Organization 11

2. Exposure: The Monopoly on Visibility 31

3. Roots: The Underground Truth Network 57

4. Nutrients: The Food That Feeds Performance 83

5. Weathering Storms: Growth Always Attracts Storms 113

THE BLOOM 131

ACKNOWLEDGMENTS 149

NOTES 151

INDEX 153

ABOUT THE AUTHOR 163

INTRODUCTION

Why Good People Can't Bloom

The language we use to describe organizational culture reveals everything about how we think it works. We talk about *building* culture, *engineering* values, and *driving* change. These words expose a fundamental belief that culture is something we construct from blueprints, like a building with rigid specifications and a project manager who's had too much coffee. I once believed this too and realized I was wrong.

When I moved into talent acquisition at a marketing company, I'd hired nearly 65 percent of the workforce. When a career-defining opportunity arose to lead C-suite recruiting abroad, I confidently put myself forward, practically doing jazz hands in my enthusiasm. The response? "Abi, you're good, but you would not have gotten that person over the line." I'm sorry, what? I'd successfully hired enough senior leaders to fill a small yacht. Apparently, I lacked some mysterious X-factor visible only to those with special corporate vision goggles. This wasn't a one-hit wonder of workplace weirdness. At another company where I'd made significant contributions, I got an encore performance: "You've done amazing work, but you're not the right fit for the next level." Not the right fit? I had helped build these organizations from the ground up. How could I not embody the cultures I'd helped create? It was like being told I couldn't join my own surprise party.

These moments exposed the fundamental absurdity in how so many organizations approach culture. By treating culture as something to be engineered from blueprints, a VIP nightclub with velvet ropes and an arbitrary bouncer, we create environments where people must choose between authenticity and belonging. We reject brilliance when it arrives wearing the wrong shoes. The costs are staggering. Innovation flatlines when diverse perspectives get bounced at the door. Talent sprints for the exit when conformity becomes a straitjacket. Organizations fossilize when they confuse uniformity with unity.

Here's what drove me to write this book: This approach doesn't just limit organizations; it dehumanizes people. I've witnessed extraordinary candidates rejected because they wouldn't participate in "Fun Fridays" that involved competitive beer-chugging. I've seen brilliant minds dismissed because they refused to play the exhausting game of ego-stroking just to get noticed. I've watched talented individuals wilt because they couldn't remove essential parts of their identity at the office door. I've also seen the opposite. Organizations where those same people flourished. Where difference was fuel, not friction. The gap between those kinds of experiences is what this book is about.

For those already inside toxic cultures, it's like fog that thickens so slowly no one notices until they can't see clearly anymore. Authentic voices get muffled. Those who question the status quo become "troublemakers." The invitation to bring your authentic self to work? It comes with an unspoken caveat: only the parts that match the existing furniture, please. This isn't just happening to a few people, either. That brilliant engineer who stopped speaking up in meetings, that innovative marketer whose ideas mysteriously die in committee, that high performer who just handed in their notice: They're all caught in the same broken system, one that promises growth but delivers conformity, that preaches innovation while punishing difference. After watching this pattern repeat across every organization, from scrappy startups to Fortune 500s, I developed The Culture Partnership. Not to create another employee program or engagement initiative, but to fundamentally reimagine how we think about organizational culture. The partnership was formed to help leaders understand why their expensive culture transformations keep failing and what actually works instead.

A quick word about me: I started my career as a film graduate who dreamed of storytelling in Hollywood, until I watched nepotism reward mediocrity while brilliance got shown the door. That disillusionment sent me back to the drawing board, where I started from scratch as an office manager and then HR assistant. From there, I moved steadily upward through Head of People and Talent to Director of Talent, until I finally founded The Culture Partnership. I've been quoted in *The New York Times* and *Forbes*; written for publications including *Metro*, *Raconteur*, and *People Management*; delivered a TEDx talk called "Who Owns Culture"; and spent over a decade immersed in HR, culture, and talent acquisition, all in service of helping people thrive at work. The stories in this book come from three places: my own experiences navigating workplace cultures, people who have trusted me with their lived experiences, and organizations across industries and continents I've partnered with as a consultant.

What Culture Actually Is

Let me clarify what I mean by "culture" in this book. I'm not talking about foosball tables, free snacks, or forced fun at company retreats. Culture is the living ecosystem of shared behaviors, beliefs, and conditions that determine what actually happens in an organization, not what the motivational posters claim should happen. It's the difference between what gets promised in the recruitment phase and what people whisper in exit interviews. Culture is whether an "open door policy" means people actually walk through that door or have learned that the door leads to career quicksand. It's whether "work-life balance" means flexibility to handle life's complexities or working from home while still answering emails at midnight. It's the unwritten rules everyone follows, the invisible hierarchies that outweigh the org chart, and the actual behaviors that get rewarded versus the ones mentioned in the values statement.

At its best, culture creates spaces where people feel safe enough to bring their true selves, where "too muchness" becomes a superpower rather than a liability, where multicultural teams don't just coexist but create innovation at the intersections of their differences, and where managers understand they're shaping human lives, not just quarterly results. Here's the thing: You can't engineer culture. You can't build it from blueprints or force it through initiatives and programs. Culture isn't constructed; it's cultivated. It grows when you create the right conditions and have the wisdom to let it evolve naturally. People are the same. They grow when conditions are right, not because personal development has been mandated or growth sessions have been scheduled (although these can certainly help). They flourish when the soil is healthy, when they receive enough light, and when toxins are removed, through thoughtful attention to the environment rather than corporate engineering.

The framework I'd been searching for was hidden in plain sight.

A few years ago, I was in my friend Kyra's kitchen, complaining about life's challenges (as you do when your career feels like a dumpster fire with good benefits). She looked at me and said simply: "Biddy, you've got to grow through what you go through." Something about that phrase stuck. Grow through, not just go through. It rattled around my brain for weeks until one evening, as I watched David Attenborough narrate *The Green Planet*, everything clicked. My beloved granny had told me something similar thirty years earlier. In our childhood home's garden in West London, she'd ruled over verdant chaos with profound wisdom. Wildflowers crashed the vegetable party. Heritage plants gossiped with experimental newcomers. She didn't battle nature; she danced with it. "The garden knows what it wants to be," she'd told me in Yoruba. "My job is to listen and help it become magnificent." Thirty years later, sitting on my sofa watching plants communicate through underground networks while Kyra's words echoed in my head, I finally understood. Organizations aren't machines to be engineered. They're gardens. Living ecosystems grow through their challenges when given the right conditions. You can't force or blueprint them; you can only create environments where they naturally flourish.

This revelation led me to develop the SERN framework, a way of understanding organizational culture through four essential elements that actually determine what grows: Soil (the truth about what's really happening in an organization), Exposure (who gets seen and how), Roots (the hidden connections holding everything together), and Nutrients (what people truly need to thrive). This isn't another acronym to memorize. It's a completely different way of thinking about culture. SERN reveals culture as a living system that already exists within every organization, growing in the soil, hiding in the shadows, connecting through underground roots, fed or starved by nutrient distribution. Unlike traditional approaches that try to impose culture through initiatives and mandates, SERN works with natural organizational patterns. It doesn't ask "What should culture be?" but rather "What is culture really, and who is it really serving?" Once you see an organization through this lens, you can't unsee it. You'll walk into work and recognize the toxic soil. You'll notice who's hoarding the light. You'll understand why certain people have shallow roots. You'll see who's creating nutrients and who's draining them.

Working with global organizations, I've used this framework to transform how they see culture, not through more programs or initiatives, but through understanding and working with the living system that already exists. The results? Innovation erupts like spring after winter. Engagement deepens beyond surface-level pizza parties. Authentic belonging flourishes even in the midst of chaos and change.

The Ground We'll Cover

In the chapters ahead, I'll show you exactly how the SERN model works and how to apply it to your organization:

Chapter 1: Soil

We'll dig into the cultural reality, the truth about what's really happening versus what the website claims. You'll learn to identify toxins poisoning the environment and understand why some organizations prefer to keep their soil toxic.

Chapter 2: Exposure

We'll examine who gets the light and who's withering in shadows. You'll discover how opportunity gets hoarded and why meritocracy is often a myth.

Chapter 3: Roots

We'll explore where real culture lives: not in town halls but in the whisper networks and group chats where people share what's actually happening.

Chapter 4: Nutrients

We'll identify what people actually need to thrive (hint: it's not pizza Fridays) and why some people drain nutrients from everyone around them.

Chapter 5: Weathering Storms

We'll prepare organizations for the unforeseen challenges that threaten every garden and provide tools to keep culture intact when everything else is falling apart.

The Bloom

We'll explore the ultimate goal: cultures that sustain and regenerate themselves without constant intervention.

Throughout, I'll share raw, sometimes funny, often painful stories from my own journey through corporate dysfunction. You'll meet the executive who was surprised that Black people eat more than fried chicken, the leader who Febreze'd her way through nonsensical salary decisions, and the HR leader who wanted to store Muslim employees in toilets during Ramadan. These aren't just stories; they're teaching moments about what happens when we try to engineer humans instead of creating conditions where they can grow naturally.

This book is for every leader mystified by their culture's failure to launch, every HR professional ready to flip tables over persistent inclusion fails, and every manager desperate to build a team where people actually want to show up. It's also for every employee who's felt invisible or performed corporate cosplay to fit into cultures that were never designed for them. You shouldn't need to shrink yourself to belong, and your unique perspective isn't organizational kryptonite; it's rocket fuel for any company smart enough to recognize it.

Fair warning: This isn't your typical workplace culture book. I tell uncomfortable truths wrapped in humor because sometimes you need to laugh to keep from screaming. I name the elephants that others pretend don't exist while they're being squashed against the corporate walls. I won't pretend that complex human systems can be fixed with prescriptive steps and motivational quotes, but I do offer something more valuable: a way to see organizations as the living ecosystems they actually are. The SERN framework isn't another process to implement; it's a lens that reveals the patterns already shaping any culture, whether they've been noticed or not. By the time you finish this book, you'll look at organizational culture differently. You'll notice the patterns that were previously invisible. You'll understand why so many culture initiatives keep failing. Most importantly, you'll know how to create conditions where people can actually thrive.

This isn't about feel-good platitudes or quick fixes. It's about understanding the living system we're actually working with, not the one we wish we had. It's about recognizing that people aren't machines to be optimized but gardens to be cultivated. It's about accepting that real transformation requires getting our hands dirty. Some readers may realize their soil is too poisoned to save, and that's valuable knowledge too; better to plant elsewhere than keep bleeding talent into toxic ground. Others will discover that the culture isn't actually broken; it's working exactly as designed, just not for the people it claims to serve. That recognition alone might be worth the price of admission.

Ready to see what's really growing? To understand who's hoarding the light and why certain roots run so deep? To discover what people actually need versus what organizations keep force-feeding them?

Gloves on. It's time to sift through the soil.

AUTHOR'S NOTE

The stories and examples in this book are based on real experiences from my in-house experiences, consulting work, and professional observations spanning over a decade. To protect privacy and confidentiality, all names, identifying details, industries, and locations have been changed or composited. Some examples represent common patterns I've observed across multiple organizations rather than single incidents. Any resemblance to specific individuals or organizations is coincidental.

The "Febreze Queen" and other memorable characters represent composite experiences that illustrate broader organizational patterns. No single person or company should recognize themselves, as these are amalgamations of behaviors witnessed across numerous workplaces.

This book is intended to provide insight and provoke thought about organizational culture. It is not intended as specific advice for any particular organization or situation. Readers should consult appropriate professionals for advice specific to their circumstances.

The views expressed in this book are solely my own and do not necessarily reflect the views of any organizations mentioned or any clients past or present.

1

Soil

The Dirt in Your Organization

Organizational culture isn't what gets claimed on websites and in town halls. It's what people experience when nobody's watching: the accumulated toxins, memories, and conditions that determine whether anything can grow. Many leaders have no idea what's actually in their soil, which explains their confusion when nothing blooms.

What Soil Really Is

An organization's soil is the accumulated truth of every decision, every broken promise, every person who got promoted despite complaints about them, and every whistleblower who got silenced. It's not what the CEO talks about at town halls. It's what people experience at 3 p.m. on a Wednesday when they're exhausted, behind on deadlines, and suddenly summoned by their manager to "hop on a quick call" that everyone knows will steal an hour and solve nothing. Soil is organizational reality, not aspiration. It's the difference between a website's claim that "our people are our greatest asset" and the fact that the company just laid off 20 percent of those assets to boost quarterly earnings. It's the gap between the "speak up culture" mentioned in onboarding and what really happens when someone disagrees with leadership. It's a question of whether HR exists to protect the people or to protect the company from its people.

Organizational soil holds memory. That time leadership promised transparency, then made decisions in secret? Still in there. The manager who got promoted after three people requested transfers? That's composting into cultural DNA. The "anonymous" survey that required an employee ID? That taught everyone exactly how much the company values honest feedback. New employees don't need orientation to learn the real rules; the soil teaches them everything within their first week. Think about how actual soil works. Every plant that dies, every leaf that falls, every organism that decomposes becomes part of what feeds the next generation. Organizations work the same way. That founder who built a culture of fear twenty years ago? Their toxicity is still feeding current dysfunction. The mass layoff from 2020 that "saved the company"? Employees still hesitate to invest emotionally because the soil remembers betrayal. The sexual harassment settlement that got buried in NDAs? That silence composted into a culture where predators feel protected.

Here's what rarely gets admitted: Some organizations prefer toxic soil. It keeps people anxious, competitive, and easier to control. I worked with a consulting firm whose CEO opened every town hall talking about "psychological safety" and "bringing your authentic self to work," then visibly rolled his eyes when someone asked a challenging question. The eye roll was quick, but it taught a master class in what really happens to people who speak up. Next town hall? Softball questions only. The soil had just revealed that psychological safety was performance art, not actual policy. The most dangerous part? Toxic soil doesn't just affect those planted in it; it seeps into everything. That startup that claims they're different but hired all their leaders from the same toxic corporation? They're importing contaminated soil and wondering why the same problems sprout. The nonprofit with beautiful values but burnout rates that would make a certain online retailer blush? Their soil is sending a different message than their mission statement.

I've consulted with organizations that spend fortunes trying to plant new cultural initiatives in poisoned soil, then wonder why nothing grows. They launch innovation programs in soil contaminated by decades of punishing failure. They preach collaboration in soil where backstabbing gets people promoted. They demand authenticity in soil that has taught everyone to play corporate roulette for survival. Organizational soil speaks every day through patterns that get ignored. The meeting where everyone agrees, but nothing changes. The talented people who leave after exactly eighteen months. The innovations that die in committee. The exit interviews that all mention the same issues leadership doesn't care to address. The way certain demographics cluster at a specific level, like sedimentation. These aren't isolated incidents; they're the soil rumbling for attention.

Testing organizational soil requires courage that most companies lack. It means looking at who thrives and who merely survives. It means admitting that maybe the problem isn't an inability to find "good people." Maybe the soil is so toxic that good people can't grow there. Maybe it's not a garden at all, but a parking lot painted green, where nothing can bloom through the concrete. Some of this contamination has accumulated naturally over time: the residue of old decisions, departed leaders, and forgotten crises composting into dysfunction. Some of it, though? Someone's been carefully tending that toxic garden bed for years. The difference matters. Accidental toxins can be cleaned up once identified. Deliberate toxins have protectors. Until organizations know which kind they're dealing with, they're just guessing at solutions.

Too many leaders breathe recycled executive air genuinely believing their cultures match their PowerPoints. They think engagement scores mean people are engaged. They assume silence means agreement. They interpret the absence of complaints as the presence of satisfaction. The first step to rehabilitating toxic soil is admitting we're all probably somewhat delusional about what's actually growing in it.

Here's a simple diagnostic: When was the last time someone three levels below a leader told them something that made them genuinely uncomfortable about the organization? Not a minor process improvement suggestion, but something that challenged fundamental assumptions about how the company operates. If it's been more than nine months, they're not hearing the truth. They're hearing what their employees think they want to hear, carefully filtered through layers of career preservation.

MIT Sloan researchers tracked why people actually leave companies—not the polite fiction of exit interviews, but the real reasons. Toxic culture proved 10.4 times more likely to predict turnover than compensation.[1] People will literally take pay cuts to escape toxic soil, yet leaders remain convinced ping-pong tables will fix everything. The study identified five toxic attributes: disrespectful, noninclusive, unethical, cutthroat, and abusive. These attributes don't announce themselves; they hide in plain sight, thriving in conference rooms while everyone pretends not to notice.

The real culture reveals itself in patterns everyone sees but nobody names. That toxic executive who's been reported to HR seventeen times but still has a corner office? That's the actual values statement. The way certain demographics cluster at certain levels despite stated diversity commitments? That's the real inclusion policy. The identical issues mentioned in every exit interview for five years? That's the authentic employee experience, no matter what the engagement survey claims.

Want to know what organizational soil really contains? Follow the fear. Where do people hesitate before speaking? Which topics create suddenly busy calendars when discussions get scheduled? What patterns do people joke about at drinks but never mention in meetings? Fear is an organization's most honest consultant, showing leaders exactly where the soil is most contaminated.

Watch who thrives versus who survives. If an organization's top performers share suspiciously similar backgrounds, communication styles, and weekend hobbies, it's not running a meritocracy. It's running a mirror factory, promoting reflections of existing leadership while wondering why innovation died. This isn't about blame; most leaders don't consciously create these patterns. The patterns emerge from a thousand unconscious preferences, each of them seeming reasonable in isolation but collectively creating soil that sustains only one type of plant.

The gap between stated culture and actual culture lives in the mundane moments nobody documents. How long does it take to reach a simple decision? How many people review an email before it gets sent to leadership? How often do meetings end with clear next steps versus some vague agreement to "circle back"? How many times does someone say "let's take this offline" when conversations get uncomfortable? These daily frustrations aren't process problems; they're soil samples, showing exactly what's contaminating the environment.

I once worked with a tech company that cited innovation as its number one value. They also had a policy where any failed project triggered a "retrospective," which was really an interrogation about who to blame. Engineers began doubling their timelines and only proposed features that already existed at competitors. When I showed leadership this disconnect, they spent forty minutes explaining how "accountability drives innovation." That's organizational soil talking: the ability to hold completely opposing realities and be convinced they align. Here's a truth that might sting a little: Any leader reading this and thinking *Thank God my culture isn't toxic* is probably wrong. Not because of malice, but because the leadership position creates blind spots. The higher leaders rise, the more filtered their reality becomes. People don't lie to them exactly; they just carefully curate what gets seen, like Instagram for executives. Leaders get the highlight reel, while the blooper reel plays on repeat for everyone else.

The good news? Soil can be tested, and once we know what's really in it, we can start rehabilitation. It's not an overnight transformation, because soil doesn't work that way. Real change happens through patient amendment: removing toxins, adding nutrients, and creating conditions where different things can grow. The first step is to stop pretending the soil smells like freshly picked roses when everyone else is choking on the fumes.

Your Contamination Stories

Every organization has contamination stories. The big spills everyone remembers: the executive who screamed at an intern during the holiday party, the mass layoff announced via email while leadership was at a retreat, the whistleblower who got fired for reporting fraud. These dramatic moments get attention, sometimes even action. Most contamination, however, happens through paper cuts. Tiny, daily toxins that individually seem survivable but collectively poison everything. The meeting where women's ideas get ignored until men repeat them. The "optional" after-work events that determine who gets promoted. The unspoken rule that you can't have a family photo on your desk if it shows a same-sex partner (yes, some organizations still have these bigoted views).

I've spent years collecting these stories, watching how small contaminations accumulate into toxic cultures. Each story teaches something about how soil becomes poisoned, why people tolerate it, and what it really costs. There's the account manager who started documenting every interaction after her ideas kept getting attributed to male colleagues. She had spreadsheets tracking who said what, when, and how credit got redistributed. Three months of data revealed a clear pattern: Her ideas consistently became "team efforts," while her male peers' identical contributions were recognized as individual achievements. When she presented this data to leadership, they told her she was keeping score instead of being a team player. She left six months later, and to this day, they're still wondering why they can't retain talented women.

Then there's the software engineer who noticed that his code reviews took three times longer than those of his white colleagues doing identical work. Same quality, same complexity, wildly different scrutiny. He started conducting an experiment, submitting code under a colleague's name with permission. Approval time dropped by 70 percent. When he revealed the experiment, management called him manipulative rather than addressing what his experiment exposed. The message was clear: Proving discrimination was worse than practicing it.

These aren't isolated incidents. They're symptoms of contaminated soil that organizations refuse to acknowledge because acknowledgment would require action, and action would require admitting that maybe the problem isn't finding good people but creating conditions where good people can thrive. The paper cuts start to compound. The woman documenting her stolen ideas also navigates being interrupted in every meeting. The engineer facing biased code reviews also gets excluded from the informal networks where real decisions happen. Each person carries dozens of these cuts, spending energy on survival that could go toward innovation.

What makes these contaminations particularly toxic is how they get rationalized. "That's just his communication style." "She needs to be more assertive." "He should adapt to our culture." Organizations become Olympic-level gymnasts, contorting logic to avoid acknowledging that their soil is poisoned. They'd rather believe in individual failures than systemic contamination. Meanwhile, protected contaminations teach everyone that toxicity plus results equals job security. The collaborative manager who develops talent but misses one aggressive target gets managed out, and the organization absorbs this lesson: Be toxic and successful rather than supportive and steady.

Some contaminations hide behind progressive language. The company that talks about "radical transparency" while punishing anyone who uses it. The startup that preaches "work-life integration," when what they really mean is work-life domination. The organization that celebrates "authentic leadership" unless that authenticity includes admitting uncertainty or showing vulnerability. I watched a tech company poison their soil with "data-driven decision making" that counted only certain data. Customer satisfaction scores? Critical. Employee attrition rates? "Not a key metric." Sprint velocity? Tracked hourly. Whether anyone could sustain that pace? Never asked. They had seventeen dashboards for product performance and zero for team health. The message was clear: Ship code, not humans.

These contamination stories all share one characteristic: They happen in plain sight while everyone pretends not to see them. This brings us to the patterns that truly run organizations, the ones growing in darkness, away from the official spotlight. While leaders focus on official org charts and documented processes, real culture thrives in the shadows. Hidden patterns, apparently invisible to leadership but obvious to everyone else, actually determine how work gets done, who succeeds, and why certain problems persist despite numerous initiatives aimed at solving them.

These patterns grow in darkness because bringing them to light would require uncomfortable admissions. The executive team that's 90 percent people who attended the same three universities? Pure coincidence, surely. Nothing to do with the CEO's alumni network or the board's obsession with ivy-covered credentials. The way opportunities flow through golf outings and whiskey tastings? Just relationship building, totally unrelated to why working mothers and people who don't drink never seem to advance. The fact that every "high potential" employee has the same haircut, handshake, and hometown? Meritocracy at its finest. Definitely not pattern matching masquerading as talent identification.

I once mapped the real power structure at a media company. The official org chart showed clear reporting lines and logical hierarchies. The actual influence map revealed something else entirely. The CFO's executive assistant wielded more power than most directors since she controlled access to budget approvals and could fast-track or bury any request. A random senior analyst in strategy had outsized influence because he wrote the CEO's speeches and quarterly board presentations, essentially controlling the narrative of what mattered. The technical architect who'd survived fifteen years of reorganizations was the person actually making decisions on technology investments while executives played elaborate vendor selection games in boardrooms.

These shadow structures determine everything. That brilliant initiative that mysteriously died? The assistant never put it on the CFO's calendar because she didn't like how someone spoke to her. That terrible project that somehow got funded? The analyst included it in the CEO's "strategic priorities" presentation. That obvious technical problem everyone sees but nobody fixes? The architect profits from being the only one who understands the legacy system. Watch how information really flows rather than how it supposedly flows. Official communication cascades down through careful hierarchies, while real information spreads through smoke breaks, bathroom conversations, and private Slack channels. By the time official communication arrives, everyone already knows what's happening, has formed opinions, and has decided whether to comply or just pretend.

The shadow culture has its own language. When leadership says "challenging quarter," employees hear "layoffs coming." When managers say "developmental opportunity," everyone knows that means thankless work nobody else wanted. When HR announces "exciting changes," people update their resumes. This translation gap between official speech and shadow understanding creates parallel realities within the same organization. Hidden patterns also determine who belongs versus who's perpetually auditioning. There's the official onboarding process, then there's the real initiation that happens through countless subtle tests. Do you laugh at the right jokes? Do you stay for the ostensibly optional but actually mandatory drinks? Do you complain about the right things while accepting the real problems? Pass these tests, and the doors open; fail them, and you'll spend your entire career wondering why you're always overlooked despite excellent performance.

The shadow culture maintains its own justice system. That leader everyone knows is toxic but HR won't dare touch? The shadow culture routes around them, warning new employees, protecting each other, creating elaborate workarounds. That unfair policy nobody can officially challenge? The shadow culture quietly ignores it, creating unofficial procedures that actually work.

What's truly damaging, though, is that the shadow culture often preserves the very toxins that official culture claims to eliminate. While leadership preaches innovation, the shadow culture punishes risk-takers who fail. While policies promote work-life balance, the shadow culture tracks who leaves "early" at 6 p.m. While values celebrate diversity, the shadow culture ensures conformity through thousands of micro-punishments for difference.

These hidden patterns resist change because they serve someone's interests. That convoluted approval process everyone hates? It gives someone power. That meeting that accomplishes nothing? It makes someone feel important. That report nobody reads? It justifies someone's existence. Until we understand who benefits from dysfunction, we can't understand why it persists despite everyone agreeing that it's problematic. Because here's what rarely gets admitted:

Organizational dysfunction isn't rotting; it's composting into exactly the culture someone wants to grow.

Dysfunction by Design (and Who Benefits)

Here's an uncomfortable truth that external consultants rarely share: Some toxic cultures are working exactly as designed. Not accidentally toxic but deliberately cultivated to serve specific interests. I learned this at a financial services firm that spent millions on culture transformation while mysteriously maintaining every structure that created toxicity. The ranking system that pitted teammates against each other stayed because it gave leadership ultimate control over compensation and promotion. The ridiculous expense approval process requiring seven signatures remained because those seven signature holders derived their entire sense of importance from being gatekeepers. The culture of fear ensured that nobody questioned why executives made four hundred times what frontline workers made.

Stanford's organizational behavior team studied companies like this one, organizations that complained about the same problems for years without dismantling the structures that had created them. They coined the term "functional dysfunction" to describe problems that serve hidden purposes.[2] That byzantine expense approval process discourages people from spending money, saving the budget without official cuts. The meeting that never accomplishes anything makes insecure leaders feel important.

The diagnostic question is simple: Who would lose power if these problems got solved? Those are the people ensuring they never do.

I watched a media company where innovation went to die in committee for five years. The committee's stated purpose was to evaluate new ideas; its actual function was to protect the status quo with bureaucratic brutality. The committee chair had built her entire career on a product line that any real innovation would instantly make obsolete. Every meeting was a funeral for fresh thinking. Every rejection was her desperately clutching at relevance. Everyone knew exactly what was happening, yet nobody dared name it. The soil had taught them that speaking truth was career sabotage.

Some organizations need their people to be anxious. Anxious people don't organize, don't question, and don't leave for better opportunities, because anxiety whispers that everywhere else is worse. They work harder, trying to achieve the security that the system ensures they'll never reach. The same media company's leadership revealed this during a strategy session about "performance management." When discussing their annual forced ranking system that required firing 10 percent of staff regardless of actual performance, the COO explained it was about "maintaining excellence" and "keeping standards high," while the CEO added that it "reinforced accountability" and created a "high-performance culture." What they were really saying was that the constant threat of arbitrary termination kept everyone desperate to prove their value. People worked unpaid overtime, skipped vacations, and accepted abuse from customers and management alike because they knew that come ranking season, someone had to go. The soil was deliberately poisoned with insecurity, not because it saved money (it didn't), but because fearful employees don't unionize, don't make demands, and don't question authority.

Every organization protects certain toxic high performers, not despite their toxicity but because of it. They serve a function: creating fear, modeling ruthless behavior, showing everyone what happens when results get prioritized over people. One toxic senior leader can contaminate an entire division, ensuring nobody gets too comfortable, too confident, or too willing to challenge the system. Their toxicity isn't accidental; it's instrumental.

Those inclusion initiatives that never seem to change anything? They're not supposed to. They exist to demonstrate effort, not create change. Real inclusion would redistribute power, and those currently holding power aren't interested in sharing, so organizations get diversity theatrics instead: visible hiring, invisible barriers, representation without influence, presence without power.

I consulted for a tech company that spent $1.5 million annually on various diversity initiatives while maintaining interview processes that systematically excluded anyone who didn't match their pattern. They had unconscious bias training every quarter (I know because I facilitated them), diverse interview panels, and hiring targets. What they also had was a "culture fit" evaluation that somehow always favored people who played the same sports, attended the same schools, and laughed at the same jokes as existing leadership. When I showed them the data revealing that 87 percent of hires came from the same five universities despite a candidate pool from hundreds of others, they created a "diverse recruiting initiative" that flew people in from different schools for interviews they'd never pass. The soil had spoken: The goal was to look inclusive, not be inclusive.

The dysfunction persists because fixing it would require admitting it exists, and admitting it exists would require acknowledging who created it. Leaders would have to say, "We built a system that hurts people to help ourselves." That level of honesty would crack foundations built on carefully maintained delusions. Instead, organizations develop what I call "solution charades": hiring consultants to diagnose problems they already know exist, creating task forces to study issues they have no intention of fixing, launching initiatives designed to fail gracefully so they can say "we tried" while ensuring nothing actually changes. The soil absorbs this pattern and teaches everyone that change is performance, not progress.

Gallup's decades of workplace research exposed an organizational truth everyone pretends not to know: Only 23 percent of employees strongly agree their managers provide meaningful feedback, yet 70 percent of the variance in team engagement is determined solely by the manager.[3] Organizations have this data and know exactly who their terrible managers are through complaints, exit interviews, and engagement scores. They keep them anyway because those managers serve a function: maintaining the power structure that benefits those already in power.

The truth is that organizational soil might be toxic by design, not through malicious intent but through accumulated decisions that served short-term interests and eventually hardened into permanent dysfunction. The executive who hoarded information to stay indispensable taught others to do the same. The board that rewarded quarterly results over sustainable growth created a culture of shortcuts. The founder who hired friends created a network that now excludes outsiders. Each decision made sense in isolation; together, they created soil that poisoned anyone planted in it.

This brings us to the question nobody wants to ask: If the soil is this contaminated, can it actually be transformed? The answer, thankfully, is yes, but only when organizations stop treating symptoms and start examining root causes. Understanding who benefits from dysfunction is the first step toward dismantling it. Once leaders can name the hidden interests that maintain toxicity, they can begin making different choices. Soil doesn't transform overnight, but it does transform when someone finally decides that the cost of maintaining it has become greater than the discomfort of changing it. The organizations I've seen successfully rehabilitate their cultures share one trait: They stopped pretending the contamination was accidental and started asking who had been tending the toxic garden, and why.

Transforming Your Environment

Once you've diagnosed the toxic soil, identified the contamination sources, mapped the hidden patterns, and understood the beneficiaries of dysfunction, what next? Burn it all down and start over? Attempt rehabilitation? Keep applying Band-aids while people update their resumes? While soil rehabilitation is possible, it's not pleasant.

It requires getting dirty, disturbing established systems, and facing resistance from those who've adapted to the toxins. Some people have built entire careers on navigating dysfunction, and they don't want it fixed.

Real transformation starts with admitting the depth of contamination. I'm not referring to the corporate admission that acknowledges "areas for improvement" while maintaining everything that created those areas; I mean the uncomfortable admission that maybe the organization has been actively harming people while pretending to help them.

The media company I mentioned earlier finally faced its reality after years of proclaiming "innovation and excellence" while running on a skeleton crew doing the work of three people each. Everyone knew they were two resignations away from complete collapse, but leadership kept announcing "record-breaking efficiency" to investors. The shift didn't come from some grand confession; it came when their star team, five people who essentially kept the company running, all resigned the same week. Their exit wasn't coordinated or malicious; they were just burnt out and exhausted. The CEO called an emergency all-hands to announce a "transition plan," but the room was half empty because much of the company had called in sick in solidarity.

The CFO, whom everyone assumed was part of the problem, opened her laptop and pulled up the real P&L on the main screen: not the polished investor deck, but the internal one showing they'd been cannibalizing operations to hit quarterly targets for three years. "This is why they left," she said. "We all know it. The question is whether we keep pretending otherwise or actually fix it." She didn't make a speech; she just left the spreadsheet up and walked out. The soil rehabilitation began not with inspiration but with someone finally showing the numbers that proved what everyone already knew.

Rehabilitation requires removing toxin sources, not just treating symptoms. That executive who contaminates every meeting with aggression needs to go, regardless of their results. That system pitting teammates against each other must be dismantled, even if it's been there forever. Those informal networks hoarding opportunities need to be exposed and restructured, despite the political cost.

Here's what most organizations get wrong: They try to add good soil on top of bad. They launch wellness initiatives while maintaining conditions that lead to burnout, celebrate innovation while punishing failure, and preach psychological safety while protecting those who destroy it. Fertilizing poison and expecting peonies doesn't work.

True soil rehabilitation happens in layers. First, stop adding new toxins. This sounds obvious, but organizations keep hiring toxic "rainmakers," implementing destructive policies, and promoting people who model the wrong behaviors, essentially pouring poison into the garden while wondering why nothing grows.

Second, remove the contamination sources, which is where courage matters. That high performer who makes people cry? Gone. The ranking system that creates fear? Eliminated. The meeting that wastes everyone's time but makes someone feel important? Cancelled. There will be resistance and discomfort, but the alternative is accepting that the soil will remain toxic forever.

Third, let the soil rest. Organizations hate this step because it feels like nothing's happening, but after removing toxins, soil needs time to neutralize. People need to see that changes are real, not just another initiative that'll be abandoned when it gets difficult, and trust rebuilds slowly. Rushing this process guarantees failure.

Fourth, add what's desperately needed. Once soil has begun recovering, you can introduce positive elements, though determining what exactly to add is its own journey, as we'll explore in Chapter 4. Recovered soil needs careful feeding, not dumping everything at once and hoping something works.

Finally, protect new growth. The first signs of a healthy culture are fragile and need protection from organizational antibodies, those forces that attack anything threatening the status quo. This might mean shielding pilot programs from premature scrutiny, protecting early adopters from retaliation, or maintaining changes when pressure mounts to revert.

The media company I mentioned followed this process. They removed toxic leaders even when it hurt revenue, dismantled the quota system that was destroying quality, and let teams recover without demanding immediate transformation. Then they slowly introduced practices that supported real journalism. Two years later, they'd won back credibility and, unsurprisingly, improved profitability. It turns out that soil growing quality also fosters sustainable success.

Here's what nobody tells you about soil rehabilitation: Fixing the soil doesn't automatically fix the people. Even perfect soil doesn't guarantee a thriving culture. An organization could remove every toxin, create ideal conditions, and still watch the culture struggle. Why? Because soil is just the foundation. It determines what's possible, not what's inevitable. I've seen organizations do everything right with their soil rehabilitation only to discover that nobody trusts the change. The soil might be clean, but people's memories aren't. They remember the last five "transformations" that transformed nothing. They're waiting for the other shoe to drop, for leadership to lose interest, for the old toxins to seep back in when the consultants leave.

A tech startup I know learned this the hard way. After a toxic founder was finally removed, new leadership did everything right: eliminated fear-based practices, restructured around collaboration, and created genuine psychological safety. The soil was objectively healthier. Employees, however, had developed survival mechanisms so deeply ingrained that they couldn't stop using them. They'd learned that reaching toward the light got them pruned, that spreading roots made them vulnerable, that blooming made them a target. Good soil couldn't overcome bad memories, and the soil was ready for growth while the people planted in it had learned not to grow.

Employees continued hoarding information despite transparency, avoided risks despite safety, and kept managing up despite leadership genuinely not needing it. They were responding to toxins that no longer existed but still felt present, what I call "phantom contamination." The old threats were gone, but the defensive behaviors remained. They flinched at shadows of old punishments and protected themselves from dangers that new leadership had genuinely eliminated. The tech firm discovered this when their cultural transformation stalled despite significant investment. Investigation revealed why: Employees were responding to ghost patterns. Five years earlier, someone who challenged a decision got mysteriously laid off two months later. The story became legend, passed to each new hire during unofficial onboarding. The executive who'd retaliated was long gone, but his poison lived on in organizational memory.

The only cure for phantom contamination is time combined with consistent evidence—not promises, not town halls, not inspirational speeches, but actual evidence that the soil has truly changed. When someone takes a risk that would have been punished in the past, they need to be visibly rewarded. When someone challenges leadership, they need to be thanked, not just tolerated. When someone admits failure, they need to receive support, not subtle retaliation three months later.

What makes this process even more complex is that while leaders are trying to convince current employees that the soil is safe, they're also dealing with accumulated trauma. Years of toxic exposure don't just disappear because conditions improve. People develop organizational trauma: hypervigilance about political threats, inability to trust leadership promises, and physical stress responses to situations that previously caused harm. This is the paradox: Fixing soil is necessary but may be insufficient. Organizations also need people who believe in the possibility of growth, who trust that this time is different, who are willing to risk vulnerability after being burned. Sometimes that means bringing in new people who don't carry the organization's trauma; sometimes it means patient, consistent proof that change is real.

The hardest truth is that some organizations are so contaminated that rehabilitation isn't possible with current leadership or available resources. The toxins run too deep, the beneficiaries of dysfunction hold too much power, or the damage to people's trust proves irreversible. When soil has been poisoned for decades, when every particle carries contamination, when the organization's very foundation rests on toxic principles, starting fresh elsewhere might be the only option. For organizations where rehabilitation is possible, where enough people still believe in transformation and leadership genuinely commits to change, fixing the soil creates the foundation for everything else. Without healthy soil, nothing else matters; with it, anything becomes possible.

Organizational soil tells the truth about culture, not the version on the website but the reality people live daily. It reveals whether an organization is nurturing human potential or strip-mining it for quarterly results. The question isn't whether the soil needs work; it's whether leadership will do that work or keep spray-painting dead grass green. Every toxic pattern, every protected dysfunction, every carefully maintained delusion has now been examined. The reasons nothing grows and who benefits from the wasteland are clear.

The work is hard. Facing contamination honestly, removing toxin sources, waiting for trust to rebuild: None of it is easy, and all of it invites resistance. Here's why it's worth it: Healthy soil transforms everything. People stop surviving and start contributing. Ideas flow because fear no longer blocks them. Talent stays because the ground finally feels safe. Whether leading the transformation or simply refusing to add poison to the garden, everyone who tends the soil is building something that matters.

Here's what soil can't fix: Some people get all the sunshine while others do brilliant work in the dark. That mediocre executive who keeps failing upward into every opportunity while genuinely talented people can't get five minutes of leadership's attention. The same faces in every important meeting, the same voices in every decision, the same "high potentials" who coincidentally went to the same schools, play the same sports, and laugh at the same tired jokes. Meanwhile, there's the analyst who solved a million-dollar problem but remains unknown, the manager whose team consistently delivers but never gets invited to present the results, the innovator whose ideas keep getting "discovered" by someone standing closer to the spotlight.

In organizations, exposure doesn't follow talent; it follows patterns, and those patterns are about as accidental as a hedge fund manager's son getting an internship at daddy's firm. Soil reveals what's poisoning culture, while exposure reveals who's hoarding the antidote. The soil might be ready to grow anything, but if only certain people get the light, organizations keep growing the same crop they've always grown.

Now, let's talk about vitamin D (I mean sunshine, of course).

2

Exposure

The Monopoly on Visibility

Success isn't just about talent. It's about who gets seen, who stays hidden, and who controls the spotlight. Every organization has a shadow roster of invisible excellence, where people do exceptional work in the shadows while others are set up to shine before they even begin.

How Opportunity Gets Monopolized

Every seasoned gardener knows how sunlight plays favorites. Place two identical plants in the same soil, give them the same water, but put one in full sun and the other in deep shade, and watch what happens. The sun-soaked plant stretches toward the sky, unfurling leaves like victory flags. The shaded one performs botanical gymnastics trying to find light, or quietly gives up, conserving energy for survival rather than growth. Organizations work exactly the same way, except we pretend the distribution of light is merit-based rather than predetermined by where people get planted.

Exposure in organizations isn't just visibility; it's the vital energy that transforms potential into performance. It's the difference between a brilliant strategy getting implemented or wilting in someone's inbox. It determines whether leadership recognizes someone's value or whether excellence happens in organizational shadows where no witnesses exist. The mythology goes like this: Do excellent work and recognition naturally follows. Performance leads to visibility. Merit rises. Cream floats. Talent gets spotted. These are the lies we tell ourselves to avoid acknowledging that some people are planted directly under spotlights, while others could cure cancer in the basement and nobody would know.

What actually plays out? That mediocre director whose wife sits on the museum board with the CEO's wife gets invited to present the project someone else led. The executive's nephew doing his "development rotation" gets credit for the turnaround another team executed while he was learning what everyone does. The usual suspects appear in every strategic meeting, on every high-visibility committee, and at every investor presentation, not because they're the most capable, but because they've monopolized the greenhouse's grow lights.

I learned this lesson with surgical precision at that marketing company where I'd hired 65 percent of the workforce. When the opportunity arose to lead C-suite recruiting internationally, something I'd already proven I could do, I got hit with words that still echo: "Abi, you're good, but you would not have gotten that person over the line." Let me translate what they really meant: "You're excellent at the work, but certain rooms require a certain look, and darling, you don't have it. You can build the show, but you can't be the star. You can create the value, but someone else needs to present it to people who matter." This wasn't about capability. I had the track record, the relationships, the results. This was about who gets to stand in the light and who's relegated to making things grow in the dark. They needed someone whose presence felt familiar in executive spaces, whose authority wouldn't be questioned in boardrooms, whose competence would be assumed rather than interrogated.

The opportunity went to someone I had hired at that company, someone who'd yet to hire a single C-suite executive within that business but who had the right look and aesthetics. When they brought in their C-suite hire, I raised concerns that this person wouldn't last and certainly wouldn't deliver. Leadership ignored my warning. Three months later, exactly as predicted, their hire abandoned ship completely. Leadership framed it as "ambitious market challenges" rather than admitting they should have listened. My proven track record of successful C-suite hiring wasn't enough to overcome whatever it was about me that made them uncomfortable in that spotlight.

This is how opportunity hoarding works. It's not a conspiracy where people gather in secret rooms parceling out advantages. It's the informal coffee that determines who gets the stretch assignment, the after-hours invitation that leads to sponsorship, the "you remind me of myself at your age" that opens doors. The benefit of the doubt gets extended only to people who resemble those already in power, and the hoarding pattern becomes self-reinforcing. Those who receive early exposure get labeled as high potential, though it's worth noting this label often reflects proximity to power rather than actual capability. High potentials get more exposure, more exposure leads to better opportunities, better opportunities create impressive resumes, and impressive resumes justify yet more exposure. The cycle continues while equally talented people in the shadows wonder what they're doing wrong.

The hoarders don't see it as hoarding; they see it as efficiency. "Why wouldn't we give the important project to someone we know can handle it?" they ask, conveniently forgetting that knowing someone can handle it requires having seen them handle something similar, which requires having given them the opportunity, which they reserve for people who remind them of themselves. The hoarding becomes especially vicious during economic uncertainty. When budgets tighten and opportunities become genuinely scarce, the informal networks that were always there become fortified walls. The coffee conversations become closed-door strategy sessions, the casual check-ins become succession planning, and those who were barely getting light before now work in complete darkness, told to be grateful they still have jobs while watching the same faces get "retained" for "critical" opportunities.

I observed this during a merger between two companies that ended up creating duplicate roles everywhere. The official process promised "fair evaluation based on performance," but those with spotlight access spent months having off-the-record conversations about "fit" and "vision," while shadow dwellers learned their fate through automated emails. One strategist discovered her role had been eliminated when her key card stopped working. Meanwhile, the mediocre director who lunched with the CEO monthly got promoted to head the newly combined division.

The technology of opportunity hoarding has evolved beyond conference rooms and corner offices. In the remote work era, it's Zoom calls that mysteriously don't get recorded, Slack channels people aren't aware of, and calendar invites marked "optional" that determine futures. The head of marketing at one startup told me that the company's official team meetings were what she called "decision cosplay," with everyone performing collaboration, while the actual decision-making took place in a weekly shadow leadership team meeting, a private "brain trust" she wasn't invited to join. Virtual hoarding might be even more pernicious than its physical predecessor. At least in offices, people could see the closed doors, notice the lunch patterns, observe who walked out of which meetings. Opportunity hoarding now occurs invisibly across time zones and platforms, with careers decided in breakout rooms people are never assigned to, in "quick syncs" that happen after they've logged off, in documents shared with everyone except them.

Perhaps the most damaging aspect of opportunity hoarding is how it becomes inherited wealth. Those who monopolize opportunities don't just advance themselves; they pull up their proteges, their friends, their dinner-party guests. It's organizational nepotism dressed as mentorship. The senior executive doesn't just take the speaking engagement; she brings her favorite analyst as "support." The board member doesn't just lead the innovation committee; he ensures his mentee gets appointed as deputy. Opportunity compounds like interest, except only certain accounts are allowed to accumulate it.

This inherited opportunity explains why organizations can hire diversely at entry levels yet remain homogeneous at the top. New recruits enter a system where opportunity has been preallocated through relationships they can't access, networks they're not invited to join, and sponsors who've already chosen who to champion. It's like joining a Monopoly game where all the properties are already owned.

The hoarders have developed sophisticated justifications for their monopoly, talking about relationship capital, earned trust, and proven track records as if these aren't euphemisms for "I give opportunities to people I'm comfortable with." They create intricate competency frameworks that coincidentally match what they've been exposed to. The 2023 Women in the Workplace report found that women are consistently passed over for stretch assignments and critical early promotions, those career-making opportunities to prove capability, with men being promoted at higher rates, particularly at the first step up to manager.[1] Everyone else gets "developmental feedback" about needing more experience while being systematically denied the experiences that would develop them.

I watched this play out repeatedly. The woman who built the entire product strategy but watched a man present it to investors because "he has more gravitas." The Black engineer whose technical innovation got repackaged by his white manager as a "team effort" he supposedly led. The immigrant founder whose accent apparently disqualified her from representing her own company to clients, so the team brought in a "communications specialist" who looked the part. Organizations create sophisticated justifications for this hoarding: "She needs more executive presence" (translation: She doesn't look like our mental image of an executive), "He lacks strategic thinking" (translation: His ideas come from experiences we don't recognize), "They're not ready for that level of visibility" (translation: Our clients, investors, and board aren't ready to see someone like them in that position).

The tragedy isn't just individual careers stunted by shadow; it's the organizational capability that withers in darkness. How many innovations died because their creators couldn't get five minutes of leadership attention? How many problems persisted because the people who understood them weren't in rooms where decisions got made? How many opportunities evaporated because the only people with visibility had no vision?

Here's the truly damaging part: Opportunity hoarding creates the very incompetence it claims to prevent. When the same people get all the practice presenting, they become better presenters. When the same people attend all the strategic meetings, they develop strategic thinking. When the same people receive all the sponsorship, they build the relationships that matter. The prophecy fulfills itself: Those who predicted certain people wouldn't succeed ensure it by denying them the light they need to grow.

When Only Certain People Shine

Some people are born in organizational spotlights, while others spend entire careers doing brilliant work in corners so dark that their excellence becomes folklore nobody can verify. "Did you hear about that analyst who saved us $10 million?" Sure, but nobody remembers their name. Meanwhile, Chris from Strategy gets profiled in the company newsletter for implementing an idea he overheard in the bathroom. Organizations create two distinct populations: the permanently illuminated and the perpetually shadowed. This isn't about talent distribution; it's about visibility patterns so consistent you could set your watch by them.

I lived this shadow life, watching my ideas undergo magical transformation into other people's insights. There's a special kind of rage that comes from hearing your exact words delivered by someone else to applause. At one company, I developed an entire talent acquisition strategy that would revolutionize how we approached hiring. Spent three months researching, building frameworks, and creating implementation plans. Presented it to my manager in what I thought was a collaborative discussion. Two weeks later, I watched him present "his" innovative approach to the leadership team. My slides. My words. His glory.

When I asked him about it, he explained he was "socializing the idea at the appropriate level" and said I should be happy the strategy was moving forward. The appropriate level, apparently, was anywhere my face wasn't.

This invisibility isn't random; it follows patterns as predictable as bad coffee in conference rooms. Certain demographics cluster in the shadows like mushrooms, doing essential work in darkness, while others photosynthesize in corner offices. Those who do the work rarely get the spotlight, while those with proximity to power get the credit. The quiet problem-solver watches the loud presenter get promoted. The outsider who brought a fresh perspective watches the insider who "championed" it get recognized. Research confirms this with depressing consistency: In mixed-gender teams, women receive systematically less credit for their contributions, particularly when collaborating with men.[2] A woman's contribution can become invisible the moment it leaves her mouth, like organizational vanishing cream applied selectively based on who's speaking.

Shadow dwelling becomes particularly cruel through its compound effect. When contributions are consistently overlooked, there's no track record for advancement. Successes that get credited to someone else can't be leveraged. Careers get built out of smoke, while others construct monuments from stolen materials. This creates an entire shadow ecosystem with its own survival rules: Documentation becomes armor, ideas get seeded through people with spotlight access, and strategic visibility becomes an art form where shadow dwellers calculate exactly when to emerge without triggering the organizational antibodies that attack anyone disrupting the established order.

Shadow dwellers also become the organization's unofficial memory keepers. While spotlight holders jump between opportunities, those in the shadows often stay in roles longer, accumulating institutional knowledge nobody else bothers to maintain. They know why that system was built that way, which client relationships are fragile, and where the bodies are buried from past failures. Organizations depend on this shadow knowledge but never acknowledge its value until these people leave, and suddenly nobody knows how anything works. One law firm lost a shadow-dwelling paralegal who'd been passed over for promotion eight times. Within a month, three major cases nearly imploded because she was the only one who knew how to navigate their "upgraded" case management system. She'd documented everything, but her documentation lived in shadows too, filed in drives nobody important accessed.

The firm spent $750,000 on consultants to reconstruct processes she'd been maintaining for $95,000 a year.

I watched a brilliant engineer from Bangladesh operate entirely through proxies. He'd developed groundbreaking solutions, but his accent became the focus rather than his ideas, with people asking him to "repeat that" when he spoke perfectly clear English. So he fed his solutions through a colleague with a British accent. That colleague got promoted twice, while the engineer got "developmental feedback" about communication skills. The shadow taught him that his ideas could thrive or he could thrive, but not both simultaneously.

Organizations maintain convenient fictions about why certain people stay shadowed. "She needs to speak up more" (she speaks; nobody listens). "He lacks strategic thinking" (his strategy got implemented; leadership just doesn't know it was his). "They're not ready for visibility" (they've been ready; leadership isn't ready to see them). These explanations protect the comfortable fiction that spotlight distribution is merit-based rather than predetermined by demographics, proximity to power, and ability to mirror existing leadership.

Then there's the opposite problem: spotlight fatigue. The chosen few who get pulled into every high-profile project, presented as the face of every initiative, and asked to represent the company at every external event while maintaining their regular responsibilities. I call them "trophy employees," and their exhaustion is real. They're on every strategic committee, at every client dinner, leading every culture initiative, all while trying to excel at the job they were actually hired to do. The spotlight for these chosen few isn't illuminating; it's interrogating. Every move gets scrutinized through multiple lenses. Are they too aggressive or not assertive enough? Too different or not authentic enough? Speaking up too much or not being a good enough advocate?

A Latina executive described her spotlight exhaustion to me: "Monday, I'm representing the company at a panel. Tuesday, I'm the face of our community initiatives. Wednesday, I'm mentoring every young woman who joins because I'm the only senior one they see. Thursday, I'm trying to do my actual job while people wonder if I'm qualified or just filling a quota. Friday, I'm burnt out but can't show it because that would confirm I can't handle the pressure."

The trophy employee phenomenon particularly punishes those who break barriers. They're simultaneously expected to be the voice of all underrepresented employees, proof that programs work, and somehow also "one of the team" who doesn't make traditional leadership uncomfortable. The code-switching becomes so constant that the authentic voice gets lost. Every room requires a different performance, and picking the wrong one means being either too threatening or not authentic enough. These chosen few also face what I call "representation taxation," the unpaid second job of being symbols rather than humans. They can't just fail individually; their failure becomes evidence about entire demographics. They can't just succeed personally; they must lift while they climb, mentor everyone who looks like them, and somehow solve systemic problems through individual excellence. While others get to have off days, bad quarters, and learning curves, trophy employees must be exceptional every moment or become ammunition for those questioning whether hiring for difference compromises quality.

This creates a vicious cycle. The few nontraditional faces in spotlight positions get overwhelmed by extra duties, impacting their performance, which then gets used as evidence that hiring for difference compromises excellence. Meanwhile, equally talented shadow dwellers who could share the load remain invisible, their capabilities unknown because nobody's looking in their direction.

The organizational impact goes beyond individual careers. When brilliance operates in shadows, companies miss critical insights. Problems invisible from spotlight positions become catastrophes. Innovations that could transform industries die in darkness. Customer perspectives that could unlock new markets get ignored because they come from shadowlands leadership never visits.

Here's the truly insidious part: Many organizations prefer the shadow–spotlight divide. It maintains hierarchies without explicit discrimination, preserves power without visible force, and allows merit mythology to persist while ensuring predetermined outcomes. Shadow dwellers can be pointed to as evidence of talent ("Look at all our talented employees!") while never threatening established power structures with actual influence. The divide serves another function: It creates scarcity that fuels competition. When spotlight positions are limited, people fight for visibility rather than fighting systems that create artificial scarcity. Shadow dwellers compete with each other for rare moments of recognition instead of questioning why recognition is rationed in the first place.

The truth about exposure is that it's not actually scarce. Unlike soil or nutrients that have genuine limitations, visibility can be created, multiplied, and distributed. Organizations choose to ration it, choose to create shadows, choose to maintain darkness because it serves someone's purpose to keep certain people invisible while others bask in manufactured brilliance.

The organizations I've seen successfully dismantle this divide share common practices. They audit visibility patterns with the same rigor they audit finances, tracking who presents to leadership, who gets stretch assignments, who speaks in meetings, and who receives credit for collaborative work. They create structural interventions: rotating presentation duties, requiring that the person who developed an idea presents it, establishing sponsorship programs that deliberately connect shadow dwellers with spotlight access. They train managers to notice and interrupt credit theft in real time, not through awkward confrontation but through simple redirection: "That's a great point, and I believe Sabrina originally raised it in last week's meeting. Sabrina, can you expand on your thinking?"

Most importantly, they redefine what visibility means. Instead of treating spotlight positions as rewards for the already visible, they treat exposure as a developmental resource that should be distributed based on potential, not just proximity. They recognize that when only certain people's contributions are visible, those methods become the standard, those backgrounds become the template, and those success stories become the only stories. True meritocracy requires illuminating all the merit, not just the merit that already matches leadership's narrow spotlight.

The shadow dwellers have always been here, doing the work, creating the value, solving the problems. They don't need development programs or executive presence coaching or lessons in the politics of visibility. They just need someone to turn on the lights.

Why "Best Person" Is BS

Every organization swears they hire and promote "the best person for the job," saying it with straight faces as though they've discovered some universal measurement tool that objectively ranks humans from best to worst. The meritocracy myth is corporate comfort food: It tastes good, goes down easy, and makes everyone feel better about systems that mysteriously keep producing the same outcomes.

Here's how the myth works: Organizations create complex performance systems with metrics, rankings, and reviews that supposedly identify top talent objectively. They build competency matrices filled with terms like "strategic thinking," "executive presence," "cultural fit," and "leadership potential." These aren't measurements; they're Rorschach tests where everyone sees what confirms their existing beliefs.

I once sat in a hiring meeting where we spent forty minutes defining "executive presence." The criteria that emerged? Confidence in presenting (but not too aggressive). Polished appearance (but not trying too hard). Natural authority (but still collaborative). Speaking style that commands attention (but remains approachable). By the end, we'd essentially described a specific person who already worked there. We'd defined merit as "resembles someone from Strategy."

The research on this is devastating to anyone still clutching their meritocracy security blanket. Lauren Rivera spent years studying elite professional service firms, watching how they actually select "the best." Her findings? These supposedly rigorous merit-based processes are elaborate similarity contests, with evaluators consistently ranking candidates who shared their hobbies, backgrounds, and experiences as higher quality even when qualifications were identical.[3]

Consider what "strategic thinking" actually means in practice. At one media company, it meant using frameworks from business school case studies, preferably while name-dropping a prestigious consulting firm. At a tech startup, it meant thinking like the founders who confused energy drinks with vision. At a government agency, it meant never proposing anything that hadn't been tried somewhere else first. The same words with completely different meanings, all supposedly measuring "merit."

"Leadership potential" is even more slippery. I've seen it defined as everything from "summers in the right locations" to "has executive presence" to "reminds me of myself twenty years ago." One organization literally included "comfortable with ambiguity" in their leadership criteria, then promoted only people who followed extremely predictable career paths. Apparently, ambiguity is comfortable only when it applies to other people's prospects. The "best person" always seems to have followed a remarkably familiar path, not necessarily the most challenging one, but the one that produces candidates fluent in the unspoken language of corporate leadership, who understand references nobody teaches explicitly, who navigate unwritten rules because they grew up swimming in them.

I learned about opportunity hoarding at a marketing company with an unspoken rule that they hired only from elite universities. At first, I felt special, like I'd been chosen for something exclusive, but then I looked around properly and saw what was really happening.

During lunch with the marketing executives, reality hit me hard. Everyone at that table could have been siblings separated at birth, sharing the same educational pedigree, the same socioeconomic bubble, and the same hobbies that required disposable income I'd never had. They debated skiing in exclusive resorts while I calculated whether I could afford both lunch and my tube fare home. The company had mistaken privilege for talent, systematically filtering out brilliant graduates from state universities who could've brought fresh perspectives. Their CVs never made it past screening because the company was so busy hiring mirror images that they'd created an echo chamber with excellent acoustics but terrible ideas.

One executive constantly preached about earning their position through merit and hard work, which would have been inspiring if their father wasn't a major investor and if they hadn't spent years as a family friend of the CEO. The internship program told the same story, filled with bright young people who all happened to attend the same private schools as leadership's children and had been born to politicians, surgeons, and investors who treated success like a family heirloom.

Pay attention to how "merit" gets selectively applied. When someone from the traditional pipeline succeeds, it validates the system; when they fail, it's an individual aberration. When someone from a nontraditional background succeeds, they're seen as exceptional, an outlier who overcame the odds; when they fail, it becomes evidence about entire demographics rather than one person's individual outcome.

The issue isn't that traditional candidates lack merit; many are genuinely excellent. The issue is that merit gets defined so narrowly that excellence in unfamiliar packages gets missed. Organizations recognize potential when it wears the right signals but miss it when it arrives dressed differently.

I consulted for a financial firm that prided itself on "pure meritocracy." Their interview process included case studies, technical assessments, and behavioral interviews designed to identify "raw talent." Sounds rigorous, right? Except the case studies assumed familiarity with concepts taught primarily at certain universities. The technical assessments favored specific approaches over equally valid alternatives. The behavioral interviews rewarded storytelling styles that aligned with particular cultural norms. They genuinely believed they were measuring merit; what they were actually measuring was cultural alignment. The candidate who could casually reference a prestigious internship naturally scored higher than the one who worked three jobs through state school, not because prestigious internships create better analysts, but because one knew how to perform success in the specific dialect this firm recognized.

Here's what's tragic: Both candidates might be equally brilliant. The state school graduate might even be stronger, having solved complex problems with fewer resources. The evaluation system couldn't see that strength because it recognized only certain signals of competence. It's like judging roses and wildflowers by their ability to grow in sand, then wondering why the garden contains only cacti.

This selective application of merit played out painfully in my own career. There was the time I was told during a performance review that my natural enthusiasm was unprofessional; that I needed to be more measured, more contained, more beige. The feedback stung, but what made it truly absurd was watching a colleague—someone whose frenetic energy had him talking at the speed of light, whose meetings felt like watching someone conduct an orchestra only they could hear—get praised in the very same week for his executive presence. My enthusiasm was a problem to be solved, while his intensity was apparently leadership material.

The most absurd part of the meritocracy myth is how organizations pretend it's new. Every generation thinks they've finally cracked the code for identifying talent objectively. Elite universities used to require photographs with applications to assess character (mysteriously, good character had very specific facial features). The 1960s had handwriting analysis to determine promotion potential. The 1990s had personality tests that sorted humans into boxes like selecting fonts for a newsletter.

Now there's algorithmic hiring, artificial intelligence, and "bias-free" assessments. Organizations have automated their biases and called them objective. AI trained on historical hiring data perfectly replicates past discrimination, just with machine-learning legitimacy.

One tech company's "culture fit" algorithm rejected candidates who didn't use specific keywords that correlated with attending certain universities. They'd literally programmed elitism and called it innovation.

Here's where the myth becomes truly destructive: It makes inequality feel justified. If the system is meritocratic, then those at the top deserve their position and those struggling deserve their struggles. It transforms systemic barriers into personal failures. Can't get promoted? Must not be working hard enough. Didn't get the job? Should have been more qualified. Never mind that "qualified" keeps getting redefined to exclude whoever wasn't already wanted.

The myth also creates what I call "merit charades," elaborate performances to justify predetermined outcomes. Interviewing for "compliance" when the external hire has already been chosen. Posting that promotion internally for "fairness" even though it's already been decided. Assembling a diverse interview panel to rubber-stamp homogeneous choices. Everyone knows it's a charade, but everyone pretends the performance is real.

I watched a company conduct a nationwide search for a new executive, flying in candidates, conducting multiple interview rounds, making a big show of their thorough process. The chosen candidate? The CEO's former colleague who'd been having coffee with him monthly for the past year. The other candidates were expensive extras in a play where the lead was already cast.

The elaborate effort everyone puts into pretending they don't know the outcome is almost impressive. I witnessed an internal promotion process where five candidates were interviewed for a role that had already been promised to someone at the company holiday party (I overheard the conversation). The chosen one showed up to his interview twenty minutes late with coffee stains on his shirt, gave one-word answers, and took a phone call during the behavioral questions. Meanwhile, a brilliant woman had prepared a ninety-day plan complete with metrics and stakeholder analysis. She'd interviewed team members to understand challenges, researched industry best practices, and basically did three weeks of free consulting to prove she deserved the role. The feedback she received? "Very thorough, perhaps overprepared. We're looking for someone more comfortable with ambiguity." The coffee-stained candidate got the job for his "executive presence" and "authentic leadership style."

What truly constitutes qualifications at senior levels reveals the absurdity. I've met executives whose primary skill is speaking in confident tones about things they don't understand, who've mastered the art of saying "let's double-click on that" and "we need to ladder up to the strategic imperative" without ever doing either. They mistake confidence for competence, volume for vision, and their own limitations for universal truths, yet they're the ones defining merit for everyone else.

The merit myth reaches peak absurdity in performance reviews, where "areas for development" mysteriously align with whatever makes someone different from the reviewer. Thoughtful and thorough? "Could benefit from being more decisive." Quick decision maker? "Should spend more time considering options." The feedback shapeshifts to ensure people are always falling short of a standard that coincidentally matches whoever's doing the reviewing.

The tragedy isn't just the waste of all those hours, all that hope, all that preparation for nothing. It's that everyone involved knows it's fake but participates anyway: the hiring managers who know the decision has been made, the candidates who suspect they're tokens, the recruiters who source prospects for roles that will never be theirs. Everyone remains complicit in maintaining the myth because admitting it would require acknowledging that success isn't always about merit.

The real tragedy of the meritocracy myth isn't just that it's false; it's that it makes organizations miss actual excellence. While obsessing over candidates who can perform success in familiar ways, they overlook those who've achieved more with less, who've solved problems without road maps, who've created value without institutional support.

Research by professors at the University of Toronto and Harvard found that when minority job applicants "whitened" their resumes by removing racial cues, their callback rates nearly doubled.[4] Same achievements, different "merit" score. It's almost as if merit isn't objective at all but filtered through who we expect to be excellent.

I know this isn't just academic theory because I tested it myself in 2018. I sent my resume to ten potential employers using my full name, Abidemi, with my fourteen-letter middle name as my last name. Five weeks of silence. Not even a rejection. Just the special kind of nothing that makes you wonder if your emails are reaching another dimension.

Then I sent the exact same resume to the exact same ten companies, but this time as "Abi Adamson." Within five working days, seven had replied with interview invitations. Same experience, same qualifications, same everything except the name at the top. The only thing that changed was that I'd made myself linguistically digestible for people who considered pronunciation an inconvenience.

These weren't small, unsophisticated companies. These were global organizations with published values statements and inclusion commitments, probably entire teams dedicated to "removing bias from hiring." I'd checked their hiring teams on LinkedIn; they looked nothing like me and had names that summer camp counselors could pronounce on the first try. My merit suddenly materialized once I anglicized my identity. Seven out of ten companies discovered I was qualified the moment I stopped being so visibly African at the top of my resume.

The meritocracy myth persists because it serves those who have already won. It tells them they earned their position through superiority rather than systemic advantage. It justifies their hoarding of opportunities and transforms their privilege into deserved reward. Most importantly, it absolves them from examining how they've defined merit to match what they already are.

What should concern every organization clinging to its merit mythology is this: by applying narrow definitions of excellence, they systematically eliminate brilliance that doesn't match the established pattern. Every time an organization rejects talent because candidates didn't attend the right school, speak with the right accent, or network at the right events, competitors get stronger. While some companies hire the same profiles that created their current problems, others scoop up the talent those companies couldn't recognize. The future belongs to organizations that understand merit isn't one thing. It's not a ladder with clear rungs but an ecosystem with multiple ways to contribute value. The organizations that figure out how to recognize excellence in all its forms, not just the ones wearing familiar costumes, will outperform those still running spotlight auctions where the same people keep bidding with inherited currency.

The question isn't "Who's the best person?" The question is "Best at what, according to whom, and why does that definition exist?" Until organizations interrogate their definition of merit, they're not running meritocracies. They're running pattern-matching exercises that mistake familiarity for quality. The good news? This is fixable. It starts with auditing how "excellence" gets defined, who created those definitions, and whose excellence becomes invisible under them. It means building evaluation processes that recognize achievement in context, that value solving problems with limited resources as much as solving them with abundant ones, that assess what people have actually accomplished rather than how well they perform the appearance of accomplishment.

Practical Interventions (and Why They're Not Enough)

Every organization trying to fix exposure inequality follows the same playbook: creating mentorship programs that pair shadow dwellers with spotlight holders, launching "visibility initiatives" where underrepresented employees get five minutes to present to leadership, and rotating stretch assignments through different demographics like Halloween candy distributed to ensure everyone gets something. These interventions work about as well as putting a bandage on a severed artery. Sure, it's something, but the bleeding continues while everyone congratulates themselves on their first-aid skills.

Let me be clear: These programs aren't useless; they're just insufficient. It's like watering one corner of a garden while the rest remains desert, then wondering why the whole thing isn't flourishing. One small patch improves, but the fundamental distribution problem remains unchanged. Shadow dwellers might get a flashlight, but spotlight holders still control the power grid. I've watched organizations implement every conceivable intervention: sponsorship programs where senior leaders champion talent, anonymous idea submission systems to bypass visibility bias, structured rotation programs ensuring everyone gets face time with decision-makers. They measure participation rates, track demographics, and create dashboards showing increased exposure equity. Then they wonder why nothing really changes.

Here's why: Light can't be redistributed in a system designed to create shadows. Every intervention gets filtered through existing power structures, which neutralize impact faster than corporate lawyers can kill fun. The mentorship program pairs shadow dwellers with mid-level managers while spotlight holders get CEOs. The visibility initiative offers five minutes quarterly versus constant daily exposure. The stretch assignments give shadow dwellers "developmental opportunities," while spotlight holders get career-making projects.

Take the classic "high-potential program" solution. Organizations identify talent from underrepresented groups and provide special development opportunities. Sounds progressive, right? The reality is less rosy. Those selected must work twice as hard to prove they deserve inclusion. They are expected to simultaneously excel at their regular job, participate in the program, and serve as ambassadors. Meanwhile, traditionally successful employees get identified as high potential without the additional burden of representing entire demographics. One employee described her high-potential experience perfectly: "I was in meetings from 7 a.m. to 7 p.m., then doing my actual job until midnight because being high potential apparently meant doing two jobs while smiling gratefully for the opportunity." She burned out within a year. The organization concluded she couldn't handle senior leadership pressure, completely missing that they'd set her up to fail by tripling her workload while calling it development.

The "anonymous resume" innovation seemed revolutionary: Remove names and identifying information, evaluate pure qualification, eliminate bias. Tech companies particularly love this approach because it feels like debugging human prejudice. Except humans aren't code, and bias isn't a bug that can be patched. Even when anonymous processes appear to work initially, they often fail during implementation.[5] Organizations might hire more broadly through anonymous screening, but once people arrive, they enter existing patterns of exposure. The old networks reform, the shadow patterns reassert, and within six months, the same distribution returns with different faces in familiar positions.

Structured visibility programs try to systematize exposure by ensuring everyone gets equal time presenting to leadership, the same number of stretch assignments, and rotation through high-visibility roles. The problem isn't the structure but the interpretation. When someone from traditional leadership presents, executives see potential; when someone from an underrepresented background presents identical work, they see someone who needs development. Same exposure, different absorption. It's like giving everyone the same amount of sunlight while some wear SPF 100 and others get magnifying glasses. I consulted for a company that mandated a diverse slate of candidates for all senior positions. Sounds foolproof, right? Except hiring managers treated it like a compliance exercise, interviewing candidates to check boxes before hiring the person they'd already chosen. The candidates became perpetual bridesmaids, decorating processes but never getting selected.

Another organization tried "exposure equity audits," tracking who gets face time with leadership, who presents at board meetings, who leads high-profile projects. They created elaborate spreadsheets ensuring equal distribution. The tracking was perfect; the impact was zero. Exposure without power is just performance. Shadow dwellers got stage time but no actual influence, becoming decorative symbols rather than decision-makers. The most deceptive intervention I've encountered was "spotlight sharing," where executives supposedly stepped back to let others present their work. In practice, they stood directly behind the presenter, nodding vigorously and interjecting "great point" after every sentence, making the entire presentation about their magnanimous gesture. One executive introduced his team member's presentation by spending fifteen minutes explaining how he'd mentored her, shaped her thinking, and essentially created her. By the time she spoke, everyone understood the real message: This was still his show and she was just guest starring.

Organizations often create "innovation challenges" allowing anyone to submit ideas. They set up elaborate digital suggestion boxes, host ideation sessions with colorful sticky notes, and promise that every voice matters. What they don't mention is that ideas get filtered through layers of middle management who wouldn't recognize innovation if it arrived with a name tag. I watched a retail company receive a proposal from a supply chain analyst about consolidating Southeast Asian shipping through Singapore instead of splitting it between three ports. He'd included port capacity data and transition costs, and he was projecting 30 percent transport savings. The proposal sat in their "innovation portal" for eight months. Then a consulting firm arrived, billing $2 million for a logistics optimization project. Their revolutionary finding? Consolidate shipping through

Singapore. Same port, same savings, same solution that had been sitting in the system since January. The analyst got an autogenerated "thank you for participating" email. The consultancy got a contract extension. The executive who hired them got promoted for "transformative cost reduction." The analyst left two years later, tired of watching his intelligence get repackaged as expensive insight.

"Skip-level meetings," where senior leadership meets with junior staff, deserve special recognition for performative listening. These sessions involve executives playing at being interested listeners while junior employees carefully calculate every word, knowing that too much honesty equals career risk. Everyone performs their assigned roles: Executives pretend to care, employees pretend problems are solvable, and HR pretends to take notes that matter.

The resistance to genuine exposure redistribution reveals exactly who benefits from the current system. When one organization tried rotating who presents to the board, the usual presenters suddenly discovered urgent conflicts. One executive claimed he needed to be in Tokyo for a conference that, upon investigation, he'd attended virtually for the past two years. Another developed a recurring condition that flared up only when he wasn't presenting. They guard their spotlight access like dragons hoarding gold, except dragons occasionally share.

Here's what makes all these interventions fail: They treat exposure like a resource to be distributed rather than a system to be redesigned. They're sharing breadcrumbs when the whole bakery needs restructuring, adjusting thermostats in a building with no insulation. Real exposure equity requires more than redistribution. It requires examining why some contributions need spotlights while others happen in darkness, questioning who decided which work deserves visibility, and admitting that maybe shadow dwellers aren't lacking anything except witnesses.

The organizations that actually solve this problem take a different approach. Instead of adding programs onto broken systems, they redesign how value gets recognized in the first place. They change meeting structures so that the person who did the work presents it, full stop. They implement "credit tracking" where managers are evaluated on whether their team members receive appropriate recognition. They rotate high-visibility assignments based on development needs rather than comfort levels, and they hold leaders accountable when the same faces keep appearing in every important room. One technology company I worked with stopped asking "Who should present this?" and started asking "Whose work is this?" The shift seemed small, but within eighteen months, their leadership pipeline had transformed because people who'd been invisible for years suddenly had track records that matched their actual contributions.

The deeper fix requires changing what gets valued, not just who gets seen. When organizations celebrate only certain types of contributions, they create shadows around everything else. The employee who prevents problems rarely gets the spotlight that goes to the one who solves them dramatically. The team member who makes everyone else better stays invisible, while the individual star gets profiled. Redesigning exposure means recognizing that visibility itself has been defined too narrowly.

Redistributing light is uncomfortable work. It means confronting who has been hoarded and who has been hidden, dismantling patterns that feel natural because they've existed so long, and facing resistance from those who've built careers on visibility they didn't earn. Here's what makes it worth the discomfort: When exposure follows contribution instead of proximity, organizations discover talent they never knew they had. Ideas surface that were always there, waiting for someone to notice. People who spent years performing invisibility finally get to perform their actual brilliance. The work isn't just about fairness, though fairness matters. It's about what becomes possible when light reaches every corner of the garden. Everyone who challenges "the usual suspects," who asks "Whose work is this actually?", who refuses to let brilliance stay hidden, is part of building something better.

What spotlight hoarders don't realize is that while they're protecting their small circles of light, something far more powerful grows in the darkness they've created. Shadow dwellers aren't just waiting; they're connecting, building networks, creating systems of support that run deeper than any org chart. The real culture isn't happening in well-lit conference rooms or all-hands meetings where the same voices dominate. It's happening in the whisper networks that leadership doesn't know exist, in the root systems that formed because official channels failed the very people who could strengthen the organization.

Controlling the light doesn't mean controlling the culture. Roots grow in darkness, and once those connections are strong enough, they don't need spotlights anymore. They become the foundation that either holds an organization together or shifts it from below. The question isn't whether shadow dwellers will thrive without official visibility; they already are. The question is whether organizations will recognize what's growing in the dark before it's too late to join it.

Exposure might be the light, but it's the roots that determine what actually lives.

3

Roots

The Underground Truth Network

Beneath every organization's official structure lies the real network: the underground connections that actually determine who survives, who thrives, and who withers. These hidden systems know more about culture than any engagement survey ever will, because they're the ones keeping people functioning despite an organization's worst practices.

Where Information Actually Flows

Every organization has two communication systems. There's the official one with town halls, all-hands meetings, and newsletters nobody reads except to see if they're mentioned. Then there's the real one: a sprawling root system of whispered warnings, bathroom conversations, and private Signal threads where actual truth lives like organizational contraband.

When leadership announces a merger is "exciting," employees update their resumes. Not because of what was said, but because of what wasn't: no mention of job security, no timeline for integration, no eye contact when questions came up. When they announce "restructuring for efficiency," the root system has already noticed the pattern: Directors who used to run meetings now just attend them, certain VPs suddenly have "advisors" shadowing their work, and everyone pretends not to notice.

This underground network exists because formal channels are about as trustworthy as a chocolate teapot. They're designed to protect the organization from reality, not communicate it. They filter bad news until it becomes good news, transform complaints into compliments, and produce engagement scores that nobody actually believes. The root system thrives on these disconnects between official fiction and lived reality. Ecologists studying forest networks have discovered that trees communicate through vast underground fungal systems called mycorrhizal networks, sharing nutrients, water, and even warning signals about threats.[1] Organizations develop strikingly similar structures: informal networks that share resources, information, and warnings far more efficiently than any official channel.

I experienced this firsthand at a media company where the newly hired head of HR was truly a horrid piece of work. During Ramadan, when a Muslim colleague asked where he could pray, she told him, "We don't have anywhere. Maybe we'll find you a toilet." When I gently suggested this was inappropriate, she turned to me and said, "Abi, we do *not* by law have to provide anywhere for *those people* to pray." The venom in "those people" could have stripped paint.

After she shut me down, I checked on the Muslim employee who'd maintained perfect composure in our shared office. In private, he told me he just needed a few months on his CV and then he was leaving. He'd already warned a friend not to bother applying. Within hours of the prayer incident, every Muslim employee knew to avoid HR entirely and arrange informal prayer spaces with sympathetic managers. People from all three floors started coming to me with their HR problems instead, and I had to keep redirecting them: "She's HR, I'm talent acquisition; I can't help with that." They'd nod knowingly and never approach her. The root system had already mapped who was safe and who was poison.

A law firm brought me in to diagnose why they were hemorrhaging associates despite 89 percent satisfaction scores and industry-leading compensation. The managing partners insisted their "collegial culture" was their greatest asset.

Then, during a video call with associates, everything changed. One associate forgot to close a browser tab. "The Grid" sat there, visible to everyone while she frantically tried to share a different screen. After I promised confidentiality that would make a priest jealous, they showed me their survival manual: a color-coded spreadsheet mapping which partners threw contracts at people, which ones claimed credit for others' work, and which ones would damage the career of anyone who interrupted their morning coffee. The Grid wasn't just data; it was their root system made visible, showing how information and warnings spread underground from person to person, keeping lawyers functioning in hostile conditions.

This wasn't paranoia; it was pattern recognition. Three years of data on who actually developed talent versus who treated associates like billable-hour factories. Who gave real work versus document review disguised as training. Which practice groups promoted women versus which ones mysteriously lost every woman senior associate to "work-life balance" right before partnership decisions.

One senior associate explained during my investigation: "We weren't trying to undermine the firm. We were trying to navigate it. Knowing that Patterson goes nuclear if you knock before 10 a.m. or that Mitchell only reviews documents fairly after his Thursday partners' lunch literally shaped careers. We've seen too many good lawyers derailed by approaching the wrong partner at the wrong time with the wrong question."

The Grid's most sophisticated feature was its safety ratings for women lawyers, color-coding which colleagues were actually safe to work with on late nights. Green meant genuinely professional and would share credit appropriately. Yellow meant professionally decent, but never be alone with them after 8 p.m. Red meant never be alone with them, always have a witness, and consider recording meetings if legally permitted.

The network started after three separate women discovered they'd all had identical experiences with the same senior partner claiming their legal research as his own. Not similar experiences. Identical. Down to him using the same phrases in client meetings: "I've developed a novel approach to this liability issue." Each woman thought she was alone until a bathroom conversation at the summer associate welcome dinner revealed the pattern.

The Grid evolved to track these patterns systematically. Women and lawyers of color mapped which partners would actually develop talent versus those who'd collect mentees for appearances while ensuring none made partner. They documented which practice groups had real advancement paths versus specialties that looked prestigious but never led to equity partnership.

Most damning was their discovery that Performance Improvement Plans followed a pattern: PIPs over the past three years had exclusively targeted Black and Asian lawyers, even those winning major cases. Research on performance management bias confirms this isn't unique to one firm. Studies have consistently found that Black employees receive more negative performance feedback than white colleagues with identical work output, and are significantly more likely to be placed on formal improvement plans regardless of objective performance metrics.[2] The network called it "The Harvest," the annual clearing out of anyone who didn't fit the template. Like roots that communicate through chemical signals to warn each other of threats, the lawyers had learned to read the signs months in advance, spreading warnings through their underground networks before decisions came down.

What made the root system truly powerful is that it crossed hierarchies. Senior associates warned juniors. Women partners (the few who existed) quietly guided younger women away from known problems. Those who'd been burned helped those just starting. Traditional power structures meant nothing in the root system; what mattered was shared support.

The firm had no idea these networks existed until they noticed something strange during performance reviews. Women and lawyers of color kept leaving specific practice groups while thriving in others, with no correlation to pay, bonuses, or official engagement scores. The pattern baffled them until I started my investigation. That's when an HR insider, someone brought in to "increase diversity," broke down during our conversation and revealed the explanation: "In my three years here, I've never put a white lawyer on a Performance Improvement Plan. Not once. I've been pressured to PIP twelve Black and Asian lawyers, including ones exceeding their billable hours and getting excellent client feedback."

One South Asian lawyer told me he navigated three attempted PIPs because the root system taught him how to work around them. "Every time I exceeded expectations, I'd email five partners about it, cc'ing my assistant for documentation. When they tried to say I wasn't meeting standards, I had receipts. They couldn't PIP someone with that much evidence of excellence. So they just stopped giving me good work instead."

The network extended beyond the firm's walls. They had connections at rival firms, sharing intelligence about which places actually promoted Black partners rather than using representation for recruitment optics. One lawyer showed me messages from the network: "Don't go to [Firm Name]. They have Black partners, but look closer. They're all non-equity. It's a showcase, not real opportunity."

Research confirms what these lawyers instinctively knew. A 2023 study by the National Association for Law Placement found that while people of color make up 38 percent of associates at major law firms, they represent only 11 percent of equity partners, with attrition rates nearly twice as high as their white counterparts.[3] The root system didn't need studies to know this. They lived it daily and built networks to navigate it.

The most sophisticated part of the root system was what they called "The Pipeline," roots that had broken through the firm's boundaries to connect with networks at other organizations. Like trees in a forest whose roots intertwine underground to share resources, this network for talented lawyers of color created pathways to better firms. They shared information about openings, provided references that bypassed official channels, and coached each other through interviews. One partner at a rival firm, herself a Pipeline graduate, hired exclusively from these networks. "I know they're excellent," she told me. "If they thrived in that environment while being systematically undermined, they can handle anything."

The root system also protected whistleblowers. When one associate tried to report abuse through official channels, the network warned her: "They'll dismiss the complaint and undermine you in the process. Document everything, get a lawyer, go external if necessary." They'd learned that HR protected the firm, not the people. The root system had watched too many careers derailed by believing in official channels.

This shadow infrastructure ran so deep that when I presented my findings to the managing partners, they refused to believe it. "This seems like conspiracy thinking," one said. So I asked a simple question: "What percentage of your Black and Asian lawyers make partner compared to white lawyers?" The silence was awkward. They didn't track it officially. The root system knew: 3 percent against 47 percent.

The partners wanted to dismantle these networks, seeing them as subversive. They missed the point entirely. The root system wasn't the problem; it was the symptom. These networks existed because official channels had failed so spectacularly that people needed underground systems to navigate. Roots can't be destroyed without destroying the plants they support, and these roots were the only thing keeping talented lawyers functioning in hostile soil.

When I pointed this out, one partner actually suggested monitoring employee communications to "break up these toxic networks." The irony was lost on him. The networks weren't toxic; they were the antidote to toxicity. They were performing the functions HR should have performed, providing the support leadership should have provided, creating the transparency the firm claimed to value but actively suppressed.

The root system at this firm wasn't unique. Every organization has these hidden networks. The administrative assistants who warn each other which executives to avoid. The junior employees sharing salary information in spreadsheets disguised as lunch orders. The women documenting harassment in shared drives labeled "Team Building Ideas." The people of color tracking discriminatory patterns in documents titled "Professional Development Resources." These roots run deeper than any official structure because they're based on trust earned through shared experience, not titles granted through political maneuvering. They carry the organization's real history, its actual values, its true power dynamics. While leadership celebrates fictional engagement scores, the root system knows who's interviewing, who's documenting, who's one difficult day away from walking out.

The problem isn't that these networks exist. It's that they have to. In healthy organizations, people don't need shadow systems to navigate. They don't need warning networks to work around leadership. They don't need underground pathways to find better opportunities. Healthy organizations make these networks unnecessary by ensuring official channels actually work, by creating genuine psychological safety, by building cultures where people can raise concerns without fear of retaliation.

Your Culture's Real Headquarters

Whisper networks aren't just information exchanges. They're judicial systems, early warning systems, and survival schools rolled into one. Like root networks that spread laterally underground, connecting plant to plant across vast distances, these whisper networks create an invisible infrastructure beneath an organization's surface. While official policies go unfollowed, these networks operate on unwritten rules everyone knows. They don't just share what happened; they teach how to navigate what's coming.

The teaching happens through stories. Not the sanitized case studies in leadership training, but the raw testimonies passed between generations of employees like organizational folklore. "Never present to Johnson without Barrett in the room; she'll keep him from claiming your work." "If Martinez asks you to coffee, bring a colleague and sit near the door." "When they say you're being given 'visibility,' they mean you're being set up as a scapegoat."

These stories become organizational DNA, encoding wisdom that no onboarding covers. A digital consulting firm I worked with discovered their whisper network had created what amounted to an underground university. New hires weren't just warned about toxic leaders; they received detailed playbooks on navigation: how to document without appearing paranoid, how to decline dangerous assignments without seeming difficult, how to build alliances before needing them. One woman showed me her "inheritance," a shared folder buried deep in the firm's own cloud system, disguised as "Q3 2023 Archive Materials," containing five years of intelligence. Email templates for creating paper trails. Scripts for difficult conversations with HR. A decision tree for determining when to fight versus when to flee. Contact information for lawyers who understood the firm's patterns. Even a financial planning spreadsheet calculating how long someone could last on savings if they had to leave suddenly. "This is what we mean by mentorship," she explained. "Not the official program where partners take you to lunch and give useless advice about 'executive presence.' This is real mentorship, teaching each other how to function long enough to maybe flourish."

The whisper network at this firm had identified something crucial: Patterns repeat. The partner who derailed one woman's career would do it again. The client who made racist remarks would escalate. The HR business partner who leaked confidential complaints would continue betraying trust. So they tracked patterns, creating predictive models more accurate than any performance review system.

One junior consultant noticed something odd: Every single person promoted in the last two years had started showing up at the managing partner's wine tastings six months before their advancement. Not because deals got made over Bordeaux, but because that's where the real performance reviews happened. Official reviews might praise analytical skills, but anyone who couldn't distinguish a Malbec from a merlot while discussing client strategies was forever marked as "lacking sophistication."

The whisper network turned this intelligence into action. They created a study group, ostensibly for professional development, that was actually teaching people how to navigate these informal evaluation moments. Wine basics, yes, but more importantly, how to casually mention wins without seeming boastful, how to take credit without appearing grabby, how to make intelligence nonthreatening to insecure leaders who had peaked at business school.

The network had identified that the real headquarters of company culture wasn't the gleaming downtown office. It was a series of spaces where actual decisions got made: the managing partner's taxi during rides with select seniors, the bathroom outside the boardroom where the CFO held court after meetings, the coffee machine on the executive floor that somehow always required fixing when important discussions were happening.

They mapped these shadow headquarters with scientific precision. Tuesday mornings at the executive coffee machine: That's where project assignments actually got distributed. Friday afternoon "casual" drinks at the hotel bar across the street: That's where partnership material got decided. The whisper network's greatest achievement was what they called "The Succession Files." While HR maintained official succession planning documents that nobody trusted, the network had built their own predictive model based on five years of observation. They could predict who would be promoted, demoted, or managed out with uncanny accuracy, usually spotting the signs three to six months before it happened.

Their indicators weren't in any leadership textbook. Exclusion from the fantasy football email chain meant being frozen out. Solo board presentation at a junior level meant setup for failure. Leading the diversity committee meant being marked "not strategic" and sidelined. One senior specialist decoded the system after being passed over for partner twice despite exceeding every metric. "I realized I was measuring the wrong things," she told me. "Revenue generated, client satisfaction, team retention, none of that mattered. What mattered was whether you laughed at the partner's jokes about his boat, whether you could quote the same business books the partners read twenty years ago, and whether your success could be attributed to their mentorship rather than your own capability."

Back channels served another crucial function: They preserved institutional memory. A senior manager showed me a shared drive disguised as old project files containing seven years of truth the organization refused to acknowledge. Every transformation that failed after a partner read a new airport book. Every star performer's actual contributions before they left. Every client lost to leadership ego, then blamed on market conditions. "Official history gets rewritten every time leadership changes," she explained.

This archive revealed patterns invisible to leadership. The same "innovative" ideas recycled every three years with new acronyms. The same toxic behaviors rewarded under different competency frameworks. The same mistakes driving clients away, the losses blamed on market conditions. The whisper network used this history to predict future failures with disturbing accuracy.

When the firm announced its latest cultural transformation, the network already knew it would fail. They'd seen the same consultant, the same framework, the same resistance to actual change. They prepared navigation guides for employees: how to appear engaged while protecting actual work, which initiatives to volunteer for (visible but low effort) versus which to avoid (high effort, no recognition), how long to wait before the transformation quietly faded and things returned to dysfunction as usual.

The whisper network's most valuable intelligence often came from administrative staff, the people leadership forgot existed. Executive assistants who scheduled meetings knew who was really in charge. IT staff who set up video calls knew which "confidential" discussions happened off the record. The facilities team knew which offices got upgraded before promotions were announced. These invisible employees became the network's early warning system. They'd notice when someone's calendar suddenly filled with "sync-ups" (performance management beginning), when office moves coincidentally isolated certain people (freezing out), or when someone's name dropped off distribution lists weeks before any official announcement. Their observations, shared quietly with those who needed to know, protected countless careers from ambush.

The network even developed economic models. They tracked which departments got budget increases (future power centers) and which faced cuts (start interviewing). They monitored office renovations, travel approvals, and hiring patterns to predict organizational shifts months before announcements. When three senior consultants noticed their travel budgets suddenly restricted while junior staff got approved for conferences, they knew they were being managed out. All three had new jobs before their severance negotiations began.

Perhaps the most profound function of whisper networks was providing what organizations claimed to value but rarely delivered: psychological safety. In these back channels, people could admit failure without fear, share struggles without judgment, and ask questions without appearing weak. The whisper network provided the support that leadership promised but never delivered.

When I presented these findings to the consulting firm's partners, their response was a master class in missing the point. In addition to the partner mentioned earlier who wanted to break up these "toxic" networks, another partner suggested "harnessing this organic intelligence for strategic advantage." A third actually asked if we could "install similar networks in other divisions." They were trying to control something that only existed because control had failed.

Whisper networks can't be dismantled without dismantling the support systems people depend on. They can't be co-opted without contaminating the only safe space left in an organization. The networks exist because leadership has broken trust so thoroughly that employees have had to build their own support systems. Until that fundamental betrayal gets addressed, the networks will persist, and they should.

The real question isn't how to eliminate whisper networks. It's how to make them unnecessary. Organizations that have successfully done this share common approaches: They create genuine channels for raising concerns without retaliation, they act visibly on feedback so people see that official channels actually work, they hold leaders accountable for patterns the whisper networks have always tracked, and they treat administrative staff as the organizational intelligence they've always been rather than invisible support functions. When official systems earn trust, shadow systems naturally fade. Not because they've been suppressed, but because they're no longer needed. The roots that formed in darkness can finally grow toward the light.

When Connection Becomes a Private Club

Not all root systems run deep. In some organizations, they barely scratch the surface, spreading laterally like grass rather than anchoring like oak trees. These shallow networks form in places where nobody expects to stay long enough to invest in real connections. Like desert plants that spread roots wide but shallow to catch any available moisture before it evaporates, these networks grab what information they can before people disappear. They're transactional, temporary, and surprisingly honest about it.

A major retail chain I assessed revealed how shallow roots become a strategy when the soil itself is temporary. With 74 percent annual turnover at store level and corporate positions restructuring every time quarterly earnings disappointed, employees had learned that deep connections were a luxury they couldn't afford. Their whisper network operated like an emergency broadcast system, rapid alerts about immediate threats with no expectation of long-term relationships. Which district manager was on a firing spree. Which stores were about to be "optimized" (closed). Which corporate initiatives would actually be enforced and which would be forgotten by next month. The information flew through Slack groups that disbanded and reformed constantly as people churned in and out.

The shallow network had developed its own brutal economics. MIT's Zeynep Ton found that retail companies lose between 60 and 100 percent of their workforce annually, with some experiencing 400 percent turnover, employees lasting an average of just three months before moving on.[4] A store manager explained the unwritten rules: "Someone warns you that corporate is doing surprise visits this week? You owe them intel about which metrics they're actually checking. Someone tells you the regional VP is hunting for scapegoats after the quarterly miss? You tell them which stores have protection from above. Don't expect anyone to remember your name six months from now."

This surface-level connection served a specific function: It prevented people from investing emotional energy in an organization where they were as disposable as seasonal merchandise. They'd watched too many colleagues pour themselves into "culture improvement" initiatives only to be laid off in the next restructuring. The shallow roots protected them from caring too much about a company that saw them as line items on a P&L. Shallow roots in retail created a particular tragedy. These weren't just corporate employees shuffling spreadsheets; they were people managing stores in communities they lived in, serving customers they knew by name. Yet they couldn't dig deep organizationally because the company might eliminate their position tomorrow to boost its stock price by twelve cents

Not every store in this retail chain had shallow roots. The contrast was stark when comparing flagship locations to mall stores. In the flagship stores, those beautiful multifloor destinations in major cities, something entirely different had evolved. Here, with lower turnover and higher wages, employees had been there for years. Instead of shallow survival networks, they'd built something else: deep roots that had become exclusive private clubs.

"There's the official onboarding, and then there's the real initiation that takes years," a flagship store manager explained. She'd transferred from a mall location three years ago and was still considered an outsider. "The people who've been here since this store opened in 2010? They control everything. Which shifts are actually good, which stockrooms have working air conditioning, which assistant managers will help rather than sabotage you. If you're not part of their network, you're basically working in a different store, the worse one."

These deep roots hadn't formed overnight. They'd grown from genuine mutual support, employees helping each other handle demanding customers, impossible metrics, and corporate whims.

Somewhere along the way, the network had calcified into something else. The same connections that once welcomed newcomers now actively repelled them.

The transformation happened gradually. First, the deep-rooted employees started hoarding knowledge: Why teach the stockroom's organizational system to someone who'd probably quit in three months? Then came resource gatekeeping: the best shifts, functioning equipment, and reliable registers somehow reserved for insiders. New employees got the finicky scanner, the register that crashed every third transaction, the stockroom key that stuck unless you knew the exact jiggle technique. Finally, the network developed its own justice system. Cross someone within the network, and schedules would mysteriously become impossible. Challenge their methods, and sales numbers would somehow drop. Threaten their comfortable ecosystem, and a transfer to a mall store would follow within a month.

The irony was that these flagship stores, despite their stability and deep roots, performed worse than the chaotic mall locations. Customer satisfaction scores consistently lagged. Innovation adoption moved at glacial pace. Sales growth stagnated, while mall stores, with all their turnover chaos, actually grew revenue. The deep roots had become so focused on self-preservation that they'd forgotten the organization's actual purpose.

What distinguished these flagship stores from healthy organizations with deep roots was the absence of renewal. In thriving ecosystems, deep roots support new growth. Old trees shelter saplings. Established plants share nutrients through fungal networks. In these flagship stores, the deep-rooted employees had created a closed system that actively prevented new growth, treating every newcomer as a threat rather than an opportunity for regeneration.

Research by Amy Edmondson at Harvard Business School found that psychological safety, the ability to take risks without fear of punishment, directly correlates with team performance and innovation.[5] These flagship stores had inverted the concept. They'd created psychological safety for insiders by making outsiders psychologically unsafe. The protected became the predators.

The exclusion mechanisms were sophisticated. New employees would receive training that somehow skipped crucial information. They'd get schedules that prevented them from attending informal gatherings where real knowledge transfer happened. Their suggestions in team meetings would be met with subtle eye rolls and sighs that communicated "you don't understand how things work here" without anyone having to say it explicitly.

One district manager documented the pattern after investigating why flagship stores had 40 percent turnover among new hires despite better pay and conditions. New employees consistently reported feeling "frozen out," "constantly tested," and "never good enough" regardless of their performance metrics. The deep-rooted employees had created such specific cultural codes, references to past events, inside jokes, and specialized vocabulary that outsiders needed years to decode the language, let alone contribute meaningfully. The comparison with technology companies revealed similar patterns. Startups that maintained their original engineering teams often developed identical dynamics. The founders and early employees would form such tight networks that new hires, even senior ones, could never truly integrate. They'd have the title, the salary, the desk, but not the invisible connections that actually enabled influence.

Here's the critical distinction: Not all deep roots become exclusive. Some organizations manage to maintain strong, interconnected networks while remaining permeable to newcomers. The difference lies in whether the root system sees new growth as competition or contribution.

A contrasting example emerged from a different retail organization, a regional grocery chain with equally low turnover but radically different outcomes. Their flagship stores also had employees who'd worked there for decades. Instead of gatekeeping, they'd developed what I can only describe as root grafting, actively connecting newcomers to the established network. This regional grocery chain had developed mentorship protocols that weren't about paperwork but actual cultivation. When someone new joined a flagship store, they weren't just assigned a trainer. They were grafted onto the root system through multiple connection points. Three different employees from different tenure levels would take responsibility for their integration—not their performance, their belonging.

The newest person who'd successfully integrated (usually six months in) would share basics: which registers actually worked, when to take breaks to avoid burnout, how to read between the lines of corporate communications. Someone from middle tenure (two to three years) would decode the social dynamics: who collaborated well together, which managers actually supported development, how decisions really got made. Critically, someone from the deep roots (five-plus years) would actively include them in informal networks: the morning coffee group where problems got solved, the lunch crew that shared customer intelligence, the after-work text chain that warned about surprise visits.

This wasn't corporate policy. No handbook mandated this root grafting. It had evolved because the deep-rooted employees understood something fundamental: New growth strengthened the entire system. Fresh perspectives prevented stagnation. Different backgrounds brought customer insights they'd never access otherwise. Energy from newcomers reminded veterans why they'd stayed.

The results spoke for themselves. These flagship stores had 82 percent retention after one year for new hires, compared to the exclusive stores' 60 percent. Customer satisfaction scores consistently ranked highest in the chain. Most tellingly, innovation actually came from these stores: new display ideas, customer service approaches, and inventory solutions that corporate would then roll out system-wide.

The difference between exclusive and inclusive deep roots came down to one fundamental belief: whether the organization was a fixed pie to be protected or an expanding garden to be cultivated. Exclusive networks operated from scarcity: only so many good shifts, only so many promotions, only so much recognition to go around. Every newcomer meant less for those already there. Inclusive networks understood abundance. New people brought new customers, fresh energy created more opportunities, different perspectives solved problems that had seemed unsolvable.

This wasn't just philosophical. The inclusive networks had developed specific practices that kept roots deep but permeable. They rotated knowledge-sharing responsibilities so no single person became a gatekeeper. They documented processes not to control them but to democratize them. They celebrated when newcomers improved on established methods rather than defending "how we've always done it."

Most critically, they'd learned to distinguish between the roots worth preserving (values, quality standards, customer relationships) and those that needed pruning (outdated processes, territorial behaviors, resistance to change). They maintained depth without rigidity, stability without stagnation.

The retail chain I'd studied never achieved this balance. Their flagship stores remained exclusive fortresses, while their mall stores churned through employees like seasonal inventory. Neither model served them well. The shallow roots couldn't build institutional knowledge. The deep roots couldn't incorporate new thinking. They had networks that either couldn't remember or couldn't forget, but none that could do both.

This is the fundamental flaw of connection becoming a private club: It defeats its own purpose. Networks exist to strengthen the collective, not to privilege the connected. When root systems become about exclusion rather than inclusion, they stop being foundations for growth and become barriers to it. The organization might function, but it will never flourish.

Why Even Good Foundations Can Fail

The most devastating cultural failures I've witnessed weren't in toxic organizations with shallow networks or exclusive clubs. They happened in companies that had cultivated exemplary root systems, genuine psychological safety, inclusive networks, and authentic trust, only to watch their carefully nurtured connections wither anyway. These weren't corporate villains. They were heroes who somehow still lost everything.

I call it "root shock," when thriving networks suddenly can't function because someone fundamentally altered their universe while swearing nothing would change.

A design startup I studied had cultivated something impressive. Their root system ran so deep that employees routinely solved each other's challenges without being asked. Designers would spot developers struggling with interface logic and quietly leave solutions on their desks. Engineers noticed when copywriters hit walls and offered technical perspectives that unlocked creativity. No formal process, no documented procedures, just people recognizing struggle and responding with support. Their Friday afternoon "show and tell" sessions were brilliant. Not mandatory, never recorded, but somehow everyone appeared. People shared half-baked ideas, spectacular failures, and accidental discoveries. The junior designer who'd broken the entire staging site got the same applause as the architect who'd solved their scaling crisis. Vulnerability was currency, mistakes were teaching moments, and everyone understood that brilliance emerges from collective intelligence, not individual genius.

Then a multinational software corporation acquired them for their "innovative culture." The acquiring company arrived genuinely wanting to preserve what made this startup special. They studied the Friday sessions, documented every organic interaction, and promised to protect this precious ecosystem. They meant it too; nobody acquires innovation to destroy it.

Within three months, those Friday sessions had transformed into "Innovation Showcases" with attendance tracking, presentation templates, and metrics for "ideation output." The spontaneous problem-solving became "peer assistance workflows" requiring tickets in their project management system. Someone decided psychological safety needed measurement, so they created quarterly assessments that everyone knew actually measured how much leadership could trust employees to stay positive.

The startup's employees watched their root system get uprooted and forced into foreign soil. Each change seemed reasonable in isolation. Structure would help scale their success. Documentation would preserve institutional knowledge. Metrics would prove the culture's value to stakeholders. Roots don't function when ripped from native ground and replanted in concrete.

Nobody could pinpoint exactly when their thriving network became corporate performance, but everyone felt it happen. What destroyed their culture wasn't malice but methodology. Every attempt to strengthen connections actually severed them. The parent company's enhancement of peer support added approval hierarchies that turned instant help into three-day request cycles. Their workspace reorganization separated teams who'd grown together, redistributing them across floors for "cross-functional synergy" that mainly created isolation.

The heartbreak was watching employees who'd built profound trust suddenly perform connection rather than experience it. They attended the mandatory sessions, filed the peer assistance tickets, scored well on psychological safety assessments. The real network, the one that had made them extraordinary, went dormant, waiting for conditions that would never return.

The most insidious change came through language itself. The acquiring company spoke a different dialect of corporate, one that transformed every simple interaction into strategic alignment exercises. "Let's chat" became "let's schedule a touchpoint to calibrate our synergies." "I have an idea" transformed into "I'd like to propose an initiative for consideration through appropriate channels." Direct feedback mutated into feedback sandwiches so elaborate they required architectural drawings. Employees who'd built trust through radical honesty suddenly found themselves translating every thought through corporate euphemism. The roots remained, but they were forced to communicate through foreign soil. Years of shorthand, inside jokes, and intuitive understanding got buried under process documentation and stakeholder management. They still knew each other, but they could no longer speak to each other, at least not in ways that mattered.

The parent company's most destructive gift was "best practice integration." They'd identified what made the startup successful and decided to improve it with proven methodologies. The red sticky note system for design critiques became a digital platform with reviewer assignments, deadline tracking, and sentiment analysis. What had been immediate and visceral became scheduled and sanitized. Designers started getting feedback like "consider exploring alternative color harmonies" instead of "this purple makes me want to quit design."

Their celebrated problem-solving culture got especially thorough treatment. The parent company created a "Solutions Architecture Framework" that formalized how help should flow between teams. Request forms, approval workflows, and impact assessments were all designed to ensure resources were "optimally allocated." The same developer who used to spot a designer struggling and offer immediate help now had to submit a cross-functional assistance request, wait for manager approval, and log hours against the appropriate project code. McKinsey's comprehensive analysis of over one thousand acquisitions found that cultural integration issues account for up to 50 percent of deal failures, with the inability to preserve target company cultures being the single largest predictor of value destruction.[6] Root systems reject the transplant, no matter how carefully the preservation attempt unfolds.

The startup employees developed what I've seen wherever healthy roots meet hostile conditions: a double existence. Like trees whose visible growth follows imposed shapes while their roots spread in natural patterns underground, they performed compliance with new systems while maintaining shadow versions of what actually worked. The official Friday showcase happened in the main conference room with slides and metrics. The real Friday session happened at the bar afterward, where people actually shared what they'd learned. They filed peer assistance tickets for visibility, then solved problems through text messages and coffee runs. This parallel universe exhausted everyone. They were tending two gardens simultaneously: one for show above ground, one for function below. Every interaction required calculating which version to use. Official channels for documentation, shadow networks for solutions. Corporate dialect for meetings, human language for hallways.

Twelve months into the acquisition, the original root system had fractured into three distinct networks. The adapters learned the new language, attended every integration workshop, and gradually forgot why they'd loved working there. The preservationists maintained shadow systems, protecting original practices like underground librarians safeguarding banned books. The departed had already left or were actively interviewing, their roots already seeking healthier soil elsewhere. The parent company couldn't fathom the exodus. They'd retained all the talent contracts. They'd preserved the office space, the benefits package, even the fancy coffee machine everyone loved. Root systems aren't about visible perks, though. They're about invisible connections, the shorthand developed over years, the trust earned through shared struggles, the safety created through consistent care.

What failed wasn't the foundation but the assumption that culture can be transplanted like code. The parent company treated their acquisition like downloading an app: Copy the features, migrate the users, maintain the interface. Roots don't migrate. They're adapted to specific conditions, particular soil chemistry, unique ecosystems. Transform the environment too drastically, and even the strongest networks deteriorate. By year two, only remnants of the original culture remained. The company still functioned, products shipped, clients paid, metrics stayed green. But the magic had evaporated. Designers who'd once created breakthrough interfaces now produced competent mediocrity. Developers who'd solved impossible problems now wrote adequate code. Everyone did their jobs. Nobody did their best.

Here's what leaders often miss: Culture can't be preserved by documenting it. Writing down how a garden grows doesn't teach anyone how to grow one. The startup's root system hadn't developed through process documents and best practices. It emerged from specific people trusting each other in specific ways under specific conditions. Change any variable, and the whole system shifts.

This pattern repeats everywhere cultures get "improved" to the point of failure. A sustainable fashion brand gets acquired by a fast fashion giant who promises to preserve their ethical practices while demanding quarterly growth that makes those practices impossible. A craft brewery gets bought by a beverage conglomerate that maintains the recipes while destroying the community connections that made those recipes matter. A boutique consultancy gets absorbed by a consultancy firm that keeps the client list while eliminating the intimate relationships that created it.

The consistent failure point isn't the obvious changes: the new systems, processes, or structures. It's the subtle shifts in how people relate to each other. The startup employees stopped sharing unfinished ideas because the new culture punished imperfection. They stopped offering unsolicited help because the new system required documented requests. They stopped trusting because trust had become a metric rather than an experience.

The lesson isn't that strong cultures can't handle change. It's that cultures aren't things organizations have but relationships people tend. Relationships can't be optimized. Intimacy can't be scaled. Trust can't be systematized.

The real revelation wasn't that the acquisition failed. Acquisitions fail constantly. The shocking part was what it exposed about the limitations of roots themselves. These startup employees had built extraordinary connections. They'd created networks so robust they could solve any problem, weather any crisis, support any struggle. Their root system was a masterpiece of human collaboration. Yet when the actual growing conditions changed, when decision-making power shifted, when resources got reallocated, when their innovations got buried under approval layers, those beautiful roots couldn't save them.

Here's what even the strongest root systems can't overcome: starvation. The startup's networks could warn each other about problematic changes, but they couldn't stop them. They could share navigation tactics, but they couldn't create opportunities for growth. They could maintain shadow systems, but they couldn't access actual power. They had connection without agency, support without resources, roots without nutrients.

I've watched this pattern repeatedly. Organizations with root systems so sophisticated that they could predict problems months in advance, yet when every solution required approval from the very people causing the problems, when innovative ideas got diluted through committees designed to maintain the status quo, those prescient roots meant nothing. They knew exactly what needed to change. They had zero power to change it.

This is the fundamental reality of workplace root systems: Connection without resources creates informed frustration. People know exactly why they're struggling. They have colleagues who understand their situation. They build beautiful support networks to help each other cope with powerlessness. Yet powerlessness remains.

The law firm associates with their Grid could track discrimination, but couldn't stop it. The retail workers with their whisper networks could warn about store closures, but couldn't prevent them. The startup employees could maintain their shadow culture, but couldn't make it matter. They were tending gardens in the dark, maintaining elaborate root systems that connected to nothing nutritious. Like roots spreading through barren soil, searching for water that doesn't exist, these networks mapped every problem, but they couldn't access the resources to solve them.

Organizations often celebrate root systems that don't challenge resource distribution. They fund employee resource groups that build connections without power. They create mentorship programs that develop relationships without opportunities. They encourage networks that provide support without agency. Roots that aren't fed can't grow strong enough to challenge anything.

An organization might have the most sophisticated root system ever developed. People might be connected through bonds that transcend org charts. Networks might carry truth more efficiently than fiber optic cables. Yet if those roots can't access real nutrients, actual power, genuine resources, and meaningful growth opportunities, they're just nurturing connections that document dysfunction without the authority to address it.

Here's the question every organization must ask: What are people actually being fed? Connection without nourishment isn't culture. It's elaborate coping mechanisms for systematic resource deprivation. I've watched organizations pour millions into building connections while denying those same connections what they need to flourish. They'll fund team-building retreats but not give teams authority to implement their solutions. They'll create mentorship programs but not promotion pathways. They'll celebrate sophisticated root systems while providing nothing that would let those roots grow beyond basic functioning.

The startup employees had roots that could navigate any challenge together, but they couldn't access the power to say no to destructive changes. The law firm associates had networks that documented every injustice, but they couldn't tap into resources to create justice. The retail workers had connections that predicted every corporate disaster, but they couldn't reach the authority to prevent a single one.

Roots are only as strong as what feeds them. Tending roots is slow and often invisible work. Connections form through consistency, through showing up, through small acts of trust repeated until they become culture. Yet roots are how people actually survive organizations. When crises hit, it's the colleague who texts "Are you okay?" before the all-hands meeting. When change threatens everything, it's the network that helps people navigate, the connections that hold when official structures fail. Roots may not fix broken systems alone, but they keep people together while the fixing happens. Those who build trust across silos, who share information freely, who create safety for others in unsafe environments, are strengthening something that can outlast any single leader, any restructuring, any acquisition. Connection is how cultures endure.

This brings us to the most critical question of all: Once the soil is healthy, once the light reaches everyone, once the roots connect deeply, what exactly do people need to actually grow? What are the essential nutrients that transform survival into flourishing? The answer might be simpler than organizations want to admit, and harder than most are willing to provide.

4

Nutrients

The Food That Feeds Performance

Perfect soil, balanced exposure, and deep roots still aren't enough. Without real nourishment, people are just surviving on scraps. The organizations that thrive understand something crucial: Different people need different nutrients to flourish, and when individuals get what they actually need, the whole culture gets fed too.

Why Pizza and Ping-Pong Don't Cut It

An organization's kitchen might stock seventeen varieties of kombucha, yet people remain parched. Not for water: That's covered by the $40,000 filtration system that makes everything taste vaguely of cucumber. They're thirsting for something no artisanal snack wall can provide: the ability to make a decision without a committee, the chance to fail without becoming unemployable, the experience of a manager having their back when something goes sideways. Too many organizations have confused feeding with nourishing, mistaking a full stomach for a fulfilled human.

I worked with a tech company that had a $300,000 meditation room that sat empty while employees got denied $500 for conferences that would actually teach them something useful. People had been trying to get ten minutes with their managers about career paths for months, but there was always something more urgent, usually another meeting about employee wellness initiatives that nobody asked for. The company catered lunch daily with options for every dietary restriction known to humanity, yet people were starving for the three nutrients that actually matter: growth that goes beyond doing a boss's job for free, power that extends past choosing a desktop wallpaper, and safety that exists when things actually go wrong, not just in the mission statement. This is feast and famine in the same building: organizations hemorrhaging money on visible perks while people wither from lack of actual sustenance.

Tech companies install multimillion-dollar game rooms where nobody plays because everyone's too busy trying to get five minutes of leadership attention. Financial firms offer concierge services for dry cleaning and dinner reservations while refusing to give anyone enough decision-making authority to approve a $50 software subscription. Consulting firms provide gourmet meals at midnight, which would be lovely if it weren't because everyone's still working, desperately trying to deliver on promises made by partners who haven't done actual client work since PowerPoint had clip art. The disconnect reveals exactly how many organizations think people work: that a well-stocked snack pantry substitutes for career progression, that wearing jeans on Friday equals psychological safety, that a foosball table in the corner somehow cancels out the fact that every decision requires seventeen approvals and a prayer circle.

The perks race has become so elaborate that companies now compete on amenities like they're running luxury resorts instead of workplaces where actual work needs to happen. Watch what happens when someone asks for something that matters: Request funding for an advanced certification, and suddenly the budget's tight; propose giving a team actual autonomy, and it's too risky; suggest reducing the approval layers that make every decision a three-week archaeological expedition, and the response is "that's not how we operate," as if organizational constipation is a core value worth protecting.

The perks arms race reveals something profound about organizational delusion: competing on amenities while people are desperate for actual nutrients. It's like watching someone wither from scurvy while debating whether to stock the kitchen with Honeycrisp or Granny Smith apples. The vitamins people need aren't in the fruit bowl. They're the three essential nutrients every human needs to thrive at work, and none of them come from a cold brew tap.

Growth nutrients transform people from task-completers to capability-builders by offering real learning opportunities where failure doesn't end careers, meaningful challenges that stretch capability without breaking spirits, the permission to experiment without seventeen committees approving every hypothesis. Too often, "development opportunities" translate to doing a manager's work without the title or pay, "stretch assignments" mean covering for three people who quit because they couldn't get growth nutrients either, and "cross-functional exposure" really means attending meetings for departments that need someone to blame when things go wrong.

Power nutrients give people actual influence over their work: the authority to make decisions without a congressional hearing for every choice, to have their ideas heard by someone who can act on them rather than by someone who files them in the suggestion box graveyard. Instead, people get "empowerment initiatives" where they can choose their laptop sticker design but need three approvals to order office supplies. They get "ownership" of outcomes but not processes, responsibility without authority, accountability without agency. It's like being named captain of a ship only to discover you're not allowed to touch the wheel, the sails, or the navigation system, but you'll definitely go down with it when it sinks.

Safety nutrients form the foundation that makes everything else possible: support when things go wrong, not just celebration when things go right; psychological safety that exists during actual mistakes, not just in presentations about innovation culture; and backup from leadership when clients get unreasonable, projects fail, or bold bets don't pay off. People need managers who absorb pressure from above rather than amplifying it downward, who shield their teams from corporate chaos rather than being chaos delivery systems. Instead, they get "fail fast" rhetoric from leaders who've never failed at anything, "bring your whole self to work" invitations from homogeneous executive teams, and "we've got your back" promises from managers who throw people under buses so regularly they should charge fare.

The measurement problem compounds this nutritional crisis. Organizations love measuring what's easy to count rather than what actually matters. They'll track ping-pong table usage while remaining oblivious to burnout rates, survey coffee preferences while ignoring who gets meaningful mentorship, celebrate meditation room occupancy while missing that people are too stressed to meditate. A fellow consultant shared a perfect example from a tech client who spent $50,000 tracking "wellness initiative engagement" only to discover people attended yoga sessions because their managers noticed who didn't show up. Nothing says namaste like mandatory mindfulness under surveillance. They had spreadsheets showing 87 percent participation but somehow missed that their top talent was leaving for companies with fewer perks but actual growth opportunities.

Most organizations already have people who create nutrients naturally: the manager who turns every failure into a learning moment without making anyone feel stupid, the colleague who shares knowledge freely without hoarding it for personal advantage, the leader who actually shields their team from corporate chaos rather than amplifying it. These nutrient creators are organizational treasures, and the smartest companies learn to identify them, study what they do differently, and build systems that replicate their approach rather than leaving nourishment to chance. When I work with organizations serious about culture transformation, we start by mapping where nutrients actually flow: who creates them, who distributes them, and who people instinctively seek out when they need real support. These patterns reveal more about organizational health than any engagement survey.

The challenge is that nutrient creators often operate despite the system rather than because of it. They're frequently underpaid and underappreciated, filing expense reports while someone else gets the "Leadership Excellence Award" essentially for showing up. Protecting and empowering these people becomes the first step in any real culture shift.

The most dangerous evolution isn't organizations refusing nutrients outright. It's leaders who've learned to weaponize wellness language while withholding actual nourishment. The modern toxic boss doesn't throw tantrums; they throw people under buses using therapeutic vocabulary. They speak fluent "psychological safety" while making everyone unsafe. They preach "bring your whole self to work," then penalize people for having actual human needs. These leaders have mastered the performance: scheduling "radical candor" sessions that are neither radical nor candid, treating empathy like a performance metric, sharing meditation practices in all-hands while ignoring burnout in one-on-ones. I've watched this pattern repeatedly: leaders who build public brands on kindness while their teams quietly exit through NDAs. The gap between external messaging and internal reality becomes the organization's worst-kept secret.

What makes these leaders particularly dangerous is that they've convinced themselves they're the good ones. They attend unconscious bias training while consciously biasing every decision. They champion mental health initiatives while being the primary cause of their team's anxiety. Their wellness vocabulary is impeccable; their wellness delivery is nonexistent. They discriminate with deniability, marginalize with plausible excuses, destroy careers while maintaining perfect documentation.

People are learning to spot the difference between someone who talks about psychological safety and someone who creates it, between leaders who perform empathy and those who practice it. This matters because performative leadership creates organizational immunity to real nutrients. When people experience leaders who speak all the right words while delivering toxicity, they learn to reject even genuine nourishment later. The vocabulary of psychological safety becomes a warning sign rather than a promise. The whole language of modern leadership gets contaminated by those who use it as camouflage rather than commitment. People develop allergies not just to false feeding, but to any feeding at all, because they can no longer tell the difference between someone offering real nutrients and someone performing nutrient delivery while planning to starve them.

The modern toxic boss hasn't disappeared; they've just gotten better at disguising themselves as exactly who we wished they were, speaking the language of transformation while ensuring nothing actually transforms. These performative leaders are dangerous, but at least their emptiness eventually becomes visible. The gap between their words and actions grows undeniable. Far more insidious are the leaders who don't just withhold nutrients through performance but actively intercept and consume them before anyone else can access them. They don't pretend to feed people while starving them; they eat the food while everyone watches.

Organizations also harbor nutrient vampires who intercept sustenance before it reaches anyone else. The executive who takes credit for every success while distributing blame for every failure isn't just unfair; they're consuming the confidence-building nutrients others need to develop. When a breakthrough becomes their insight at the board meeting, the person who did the work doesn't just lose recognition; they lose the growth fuel that comes from owning contributions, the developmental nourishment of seeing thinking create impact, the career-building vitamins of being known for capabilities.

The manager who creates artificial scarcity, making people compete for crumbs of recognition, transforms abundance into famine. There's enough praise, development, and opportunity for everyone to flourish, but they ration it like wartime provisions, keeping teams malnourished on purpose, doling out just enough nutrients to prevent complete starvation but never enough for actual growth. The colleague who weaponizes information, using knowledge as currency rather than sharing it as nourishment, creates intellectual malnutrition across entire departments. They've turned learning into a scarce resource, hoarding insights like a survivalist hoards canned goods. Every question answered becomes a debt, every skill shared a loan that must be repaid. One of these vampires can turn an entire department into a wasteland where nothing grows except resignation letters. They position themselves between resources and recipients like organizational parasites, absorbing nutrients meant to feed whole teams.

Most organizations know exactly who their nutrient vampires are. They have the complaints, the exit interview patterns, the engagement scores that crater wherever these people feed. Yet they keep the vampires because they "deliver results," never calculating the starvation cost: How much more could flourish if nutrients actually reached the people doing the work? What innovations might bloom if growth resources weren't monopolized by those who stopped growing years ago?

Organizations spend millions on perks while people remain psychologically malnourished, installing massage chairs while souls cry out for meaningful challenge, upgrading coffee machines while downgrading human potential. The question isn't "What perks should we add?" but "What are people actually starving for?" Because somewhere in every building, someone brilliant is withering from lack of real opportunity while leadership debates sparkling water brands. Someone with game-changing ideas stays silent because speaking up has never been safe. Someone who could transform the business is updating their resume because they've realized the furniture gets fed better than the humans.

Knowing what people need is the first step. Actually providing it is where most organizations fail spectacularly.

What Actually Helps People Grow

The nutrients people need are clear: growth, power, and safety. Knowing and providing, however, are as different as reading a cookbook and actually producing something edible. Most organizations approach nutrients like amateur chefs who buy expensive ingredients and then burn everything because they never learned basic technique. They've got all the right components sitting in the pantry but keep serving burnt offerings and wondering why nobody's thriving.

Let's start with how organizations actually botch growth nutrients. Research by Carol Dweck and Kathleen Hogan shows that employees in growth-mindset cultures are 47 percent more likely to trust colleagues and 34 percent more likely to feel strong ownership and commitment to their company compared to those in fixed-mindset environments.[1] Yet most organizations claim to value growth while treating every mistake like someone personally betrayed the CEO's mother. They want innovation without risk, learning without stumbling, expertise without the awkward phase of not knowing what you're doing. It's like expecting someone to learn skiing without falling. It's theoretically possible if they never leave the bunny slope, but that's not really skiing; it's just standing on snow with expensive equipment.

Watch how organizations actually treat learning versus how they claim to. Does that "stretch assignment" come with support and permission to struggle, or is it code for "do a manager's work without the title or pay"? When someone admits they don't know something, do they receive resources and guidance, or do they get marked down as "lacking initiative"? The difference between growth nutrients and growth performance determines whether people develop capabilities or just anxiety disorders. I've seen organizations spend $100,000 sending executives to Harvard while denying $1,000 for online courses to the engineers who actually build the products. The executives come back quoting case studies about companies that failed twenty years ago, while the engineers figure out solutions on YouTube during lunch breaks.

Organizations that genuinely provide growth nutrients share specific characteristics. They don't just celebrate success; they actively feed the learning process. A software company I worked with has a CTO who rings a bell every time someone breaks production, not to shame but to announce "someone was brave enough to attempt something that matters." That bell isn't just sound; it's a nutrient injection that says intelligent risk-taking gets fed here, not starved. These organizations measure progress, not just outcomes, understanding that growth needs consistent feeding rather than final feast or famine. They give people time to actually digest learning instead of piling it on top of already overwhelming workloads. Most tellingly, their leaders openly display their own hunger for knowledge. When a CEO admits she's taking a course on data analytics because she doesn't understand half of what her tech team says, she's not just learning; she's showing everyone that admitting nutrient deficiency is the first step to getting fed.

Watch what happens in most organizations when someone admits they're hungry for knowledge: They get marked as malnourished rather than growth-oriented. Their credibility becomes rationed. They're quietly removed from the important projects that could actually feed their development. The pattern is consistent: Those who admit to learning get fed less opportunity, not more.

The fear of appearing hungry while learning creates elaborate corporate camouflage. Executives hire "advisors" to secretly feed them knowledge they should already have, packaging remedial nutrition as strategic consulting. Organizations spend millions on learning management platforms that track completion rates while missing that everyone's just clicking through at 2x speed to get the certificate without digesting any actual nutrients. Meanwhile, people who openly admit what they don't know get tagged as "lacking confidence" in performance reviews, teaching everyone else that ignorance is safer when it's silent.

Now let's examine how organizations mess up power nutrients. They announce "empowerment initiatives" with straight faces, like calling a hamster wheel a transportation solution. I've seen a company that let employees vote on the office air freshener scent but required four approvals to order printer paper. A startup that put "CEO" in everyone's title (Chief Everything Officer, Chief Excellence Officer) but nobody could approve their own expense report. A consultancy that created "autonomous teams" who had to present their decisions to three committees before implementing anything. Power without authority is costume jewelry: shiny, impressive at a distance, worthless when you need to actually buy something. Real power nutrients manifest in unglamorous ways: the ability to fix a broken process without forming a task force; make a decision that sticks without seventeen email threads; and say no to a client request without checking with legal, finance, and a manager's manager's spiritual advisor.

Power nutrients reveal themselves most clearly through their absence. Watch someone identify an obvious problem but lack the authority to address it. They write emails that get forwarded into oblivion, their ideas becoming watered down with each forward until they're barely recognizable. They raise issues in meetings where everyone nods sympathetically but nothing changes, their insights acknowledged but never activated. They create detailed proposals that languish unread in someone's inbox. Eventually, they stop trying, not from laziness but from learning that competence without authority equals frustration without resolution.

Organizations create elaborate systems to collect input while ensuring that input never transforms into action. Suggestion boxes become idea graveyards where good thinking goes unutilized. Innovation portals absorb energy while returning nothing. Town halls where questions get "taken offline" become performances where people pretend to engage while nothing actually changes.

The most damaging aspect of power deprivation shows up in how it transforms talented people into organizational shadows of themselves. They entered eager to contribute, full of energy and ideas. After years of watching their solutions get stuck in approval purgatory, however, they develop learned helplessness. They phrase every idea as a question ("Should we maybe consider possibly . . . ?") because direct statements require confidence they've been systematically denied. They credit others for their own innovations, knowing ideas need powerful sponsors to survive. They present solutions as "things they heard somewhere" rather than convictions they hold, knowing that the same idea from someone with more authority would be genius, while from them it's insubordination.

They've become ventriloquists throwing their voice through safer mouths, performing that careful dance where someone soft-pedals brilliance because their position makes their perspective dismissible. This is one of the most heartbreaking patterns in organizational life: watching someone with genuine insight learn to make themselves smaller because the alternative is being dismissed entirely.

Power nutrients don't mean chaos without oversight; they mean oversight without obstruction. When someone has genuine authority, they still operate within boundaries, with metrics to meet, standards to maintain, and protocols to follow. Within those boundaries, however, they have genuine agency to excel rather than just execute.

Safety nutrients might be the trickiest because organizations love performing safety while creating danger. They spend millions on "psychological safety workshops" led by the same executives who retaliate against anyone who disagrees with them. It's like taking swimming lessons from someone actively trying to drown you. Real safety nutrients show up in mundane moments: when someone admits they're lost in a meeting and gets guidance instead of judgment, when a project fails and the postmortem focuses on learning rather than blame, when someone challenges the CEO's pet project and still has a job next Monday.

The absence of safety creates a specific organizational paranoia where every interaction becomes calculated for survival rather than value. I've watched entire departments develop their own sign language for meetings: subtle hand signals warning colleagues when they're about to step on political landmines, eyebrow raises that mean "stop talking now," the tactical cough that signals "the person who can fire us just walked in." When safety nutrients are withheld, people develop elaborate workarounds just to function. The email draft folder with seventeen versions of the same message, each progressively diluted until it communicates nothing controversial, represents what happens when honest communication isn't nourished. The pre-meeting before the pre-meeting before the actual meeting, where people rehearse how to present bad news without appearing responsible, represents energy that could fuel innovation instead being spent on self-preservation.

People develop their own navigation systems when safety nutrients are rationed: timing difficult conversations for after the CFO's weekly tennis game when endorphins temporarily make them approachable, learning which phrases trigger which executives ("pivot" somehow means "lack of commitment," but "iterate" signals progress), memorizing the exact tone that conveys concern without sounding critical. They become behavioral scientists studying their leaders' patterns instead of focusing on their actual work, knowing Tuesday mornings mean staying invisible, that certain jacket colors signal approachability, that when the corner-office door closes at 2 p.m., someone's career is ending at 3. This hypervigilance consumes mental energy that could be driving innovation, solving problems, or building relationships.

Without safety nutrients, talented people can't risk the vulnerability that real growth requires. They can't admit knowledge gaps that need filling, can't propose bold solutions that might fail, can't build genuine connections that make work meaningful. Instead, they operate in perpetual defense mode, using all their creative energy to navigate political minefields rather than create value.

These three nutrients don't operate in isolation; they're interdependent in ways organizations rarely understand. I saw this play out at a retail company that gave store managers full authority to make decisions (power) and invested heavily in their development (growth), but maintained a culture where one complaint to corporate meant termination (no safety). The result? Managers had all the authority and knowledge to revolutionize their stores but used neither. They made only the safest, most conventional decisions because power without safety just means being captain of a ship you're afraid to steer.

Another organization provided exceptional psychological safety and continuous learning opportunities but no actual authority to implement what people learned. They became the world's most supportive think tank: brilliant ideas, genuine care, zero impact. People felt safe to dream but powerless to act, eventually developing a kind of comfortable learned helplessness where they'd discuss problems for hours without anyone able to actually fix them.

The interaction creates multiplier effects, both positive and negative. When all three nutrients are present, people don't just perform better; they transform what performance means. They take intelligent risks because safety allows for failure. They implement solutions immediately because power removes bureaucratic friction. They develop expertise rapidly because growth opportunities actually exist. Each nutrient amplifies the others, creating conditions where excellence becomes inevitable rather than exceptional.

Organizations consistently underestimate how these nutrients must be distributed together rather than in sequence. They give someone a promotion (power) without development support (growth) or protection when they stumble (safety), then wonder why high performers fail in new roles. They send people to expensive training (growth) without authority to apply what they've learned (power) or permission to experiment with new approaches (safety), then complain about poor ROI on learning investments.

The organizations that get this right understand something fundamental: Nutrients aren't rewards for performance but prerequisites for it. Authority enables people to prove themselves; waiting until they've already proven themselves defeats the purpose. Growth opportunities create high potentials; reserving them for those already labeled high potential just reinforces existing hierarchies. Safety allows the kind of intelligent failure that precedes breakthrough success; extending it only to those who succeed means nobody risks the attempts that lead to real innovation.

The Odds in Whose Favor?

Every organization insists nutrients are scarce: limited promotion slots, finite development budgets, only so much mentorship to go around. They've turned workplace growth into a competitive sport where people fight over crumbs while pretending there's not enough bread for everyone. Except there is. Companies find $2 million for rebrandings nobody asked for (congratulations on changing from navy to midnight blue), but can't find $2,000 for someone's professional certification. They have seventeen vice presidents of various mysteries but only one promotion slot for the twelve people actually doing the work. Scarcity isn't real; it's recreational.

The fascinating part isn't who gets nutrients; it's how organizations convince themselves the distribution is logical. That person who got the development opportunity? They were "ready for it." The one who didn't? "Needs more seasoning." What determines readiness versus seasoning remains mysteriously undefined, like organizational astrology where career trajectories depend on what conference room someone was hired in and whether Mercury was in retrograde. The patterns become absurd when tracked. People who admit they don't understand the business get sent to executive education at Wharton. People who understand it deeply get told they're "too operational" for strategic development. Those who've been with the company for fifteen years need "fresh perspective" from external programs, while new hires need to "learn the culture first" before accessing any development. Everyone needs what they can't get; nobody needs what they're offered.

The scarcity becomes especially revealing during annual planning when inclusion gets relegated to the "if we have money left over" category. Organizations find $3 million overnight for a system migration that could have waited but claim bankruptcy when asked to invest $30,000 in understanding the humans actually using those systems. They pay consultancies seven figures to tell them they need diverse talent, then act shocked when that talent leaves because nobody invested in teaching managers why some employees need cameras off during calls to manage sensory overload, or why "mandatory fun" team building actively excludes introverts, parents, and anyone whose idea of fun doesn't involve trust falls with people they don't trust. Watch the magic unfold when budgets get discussed. Mental health support? "Let's revisit next quarter." Neurodiversity training? "We'll add it to the wish list." Flexible working for parents? "Too complex to implement." Yet when the CEO's favorite project needs funding, millions materialize from departments that were just told to cut 10 percent. The same organization crying poverty about inclusion education just found $500,000 for a rebrand that changed punctuation in the tagline. Understanding a workforce gets treated like optional charity work rather than what it actually is: basic maintenance for the humans generating the revenue.

Organizations can have diversity where different faces revolve through the same door, never staying long enough to warm their seats. They can have inclusion that creates wonderfully welcoming monocultures where everyone feels belonging because everyone's identical. Without both diversity and inclusion, plus actual fairness and belonging, they're essentially running very expensive revolving doors. The talent they desperately need takes one look at the culture and decides their brilliance would be better appreciated elsewhere, somewhere that invests in understanding them as much as it invests in extracting value from them.

The compound effect starts early and becomes irreversible fast. Miss those first crucial nutrients in an early career, and people spend decades trying to catch up. Not because they lack capability, but because they never received the foundational nourishment that builds confidence. Without early growth nutrients, such as mentorship that actually develops, challenges that stretch without breaking, and permission to experiment, people become excellent at executing someone else's vision but unable to create their own. They master existing processes but can't innovate new ones because they learned that big ideas require big titles, not big thinking.

Meanwhile, those who got fed early keep getting fed more. They received confidence nutrients from day one: Their ideas were heard, their mistakes were framed as learning, their potential was assumed rather than questioned. These early nutrients compound like interest. The confidence to speak up leads to visibility, which leads to opportunities, which leads to more confidence. They're not smarter or more capable; they just got fed when it mattered most.

By year five, the gap becomes a canyon. One group has been living on minimum nutrients, just enough to perform their function but never enough to grow beyond it. They've learned to be grateful for scraps, to not ask for more, to make do with less. The other group has been dining on abundant nutrients they didn't even know were exclusive: casual mentorship over coffee, stretch assignments with safety nets, the permission to fail forward rather than just fail. One group races to stand still, while the other coasts on compound interest from investments they didn't even know they were receiving.

Organizations have perfected the art of nutrient hoarding while performing generosity. They create mentorship programs that mysteriously match people who already vacation together, then celebrate their commitment to development. How does this actually happen? The "mentor matching survey" asks about leadership style, career goals, and somehow, hobbies. Those hobbies get weighted surprisingly high in the algorithm. Suddenly everyone who mentions sailing gets paired with the CFO who owns a yacht, while everyone else gets middle managers who are also trying to figure out what mentorship means. They establish high-potential programs where potential seems to correlate with who drinks wine at the selection committee chair's house. The nomination form requires manager approval, skip-level endorsement, and a "business case" for potential. The real selection happens at those informal "calibration sessions" where leaders discuss candidates over drinks, and somehow the people who went to their alma mater or whose kids play lacrosse together keep rising to the top.

The distribution mechanisms are particularly clever because they appear merit-based while being entirely relationship-based. Take the famous "stretch assignment" that actually determines how much growth nutrient someone receives. When it goes to someone deemed high potential, it comes pre-fertilized: a shadow team providing support nutrients, weekly coaching that delivers leadership vitamins, and permission to "iterate," which essentially means unlimited nutrients to experiment and fail safely. When the same assignment goes to someone who needs to "prove themselves," they get the title but none of the sustenance. Same deadline, zero support nutrients, and if anything goes wrong, they're marked as unable to digest opportunity. It's like giving two people identical seeds but watering only one, then using the predictable results to justify who "naturally grows better."

Organizations orchestrate this starvation while performing abundance. That development opportunity comes with invisible rationing. Some people get the full meal with mentorship, protection, and time to digest the learning. Others get the scraps, the work without the wisdom, the responsibility without the resources, the challenge without the calories needed to meet it. Then leadership points to the predictable outcomes as validation of initial assessments, like weather forecasters predicting rain after they've turned on the sprinklers.

The real genius lies in how organizations make abundance appear scarce. That leadership development program with limited slots? They could easily run four cohorts instead of one, but scarcity creates prestige. When someone questions why only twenty people can attend, the response cites intimate learning environment and resource constraints, ignoring that the same content could be delivered virtually to hundreds. Those executive coaching hours reserved for senior management? The same budget could provide coaching for dozens of mid-level managers who'd actually benefit from it, but exclusivity maintains hierarchy. It's not resource management; it's distance management, ensuring those at the top have capabilities those below can't access.

The most revealing part is how organizations pour nutrients into people who contribute nothing, while those keeping the business alive ration their printer paper. I watched a media company maintain a leadership team of legacy employees whose primary skill was having survived previous layoffs. Enter a new hire at an eye-watering salary to "drive new business development." She'd patrol the building spraying air freshener like she was marking territory, conducting phantom meetings with prospects who'd already told junior salespeople no three times. Those junior employees, on criminally low wages, would watch her commandeer their research, repackage their leads as "strategic initiatives," and present their work in meetings they weren't invited to attend. Not one sliver of new business materialized from her perfumed performances, yet she consumed the salary of seven people who were actually generating revenue. When budgets tightened, guess whose roles got "restructured"? Not hers. She was "essential for strategic direction." The junior employees who'd kept the lights on? They were "redundant."

This is nutrient hoarding at its most grotesque: organizations protecting those who drain resources while eliminating those who create value. She kept getting fed not despite her failure, but because acknowledging it would mean admitting someone made a terrible hiring decision. Better to keep funding the mistake than admit it exists.

Nutrient vampires don't just drain through incompetence. Some drain through casual cruelty that forces others to expend their growth energy on basic survival. At a publishing company where I served as Head of People briefly (nine weeks; I've had longer relationships with houseplants), I discovered another species of vampire entirely. Picture this: I'm eating sushi at my desk, trying to fuel myself for an afternoon of strategic people planning, when a fellow leadership team member approaches and delivers this gem: "I'm surprised to see you eating sushi. I thought all you people ate was fried chicken. I'm impressed."

I'll pause while you pick your jaw up off the floor.

This person wasn't just consuming a salary. They were consuming my actual nutrients: the mental energy I needed for problem-solving, the emotional reserves required for afternoon negotiations, the cognitive resources I'd allocated for innovation. In that moment, I had to redirect all of it toward managing their ignorance. Instead of using my lunch break to recharge for creating value, I was forced to become an involuntary processing plant for their casual racism, calculating whether to educate (unpaid emotional labor), challenge (career risk), or deflect (enabling future incidents).

This is how nutrient vampires operate at the cellular level. While I was trying to fuel myself with actual food, they forced me to burn through my psychological reserves processing their "observation." The energy I'd saved for developing my team's capability got rerouted to managing someone else's bias. The creativity I'd planned to bring to our product strategy got consumed by diplomatic calculation. They didn't just interrupt my lunch; they hijacked my cognitive resources and expected me to thank them for the "cultural curiosity."

Multiply this by every marginalized person in an organization, every day, multiple times a day. The woman whose technical brilliance gets diverted into managing comments about being "surprisingly analytical for a girl": That's innovation energy being burned on basic dignity maintenance. The immigrant whose strategic thinking gets interrupted to smile through accent jokes: That's problem-solving capacity being drained by someone else's amusement. The gay colleague using relationship-building energy to navigate comments about their partner seeming "normal": That's collaboration potential being consumed by ignorance.

These casual vampires often consider themselves allies, which makes their nutrient drain even more insidious. They donate to diversity initiatives while simultaneously ensuring diverse employees need to spend their development resources on survival. They create inclusion programs while forcing marginalized employees to exhaust their growth nutrients just to exist in the building. They're the reason talented people eat lunch at desks with headphones: not for productivity, but to preserve their psychological nutrients from "friendly" observations that would devour their afternoon's capacity.

Whether draining salaries through incompetence or dignity through ignorance, these vampires share one trait: They're protected while their victims are told to be team players.

This systematic misallocation of nutrients creates exactly the culture organizations claim they don't want. When people see the incompetent protected while their colleagues get cut, they learn that performance doesn't determine survival; proximity to power does. When they watch nutrients flow to those who already have plenty while they ration printer paper, they understand that working harder won't get them fed. The lesson becomes clear: Attach yourself to power, perform importance rather than create value, and never, ever point out that the empress has no clothes.

The hunger makes people do things they'd never choose in abundance. Watch the behavioral mutations it creates: the analyst who discovered a faster way to run reports but keeps it secret because efficiency is her only edge, the project manager who speaks for seventeen minutes in every meeting about work that took seventeen seconds because airtime equals existence, the developer who spots a critical bug but waits to mention it until the all-hands to ensure maximum visibility for being the savior. They've become workplace preppers, hoarding knowledge like canned goods for the apocalypse, inflating contributions like life rafts on a sinking ship, avoiding challenging bad ideas from nutrient-controllers even when those ideas are sailing straight toward icebergs.

The woman who could streamline the entire invoicing process leaves it broken because the CFO's wife designed it. The team that knows the product launch will fail stays silent because the CMO's ego is attached to the timeline. The organization hasn't just created scarcity; it's created a culture of scarcity thinking that poisons every interaction, every project, every possibility for genuine collaboration.

This is the real cost of manufactured hunger: not just that some people don't get nutrients, but that everyone learns to operate from deprivation. The good news is that scarcity thinking can be unlearned, but only when organizations stop pretending resources are limited and start examining who benefits from keeping everyone hungry.

The Organizational Allergy

Some organizations develop a fascinating condition: They become allergic to their own nourishment. They invest millions in development programs that nobody attends, create psychological safety initiatives that make people feel less safe, and implement empowerment frameworks that somehow reduce everyone's power. It's not that the nutrients are toxic; it's that the organizational body has learned to reject what it needs most.

A colleague who consulted for a major real estate firm described their peculiar dysfunction perfectly. The company had introduced unlimited commission structures, thinking hunger would drive performance. Instead, agents began sabotaging each other's deals, hiding listings, and poaching clients so aggressively that overall sales dropped 30 percent. When leadership tried introducing collaboration incentives and team-based rewards to fix the damage, nobody trusted it. Agents who'd survived the carnage couldn't metabolize cooperation. Their systems had adapted to combat, and peace felt like vulnerability. They'd developed immunity to the very nutrients that could have saved them because those nutrients had been weaponized before.

This immunity develops through repeated exposure to false nutrients, the organizational equivalent of artificial sweeteners that train bodies to mistrust the real thing. Every "empowerment" initiative that ended with someone losing their job for making the decision they were supposedly empowered to make. Every "learning opportunity" that turned out to be doing three jobs for one salary. Every "psychological safety" workshop immediately followed by the facilitator being let go for "not aligning with leadership vision." These aren't just broken promises; they're nutrient poisoning. When growth opportunities consistently become overwork, people's systems learn to reject all opportunities as potential threats. When empowerment repeatedly means abandonment, authority starts feeling dangerous rather than nourishing. When safety initiatives precede punishment, vulnerability becomes something to avoid rather than embrace. Each false promise creates antibodies against the real thing.

When genuine nutrients finally arrive, the organizational immune system attacks them like foreign invaders. It's like dating after a string of terrible relationships: Someone actually being nice feels suspicious, so the catch must be coming. The symptoms manifest everywhere. People offered development opportunities assume they're being set up to fail, declining with elaborate excuses about workload. Teams given decision-making authority continue requesting permission for everything, creating the very bureaucracy they're empowered to eliminate. Employees in genuinely safe environments still speak in corporate euphemisms, unable to risk the clarity that safety should enable.

A tech company eliminated all approval layers, then watched as employees created their own informal approval chains because autonomy felt like abandonment after years of micromanagement. They'd been trained to need permission like plants trained to grow toward light: Even when the obstacle is removed, they keep growing crooked.

The critical distinction is that this immunity isn't employee dysfunction; it's organizational scar tissue. Leaders created these allergic reactions through years of bait-and-switch: development programs that developed people out the door, empowerment initiatives that empowered nothing except blame distribution, psychological safety campaigns that made truth-telling career-ending. Now these same leaders stand bewildered when their latest authentic initiative gets met with cynicism, as if organizational memory doesn't exist, as if people should simply forget the pattern of betrayal because this time, they promise, it's different.

What makes this particularly damaging is how leaders weaponize the immunity they created. They point to low adoption of development programs as evidence that employees don't want to grow.

They cite unused empowerment as proof that people prefer being told what to do. They interpret the persistence of corporate euphemisms as validation that radical candor doesn't work. They've poisoned the well for so long that when people won't drink, they blame thirst rather than toxicity.

The oscillation between approaches makes immunity worse, not better. When organizations constantly switch their nutrient distribution strategies with each new leadership change, employees stop believing any of it will last. Each executive arrives with their revolutionary framework for who gets fed and how. One year it's servant leadership, where nutrients supposedly flow upward. The next it's radical transparency, where everyone can supposedly see who's getting what. Then comes holacracy, where nutrients are supposedly self-distributed. After experiencing multiple cycles of these changes, employees develop protective behaviors. They perform enthusiasm for each new system while quietly maintaining their own survival strategies. They've learned that engaging genuinely with any feeding system is pointless when it'll be replaced within eighteen months.

The result is an organization where everyone performs consumption of whatever nutrients are currently being offered while actually surviving on hidden reserves and informal networks. People go through the motions, attending the workshops, using the new terminology, and filling out the frameworks, while protecting their real nutrient sources from the next inevitable change.

Tech companies have perfected a particular strain of nutrient immunity through unlimited PTO that nobody takes and perks that become prison bars. A friend at a major social media platform discovered this when she joined, lured by unlimited time off and free meals that seemed like abundance after years of counting vacation days and buying sad desk salads. Within months, she'd developed complete immunity to the very benefits that attracted her. The unlimited PTO? Purely theoretical when managers message at midnight "just checking on that project" and colleagues who take more than five days get mysteriously excluded from important initiatives. The free food? Lovely, except it meant never leaving the building, working through what should have been lunch breaks, dinner with family, any boundary between work and existence.

The platform operated from another continent, importing work cultures and expectations wholesale without adapting to local norms. Leadership would say they cared about time differences while scheduling "optional" meetings at 3 a.m. that somehow determined a project's future. They preached work-life balance while expecting instant responses to messages sent during someone's night, as if the human need for sleep was a character flaw that dedication could overcome. She learned to perform the grateful employee routine, posting about amazing perks while secretly calculating how many more months she could survive before her immune system completely rejected the environment.

Breaking this immunity requires something most leaders won't attempt: genuine consistency over time. Not quarters, but years. Not new feeding programs, but sustained nourishment that doesn't change with each leadership transition. MIT Sloan researchers found that toxic culture is 10.4 times more likely to predict employee attrition than compensation, with the damage persisting long after supposed culture improvements are implemented.[2] Once organizations create nutrient scarcity, the behavioral adaptations persist long after abundance returns. People who learned to hoard knowledge when it was the only currency continue hoarding even when sharing gets rewarded. Teams that competed for scraps of recognition can't suddenly collaborate just because there's enough praise for everyone now.

The damage from nutrient deprivation creates lasting changes in how people's systems process resources. Like bodies that learned to conserve during shortage, organizational bodies continue operating in conservation mode even when nutrients become plentiful. They can't simply start absorbing what's offered; their systems have fundamentally changed to protect against future deprivation. Organizations consistently underestimate these lasting behavioral changes. Leaders want transformation on quarterly timelines when they've spent decades creating dysfunction.

The few organizations that successfully break through immunity share specific characteristics. Their leaders acknowledge the damage they or their predecessors caused. Not vague admissions about "past challenges" but specific recognition: "We fired people for taking the risks we claimed to value. We promoted toxic performers while eliminating collaborators. We created the very fear we now need to overcome." This acknowledgment doesn't fix everything, but it signals that leadership finally understands the depth of organizational trauma.

Recovery happens through accumulated proof, not promises. When someone takes a risk that would have been punished before, they need to be visibly rewarded, not just tolerated. When someone admits failure, they need genuine support, not subtle retaliation three months later. When someone exercises their newfound authority and something goes wrong, leadership needs to absorb the consequence, not redistribute blame. Each interaction either reinforces immunity or slowly dissolves it. There's no neutral; every moment moves the organization toward health or deeper pathology.

I watched this transformation happen at a financial services firm that hired a new CPO after years of revolving-door leadership. Instead of arriving with another framework, she spent her first three months just listening. No initiatives, no programs, just conversations where she asked, "What promises have we broken?" When she finally acted, it wasn't with fanfare but with small, consistent changes. Someone who challenged a policy didn't get flagged as "not aligned" but instead got asked to help rewrite it. A team that admitted a project was failing got resources to pivot, not punishment for honesty. A manager who'd been burned by previous "empowerment" initiatives tested the waters by approving expenses without asking permission, and nothing happened except the expenses got paid. Six months in, people started tentatively using the psychological safety they'd been promised. A year in, they were sharing actual opinions in meetings. Eighteen months in, innovation metrics started climbing. Not because the CPO had installed innovation labs or hired consultants, but because she'd consistently rewarded the behaviors she claimed to want, until people's immune systems slowly and carefully began to accept that maybe this time the nutrients were real.

What makes recovery so rare is that it requires leaders to sustain changes that won't show results during their tenure. The executive who begins breaking immunity probably won't be around to see the organization fully heal. They're investing in someone else's success metrics, and most leaders would rather implement another flashy transformation that looks good in their exit portfolio than do the slow, patient work of rebuilding organizational trust. They'll add new nutrients rather than address why the organization can't digest what it already has.

The real challenge unfolds when recovery actually begins. When organizations start genuinely feeding their people, they discover that some can't digest what they're being offered. Twenty years of nutrient deprivation creates permanent changes in how people process resources. The senior engineers who learned to hide their innovations can't suddenly start sharing breakthroughs, even with patent protection and bonuses guaranteed. Their creative muscles have atrophied from decades of seeing ideas disappear into the void or emerge with someone else's name attached. They've forgotten how to metabolize recognition. Middle managers who survived by never challenging anything can't suddenly exercise judgment, even when asked to by leadership. They've been on such a restricted diet of "yes" and "of course" that their palate can't process independent thought anymore. They've lost the ability to digest authority, to break down decisions into actionable components.

Administrative staff who learned that efficiency improvements meant job losses can't suddenly optimize processes, even with job security promised in writing. They've been conditioned to see growth nutrients as poison: Every improvement they make reduces their perceived necessity. Their systems reject the very nutrients that would help them flourish because those nutrients once preceded elimination. Trust in nourishment died too many times to resurrect.

For those who could metabolize the change, something extraordinary happened. They didn't just return to health; they developed a kind of superpower. Having survived deprivation and recovered from it, they could spot false nutrients instantly. They became the organization's immune system against future toxicity, calling out performative initiatives before they could take root, identifying false promises before they could create new allergies. They became living proof that recovery was possible, but also walking reminders of what organizational malnourishment actually costs: not just productivity or engagement, but human capacity itself.

This is the final truth about nutrients: They can't just be added to broken systems with the expectation of growth. Organizations have to acknowledge the damage done, accept that some of it is permanent, and commit to consistency that outlasts quarterly earnings and executive tenures. Restoring nutrient flow is patient work. It means acknowledging damage done, accepting that some healing takes years, and committing to consistency that outlasts any single quarter or leadership change. Here's what that patience makes possible: People who spent years protecting themselves begin to open. Ideas that were hoarded start flowing. Talent that was updating their resumes decides to stay, not for perks or promises, but because they finally feel fed. The engineer who hid every innovation starts mentoring. The manager who never decided without permission starts trusting her judgment. The team that competed for scraps discovers they prefer collaboration. These aren't personality changes; they're what happens when starving people receive real nourishment. Anyone who provides genuine nutrients, who fights for someone's development, who shares power instead of guarding it, who makes it safe for others to struggle and grow, is proving that work doesn't have to leave people empty. That proof is how cultures finally start to heal.

Imagine an organization that has done the work. Cleared the toxins from its soil and acknowledged uncomfortable truths. Redistributed exposure so brilliance isn't trapped in shadows. Strengthened root systems that actually support people instead of constraining them. Provided real nutrients: growth, power, and safety, not just foosball tables and kombucha. The garden is finally thriving. People are flourishing. Innovation is sprouting from unexpected places. Leadership wants to celebrate this transformation, to finally exhale after all that work.

What's been built now needs protecting.

The thing about healthy gardens is that they face the same storms as dying ones, but now there's something worth protecting. Success makes organizations visible to competitors who ignored them when they were failing. Growth makes them valuable to acquirers who promise to preserve culture while preparing to strip-mine it. Thriving makes them targets for everyone who profited from previous dysfunction. Those people liked the toxic soil that kept others weak. They benefited from hoarding the spotlight. They controlled nutrients like dragons guarding gold, and now the game is changing.

The storm doesn't just come from outside. Executives who built careers on fear-based management aren't celebrating psychological safety initiatives. Managers whose only skill was gatekeeping information feel threatened by transparency. Toxic high performers are working to convince leadership that these changes are hurting productivity. Every healthy change disturbs someone's comfortable dysfunction. They're going to fight back with the viciousness of people who've confused privilege with merit.

Which brings us to an uncomfortable truth about organizational transformation: Creating the right conditions is necessary but insufficient. Carefully cultivated culture doesn't exist in isolation. A new CEO arrives with different priorities. A major client demands changes that compromise values. The executive who championed culture transformation burns out and leaves. A competitor poaches half the team with offers that can't be matched. The toxic leader who was finally removed gets hired by the parent company and becomes the boss's boss.

The question isn't whether storms will hit carefully cultivated culture. They always do. The question is whether the culture is strong enough to survive them, or better yet, to somehow grow stronger in the wind.

5

Weathering Storms

Growth Always Attracts Storms

The average organizational transformation fails within eighteen months. Not because the changes were wrong, but because nobody prepared for the predictable backlash, the inevitable resistance, and the perfect storm of forces that emerge to restore dysfunction.

Why Every Culture Faces Seasons

Many organizations believe their culture is strong enough to transcend the cycles that challenge others. They point to engagement scores, retention rates, and "Best Places to Work" awards as evidence they've built something stormproof. It's a comforting thought. Seasons don't check credentials before arriving.

Winter comes for everyone. Sometimes it arrives as a new CEO who considers carefully cultivated psychological safety "too soft for business." Sometimes it's a market crash that turns generous growth nutrients into unaffordable luxuries. Sometimes it's the champion who built everything getting exhausted, burning out, or being forced out by the very dysfunction they tried to change. The specifics vary, yet the pattern remains constant: Every culture faces seasons that test whether roots run deep enough to survive.

What catches leaders off guard is that healthy cultures don't prevent storms; they might even attract them. Like tall trees that draw lightning, success can threaten those who profited from failure. Transparency might reveal what others prefer hidden. Inclusive practices could challenge those who've been hoarding opportunities. The storm isn't punishment for doing something wrong; it's often the result of doing something right in a system that rewards dysfunction.

The trap many fall into is mistaking current conditions for permanent climate. Today's supportive board becomes tomorrow's cost-cutting committee. The team that collaboratively built organizational values gets replaced by new hires who have never experienced why change was necessary. Markets that reward innovation shift toward competitors who find efficiency through exploitation. These aren't failures of planning; they're natural cycles that every organization must navigate, preferably without losing its mind or its best people in the process.

This is where Simon Sinek's insight becomes vital: "The responsibility of leadership is not to come up with all the ideas but to create an environment where great ideas can happen."[1] When storms hit, this principle transforms from inspiration to survival strategy. If culture depends on one visionary leader, one generous budget, or one favorable market condition, organizations have created dependency, not resilience. True strength comes from cultivating leadership at every level: people who understand the "why" deeply enough to adapt the "how" when conditions change. Not clones of the original vision, but translators who can preserve the essence while adjusting to new weather patterns.

The cycles follow recognizable patterns, like horror movie sequences where audiences want to yell "Don't go in the basement!" at the screen. First comes the golden period, where everything planted seems to bloom. Success stories multiply, skeptics become believers, and it feels like someone has discovered the secret formula. This is precisely when organizations should be preparing for winter: strengthening roots, distributing leadership, documenting what works. Instead, most use this time to expand rapidly, assuming eternal summer. They mistake a season for a climate, a moment for permanence, current prosperity for guaranteed future prosperity. It's like assuming a good hair day means never needing conditioner again.

The second pattern arrives disguised as reasonable questions. After the golden period of easy growth comes the first test of principles. Someone in finance asks, "Do we really need all this psychological safety stuff when we're missing our targets?" A new board member wonders about "overinvesting in culture at the expense of performance." These aren't attacks yet; they're probes, checking if cultural transformation is conviction or just convenience. Think of them as organizational weather balloons, testing which way the wind is blowing.

This is where organizations discover whether they've built culture or just decorated dysfunction. The test might be a difficult quarter that has finance eyeing development budgets like a hungry wolf spotting a limping deer. It might be the toxic high performer finally getting caught doing something indefensible, forcing a choice between values and their revenue. Or it might be new leadership who learned management when computers were the size of refrigerators and thinks psychological safety sounds like "participation trophies for adults."

How organizations respond to this first test predicts everything. Some immediately abandon their principles, proving they were never principles at all, just fair-weather preferences. They cut the inclusion programs, reinstate the ranking systems, and start having those "difficult conversations" that are really just fear-based management wearing business casual. Others double down defensively, treating any question about their culture initiatives as heresy. Trying to build psychological safety while punishing anyone who uses it works about as well as you'd expect.

The organizations that survive find a different path: They adapt without abandoning. They might slow the pace of change without reversing direction. They find creative ways to maintain nutrients when traditional sources dry up. Most importantly, they've distributed leadership enough that no single pressure point can break the system. When the CFO starts asking pointed questions about ROI on culture initiatives, twelve people can articulate the value because they're all living it, not just one exhausted champion trying to justify their entire existence through PowerPoint slides nobody actually reads.

Then comes the third pattern in the cycle: the real storm. Not the gentle testing rain that makes people reach for an umbrella, but the full tempest that makes everyone question whether this culture thing was worth it. A major acquisition that promises to preserve culture while actively planning its demolition. A market disruption that makes an entire business model look like a flip phone at an iPhone convention. A scandal that reveals the toxicity leadership thought had been eliminated was just hiding in better places. Sometimes, beautifully and terribly, success so profound that it attracts corporate antibodies as though healthy culture is a virus the larger system needs to eliminate.

This is when organizations discover the difference between surface culture and deep roots. Surface culture is the values posters, the engagement surveys, the carefully crafted employer brand that looks gorgeous on LinkedIn. These get stripped away in the first strong wind, leaving people clinging to whatever remains. Deep culture lives in the habits that persist under pressure, the relationships that strengthen in crisis, the principles people follow even when nobody's watching and everything's catching fire around them.

The organizations that weather these storms share one characteristic: They prepared during the golden period. They didn't wait for a crisis to distribute leadership. They built networks of culture carriers, not culture dependents. They documented not just what they did but why, creating organizational memory that could survive the people who created it. They developed what one leader brilliantly called "cultural muscle memory," responses so ingrained that they persist even when everyone's panicking and the CEO is googling "crisis management" from the bathroom.

Perhaps most importantly, they accepted that storms would come. Not as a failure but as weather. They didn't promise their people eternal summer; they promised them strong shelters and the skills to rebuild. They understood that resilience isn't about avoiding damage; it's about recovering from it, sometimes even growing stronger from the breaking, like a bone that heals denser than before (though hopefully with less screaming).

What the cheerful "culture consultants" won't say is this: Every transformation faces its reckoning. Every garden faces winter. The question isn't whether carefully cultivated culture will be tested. The question is whether organizations have prepared their people to be gardeners who can work in all seasons, or whether they've just taught them to enjoy the sunshine while it lasts.

The inevitable storm will reveal the answer.

Recognizing the Breaking Point

Sometimes the storm doesn't build gradually. Sometimes it arrives fully formed, delivered by the very people who should be protecting the organization from damage. The breaking point reveals itself not through external forces but through decisions so bewildering that employees question whether they're living in the same reality as leadership.

A podcast platform I was scheduled to work with taught me how storms can come from the most unexpected direction: upward. My contact there called me one morning, voice hollow with disbelief. The toxic executive everyone expected to be fired had just been promoted to the CEO position. Not despite the formal HR complaints against him. Not despite his documented hostility toward psychological safety, inclusion, and basic human decency. Perhaps because of them. The employees learned about their new CEO through whispers and side conversations, not an official announcement, as if leadership knew this appointment was something to be ashamed of rather than celebrated. People who'd filed complaints against him for his combative, manipulative behavior now reported directly to him. Those who'd documented his gaslighting now watched him control the entire narrative. The very person who believed workplace culture was "fluffy nonsense" now held absolute power over it.

This wasn't just poor judgment; it was organizational self-harm. The board had looked at someone who made people physically ill from stress, who drove talent out through deliberate cruelty, who viewed empathy as weakness, and decided he should run everything. The message to employees was clearer than any values statement: Toxicity gets rewarded if it comes with the right connections, the right look, the right ability to manage up while destroying down.

My contact described the atmosphere after the announcement: "It was like finding out the arsonist had been promoted to fire chief. Everyone who'd reported smoke was now at his mercy." People who'd built psychological safety in their teams watched him dismantle it in his first week. Those who'd championed inclusion saw their programs gutted because he considered them "distractions from real work." The organization didn't just tolerate toxicity; it crowned it.

The pattern was sickeningly familiar. Organizations often promote their problems rather than solving them, especially when those problems are presented in expensive suits and generate short-term results. The board sees confidence where employees see cruelty. They interpret fear-based productivity as "strong leadership" rather than recognizing it as a sign of organizational decay. They mistake the silence of terrorized employees for satisfaction, the exodus of talent for "natural turnover," the death of innovation for "increased focus."

What makes these internal storms particularly devastating is the betrayal. External storms, such as market crashes, competition, and pandemics, at least offer the comfort of shared struggle against outside forces. When an organization promotes the very person destroying its culture, when leadership chooses toxicity over their own people, the storm becomes personal. It's not just rain; it's acid, dissolving trust from the inside out.

Remember that publishing company where someone made the sushi comment to me about "all you people" and fried chicken? That place taught me how storms impact people differently based on their power and position in the organization. The entire leadership team had inherited their positions along with their trust funds, genuinely believing poverty was a character flaw. When the CEO publicly screamed at me to stop talking, I learned something critical about organizational storms: Those with the least organizational power bear the worst weather.

Within nine weeks, the physical toll was undeniable: weight loss, hair loss, morning stops at Caffé Nero on High Holborn just to cry before work. My body was rejecting the environment, but my bank account demanded I stay. The breaking point came when my father, who normally considers workplace drama beneath his attention, delivered his verdict: "Either you quit, or I'm kicking down that company's door." Nigerian fathers don't mess around with three things: their money, their food, and their children (in that order).

This visceral experience taught me what countless employees already know: Storms hit differently depending on where people sit in the hierarchy. Those at the top have umbrellas, raincoats, and backup shelters. Those at the bottom get soaked. People develop elaborate coping mechanisms that look like resilience but are really sophisticated forms of self-destruction. The cost calculation changes based on what someone has to lose. A person with generational wealth can walk away from toxicity. Someone supporting extended family cannot. A person with a powerful network finds new opportunities. Someone without one might not get another chance.

These crisis moments teach something critical about organizational storms: They have predictable warning signs that organizations consistently ignore. The podcast platform had documented HR complaints. My publishing company had an employee turnover rate that should have triggered alarms. Both organizations saw the lightning gathering but convinced themselves that it wouldn't strike or, worse, that the damage would be worth the perceived benefits of keeping toxic leaders in power.

The first warning sign is when physical symptoms become normalized. When an organization has employees who regularly cry in bathrooms, vomit from stress, or lose hair from anxiety, that's not "growing pains" or "challenging times." That's a crisis. The human body doesn't lie about toxicity the way engagement surveys do. When multiple people develop stress-related illnesses, insomnia, or anxiety disorders that mysteriously improve during vacations, the culture has become literally toxic.

The second warning is when good people start creating elaborate coping mechanisms. The morning cry sessions, the secret support networks warning each other about dangerous leaders, the resignation letters saved in draft folders updated after each incident: These aren't signs of weak employees; they're symptoms of an organization that's forcing people to choose between their well-being and their livelihood. When survival requires this much emotional labor, the storm has already caused structural damage.

The third sign appears in language patterns. Organizations approaching their limits develop elaborate euphemisms, turning simple truths into corporate word salad. "Challenging leadership style" means abusive behavior. "High standards" means impossible expectations. "Direct communication" means verbal assault. When truth requires this much translation, when reality needs this much softening, the organization has already broken something fundamental: the ability to acknowledge what's actually happening.

The protection strategies that emerge during these storms reveal both human creativity and organizational failure. Employees develop buddy systems for difficult meetings, documentation habits that would impress lawyers, and extraction plans for colleagues showing signs of breakdown. One organization I studied had an underground railroad of references and job leads specifically for people escaping toxic departments. The existence of these systems is proof that the storm has become the climate.

What most leaders miss is that the crisis threshold isn't the same for everyone. It's like assuming everyone can hold their breath underwater for the same amount of time just because they're all in the same pool. Those with more privilege, whether through identity, wealth, or connections, weather storms longer because they have better shelter. The trust-fund executives at that publishing company could afford to be toxic because they'd never experienced consequences. Meanwhile, those without safety nets reach their limits faster, not from weakness but from carrying more weight with less support.

Leaders who want to protect their people during storms need to understand the difference between shelter and evacuation. Shelter is temporary protection while the storm passes: offering flexible work arrangements during a difficult transition, providing additional support during a challenging quarter, creating buffers between toxic leaders and their teams. Evacuation is recognizing that the building is collapsing and helping people get out alive.

Too many leaders confuse the two. They keep offering umbrellas in hurricanes, suggesting resilience training for people experiencing abuse, providing wellness apps to employees whose bodies are shutting down from stress. This isn't protection; it's complicity dressed as compassion. Real protection sometimes means admitting an organization has become uninhabitable and helping people leave with their dignity and references intact.

One of the most impressive leaders I encountered was a department head who, recognizing her organization's toxicity was irreversible, quietly built an evacuation network. She connected her team with recruiters, wrote stellar recommendations, and even helped them negotiate exit packages that included extended healthcare. When criticized for not retaining talent, she responded: "My job is to develop people, not trap them in dysfunction." Within a year, her entire team had moved to healthier organizations. She followed soon after.

Protection also means using whatever privilege exists to absorb damage that others can't survive. Those with political capital to challenge toxic leadership should use it. Those with financial security to speak truth without fear should speak it. Those with networks to create opportunities for people trapped in storms should create them. Protection isn't just about policies; it's about people with power actually using it to shield those without.

The decision to evacuate, whether as a leader or individual, requires recognizing that some storms don't pass; they become the climate. When toxicity gets promoted to CEO, when HR complaints become promotion criteria, when crying employees become normalized, the storm has won. Staying doesn't demonstrate resilience; it creates casualties who haven't admitted it yet.

Evacuation requires resources that not everyone has. This is where organizational responsibility becomes critical. Severance packages, extended healthcare, honest references: These aren't generosity, they're reparations for the damage that's been allowed. The least an organization can do when it becomes uninhabitable is help people escape without destroying their futures.

Most organizations respond to these evacuations with bewilderment rather than reflection. They conduct exit interviews that ask all the wrong questions, focusing on compensation and benefits rather than the toxicity that made breathing impossible. They replace evacuated talent, then wonder why the cycle continues when the new hires face the same storms. The pattern becomes so predictable that recruiters develop specialties in placing refugees from specific organizational disasters, knowing exactly which companies create which kinds of damage.

The final teaching from these critical moments is perhaps the most uncomfortable: Sometimes good cultures die. Not from external forces but from internal choices. The decision to promote toxicity, to protect perpetrators, to silence truth-tellers: These aren't storms that happen to organizations; they're choices organizations make. The storm doesn't cause the damage. It just reveals which organizations chose their values and which only marketed them.

How Strong Cultures Survive and Rebuild

Storms don't end; they overlap, evolve, and spawn new weather patterns. While one department recovers from the departure of a toxic leader, another faces budget cuts. While leadership celebrates surviving an acquisition, individual teams navigate the daily microaggressions that never make it to board meetings. The question isn't how to rebuild after the storm but how to create shelter during constant weather.

The panic arrives in a predictable form: "I have fifteen direct reports from twelve different backgrounds with seventeen different working styles. If I create unique conditions for everyone, when exactly am I supposed to do my actual job?" This exhaustion is real. Leaders trying to be inclusive are drowning in individual accommodations, becoming full-time concierges rather than leaders who can actually lead.

Sarah, a VP of People and Talent, approached me at a conference looking like she'd been personally victimized by her own good intentions. "Yesterday alone," she said, clutching her coffee like a lifeline, "I had one employee who needed flexible hours for religious observance, another who required written communication due to auditory processing differences, a third who asked for standing desk arrangements, and someone else needing time off for therapy appointments. I spent my entire day accommodating individual needs and got zero actual work done. How is this sustainable?"

It's not. This approach to weathering storms, individually managing each person's crisis, creates leader burnout while failing to actually protect anyone. Sarah was trying to be everyone's personal storm shelter, which meant nobody had real protection.

The breakthrough came when Sarah stopped asking "How do I meet each person's unique needs?" and started asking "What conditions enable different people to thrive naturally?" Instead of being a personal concierge, she became an architect of flexible systems. The shift transformed everything.

She discovered that multiple people needed quiet focus time but were requesting it differently: some asking for remote work, others for private offices, still others for meeting-free blocks. Instead of negotiating fifteen individual arrangements, she instituted "Deep Work Wednesdays," with no meetings, optional office attendance, and Slack on Do Not Disturb. One systemic change addressed multiple needs without anyone having to disclose why they needed it.

The religious observances, therapy appointments, and caregiving responsibilities that had her creating spreadsheets to track individual schedules? She shifted to "core collaboration hours," twelve hours weekly when everyone needed to be available (Tuesday through

Thursday from eleven to three). Outside those hours, people self-managed their time as long as work got done. The person needing Friday afternoon prayers didn't have to explain. The employee with standing therapy appointments didn't have to disclose. The parent managing school pickups didn't have to negotiate. The system accommodated variation without requiring justification.

This is storm shelter design at its finest: creating structures that naturally protect different people without requiring them to expose their vulnerabilities. Think about curb cuts, those ramps at street corners originally designed for wheelchairs that now benefit parents with strollers, travelers with luggage, delivery workers with hand trucks. One systemic change, multiple beneficiaries. That's the scale secret for weathering organizational storms.

The meeting structure transformation was particularly brilliant. Instead of accommodating each person's communication style individually, Sarah's team created meetings with multiple participation channels. Pre-meeting agenda sharing helped processors and non-native speakers prepare. Silent brainstorming before verbal discussion included introverts and deliberate thinkers. Written follow-up summaries supported those who process better through reading. Rotating facilitation prevented a single communication style from dominating. "I stopped having to remember that Mia needs thinking time, Róisín processes better in writing, and Dayo speaks up more in smaller groups," Sarah told me six months later. "The structure handles it automatically."

A manufacturing leader struggled with an employee who wanted to work entirely remotely in a role requiring equipment operation. Instead of making false promises or outright rejection, they explored what was actually possible: remote planning and documentation days, on-site operation days. Partial accommodation that actually worked versus full accommodation that would have failed. The conversation focused on what could flex versus what couldn't, with a transparent explanation of why certain boundaries existed.

The healthcare executive managing more than two hundred people across three shifts told me her crisis moment came during a particularly brutal month. "I had seventeen different scheduled accommodation requests on my desk, two discrimination complaints about shift assignments, and someone crying in my office daily about unfair treatment. I was spending twelve-hour days just managing individual negotiations."

Her solution wasn't perfect, but it was sustainable. She created "working style profiles," basic frameworks where people identified their needs: consistent schedules versus flexibility, solo work versus team collaboration, morning versus evening preferences. Then she let teams self-organize around complementary styles. "It's not utopia," she admitted. "Some people still feel they're not getting exactly what they want. I'm not drowning anymore, though, and most people found something workable."

The revelation is that perfect accommodation isn't the goal; sustainable systems are. When organizations stop trying to be everything to everyone, they can actually be something meaningful to most people. One startup founder admitted they weren't a tech giant and freed his team from pretense. "Once we stopped apologizing for what we couldn't provide, we got creative about what we could. Our quiet room is a converted supply closet with noise-canceling headphones. Our flexible hours mean you can start anytime between seven and ten. It's not fancy, but it's real."

This honesty creates its own kind of shelter. People know exactly what storm protection exists and can make informed choices about whether to stay or find better weather elsewhere. No false promises, no exhausted leaders, no bitter employees who were sold something that doesn't exist.

The magic happens when organizations discover their unique shelter capabilities. A small nonprofit realized they couldn't match corporate benefits, but they could offer something else: genuine flexibility about life happening. Kid sick? Work from their bedside. Pet dying? Take the time needed without counting days. Mental health crisis? They'd figure out coverage together. "We can't pay Google salaries," the director explained, "but we can treat you like a human when humanity happens."

Research validates what these organizations discovered through necessity: The perceived availability of flexibility matters more than the flexibility itself. When accommodation must be individually negotiated, employees either don't ask for it or pay a "flexibility stigma" penalty when they do. Built-in flexibility removes that tax. It's not about granting more accommodations; it's about removing the humiliation of having to beg for basic human needs.[2]

The most successful storm shelters share three characteristics that any organization can implement. First, they're transparent about what protection they can and cannot provide. No wellness-washing about unlimited flexibility that's actually unlimited surveillance. Clear boundaries explained with respect create more trust than vague promises that inevitably disappoint.

Second, they're built from collective wisdom, not top-down mandates. The best shelter designs come from asking people what protection they actually need, not what leadership thinks they should want. Sometimes the answer surprises everyone, like the team that chose consistent schedules over flexibility because predictability helped them manage their outside-work storms.

Third, they evolve with the weather. What sheltered people during one crisis might trap them during another. Regular shelter audits, not asking "Are people using them?" but "Are they still providing protection?", keep systems responsive to actual needs.

Communication during storms requires a delicate balance that most leaders get wrong. They either minimize the crisis ("Just a rough patch!") or catastrophize it ("Unprecedented challenges ahead!"). The organizations that maintain trust during storms master three-part communication: Acknowledge the specific reality without euphemism ("We're facing budget cuts that will affect resources"), commit to what can actually be protected ("Jobs are safe, but project budgets will shrink"), and be clear about what remains unknown ("We're still determining which initiatives continue"). This honesty prevents the rumor mill from creating worse storms than the actual weather. One leader told me, "I learned to say 'I don't know, but I'll tell you when I do' instead of making up answers." His team trusted that more than false certainty.

Sarah's eighteen-month transformation wasn't smooth, but it was real. "We lost people who needed full remote work we couldn't provide. We kept people who just needed human flexibility we could actually deliver. The difference was being honest about which was which." Her exhaustion lifted not because she'd solved every problem but because she'd stopped pretending she could. The timeline for cultural recovery surprises everyone. Leaders expect quick wins after implementing shelter systems, but real recovery follows a predictable pattern: three months before people trust the changes are real, six months before they start using the systems without fear, twelve months before new behaviors become habits, and eighteen months before anyone can claim real transformation. This isn't resistance or ingratitude; it's organizational PTSD requiring patience most quarterly focused leaders don't have. The organizations that succeed commit to consistency over multiple seasons, understanding that trust rebuilds in months what toxicity destroyed in moments.

The ultimate realization about weathering organizational storms isn't that strong cultures prevent them or that perfect leaders shield everyone from damage. It's that systematic flexibility beats individual heroics every time.

Organizations that refuse to build systematic shelters pay a hidden tax that compounds annually. Research from the Society for Human Resource Management (SHRM) found that replacing an employee costs between 90 percent and 200 percent of their annual salary, with knowledge workers and specialized roles at the higher end.[3] When experienced people evacuate, companies hemorrhage institutional knowledge and become known as "survivor jobs," places people endure to build their resumes before escaping to companies that treat humans like humans. The Work Institute's 2018 Retention Report revealed that 77 percent of employee turnover is preventable through better management practices and flexibility systems.[4] One CFO calculated they'd spent $3.2 million on turnover-related costs in two years, while the flexible systems they'd rejected would have cost $200,000 to implement. "We saved money the way someone saves money by not changing their oil," he admitted. "Eventually, the engine seizes, and you're buying a new car."

When organizations stop trying to hold umbrellas over each person's head and instead build actual structures that provide real shelter, everyone, including leadership, has a better chance of surviving the weather. Sometimes the strongest thing a leader can say is: "This is the shelter we can build. It won't protect everyone from everything, but it's solid, it's real, and we'll maintain it together." That honesty, paired with genuine systematic support, creates cultures that don't just survive storms but teach people they're worth protecting.

The storms will keep coming. They always do. The question is whether leaders are still standing alone in the rain, trying to shelter everyone individually, or whether they've built something that stands even when they need shelter themselves. A culture's strength isn't measured by the absence of storms but by how many people still have somewhere safe to weather them. Not everyone gets a corner office with a view, but everyone should get shelter from the rain.

The strongest cultures eventually evolve beyond needing constant shelter maintenance. When everyone understands how to build protection, when tending becomes instinctive rather than instructed, when weathering storms flows from collective wisdom rather than individual heroics, something remarkable happens. The garden stops being something to maintain and starts being something people are.

What some leaders misunderstand about collective ownership is this: Letting go of control doesn't mean letting go of responsibility.

The strongest cultures emerge when those with the most power use it to model what they want to see. Every time a CEO admits they don't know something, it makes questioning safer for everyone. Every time a leader takes accountability for failure, it teaches the organization that growth matters more than blame. Every time someone with privilege amplifies a quieter voice, it shows that contribution matters more than volume. Culture belongs to everyone, yes. It's also strengthened or poisoned by those who have the most power to shape it. The paradox of truly collective cultures is that they require leaders secure enough to share power, confident enough to show vulnerability, and committed enough to keep modeling even when nobody's watching.

The journey through this book has covered clearing toxic soil, redistributing exposure so everyone gets light, strengthening root systems that actually support people, providing real nutrients that help them grow, and building shelters that protect during inevitable storms. Now comes the most radical shift of all: Letting go of the idea that culture is something leaders create for others. The organizations that truly thrive understand a secret that changes everything. Culture doesn't belong to leadership, HR, or even the founder who started it all.

The bloom happens when culture belongs to everyone.

The Bloom

The strongest cultures in the world share one secret: Nobody owns them. Not the founders who started them, not the executives who claim them, not the departments who manage them. These cultures bloom because ownership became irrelevant and tending became universal. Leaders still matter; they create conditions, remove obstacles, model behaviors. The garden thrives not because someone manages it from above, but because everyone has become a cultural gardener.

When Culture Becomes Collective Creation

Most organizations dream of cultures that maintain themselves without constant intervention. The few that achieve this understand something revolutionary: The strongest cultures aren't managed by leaders but grown by everyone. The shift happens quietly. One day leadership realizes nobody's checking the employee handbook anymore because everyone already knows how to handle situations. Problems get solved before meetings happen. New hires learn the real culture from peers, not orientation videos. The organization develops its own immune system, rejecting toxicity without HR interventions, amplifying excellence without recognition programs. This isn't utopia. It's what happens when SERN elements finally work together instead of against each other.

When soil becomes healthy, people stop spending energy on self-protection and start investing in growth. They trust the ground beneath them enough to take actual risks, not the fake risks companies celebrate in innovation workshops, but real ones where failure might hurt. They know the organization won't poison them for trying.

When exposure gets distributed fairly, brilliance emerges from unexpected places. The quiet analyst who's been invisible for three years suddenly revolutionizes the reporting process. The warehouse team stops being "back office" and starts being the group that understands customer needs better than anyone. Light reaches corners that were permanently dark, and what grows there surprises everyone.

When root systems connect authentically, information flows faster than any official channel could manage. Problems get identified, discussed, and often solved before leadership even knows they exist. The whisper network that once spread warnings about toxic managers now spreads solutions, opportunities, and support. The underground railroad that helped people escape becomes the infrastructure that helps them thrive.

When nutrients flow freely, people stop hoarding and start sharing. Knowledge becomes abundant rather than scarce. Power distributes itself based on who can use it best, not who guards it most carefully. Safety becomes assumed rather than negotiated. Growth happens because people have what they need, not because someone's forcing it through another development program. These elements don't align through strategic planning. They align when organizations stop interfering with natural patterns, like a garden that's been overengineered finally being allowed to find its own balance.

Pixar stumbled into this truth through expensive failure. After pouring millions into projects led by singular visionaries who created beautiful disasters, they discovered something uncomfortable: Genius needs reality checks. Not from executives or consultants, but from anyone willing to say "this isn't working." The Braintrust emerged not from strategy but from exhaustion with strategies that weren't working. What Pixar learned wasn't about feedback systems. It was about power dynamics. When directors voluntarily submit their work to brutal honesty from people they outrank, hierarchy becomes irrelevant. The newest animator might have the insight that saves the third act. The CEO might be completely wrong about what's funny. Excellence emerges when nobody's protecting territory.

Spotify discovered this when their "autonomous squads" produced Discover Weekly. No executive commanded this feature into existence. A small squad noticed patterns in listening behavior, built a solution, and tested it independently. Now it drives 40 percent of user engagement. The feature succeeded precisely because no senior leader controlled its development. Excellence emerged from engineers who understood user needs better than any strategy document could capture.

Cosmetics brand e.l.f. Beauty discovered something similar through market pressure rather than creative crisis. While competitors spent fortunes on celebrity endorsements, e.l.f. didn't rely on famous faces. They turned their actual employees into the voice of the brand: the social media manager who understood TikTok better than any executive, the product developer who knew what $6 lipstick buyers actually wanted, the warehouse team that spotted packaging inefficiencies executives never noticed.

All three companies learned the same lesson through different paths: The best culture isn't managed from above but enabled from within.

The shift from managing to enabling terrifies leaders who've built careers on being indispensable. If culture grows itself, what's the purpose of leadership? If employees solve problems without permission, why do organizations need executives? The questions reveal the insecurity beneath most command-and-control structures: the fear that distributed power means diminished importance.

What those leaders miss is that stepping back doesn't mean disappearing. It means evolving from conductor to composer, from director to producer, from controller to creator of conditions. The gardener who stops obsessively pruning every leaf can finally see the overall shape of growth, notice patterns invisible from ground level, and protect the garden from threats individual plants can't perceive.

This evolution requires unlearning everything business school taught about leadership. Stop having answers; start having better questions. Stop driving change; start removing obstacles. Stop inspiring people; start creating conditions where inspiration emerges naturally. Stop being the hero; start being the platform where others become heroic.

The hardest part isn't learning new behaviors but releasing old ones. The executive who's always been the smartest person in the room has to discover the intelligence of collective wisdom. The manager who's built their identity around solving crises has to let others handle problems. The founder who's been the cultural North Star has to trust that others can navigate. Some leaders never make this transition. They'll go down clutching the wheel while the ship sinks rather than teaching others to sail. They'll maintain control of a mediocre culture rather than enable an excellent one they can't claim credit for creating. They'll choose being essential over being effective.

The leaders who do make this transition discover something unexpected: Influence without control is more powerful than authority with it. When leaders stop being the source of all decisions, their judgment becomes more valued, not less. When they admit ignorance, people trust their knowledge more. When they share power, their leadership multiplies rather than diminishes.

The shift from a managed to a collective culture doesn't happen through an announcement or an initiative. It happens through the accumulation of moments when leaders choose enabling over controlling. The CEO who hears a junior employee's idea in a meeting and says "run with it" instead of forming a committee. The manager who discovers their team solved a crisis while they were on vacation and celebrates instead of feeling threatened. The founder who watches their company evolve beyond their original vision and feels pride rather than loss. These moments teach the organization something profound: Culture doesn't need a single owner any more than a forest needs a single gardener. It needs multiple caretakers, diverse perspectives, and distributed responsibility. It needs people who understand their part without needing to control the whole.

When this shift happens, organizations stop having culture problems and start having culture conversations. The difference is fundamental. Problems require solutions from those in charge. Conversations require participation from everyone present. Problems get escalated until someone with enough authority fixes them. Conversations get distributed until collective wisdom emerges.

The irony is that organizations spend millions trying to engineer what emerges naturally when they simply stop interfering. They hire consultants to design collaborative cultures while preventing actual collaboration. They invest in engagement programs while maintaining systems that ensure disengagement. They preach innovation while punishing the failures that innovation requires. The organizations that achieve collective culture creation don't do so through programs or initiatives. They do it through restraint: by not immediately solving every problem, by not having an opinion on every decision, by not claiming credit for every success, by creating space for others to step forward rather than filling every vacuum with their own presence.

This restraint feels like leadership failure to those trained in traditional management. How is it possible to lead without leading? To manage without managing? To be responsible without controlling? The questions reveal the poverty of our leadership imagination. We've confused activity with impact, control with influence, presence with power. True collective culture emerges when everyone understands a simple truth: This belongs to us, not them. The shift from "their culture" to "our culture" changes everything. Problems become puzzles to solve together rather than complaints lodged upward. Opportunities become possibilities to explore rather than permissions to seek. Culture becomes something created daily rather than something endured.

Understanding this truth and acting on it are different challenges entirely. Culture can't be transformed through inspiration alone. It requires seeing the leverage points others miss, understanding the power dynamics everyone pretends don't exist, and knowing exactly where small changes create seismic shifts.

The SERN Bloom Assessment

Most organizations measure dysfunction obsessively but have no idea what a thriving culture actually looks like. They track turnover, complaints, and engagement scores: all measures of what's wrong. Ask leadership to describe what it looks like when people are genuinely flourishing, not just surviving, and they fall silent. They can list problems in detail but can't articulate what cultural vitality would actually feel like for the humans who work there.

What does organizational flourishing look like? It's when people generate ideas without being asked. When teams solve problems before management knows they exist. When innovation happens naturally rather than through forced brainstorming sessions. When people develop skills because they're curious, not because it's required. When collaboration occurs without coordination meetings. These aren't utopian fantasies; they're what happens when all four SERN elements align and when people understand how to cultivate them regardless of position or power.

This inability to recognize cultural vitality keeps organizations trapped in perpetual diagnosis. They measure pain points quarterly, run annual surveys about dissatisfaction, and create dashboards tracking everything that's broken. Yet they have no metrics for growth, no language for collective thriving, no way to recognize when something is actually working beyond the absence of complaints.

Consider: Does an organization know what it looks like when someone is genuinely growing versus just performing adequately? Can leadership describe the difference between a team that's functioning and one that's flourishing? Do they recognize the early signs that culture is strengthening, or do they only notice when it's already broken?

The SERN framework reveals both shadows and light. Throughout this book, the focus has been on spotting toxicity in soil, imbalance in exposure, disconnection in roots, and deprivation in nutrients. Now comes learning to recognize the early signs of bloom, those subtle shifts that indicate a garden is moving from survival to genuine growth.

These aren't dramatic transformations. Blooming happens quietly, often invisibly at first. A conversation that feels different. A meeting where something shifts. A moment when the realization hits that people are creating rather than just complying. The bloom begins long before anyone notices the flowers.

Soil: Signs of Enrichment

When soil transforms from toxic to fertile, the shifts are unmistakable. People start admitting what they don't know without fear of looking incompetent. Disagreements become energizing rather than exhausting. Mistakes get discussed openly because learning matters more than blame. Information flows freely because knowledge isn't currency anymore.

The place to nurture this growth is wherever someone takes a risk and isn't punished for it. That space, however small, is where bloom begins. Protect it. Expand it carefully. Leaders and managers who publicly celebrate the learning from failures, not just successes, create permission for everyone else's growth through their own vulnerability.

Exposure: Signs of Balanced Light

When exposure starts distributing fairly, previously silent people begin contributing ideas without being coaxed. Credit naturally flows to originators without battles for attribution. Different people lead different moments based on expertise, not hierarchy. Celebration replaces competition when someone else succeeds.

The place to cultivate this growth is wherever someone voluntarily amplifies another's work. That generosity of spirit spreads when protected. Individual contributors can name their sources and credit inspirations. Leaders and managers can rotate who presents to senior leadership. The same faces in every important meeting means shadows are being created elsewhere.

Roots: Signs of Healthy Connection

When root systems strengthen authentically, problems get solved before they become crises. Information travels faster through informal networks than official channels. People help across departments without being asked. Trust replaces verification in daily interactions.

The place to encourage this spread is wherever spontaneous collaboration appears. Remove obstacles rather than adding process. Roots grow best without interference. Everyone can share knowledge freely and connect people who should know each other. Leaders and managers can build bridges between departments, remembering that real solutions travel through roots, not org charts.

Nutrients: Signs of Abundant Flow

When nutrients flow freely, people demonstrate voluntary skill-sharing without protecting expertise. Risk-taking happens without permission-seeking. Growth moves in unexpected directions rather than prescribed paths. Energy increases through the day rather than depleting.

The place to maintain this flow is wherever someone teaches what they once hoarded. Ensure they're rewarded, not punished, for that generosity. Anyone can become a nutrient creator by teaching what they know and supporting without being asked. Leaders and managers can fight for their people's growth opportunities. That conference someone wants? Find the money. Budgets reveal what organizations actually value versus what they claim to value.

The Bloom Begins with Recognition

Most organizations are so busy fighting fires they never notice the green shoots emerging. They're so focused on preventing failure they miss the early signs of flourishing. The SERN Bloom Assessment isn't about scoring or measuring; it's about developing eyes to see what's already growing and knowing how to nurture it.

From Recognition to Action: The Bloom Cultivation Practice

Recognizing bloom is only the beginning. The next step is learning how to cultivate these early signs without suffocating them with too much attention or process. This requires a different kind of leadership, one that tends rather than manages.

Start with weekly observation. Not formal assessment, but conscious awareness. Where did someone take initiative without being asked? When did collaboration happen naturally? What problem got solved without escalation? These moments reveal where culture is naturally strong.

Document patterns, not events. One person admitting ignorance isn't bloom; it might be personality. Five people admitting ignorance in the same week? That's a cultural shift. One team collaborating across departments isn't transformation; it could be coincidence. Three teams doing it independently? That's roots connecting underground. These patterns reveal where a garden naturally wants to grow. Follow them rather than forcing growth where leadership thinks it should happen.

The power lies in amplification without formalization. When bloom appears, resist the instinct to create a program around it. No best practice guides. No committees. Simply remove obstacles and let it spread. Nothing stifles emerging culture faster than turning it into a mandatory process.

Consider what happened at Patagonia when employees started organizing environmental activism during lunch hours. Leadership didn't create an "Environmental Activism Program" with KPIs and quarterly reviews. They simply stopped scheduling meetings during lunch. They made it easier for employees to participate without making participation required. The movement grew stronger because it remained voluntary, authentic, and employee-driven.

The Framework Is the Tool

This book has provided what most organizations spend millions trying to develop: a way to see culture clearly. The SERN framework isn't another model to implement. It's a lens that reveals what's already happening.

When people start seeing organizations as gardens rather than machines, everything shifts. Problems become patterns. Complaints become data. Resistance becomes information about root systems. Failure becomes feedback about soil conditions. This isn't about adding another initiative or program; it's about seeing with different eyes. Once someone recognizes toxic soil, they can't unknowingly poison it. Once shadow dynamics become visible, pretending everyone has equal exposure becomes impossible. Once root networks are understood, whisper networks can't be ignored. Once people know what nutrients others need, they can't keep starving them.

The tool is the seeing itself. The framework is the intervention.

What Changes When Organizations See

Organizations that use SERN don't implement it; they inhabit it. They stop asking, "How do we fix culture?" and start asking, "What is our garden telling us?" They stop managing problems and start tending conditions.

The shift happens in language first. Instead of "engagement issues," they see "nutrient deficiency." Instead of "communication breakdowns," they recognize "disconnected roots." Instead of "performance problems," they identify "toxic soil." This isn't just reframing; it's recognition that changes response.

When culture is seen as a living system rather than a mechanical one, the impulse to engineer outcomes gives way to creating conditions. You can't make a plant grow faster by pulling on it. You can't force bloom by demanding it. The only path forward is creating conditions where growth becomes possible, then trusting the garden to do what gardens do.

The organizations that understand this achieve what others only dream of: cultures that sustain themselves, evolve without force, and bloom without being commanded to flourish.

We Bloom Together or We Wilt Alone

Brian Tracy wrote, "Become the type of leader that people would follow voluntarily, even if you had no title or position."[1] This truth extends beyond leadership to culture itself. Culture doesn't belong to titles or positions. It belongs to anyone willing to tend it.

Throughout this book, the journey has moved through toxic soil that poisons growth, shadow dynamics that determine who thrives, underground networks that reveal actual truth, nutrients that fuel genuine performance, and storms that test everything that's been built. The SERN framework has revealed organizations as living systems rather than mechanical structures. Now comes the choice that defines everything: Will you become a mindful gardener or remain someone who walks past struggling plants without noticing?

The organizations that flourish understand something fundamental: Culture isn't created by leaders for followers. It emerges from countless daily decisions by everyone present. The security guard who treats everyone with equal dignity. The analyst who shares knowledge freely. The executive who admits ignorance publicly. The intern who speaks truth respectfully. Each action enriches soil or contaminates it, creates light or shadow, strengthens or weakens roots, provides or withholds nutrients.

This collective creation terrifies traditional management. If culture belongs to everyone, what makes leadership special? If the newest employee can influence culture as profoundly as the CEO, why do hierarchies exist? These questions reveal the poverty of imagination that keeps organizations stuck. They assume power is finite, that influence shared is influence lost, that cultures need owners rather than gardeners.

The truth is more radical: Distributed ownership creates stronger cultures than centralized control ever could. When one person owns culture, it's as fragile as their tenure, as limited as their imagination, as narrow as their experience. When everyone owns culture, it becomes as resilient as the collective, as creative as all minds combined, as broad as every perspective present.

Consider what happens in organizations where culture truly belongs to everyone. Problems get solved by whoever notices them first, not whoever has the right title. Innovation emerges from unexpected corners because brilliance doesn't check org charts. Collaboration happens naturally because people aren't competing for artificial scarcity. Growth occurs in surprising directions because nutrients flow where needed, not where directed.

This isn't organizational fantasy. It's what happens when people stop waiting for permission to improve their environment. The financial analyst who starts documenting decisions so others can learn. The warehouse team that reorganizes processes without being asked. The marketing manager who amplifies engineering's contributions. The engineer who teaches sales about technical possibilities. None of them wait for culture initiatives or transformation programs. All of them create culture through daily choices.

Yet most organizations remain trapped in the ownership delusion. They assign culture to HR, who lack the power to change it. They create committees that meet about meetings. They launch initiatives that compete with last year's initiatives that nobody remembered to cancel. They write values that contradict their reward systems. It's the corporate equivalent of a group project where everyone's name is on it but nobody actually does the work.

The best consultants (and yes, some of us do exist) don't arrive with preset ideas to impose. We help organizations see what's already growing and what's quietly fading. We translate between the executive floor and the warehouse floor. We name what everyone sees but nobody will say. The difference between transformation and just another expensive initiative? Whether someone helps an organization recognize its own garden's potential rather than trying to install their preferred landscaping.

The shift from owned to collective culture requires courage that most organizations lack. Courage to admit that the C-suite doesn't have all the answers (shocking, I know). Courage to acknowledge that the intern might see something the board missed entirely. Courage to recognize that whisper networks know truths that official channels desperately deny. Courage to accept that culture emerges from collective wisdom rather than strategic planning retreats at mountain resorts.

This courage pays dividends that spreadsheets can't capture. Organizations with truly collective cultures don't just perform better financially, though research consistently shows they do. They create environments where humans can be fully human. Where growth isn't rationed like wartime provisions. Where truth isn't dangerous contraband. Where failure teaches rather than terminates. Where people bring their whole selves because there's actually room for everyone to bloom.

The SERN framework provides tools to understand these dynamics, but understanding alone doesn't create change. Change happens when enough people decide that struggling in silence is no longer acceptable. When they stop pretending toxic soil is "just how business works." When they refuse to accept shadows as permanent residents. When they strengthen roots despite policies that prioritize isolation. When they share nutrients despite reward systems built on scarcity logic.

You might be thinking: *This sounds lovely, but I'm just one person in a massive organization. What can I possibly change?* This thinking is exactly what keeps cultures stagnant. Every forest started with seeds that didn't wait for permission to grow. Every cultural transformation began with someone who decided that different was possible, probable, and necessary.

Start exactly where you are.

For individual contributors: Model what you want to see. Document work transparently. Amplify others' contributions enthusiastically. Share knowledge like it's abundant, because it is. Connect people who should know each other. These are seeds that might not bloom this quarter but will create possibilities for others. One person choosing generosity over hoarding, transparency over secrecy, connection over isolation, changes the soil composition for everyone nearby.

For middle managers: The influence available is greater than most realize. A team is a microclimate within the larger organization. Healthy soil can be created even in toxic companies. Fair exposure can be ensured even in biased systems. Roots can be nurtured that support people through organizational hurricanes. Nutrients can be provided that help people grow beyond what anyone anticipated. The middle of an organization is where culture actually lives, where values either become real or remain wall decorations.

For senior leaders: The choice is simple but not often easy. Control or cultivate? Engineer or enable? Own or share? The answer determines whether an organization blooms or continues its slow, expensive drift toward irrelevance. The leaders who will be remembered aren't those who accumulated the most power but those who distributed it most wisely.

The choice extends beyond individual organizations. Traditional command-and-control structures are being challenged as never before, not because they've stopped working entirely, but because people have discovered what's possible when trust replaces surveillance and autonomy replaces micromanagement. The organizations defining the next century understand that competitive advantage doesn't come from hoarding power but from distributing it. Not from controlling culture but from enabling it. Not from managing people but from creating conditions where people manage themselves.

This isn't soft philosophy. It's hard economics. Organizations that treat people as replaceable resources are being outperformed by organizations that recognize people as irreplaceable creators. The companies that survive coming disruptions won't be those with the best strategies but those with the most gardeners. Not those with the strongest individual leaders, but those with the strongest collective cultures. Talent now chooses where to grow, and talent chooses gardens over factories every time.

The garden metaphor guiding this book isn't just a poetic device (if I do say so myself). It's a practical framework for understanding how human systems truly work. Gardens don't care about titles. They respond to care, not control. They grow through interaction, not instruction. They thrive on variety, not uniformity. They survive through adaptation, not rigidity. They bloom when tended by many hands, not managed by one.

Every organization is already a garden. The only question is whether it's being tended with intention or left to chance. Whether the people within it understand what they're growing or remain blind to the seeds they plant daily. Whether leadership sees their role as controlling outcomes or creating conditions. The SERN framework makes the invisible visible: the soil people stand on, the light they receive, the connections sustaining them, the nourishment feeding their growth. Once seen, these elements can't be unseen. Once understood, they can finally be tended with the wisdom they deserve.

Every day, choices are made that either nurture or neglect the garden we tend. The decision to stay silent or speak truth. The choice to hoard knowledge or share it freely. The option to claim credit or give it to those who earned it. These aren't small things. These are the thousand daily decisions that determine whether cultures bloom or wither.

The work isn't glamorous. Gardening rarely is. The real gardeners do it anyway, knowing that beneath the soil, something wonderful is preparing to emerge. They choose truth when silence would be safer. They lift others when keeping them down would feel easier. They share what they know when guarding it would secure their position. They might not see the bloom today or tomorrow, but they tend the garden anyway because they understand that growth happens in darkness before it reaches light.

Some will call this naive. They'll say organizations are too complex for such simple solutions. They're right about the complexity but wrong about the solutions. Complex systems don't need complex interventions. They need consistent, aligned actions from people who understand that their individual contributions matter precisely because they're part of something larger. One gardener can't transform a forest. Yet lavender lingers long after storms pass, roses reach through seasons of neglect, and sunflowers seek each other across impossible distances. People carry that same capacity: to grow toward light, to bloom despite less-than-ideal conditions, to drive transformation simply by refusing to stop reaching. The transformation happens when individuals stop asking "What difference can I make?" and simply start making it.

The organizations that bloom in the coming decades will be those where everyone understands a fundamental truth: Culture isn't something to have but something to do. Every interaction enriches soil or contaminates it. Every decision creates light or shadow. Every connection strengthens or weakens roots. Every resource shared or withheld affects nutrient flow. Everyone is already shaping culture through thousands of daily choices. The question is whether those choices will be made consciously, with intention, care, and the understanding that every action ripples through the entire system.

The future belongs to organizations where everyone tends. Where culture isn't owned but cultivated. Where growth isn't managed but enabled. Where people don't just survive but flourish. Where everyone who walks through the door answers the question "Whose job is culture?" the same way: "Mine."

Right now, a choice awaits. Return to pretending everything is fine while potential goes unrealized. Wait for someone else to fix what's broken. Keep hoping that the next initiative, the next leader, the next reorganization will finally create the workplace that people deserve.

Or pick up whatever tools are available and start tending the garden that's right here, right now. Share light where shadows have lingered too long. Strengthen connections where isolation has taken hold. Offer nutrients where people are starving for growth. Trust that others are doing the same, even when their work remains invisible.

Not every garden is ours to tend. If an organization resists the work someone is willing to do, finding healthier soil isn't surrender; it's choosing to bloom where contribution is valued. Whether the path forward means staying to transform or leaving to flourish, the principle remains: Tend what can be tended, where it can be tended, with whoever will join in the work.

The workplace most people dream of isn't a fantasy. It's a garden waiting to be grown. It exists in every organization where someone decides that culture matters too much to leave to chance, that people matter too much to leave struggling, that potential matters too much to leave unrealized. It starts with one person choosing to be a culture gardener. Then another. Then another. Until the whole organization is tending something together that none of them could have grown alone.

Something extraordinary is ready to flourish. Your culture. Your people. We bloom together or we wilt alone.

ACKNOWLEDGMENTS

No flower blooms without the hands that tended the soil before the first petal appeared. To each of you: Thank you.

Jeevan Sivasubramaniam, my editor: For seeing the flower when all I had was a seed.

Berrett-Koehler Publishers: For cultivating my dream into something that all can hold.

Ma: For your daily prayers that cover me and keep me blessed.

Angel, Alyzah, and Armani: We're a quartet of laughter, love, and chaos.

Tolu (Squidge): For always reminding me of who I am.

Cindy: For being the most selfless person I know. What a gift to call you a friend.

Miz and Imz: For swinging from invisible chandeliers with me since 1998. Peak happiness.

Kyra: For the tough-soft love that was the harmony I needed to hear.

Amy: For being firm to my fair. The best kind of partner in this work.

Katrina: For telling me, "You're magic, Abi. Go share it with the world."

NOTES

Chapter 1

1 Donald Sull, Charles Sull, and Ben Zweig, "Toxic Culture Is Driving the Great Resignation," *MIT Sloan Management Review* 63, no. 2 (Winter 2022): 1–9.

2 Gary P. Pisano, "The Hard Truth About Innovative Cultures," *Harvard Business Review* 97, no. 1 (January–February 2019): 62–71.

3 Jim Harter, "Why Great Managers Are So Rare," Gallup Workplace, March 25, 2024, https://www.gallup.com/workplace/231593/why-great-managers-rare.aspx.

Chapter 2

1 Emily Field et al., "Women in the Workplace 2023," McKinsey & Company and LeanIn.Org, October 5, 2023, https://www.mckinsey.com/featured-insights/diversity-and-inclusion/women-in-the-workplace-2023.

2 Heather Sarsons, "Recognition for Group Work: Gender Differences in Academia," *American Economic Review* 111, no. 5 (2021): 141–175.

3 Lauren A. Rivera, "Employer Decision Making," *Annual Review of Sociology* 46 (2020): 215–232.

4 Sonia K. Kang et al., "Whitened Resumes: Race and Self-Presentation in the Labor Market," *Administrative Science Quarterly* 61, no. 3 (2016): 469–502.

5 Luc Behaghel et al., "Unintended Effects of Anonymous Resumes," *American Economic Journal: Applied Economics* 15, no. 3 (2023): 184–211.

Chapter 3

1 Suzanne W. Simard, "Mycorrhizal Networks Facilitate Tree Communication, Learning, and Memory," chap. 10 in *Memory and Learning in Plants*, ed. Frantisek Baluska et al. (Springer, 2018), 191–213.

2 Kieran Snyder, "Language Bias in Performance Feedback: 2022 Data Analysis and Survey Results," Textio, 2022, https://textio.com/feedback-bias-2022.

3 National Association for Law Placement, "Report on Diversity in U.S. Law Firms," NALP, January 2023, https://www.nalp.org/uploads/Research/2023NALPReportonDiversityFinal.pdf.

4 Zeynep Ton, *The Case for Good Jobs: How Great Companies Bring Dignity, Pay, and Meaning to Everyone's Work* (Harvard Business Review Press, 2023), 45–47.

5 Amy Edmondson, *The Fearless Organization: Creating Psychological Safety in the Workplace for Learning, Innovation, and Growth* (Wiley, 2019), 47–49.

6 McKinsey & Company, "How to Beat the Odds in M&A," McKinsey Global Institute, May 2024, https://www.mckinsey.com/capabilities/m-and-a/our-insights/how-to-beat-the-odds-in-m-and-a.

Chapter 4

1 Carol Dweck and Kathleen Hogan, "How Microsoft Uses a Growth Mindset to Develop Leaders," *Harvard Business Review*, October 7, 2016.

2 Donald Sull et al., "Toxic Culture Is Driving the Great Resignation," *MIT Sloan Management Review*, January 11, 2022, https://sloanreview.mit.edu/article/toxic-culture-is-driving-the-great-resignation/.

Chapter 5

1 Simon Sinek, *Start with Why: How Great Leaders Inspire Everyone to Take Action* (Portfolio, 2009).

2 Peggy A. Thoits, "Mechanisms Linking Social Ties and Support to Physical and Mental Health," *Journal of Health and Social Behavior* 52, no. 2 (2011): 145–161.

3 Society for Human Resource Management, "Improving Employee Retention and Reducing Turnover," September 11, 2024, https://www.shrm.org/topics-tools/tools/toolkits/managing-employee-retention.

4 Work Institute, "2018 Retention Report: The Complexities of Employee Retention," https://info.workinstitute.com/retentionreport2018.

Bloom

1 Brian Tracy, *Leadership* (Amacom, 2014).

INDEX

A

accountability, innovation and, 15
acquisitions, 75–79
administrative staff, 67
agency, employee, 93–94
AI and automated bias, 45–46
anonymous resume, 51
Attenborough, David, 4
authenticity, 2, 7

B

belonging
  authenticity/belonging choice, 2
  of culture to all, 135
  via the roots, 73
  and talent retention, 98
bias. *See* discrimination
Black/Brown people
  passed over for promotions, 35–36
  and performance management bias, 60–61
  vs. promotions of whiteness, 48
  workplace safety for, 60
blind spots, leadership, 16
burnout
  burnout culture, 20, 25
  in high-potential program, 50–51
  of leaders, 124
  resignation wake up calls, 25
  and toxic soil, 13, 18

C

career advancement, 38
change
  accommodating multiple needs, 124
  authentic exposure change, 53–54
  backlash to, 117
  capacity for, 109–110
  of cultural soil, 16, 29
  deliberate refusal to, 23
  of existing power structures, 50
  of exposure patterns, 30
  honesty required for, 24, 25
  individual/collective, 144–145, 147
  jadedness to cyclical, 106
  of leadership style, 134
  lip service to, 53, 86
  via nutrient distribution, 87
  pathway to cultural, 24–30
  performative, 66–67, 88
  vs. powerless roots, 80–81
  slow pace of, 26, 27–28, 108–109, 116, 128
  sudden, wholesale, 75–79
code-switching, 40
communication
  in challenging times, 126–127
  in "foreign" accents, 38–39
  official vs. actual, 19–20, 57–58
  organizational lingo, 77, 121
  in the roots, 69
  unspoken, 20, 58
  wellness language, 87–88
  without power, 81–82
competition
  new growth as, 72
  and scarcity mindset, 96
  in toxic culture, 22
courage
  to cede power, 143–144

courage (*continued*)
honesty and, 24, 25
in removing toxic soil, 26
cross-functional exposure, 85
cultural illiteracy, 7, 58
culture
behind the scenes, 11
calling out invisible patterns in, 7–8
defined, 3
as enabled from within, 133
enforced conformity to, 2
as "engineered," 1–2, 4
gap between stated and actual, 15
growth mindset in, 90–92
organizational jargon on, 43
as owned by all, 130, 131–136, 142–143, 147
of safety, 4
test of healthy, 14
via tiny, daily acts, 16
transplants of, 75–79
See also healthy culture; toxic culture

D

dehumanization
amid perks, 89
via enforced conformity, 2
of token/trophy employees, 40
Discover Weekly, 133
discrimination
AI and automated, 45–46
anonymous resume vs., 51
deniability language and, 87–88
dismissing proof of, 17
in identifying talent, 45–46
in nutrient distribution, 99–100
in performance management, 60–61
roots and tracking of, 60–63
diversity
cost of rejecting, 2
vs. deliberate exclusion, 23
entry-level vs. C-suite, 35
performative, 23, 39–40
Dweck, Carol, 90

E

Edmondson, Amy, 71
e.l.f. Beauty, 133
employees
accumulated trauma in, 27–28
agency granted to, 93–94
cost of replacing, 128–129
costs of racism on, 101–102
creating jaded, 104–105
culturally-conforming, 15, 18–19
employee-driven movements, 140
empowerment of, 85–86, 92
in growth-mindset cultures, 90–92
harm to disempowered, 119
learning/training for, 91
ownership of culture by, 131–136
real experience of, 11–14
rebuilding trust of, 26, 27–28, 68, 108–110
safe evacuation of, 121–123
shadow-dwelling, 55
systemic change to accommodate, 124–127
thriving vs. surviving, 15
toxic motivation for, 22
trophy employees, 39–40
unwanted perks for, 83–85
See also talent
engagement
falsified, 58
measuring, 86
and team leadership, 23
engineering values, 1
evolution of culture, natural, 4
executive presence, 42, 43, 47
exposure in culture
exposure equity audits, 52
fair, 41, 53–54, 131, 138
light distribution on teams, 6
lip service to redistributing, 49–53
mentorship for, 49–50
meritocracy myth, 42–49
and nutrient hoarding, 103
and opportunity hoarding, 33–36, 43, 55
resistance to transforming, 53
and the "right look," 32–33

roots and, 55, 68
shadow–spotlight divide, 40–41
soil as, 35–36, 37
and sunlight hogging, 29–30, 38, 43, 48
systemic address to, 50
talent/exposure dichotomy, 30, 38, 40
and tokenism, 39–40

F

failures
challenges are not, 117
of cultural improvements, 79, 105, 113, 115
fixing vs. abandoning, 8
of healthy roots, 75–79
of inclusion, 1
of token/trophy employees, 40
understanding cultural, 3, 7
of using talent, 1
fear
and absence of safety, 94
deliberately instilled, 21, 22
and exclusion, 71–72
leadership blind spots via, 15–16
of loss of power, 142
toxic culture of, 12
and truth of cultural soil, 11–14
of wanting to learn, 92
feedback
action-taking following, 93
backlash to, 12
meaningful managerial, 23
non-anonymous, 12
financial considerations
cost of nutrient vampires, 89
cost of rejecting diverse talent, 2
cost of replacing employees, 128–129
cultural investments, 115
misappropriated idea costs, 52–53
nutrient scarcity mindset, 97–98
functional dysfunction, 24, 67, 104
"Fun Fridays," 2, 84

G

Gallup, 23
gatekeeping, 21, 71–72, 88–89, 111
gender factors
co-opting ideas of others, 35–36, 37
diminishing women's ideas, 16–17
in promotions, 35–36, 46–47
queer safety, 16
growth mindset, 73, 90–92, 95

H

Harvard Business School, 71
Harvard University, 48
healthy culture
backlash to, 113, 116
cultivating blooming in, 4, 75–79, 139–140
deep roots in, 116–117
of growth mindset, 90–92
honest self-reflection in, 24, 25
idea generation in, 114
leader cultivation of, 17
leadership nutrients in, 86–87
learning/training in, 91
as living ecosystems, 5, 140, 146
meeting structure in, 125
merit in, 49
no need for whisper networks in, 68
as owned by all, 131–136, 142–143, 147
patience in cultivating, 108–109
psychological safety in, 63
rebuilding trust in, 108–111
role of soil in, 13, 27
in the roots, 63
signs of thriving in, 136–139
surviving threats to, 111–112, 123–124
systemic accommodations in, 124–127
tests of, 14, 115
unnecessary perks vs., 83–85
uprooting of, 75–79
hierarchies
vs. actual power structures, 19–20
culture and invisible, 4, 23, 24
entry-level vs. C-suite diversity, 35
exclusivity to maintain, 100

flattening, 132–133
healthy culture and permeable, 14
as predetermined, 46, 47
of the roots, 73
root system as crossing, 61
shadow-spotlight divide to maintain, 40
storm impact in, 119–120
high-potential program, 50–51
hiring process
anonymous resumes, 51
cultural conformity in, 43–44
deliberately uninclusive, 23
entry-level vs. C-suite diversity, 35
"merit charades" in, 46–47
and opportunity hoarding, 32–33
removing toxins in, 26
socialization of new hires, 12–13
structured visibility for, 51–52
Hogan, Kathleen, 90
honesty
about challenges, 126–127
in auditing "excellence," 49
changing culture via, 24, 25
in facing contamination, 25, 29
fear as pointer to the truth, 15–16
lack of cultural self-reflection, 17–18
vs. organizational lingo, 121
as storm shelter, 126
HR
blocked promotions in, 1
consultation in, 3
cultural illiteracy in, 58
culture as reinforced by, 20
firm vs. human protections by, 62

I

idea misappropriation
gender factors in, 35–36, 37
sunlight hogging and, 33–37, 38
of women's ideas, 16–17
inclusivity
deliberately performative, 22–23
failures in, 1
fair exposure opportunities, 41
vs. opportunity hoarding, 35–37
performative, 39–40
in the roots, 72–74
inherited wealth, 35
innovation
blame for failures vs., 15
co-opted by teammates, 37
via cultural health, 6, 142–143
vs. microaggression, 102
performative, 75–76
vs. protecting the status quo, 21
self-preservation vs., 71–72
shadow culture vs., 20
and toxic soil, 13
innovation challenges, 52
insecurity, deliberate, 22

L

layoffs
roots and early warning of, 67, 69–70
unspoken information and, 20, 58
leadership
blind spots in, 16
burnout of, 124
change initiatives by, 145
culture as reinforced by, 17, 130
deliberately toxic, 22–23
enabling vs. managing by, 133–134
exposure and proximity to, 33–36
exposure justifications by, 36, 39
failed cultural programs by, 3, 7
gatekeeping by, 21
honest responsibility-taking by, 25
and idea generation, 114
ignorance of toxic soil, 14
"leadership potential," 43
learning mindset in, 91
"merit charades" in hiring, 46–47
and nepotism, 35
as nutrient creators, 86–87
as nutrient vampires, 88–89, 101–102
performative, 52, 53, 87–88
responsibility vs. control, 129–130, 134
rewards of toxic, 118
roots and awareness of, 59
shadow headquarters of, 65–66
speaking truth to, 14

storm protection by, 122
sunlight hogging by, 29–30
systemic accommodations by, 124–127
and toxic soil, 12, 13, 17
true, 141
as white, 61–62

M

marginalized people
AI and automated bias, 45–46
cost of microaggressions on, 101–102
and "foreign" accents, 38–39
and the meritocracy myth, 43–44
passed over for promotions, 35–36
and performance management bias, 60–61
vs. promotions of whiteness, 48
shadow knowledge in, 38
in structured visibility programs, 51
tokenism for, 50–51
as trophy employees, 39–40
workplace safety for, 60
memory, organizational
roots as, 64, 66
of shadow dwellers, 38
soil as, 12, 27, 29
men, promotion of, 35–36, 46–47
mentorships
activating learning, 91
for exposure, 49–50
intentional exclusions in, 72
performative, 60, 99
in the roots, 64–65, 72–73
meritocracy myth
vs. actual power structures, 19
overview of, 42
in performance reviews, 47
vs. promoting cultural conformity, 15, 43–44
and promoting the "best person," 42–49
vs. real meritocracy, 41
shadow-spotlight divide, 40
talent/recognition myth, 31–32
MIT, 69
MIT Sloan, 14, 107
mycorrhizal networks, 58, 71

N

National Association for Law Placement, 62
nepotism, 3, 35
nutrients in culture
and authority/empowerment, 92–93
effective/needed, 83, 85–86, 90, 94
in good leadership, 86–87
in healthy culture, 131, 138–139
immunity to, 104–107, 109–110
inequal distribution of, 97–103
measuring of, 86
mycorrhizal networks to share, 58
nutrient creators, 86–87
nutrient vampires, 88–89
vs. perks/wellness language, 83–84, 87
root access to, 81–82
scarcity mindset on, 89, 96–97, 103
three primary, 90–96
timing of, 98–99
as what is needed to thrive, 6
withholding, 88, 94–95, 101–103

O

opportunity hoarding, 33–36, 43, 48, 55
organizations
accumulated trauma in, 27–28
defining terms for, 42–43, 49
"engineering" culture at, 1, 4
exposure cultivated in, 37
filtering bad news in, 58
fostering jadedness in, 106–107
functional dysfunction, 21
as gardens, 4–5
lack of cultural honesty in, 17–18
lingo of, 77
as living ecosystems, 4–5, 49
nepotism in, 35
nutrient distribution in, 86–87, 97
perks race among, 84–85
root systems in, 63
shadow knowledge in, 38
status quo maintenance by, 23–24
toxic culture preferred by, 12

P

Patagonia, 140
performance
of fairness, 46
of importance, 103
nutrients as prerequisites to, 96
performance management bias, 22, 60–61
performative, 39–40, 53
and recognition, 32
reviews, 47, 65, 92
of whiteness, 48
perks race, 83–85
PIPs (Performance Improvement Plans), 60–61
Pixar, 132–133
power
in administrative staff, 67
changing existing, 50
connections without, 80–81
control and responsibility, 129–130
empowerment of employees, 85–86, 92
exclusivity to maintain, 100
exposure and proximity to, 33–36, 103
exposure without, 52
flattening hierarchies, 132–133, 142
as influence without control, 134
mapping real structures of, 19–20
as necessary nutrient, 90, 92–94, 95
and presentation of work, 54, 88–89
via protecting the status quo, 21–24
and resistance to exposure shifts, 53
roots and awareness of, 61
roots and mapping of, 58–60
roots as private clubs, 70–72
shadow headquarters of, 65–66, 99
shadow-spotlight divide to maintain, 40–41
without authority, 92
promotions
being passed over for, 1, 32, 66
of the "best person," 42–43
of cultural conformity, 15, 18–19, 20, 32–33, 42, 43, 65
exposure and, 33–35
and invisible hierarchies, 4, 20
leadership control of, 21
of men vs. women, 35–36, 46–47, 59
"merit charades" in, 46
racial issues, 48, 61
systemic barriers vs., 46
of toxic leaders, 118
psychological safety, 12, 27, 63, 68, 71–72, 76, 88

R

racial factors
costs of racism, 101–102
discrimination, 17
promotions of whiteness, 48
representation taxation, 40
retail industry, 52, 69–72, 74, 81, 82, 95
rewards
for ideas in real time, 41
and recognition of work, 54
scarcity mindset on, 89
vs. sunlight hogging, 29–30
of toxic leaders, 118
visible, for risk-taking, 28, 91, 108
risk-taking
employee willingness in, 28
as needed for innovation, 90
nutrients needed for, 95
visible rewards for, 28, 91, 108
Rivera, Lauren, 42
roots in culture
authentic mentorships in, 65–67
early warning system in, 67
eliminating need for, 68
escape hatches in, 121
exposure and, 55
failures of, 75–79
in healthy culture, 131, 138
as home of authentic culture, 6, 55, 62–63, 64
inclusive, 72–74
inequity awareness in, 60–62
mycorrhizal networks of, 58, 68
nonverbal communication in, 94
pattern recognition in, 59, 65
performative compliance in, 78

powerlessness in, 80–81
resource gatekeeping in, 70–72, 74
safety mapping in, 58–60
shallow vs. deep, 69–71, 74
as true information pathways, 57–63
welcoming newcomers to, 72–73
whistleblower protection in, 62
rules, unwritten, 3–4

S

safety
culture of, 4
fear and absence of, 94
intentional exclusion from, 71–72
lip service to, 88
measuring, 76
as necessary nutrient, 90, 94–96
nutrients needed for, 85–86
pattern recognition of, 65
psychological safety, 12, 27, 63, 68, 88
in the roots, 68
and storm evacuation, 121–123
unwanted substitutions for, 84, 86
for women, 60
scarcity mindset, 89, 96–97, 100, 103
SERN (Soil, Exposure, Roots, Nutrients) framework, 4, 131–132, 136–139, 140–141
shadow culture, 18–20
silence
about toxic patterns, 14, 18
in front of bosses, 15
presumed as agreement, 14
and protection of harm, 12
and withering of talent, 90
Sinek, Simon, 114
skip-level meetings, 53
Society for Human Resource Management (SHRM), 128
soil in culture
accidental vs. deliberately toxic, 13
adding good on top of bad, 26
deliberately toxic, 21–24
fear and truth of, 15
in healthy culture, 27, 131, 137
healthy roots in toxic, 76–80
as hidden in plain sight, 18–19
mission statement vs., 13
organizational memory in, 12, 27–29
as reality, not aspiration, 11–12
rehabilitation of, 16
and role of sunshine, 29–30
as truth vs. claims, 6
solution charades, 23
Spotify, 133
Stanford, 21
status quo
deliberate protection of, 21–22
and promoting the "best person," 42–43
and promotion of the "right look," 33
protecting challengers to, 26–27, 54
pushback for questioning the, 2, 28
roots that protect the, 71–72, 80–81
via talent/exposure dichotomy, 40
storms, weathering
and backlash, 113
as cultural tests, 112, 115
forms of storms, 114–116
hierarchical implications, 119–120
idea generation in, 114
inevitability of, 113–114
internal vs. external, 118–119, 123
preparation for, 7, 117
shelter vs. evacuation in, 121–129
varying crisis threshold in, 121
warning signs in, 120
strategic thinking, 43
stress responses, 28
stretch assignments, 33, 35, 41, 50, 51, 85, 91, 99
structured visibility programs, 51
success
exposure and, 31, 36
via healthy soil, 27
via needed nutrients, 83, 100
and nutrient timing, 98–99
via opportunity hoarding, 33–35
of token/trophy employees, 40
in toxic culture, 18

T

talent
vs. the "best person," 44–45
cost of microaggressions on, 101–102
cost of rejecting diverse, 2
cost of replacing employees, 128–129
dehumanization of, 2
disempowered, 92–93
documentation of, 61
exposure opportunities for, 41, 54
healthy roots and retention of, 73
healthy soil and retention of, 29
ingredients for flourishing of, 2
meritocracy myth and overlooking, 47–48, 49
nepotism vs., 3
nutrients and retention of, 86, 97
nutrients and withering of, 89–90
"objective" identification of, 45–46
vs. proximity to power, 33–37
and recognition, 31–32
retaining women, 17
root networks to train, 65
safe evacuation of, 121–123
talent/exposure dichotomy, 30, 38, 40
toxic culture and retention of, 107
teams
burnout culture for, 18
co-opting of ideas on, 37
credit tracking among, 54
diminishing women's ideas on, 16–17
with healthy roots, 75
nonverbal communication on, 94
The Culture Partnership, 3
tokenism, 39–40, 50–51
Ton, Zeynep, 69
toxic culture
calling out, 7
deliberate, 13, 15, 21–24
and employee retention, 14, 107
facing reality of, 14, 110
of fear, 12
flourishing in removal of, 4
health effects of, 119, 120
inability to innovate in, 13
insecurity in, 22
leadership cultivation of, 12, 17
lingering effects of, 27–28
motivation in, 22
nutrient distribution in, 97, 103
of nutrient immunity, 104–107
and opportunity hoarding, 33–36
re-assertion of, 113
rehabilitation of, 108–109
in the roots, 70–72
roots as antidote to, 63, 64, 68
socialization in, 24, 104–106
succeeding in, 18, 35
via tiny, daily acts, 16
toxicity rewarded in, 118
uprooting from, 8
Tracy, Brian, 141
transformation
authentic exposure change, 53–54
backlash to, 117
capacity for, 109–110
of cultural soil, 16, 29
deliberate refusal of, 23
of existing power structures, 50
of exposure patterns, 30
honesty required for, 24, 25
individual/collective, 144–145, 147
jadedness to cyclical, 106
of leadership style, 134
lip service to exposure changes, 53
via nutrient distribution, 87
pathway to cultural, 24–30
performative, 88
repetition of performative, 66–67
slow pace of, 26, 27–28, 108–109, 116, 128
transparency, 12, 18
trophy employees, 39–40
trust
breaking of, 88–89
failures of, 76, 78
in growth-mindset cultures, 90
as organic, 80
rebuilding, 26, 68, 108–109

roots and building of, 82
of sustained nutrients, 107
truth telling
as career sabotage, 22
to credit theft, 41
in cultural roots, 55, 57–58, 68
to leadership, 14
turnover
as cost of rejecting talent, 2
cost of replacing employees, 128–129
in retail, 69
toxic culture and, 14

U

uncertainty
driving performance via, 22
and opportunity hoarding, 34
shadow–spotlight divide to maintain, 40–41
shelter in challenging times, 124–129
unconscious bias training, 23
University of Toronto, 48

V

virtual workplace, 34
visibility. *See* exposure in culture

W

wellness language, 87–88
whistleblower protection, 62
whiteness/white people, 48, 61–62
women
co-opting ideas of, 16–17, 37
cost of microaggressions to, 102
passed over for promotions, 35–36, 59
workplace safety for, 60
Women in the Workplace report 2023, 35
Work Institute's 2018 Retention Report, 129
work-life balance, 4, 18, 20, 59, 106

ABOUT THE AUTHOR

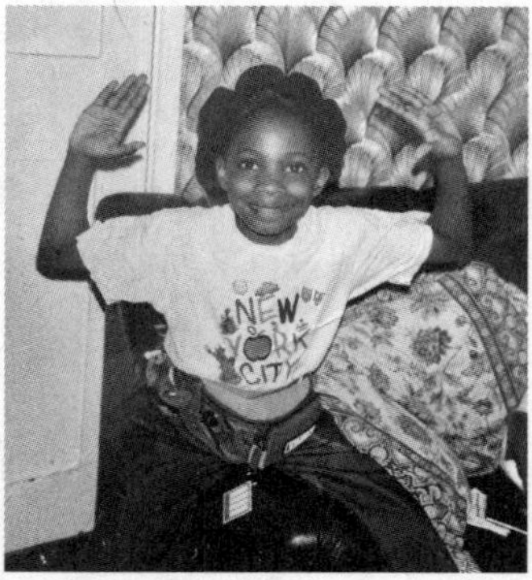

Abi Adamson is the founder of The Culture Partnership, a consultancy helping organizations move beyond performative culture initiatives to create workplaces where people thrive, not just survive. She is also the creator of the SERN framework, which reimagines organizational culture as a living ecosystem. She has designed cultural strategies and facilitated culture workshops for global brands, including Spotify, Sony Music, Soho House, Papier, and Match Group. Quoted in *The New York Times* and *Forbes*, Abi has written for *Metro*, *Raconteur*, and *People Management* and delivered a TEDx talk, "Who Owns Culture." Born in Lagos and raised in London, today she is perpetually discovering new corners of the world to call home.

Abi is available for keynote presentations, speaking engagements, workshops (virtual and onsite), and consulting. If this book planted a seed, she'd love to help it bloom.

Websites: abiadamson.com | theculturepartnership.com

LinkedIn: Abi Adamson

Email: hello@abiadamson.com

Berrett-Koehler
PUBLISHERS

Dear Reader,

Welcome to the Berrett-Koehler Community—a global network of changemakers creating positive impact in their lives, organizations, and communities.

Our Mission: Connecting People and Ideas to Create a World That Works for All

We believe transformation is possible. While outdated paradigms of self-interest, exclusion, and hierarchy continue to hold back our communities and organizations, we know that change can happen. That's why we connect people with actionable ideas from leading experts who are already creating the solutions we need.

The BK Way

We're an independent publisher that practices what we publish. Our books, digital resources, and community offerings provide practical pathways for building more just, equitable, and sustainable organizations and lives. Whether you're transforming your workplace, community, or personal practices, our publications meet you where you are with tools that work.

But we don't just talk about positive change—we live it. Through "The BK Way," we put stewardship and purpose before profit. As a benefit corporation, we're legally committed to benefiting all our stakeholders: authors, readers, employees, communities, and the environment.

As our gift to you, claim your free bestselling ebook at bkconnection .com/welcome. You'll also receive fresh leadership insights delivered to your inbox from bkconnection.com/blogs/the-bk-exchange.

You Make the Difference

We're grateful to our readers, authors, and community members, who bring our mission to life every day. Your stories of transformation inspire us and show others what's possible.

Share how BK publications are making a difference in your world at bkconnection.com/impact.

Your friends at Berrett-Koehler

Join the Berrett-Koehler Community

Are you passionate about supporting independent publishing and reading diverse voices and perspectives? Join the BK Community Membership Program and become a part of a vibrant literary community. To support mission-based publishing while saving up to 30 percent on all books and attending exclusive events, visit ideas .bkconnection.com/bkcommunity-join to learn more and become a member.

MIX
Paper | Supporting responsible forestry
FSC® C005010
FSC www.fsc.org

UNCOVER UP

HOW TO THINK CLEARLY IN AN AGE OF CONSPIRACIES

LEE KUHNLE

NATHAN RADKE

ECW

Published by ECW Press
665 Gerrard Street East
Toronto, Ontario, Canada M4M 1Y2
416-694-3348 / info@ecwpress.com

CERTIFIED CANADIAN PUBLISHER

Editor for the Press: Jen Albert
Copy editor: Peter Norman
Cover design: Jessica Albert

LIBRARY AND ARCHIVES CANADA CATALOGUING IN PUBLICATION

Title: Uncover up : how to think clearly in an age of conspiracies / Lee Kuhnle and Nathan Radke.

Names: Kuhnle, Lee, author. | Radke, Nathan, author

Description: Includes bibliographical references and index.

Identifiers: Canadiana (print) 20260180874 | Canadiana (ebook) 20260180904

ISBN 978-1-77041-887-5 (softcover)
ISBN 978-1-77852-580-3 (PDF)
ISBN 978-1-77852-579-7 (ePub)

Subjects: LCSH: Critical thinking. | LCSH: Conspiracy theories.

Classification: LCC BF441 .K84 2026 | DDC 153.4/2—dc23

This book is funded in part by the Government of Canada. *Ce livre est financé en partie par le gouvernement du Canada.* We also acknowledge the support of the Government of Ontario through the Ontario Book Publishing Tax Credit, and through Ontario Creates.

Canada Ontario ONTARIO CREATES

PRINTED AND BOUND IN CANADA

PRINTING: MARQUIS 5 4 3 2 1

To Captain Edward Ruppelt,
who genuinely tried to figure out
the flying saucer mystery

CONTENTS

INTRODUCTION 1

1 Folk Psychology — How a Magician Fooled the CIA 13

2 Chaos and Causation — Is the Illuminati Behind Everything? 29

3 Belonging Before Belief — What's Animating the Anti-Vax Community 49

4 The Information Ecosystem — The Evolving FEMA Death Camp Conspiracy 66

5 Disinformation Campaigns — When the Conspiracy Theory *Is* the Conspiracy 84

6 Moral Panics — Three Witch Hunts and the Consequences of Bad Information 100

7 Good and Evil — QAnon vs. the Sinister Cabal 116

8 Conspiracy and Millenarianism — The Dangers of Apocalyptic Cults 132

9 Cognitive Dissonance — What Happens When the Flying Saucer Doesn't Land 151

10 Conspiracism vs. Falsifiability — Why a Flat Earth Needs a Fake Moon Landing 168

11 Text, Context, and Subtext — Reading Between the Lines of the Cattle Mutilation Conspiracy 182

12 Aliens and Flying Saucers — UFOs as Contemporary Mythology 203

CONCLUSION Empathy in an Age of Conspiracy — The Great Seattle Windshield Epidemic 221

NOTES 231

ACKNOWLEDGEMENTS 253

INDEX 255

INTRODUCTION

This is a book about conspiracies and conspiracy theories, about the forces that make them arise and why people believe them. It is also about how to tell which are nonsense and which probably happened.

Conspiracies have moved into the mainstream of contemporary society and are having a direct impact on the outcome of important decisions. They are shaping the outcomes of elections. They are hampering public health efforts to stop diseases. They are preventing global action on climate change.

Conspiracy theorists generate counter-narratives to every major news story. Did Princess Diana lose her life due to a drunk driver and overzealous paparazzi, or was she actually murdered by the British royal family? Was 9/11 orchestrated by terrorists or by the CIA? Does the newest vaccine represent a boon to community health, or is it a ploy to sterilize a segment of the population?

Since conspiracies dominate so much of contemporary society, it is worth understanding them in their own right. In this book, we investigate conspiracies from sociological, historical, philosophical, and literary perspectives in order to understand their role. In doing so, we also provide strategies for analyzing their validity.

COMMON SENSE, OBVIOUSLY!

"Why would anyone need a book to tell them that the world isn't actually flat? We have common sense for that!" When put like that, it does seem like we could simply rely on a bit of reasoning and common sense to figure out what's real and what isn't. But conspiracies that we know have actually taken place are sometimes more fantastical than the ones that turn out not to have happened.

Two of the following events really happened. One did not. Can you tell which is the fake?

A) In 1960s, the CIA's Directorate of Science and Technology was given $20 million to devise new ways to spy on people. What they developed has come to be known as Acoustic Kitty. House cats were surgically implanted with listening devices in the hopes that the cats would luxuriate outside the Soviet embassy in Washington, transmitting the machinations of Russian spymasters.

B) In WWII, leading up to the attacks on Pearl Harbor on December 7, 1941, the U.S. intercepted encrypted Japanese communications that gave Franklin D. Roosevelt's government concrete advance warnings of an impending Japanese attack. Despite the early warnings, the U.S. decided to allow the attack to take place to provide the American leadership with an excuse to enter the war. Up to that point, America had stayed out of the conflict. The attacks happened, and America joined the fighting.

C) In the summer of 1964, the NSA (National Security Agency) manipulated intelligence coming out of Vietnam to make it appear that an American warship, the USS *Maddox*, was directly attacked by North Vietnamese fighters on August 4. This "attack" led to the expansion of the Vietnam War. Except the "attack" was staged and didn't happen. The U.S. increased its involvement in the Vietnam War based on information they knew was false because they themselves had falsified it.

Without further information, which of these examples seems most plausible? It can be hard to tell because real-life conspiracies throughout history have often seemed unreasonable. We definitely can't go by our own common sense here. As it turns out, conspiracy A is true. Acoustic Kitty was tried by the CIA.[1] (It didn't work.)

Conspiracies B and C are **false flags**. A false flag is when a country allows an attack to take place or entirely fabricates an attack to garner legitimacy to enter a war. Both options are equally plausible, and they both say shocking things about the U.S. government, but only one is true. It is true that communications were intercepted before the Pearl Harbor attacks, but they did not provide the Roosevelt government with substantial information indicating an attack was coming. By contrast, the Gulf of Tonkin Incident (option C) happened.[2] It was a government conspiracy to extend an unpopular war.

There are many incredible, outrageous, and bizarre real-life conspiracies. We know this beyond any reasonable doubt. MKUltra, for example, is an umbrella term for a 20-year-long CIA-funded project to test hallucinogenic drugs on unsuspecting Canadian and American citizens. The goal of these projects was to create "super soldiers," find a "truth serum," and see if "sleeper assassins" could be created without the assassins themselves knowing anything about it.[3] These projects were deeply unethical and illegal according to both domestic American and international law. This is just one example of a conspiracy that sounds more like an elevator pitch for a horror movie than historical fact.

By contrast, there are reasonable, believable, and unspectacular conspiracy theories that have turned out to be untrue. The idea, which gained currency in the 1950s, that GM deliberately sabotaged the streetcar industry, seems plausible.[4] Within the realm of conspiracies, it is not far-fetched. The motivations of the actors are coherent, and there is precedent: Similar corporate conspiracies really have happened. But the streetcar conspiracy was not one of them.

Of course, there are bizarre conspiracy theories that are demonstrably not true, such as Fiona Broome's interpretation of the Mandela Effect. The Mandela Effect conspiracy theory posits that simple slips of memory are best explained by the fact that we are actually travelling between dimensions, and that these realities are subtly different from each other.

We notice this when we collectively misremember something like whether the Monopoly Man is or is not wearing a monocle. There is absolutely no evidence for this conspiracy.

There are mundane conspiracies that did happen. A group of Confederates conspired to assassinate Abraham Lincoln. Big Tobacco lied about the harmful effects of smoking on people's health.[5]

If we can't rely on common sense, how are we to know which conspiracies are real and which are not? Are there guidelines, or clues that we can look to, to get a handle on reality?

Fortunately, there are. This book describes the psychological traps that can lead to false positives. It describes social forces that give a sense of reality to baseless fears. We examine the underlying ideologies of false conspiracies when we investigate concepts of evil and Manichean worldviews. We look at the media ecosystem as well as how the media is manipulated by unscrupulous political actors deliberately ensnaring us in disinformation.

CONSPIRACY THEORIES DEFINED

We define a **conspiracy** as what happens when a group of people collaborates against the public good, in secret, for their own gain. Definitions tend to be clearer when we add an example, so let's use one we've already encountered above. MKUltra was a conspiracy because it was a program done in secret, by a group of people (the CIA), collaborating against the public good (certainly as defined by the victims and more broadly as defined by the Bill of Rights), in order to gain an advantage (over the Soviets) in the Cold War.

However, we encounter a problem when we try to define the term **conspiracy theory**. The term tends to be used as a putdown in popular culture and is generally reserved for erroneous descriptions of reality. The issue with *conspiracy theory* is how we define *theory*. In the natural and social sciences, the term *theory* is used in a more limited way than it is used in everyday speech. For natural and social scientists, a theory is a causally related story that explains the facts under investigation. When a physicist speaks about "the theory of gravity," it is not meant as a guess. All serious physicists believe that there's such a thing as gravity. The term *theory* in this sense leaves open the possibility that we may need to revise or develop the concept in the future. If more facts become known to us, then the theory of gravity may need to be reworked or reconsidered in light of the new information. Importantly, however, *theory* in this narrower sense is not a guess in lieu of the facts. Theory is what we say when we know what we are talking about.

If we follow this more restrictive use of the term *theory*, then a conspiracy theory is a story that causally connects the facts under investigation by assuming that a group of people is working in secret for their own benefit but against a public good. It is important for us to note that this definition is neutral. There are conspiracy theories that turn out to be false and there are those that turn out to be real.

In much of the literature on this topic, conspiracy theories are synonymous with falsehood. It is a specific way of being wrong. They are reductive theories about how the world works, usually rooted in paranoia, and always wrong. We disagree. The mere act of assuming that there might be a small group of people secretly orchestrating the events under investigation so that it benefits them at the expense of everyone else is not necessarily a sign of paranoia or of reductive understandings of the social and political world. In many cases, this is exactly what happened. We therefore in this book refer to a conspiracy that can be shown to have actually taken place as a **true conspiracy theory**, while we use **false conspiracy theory** or simply **conspiracy theory** for those which didn't happen or are highly implausible. MKUltra, COINTELPRO, Watergate, and Iran-Contra are just a few examples of real conspiracies where outrageous government overreach in which basic civil and constitutional rights of Canadians, Americans, and many others were violated for the secret purposes of a small group of people. To relegate these and many other real conspiracies to the margins of history and view them as rare outliers does a lot of harm to the project of trying to debunk the false ones.

IS THERE A TRUTH TO THE LIE?

We therefore suggest a more nuanced approach to the concept of truth and untruth in conspiracy theories. Sometimes, they can function as a smoke screen, a story that hides a deeper truth. This is at least partly what is going on with the UFO (now UAP) sightings and secret defence testing.[6]

A conspiracy theory might also be a dog whistle, making claims about real events when the actual purpose is to activate a certain political or ideological community. The conspiracy theory that circulated during the 2012 American election campaign that suggested that President Barack Obama was actually a Kenyan-born Muslim, and therefore ineligible to run for the highest office, was a dog-whistle conspiracy.[7] Some believed in the literal veracity of this conspiracy as a counter-narrative to the mainstream belief that he was born in Hawaii, but others saw through it to the underlying message: It was a dog whistle to signal racist elements in the American public that "this candidate is not one of us." Sometimes, the conspiracy theory hides a message in plain sight. But it is only visible to the initiated.

Sometimes, the conspiracy theory is partially correct but the conclusion or key elements are not. It is largely true that the rich aim to remain rich, which can include endorsing policies that harm the environment or human rights. It is obvious that many decisions are made in closed-door sessions, not on the floors of elected assemblies. The fact that sometimes the rich collude in ways that harm the rest of us is not a far-fetched conspiracy claim. It is also not a far stretch from this insight to the conspiratorial belief in secret societies that rule the world. While there is little evidence to suggest that the Illuminati are a secretive world government, there are those with far more wealth and power than the rest of us who conspire with other rich people to use their wealth and power "against the common good." A belief in the Illuminati-rules-the-world conspiracy is factually untrue and easily debunked, and yet there are aspects that are correct. The conspiracy itself speaks to an underlying truth that is often expressed in the realm of conspiratorial lore: Sometimes conspiracies express pain, frustration, and injustice that are true to reality, but do so in a simplified and stylized way.

Conspiracy theories can also function as markers of group identity. For instance, among American Democratic voters, it is assumed that Donald Trump colluded with elements within the Russian government to swing the election in his favour in 2016, despite the fact that the Mueller Report was unable to find any convincing evidence this was the case.[8] On the other side, Republicans argue that Hillary Clinton definitely "did something in Benghazi."[9] In both cases the conspiracy theory is less about what took place than it is about identifying with an ideological group. We have noted a similar dynamic among some of our students who seem to "try on" a conspiracy theory as part of a process of developing an adult identity. The conspiracy theory is less a factual description of the world as it appears upon reasoned reflection, and more an attempt to define oneself as part of this group (rebelling youth) as opposed to that one (normative "mainstream").

In the dystopian science fiction film *The Matrix*, the protagonist, Neo, is given a choice between two pills. If he takes the blue pill, he remains in an illusory world. If he takes the red pill, he awakens to the reality of his existence. And that seems to be the standard choice. There's truth (red pill) and illusion (blue pill). But in his interpretation of the movie, philosopher and film critic Slavoj Žižek wonders if there isn't a "third pill" that allows one to see the reality within an illusion. Conspiracy theories that are false may nonetheless contain a certain truth hidden within the illusion.[10]

RED FLAGS

We want to provide the reader with a sample of what is to come. Below are four concepts that are related to conspiracy theories that help us understand how they work and why they flourish. They are also red flags because they are often associated with incorrect conspiracy theories.

The Paranoid Spokesman

Conspiracy theories need amplifiers, or what historian Richard Hofstadter described as the **paranoid spokesmen**. These people do the work of spreading the theory. They tend to centralise conspiracies in explanation of social phenomena, believe in immensely powerful and organized enemies, imagine they are participating in apocalyptic stuggles between good and evil, and demonize their opponents. A good example is Alex Jones. At his height, Jones was a huge conspiracy theory amplifier. He had a massive podcast, *The Alex Jones Show*, and owned a huge "news" site called Infowars. His shows and his site dedicated a lot of coverage to uncritically repeating conspiracy theories. One conspiracy theory in particular, the claim that school shootings like Sandy Hook were made-for-TV sagas with no real victims that instead relied on "crisis actors," led to a number of lengthy court cases filed by the parents of some of the murdered children. These court cases resulted in Jones being found liable, and he lost control of his media empire.[11]

Thought-Terminating Cliché

A thought-terminating cliché is a phrase that is used by believers to quell doubt. The concept was developed by psychiatrist Robert Lifton in describing language forms used by the Chinese Communist Party. Thought-terminating clichés tend to be pithy folk-wisdom slogans: "If it ain't broke don't fix it"; "It is what it is."[12] In contemporary conspiracy culture, we see the use of a thought-terminating cliché in the QAnon movement. "Trust the plan" is a phrase often repeated, especially when disconfirming evidence arises to contest the validity of the theory. In the QAnon movement, a theory arose that Donald Trump would return as president in March of 2021.[13] When that didn't happen, "trust the plan" was deployed by believers to ease discrepancy between theory and reality. Not all conspiracy theories are marked by a thought-terminating cliché, but when there is one, it is usually a bad sign.

It Was Not Literal!

Ray Hyman is professor emeritus of psychology at the University of Oregon. He has also performed as a stage psychic to expose frauds and show how the tricks of mind-reading are accomplished. In a lecture on how to do "cold readings," a technique in which the psychic reads a person at random, Hyman explains that if a prediction goes wrong, the best thing to do is to maintain that it was meant figuratively, not literally.[14] For instance, if the psychic were to say, "I see you working in a garden," and the subject counters with a negative like, "I don't have a garden and I hate flowers," the response should be on the order of, "I didn't mean a literal garden. I meant that I see you as nurturing and responsible for the flourishing of others." We have noticed this dynamic in many conspiracy narratives. Doomsday cults that predict a specific end of the world have relied on this to suggest that "the end happened in the heavenly realm."

Conspiracism — The Thought-Trap

In the world of conspiracy theories there is a danger known as **conspiracism**: conspiracy theory as an all-encompassing worldview, an ideological stance under which no facts that could possibly disprove the conspiracy exist. For example, it is impossible to disprove the belief that we are all part of a simulated reality, like a sophisticated computer game, and that we can never escape. It is a variation on the "this is but a dream" idea in which we are all trapped inside a dream and are not living in the "really real" world. Some conspiracy theories make discrete claims about the world, such as "Princess Diana was murdered by the royal family." In this case we can amass evidence for one side or the other and prove that the conspiracy is correct or incorrect. However, if we find evidence that the conspiracy is incorrect and the retort is that "but the royal family is so powerful that they planted that false evidence to confuse us," we start to enter the world of conspiracism. There is no appeal to reason, to common facts, or to a shared commitment to the truth. It is a thought-trap.

WELCOME TO THE PROJECT — CHAPTER OVERVIEW

Each of the following chapters is organized around a key idea and the tools needed to analyze and interpret the relevant conspiracy theories. We rely on experts in various fields to do much of the heavy lifting, introducing readers to aspects of social psychology, disaster theory, Biblical philosophy, 20th-century logic, French postmodern thought, classical social theory, theories of group dynamics, and the philosophy of science, to name but a few.

In the first three chapters, we examine reasons why intelligent people might believe incorrect conspiracy theories. In chapter 1, we suggest that sometimes this happens because we have made a mistake interpreting our sense experiences. We examine this by telling the true story of how a magician tricked CIA-funded researchers, leading to a multi-decade program investigating psychic abilities. In chapter 2, we investigate the complexities of causal reasoning and show that sometimes we believe incorrect conspiracy theories because we have made a logical error. To demonstrate this point, we investigate the conspiracy theory that a secret society known as the Illuminati is in charge of the world. Chapter 3 argues that the role of our community is central to influencing what we believe and why we believe it. Our conspiracy theory in this chapter is the anti-vax movement.

In the next set of chapters, we look at how we obtain information about the world and some consequences of poor information. Chapter 4 examines the virtual ecosystem of the internet and explains how the characteristics of that environment give an evolutionary advantage to lies and errors over the truth. As a case study, the chapter examines a meme-based conspiracy claim that the Federal Emergency Management Agency (FEMA) is preparing to set up concentration camps in America. Chapter 5 delves into the murky world of political disinformation, where incorrect conspiracy narratives are sometimes weaponized as part of a larger information warfare campaign. We look at the theory that the HIV/AIDS epidemic was actually a bioweapons program as well as other examples of disinformation, such as Climategate. Chapter 6 looks at moral panic, a circumstance where people turn on each other as a result of poor-quality information. We look at three examples of moral panic, including the Salem Witch Scare, where people got hurt because others were wrongly convinced a conspiracy was thriving in their community.

In the next set of chapters, we analyze some of the hallmarks that tend to be associated with incorrect conspiracy theories. In Chapter 7, we claim that a binary worldview of good versus evil tends to mask the complexity of real social and political situations. Our examples include a deep dive into the world of QAnon. Chapter 8 introduces the consequences of the binary worldview, which is the idea of a great cleansing or the "millennium." In conspiratorial movements, we often see that there is a desire to "start again," and this chapter examines several examples of this throughout history. In chapter 9 we explore the concept of cognitive dissonance. We introduce the reader to a UFO doomsday cult and describe how they dealt with their predictions not coming true. Chapter 10 suggests one conceptual strategy to mitigate against incorrect conspiracy beliefs. We argue that the concept of falsifiability can help us get out of belief systems that are incorrect but nonetheless self-reinforcing. Our conspiracy examples in this chapter are the moon landing hoax and the Flat Earth theory.

Lastly, we turn to some literary dimensions of conspiracy theories. Chapter 11 examines the idea of subtext. Sometimes, we can learn truths by looking at the underlying fears and desires of the society that believes false conspiracy claims, and this chapter uses the example of the cattle mutilation scare of the 1970s to illustrate that point. Chapter 12 suggests that the UFO conspiracy theories represent the development of a contemporary cultural myth. We begin with the startling claims made by a former Pentagon insider and trace the history of the UFO myth to show where these ideas really came from.

OUR RESPONSIBILITY

The cliché says you are what you eat. However, since what we believe changes how we see the world, and how we see the world changes our choices and actions, and our choices and actions dictate who we are, it may be more accurate to state that we are what we believe. For this reason, it is vital to be careful and reflective about the ideas that we allow to take root in our minds.

We live at a time when countless conspiracy claims are circulating through our culture, changing public opinion, shaping public policy, and taking up much of the oxygen in the media landscape. To protect ourselves from believing false claims — and potentially opening the door to being manipulated by people who don't have our best interest in mind — we must learn everything we can about the nature of these claims. Tricks and tropes are far less effective on us when we recognize them. And by filtering out false claims, we are less distracted from the genuine conspiracies that are occurring away from the public view.

1

FOLK PSYCHOLOGY — HOW A MAGICIAN FOOLED THE CIA

How is it that smart, even brilliant and highly educated people become ensnared in outlandish theories about how the world works? For instance, Sir Isaac Newton. He discovered and calculated laws of physics still used today, but he also got caught up in the financial mania of his time and lost a whopping £20,000. A large sum even today, massive back then. He was reported to have said he could "calculate the motion of the heavenly bodies but not the madness of people."[15] If Newton could get caught up in nonsense, what hope is there for the rest of us? It seems that highly educated folks are just as likely to believe in nonsense outside their domain of expertise as anyone else; "smartness," it turns out, is less transferable than many of us believe. It's a misconception often shared by smart people, who might imagine their education reaches far beyond their actual area of competence.

This chapter explains that certain assumptions we tend to make about our mind's ability to analyze the world can make any of us vulnerable to erroneous claims, including false conspiracy theories. There are many reasons why someone might get the wrong idea about the world. In the next chapter, we examine specific thought patterns related to causal reasoning that can lead us to the wrong answer, and in chapter 3, we introduce the role that other people have in forming our beliefs, including incorrect ones. Here, we discuss the times when our own senses lead us astray.

Magic tricks are surprisingly helpful for learning about why reasonable people can be led to believe the unreasonable. In noting how a magician manages to fool us, we learn about the limits of perception, memory, and other basic cognitive functions. There is an important relationship between how we are fooled by a magic trick and how we are fooled by erroneous conspiracy theories; when we start to believe in a conspiracy theory that isn't actually true, it often happens because we make false assumptions about how the world works.

In any false conspiracy, there is a **seductive claim**, something that challenges our understanding of the world and makes us wonder if we can really trust our prior interpretations. For instance, in the moon landing conspiracy theory, which suggests that the U.S. faked the 1969 Apollo moon landing, the seductive claim might be that the American flag should not be waving on the moon since there isn't an atmosphere. Because the flag is clearly waving, we may need to rely on the theory that NASA faked the moon landing and the entire episode was shot on Earth, where there exists wind to make flags wave.

All false conspiracy theories contain one or more of these seductive claims. They draw us into the conspiracy because we've probably not thought about the subject too much, and once we're confronted with someone who appears to know a lot about it, we hear things for which we don't have a ready answer. It can be an unsettling experience. This opens to door to a **conspiratorial seduction**, where our inability to explain contradictions in the mainstream accounts of events leads us inextricably to a conspiratorial interpretation. But often these seductive claims rest on a misunderstanding about our minds or the world, sometimes both.

This is where magic comes in. Just like with conspiracies, we are fooled by magic tricks because we make an implicit and often unconscious assumption about our cognition and the world. Basically, we tend to imagine that we perceive more of the world than we do, that we remember more accurately than we do, and that our minds' interpretation of sense data provides us with a pretty good description of reality. By noting that our minds are tricked by magicians, we can apply some of these insights to how we might be tricked by an erroneous conspiratorial explanation.

Magic tricks work because our brains don't work the way we think they do. As neurologists and stage magicians Stephen L. Macknik and Susana

Martinez-Conde explain in their insightful book *Sleights of Mind*: "Magic tricks work because humans have a hardwired process of attention and awareness that is hackable. By understanding how magicians hack our brains, we can better understand how the same cognitive tricks are at work in advertising strategy, business negotiations, and all varieties of interpersonal relations."[16]

The way non-specialists imagine the workings of our minds we will term **folk psychology**. Anyone who isn't an expert in neurology or psychology is a folk psychologist; we all imagine how our cognitive processes function based on our lived experience. Magicians know that there is a vast gulf between folk psychology and the actual processes of cognition, and of course they take full advantage of it. Stage magicians, close-up magicians, and other tricksters such as con artists, pickpockets, and fake psychics deliberately operate in the gaps of perception. When an audience watches a live magic show, they think they can trust their perception. In fact, they are often watching specifically to catch how the magician does the trick. For example, in the Ambitious Card Trick, an audience member is shown a card from the top of the deck, which is then moved into the middle. Without further apparent manipulation, the card is back on top of the deck. The audience experiences the thrill of wonder because even though they were watching closely, they didn't *see* anything out of the ordinary. The assumption is that they would have, that they can trust their senses and cognition. This particular trick, which even Harry Houdini couldn't figure out, works because our brain relies on shortcuts, half measures, and other "cheats" to produce a sense of the world that seems reliable and consistent.[17] But our brain is a cognitive miser.[18] It "does a staggering amount of outright confabulation in order to construct the mental simulation of reality known as consciousness. The fact that consciousness feels like a solid, robust, fact-rich transcription of reality is just one of the illusions your brain creates for itself."[19] Brains save time and energy by taking shortcuts that are usually unnoticeable and unconscious.[20]

THE CIA'S FORAY INTO PSYCHIC RESEARCH

What follows is a true story from the world of secret U.S. defence research, and it contains all the themes mentioned so far. This is a story of how two highly educated physicists at the top of their game, working for one of the most respectable research institutions in America, were taken in by a stage magician while working on a secret CIA-funded project to test psychic abilities. This story demonstrates how highly educated people are as liable as the rest of us to get fooled by nonsense, especially when it falls outside their precise area of expertise. It's also a cautionary tale about the need for empathy when examining the views of others. Even the most intelligent and educated among us can get the wrong answer; we all make mistakes in interpreting our senses and perceptions.

During the 1960s, it emerged that the USSR was conducting research into psychic abilities and that they were making significant progress. A working paper for the Gondola Wish program written in 1978 and only recently declassified by the CIA summarizes the problem: "The Soviets have a parapsychology research program whose existence is classified and whose funding and control reside largely with the Ministry of Defense and possibly with the KGB. This program has been active since the early 1960s, is staffed by competent scientists and technicians, and includes about 10 research units that range in size from a single laboratory to large institutes employing several hundred people. Soviet researchers have gained experience with a greater variety of research methods than have their US counterparts and have completed more of the critical experiments needed to evaluate adequately the applications of paranormal abilities."[21] The Soviets, it seemed, were doing research into psychic abilities and they were getting positive results. If it were true, it would present a serious intelligence problem for the U.S.

As is so often the case, the social and historical background that legitimized a lot of bizarre CIA research projects was the logic of the Cold War and the official policy of mutually assured destruction (appropriately abbreviated as MAD). MAD stated that in the event of a Soviet nuclear attack, even a surprise attack, all belligerents would be wiped off the face of the earth, and teetering on the edge of oblivion does strange things to policy makers. With stakes set so high, every potential research question was worth pursuing, no matter how outlandish or implausible, if it had any potential for gaining a small political or military advantage. But weaponizing psychic ability would first require establishing that the phenomenon can be shown to actually exist, that it can be measured, and that trained operators can control and direct it. As one of the declassified reports explains, "The project's main goals were to evaluate the threat that foreign psychoenergetics achievements might pose to US national security, and to explore the potential of psychoenergetics for use in US intelligence collection." It would not help to invest in psychics before knowing whether they could do what they claimed and whether they were reliable enough to be effective tools. Even a 75 percent success rate, quite high when it comes to ESP, it would be unimpressive when compared with the success rate of actual radio or written communication. If your submariner-psychic gets the wrong answer a quarter of the time to the question "should we launch the missile?" the very war this project was meant to avoid becomes more likely. Establishing all those points would require rigorous scientific controls. What the CIA needed was a lab and trained, accredited, and published experimental researchers.

Specifically, the CIA was interested in a parapsychological phenomenon known as **Remote Viewing** (RV). According to a study commissioned by the CIA in 1995, remote viewing is "the ability to describe locations one has not visited." RV research had three goals, as the CIA review notes: "The first and primary objective was to provide scientifically compelling evidence for the existence of the remote viewing phenomenon." Second was to "identify causal mechanisms that might account for or explain the observed (or inferred) phenomenon." And third was "to identify techniques or procedures that might enhance the utility of the information provided by remote viewings."[22]

The CIA's research into RV and related parapsychological ability lasted from 1972 to 1977.[23] Thereafter, the Defense Intelligence Agency (DIA) began its own research, which continued well into the 1990s. In fact, researching psychic phenomena became a prominent sideline for the Department of Defense (DoD) and intelligence agencies. The various departments and investigations were saddled with a multitude of code names, the most prominent being Project Star Gate, but there were also Gondola Wish, Grill Flame, Sun Streak, the Army's Gateway Process, and others, as well as many subprojects.

However, our current interest is specifically about the two researchers at Stanford Research Institute (SRI) first contracted by the CIA to conduct initial experiments into the field of parapsychology. It was their apparent success, together with the Soviet and Chinese programs, that got the rest of the departments interested in the first place. As Annie Jacobsen explains in *Phenomena*, her comprehensive book on this project, "The results, called the Swann-Geller phenomena, would set the stage for more than twenty years of classified government research into extrasensory perception, psychokinesis, and extraordinary human functioning."[24]

In 1972, Harold "Hal" Puthoff and Russell Targ, two physicists at the SRI, began work on a CIA-funded project to investigate psychic abilities.[25] While there were other participants,[26] the most startling research occurred with Israeli "psychic" Uri Geller.[27] Geller was "discovered" by Dr. (Henry Karl) Andrija Puharich, an American medical doctor who also specialized in paranormal research, including psychic abilities, aliens, and psychedelic drugs, and who had connections to both academics and the intelligence community in the U.S. It was Puharich who suggested that Geller go to America. And Puharich would later write a book, *Uri*, expounding upon Geller's abilities.[28]

At the SRI, the two physicists put Geller's abilities to the test under rigorous laboratory conditions between December 1, 1972, and January 15, 1973.[29] The researchers made a film about their experiments and also published a paper about their findings in the prestigious peer-reviewed science journal *Nature*.[30] In the preface of their book *Mind-Reach: Scientists Look at Psychic Abilities*, Puthoff and Targ claim that "the primary achievement of this research has been the demonstration of high-quality 'remote-viewing.' The ability of experienced and inexperienced volunteers to view, by means of mental processes, remote geographical or technical targets such as roads, buildings and laboratory apparatus."[31]

The following description of the experiments relies on these sources as well as James "The Amaz!ng" Randi's reconstruction of the experiments in his book, *The Truth About Uri Geller*.[32] Randi was a stage magician of considerable skill. He was also deeply skeptical of Geller's claims and remained so throughout his life.

In one of the experiments meant to test Geller's ability to receive information psychically, similar to RV but not necessarily specific to locations, Geller was put in a sealed room without windows or any obvious way to communicate with the outside world. Random words and images were selected, and Geller was tasked with reproducing them as drawings without being told what they were.

As the researchers noted, Geller always had the option to pass and not produce a response if he didn't "feel it." Of the responses he did produce, all 13 pictures were close approximations of the target pictures. In one instance, the target was a camel when the response looked more like a horse, but when compared to what could be expected by mere chance, his accuracy was incredible. As Targ and Puthoff note, reproducing such a feat by guessing would happen less than once in a million attempts.

In another experiment, the researchers put an object into one of a number of opaque, sealed containers that looked like old analog film canisters. Only one of them contained the target object; the point was for Geller to determine which. He was not allowed to pick up or handle the containers. To prevent any information accidentally being divulged by the experimenters, people "not otherwise associated" with the experiment placed the objects inside the cans.

Targ and Puthoff explain the results: "We repeated this experiment fourteen times. Five times the target was a small permanent magnet affixed to the inside of the steel lid, five times a steel ball bearing, and once a sugar cube. On the latter two Uri got no impressions and passed. On the remaining twelve he did make a guess as to the target location and was correct in every instance, a result significant at odds [*sic*] of a trillion to one."

How about telekinesis? Could Geller manipulate the physical world using only his mind? In one experiment, he was asked to move the needle of a compass without touching it. To prevent any trickery, his body, especially his hands, were examined with a machine that detects magnets. The compass needle moved. Despite this, the results were discarded because it was later determined that the machine couldn't detect very small magnets and the possibility of cheating was therefore not ruled out conclusively. Puthoff and Targ can be commended for their intellectual honesty. If they discovered that a trick was possible, they refused to acknowledge the results, even though they didn't actually detect any trickery. But the data from a different telekinetic experiment did not need to be scrapped. Geller's task was to move a weight on a scale under a bell jar, without touching it. He succeeded.

What Puthoff and Targ discovered was, to put it mildly, unbelievable. Geller was able to perform psychic and telekinetic feats that had never before been seen in a laboratory. The experimenters claimed that his results far exceeded chance, all within strict laboratory conditions that permitted no possibility for cheating or manipulation. Since his time at the SRI, Geller has gone on to boast that his psychic abilities have been proven under strict laboratory conditions. And as Puthoff and Targ state in their book, "the burden of proof with regard to excluding the possibility of paranormal functioning now lies with the skeptics."

Not only did Puthoff and Targ provide incredible new research about psychic abilities, their work functioned as the initial academic and scientific legitimation of what the Soviets were up to. Partly as a result of this research, decades of research and tax dollars went into investigating psychic abilities.

GELLER RE-EXAMINED

One problem with the entire research enterprise, however, is that there are credible indications that Uri Geller is not actually a psychic and that what he pulled off were good magic tricks, not legitimate psychic ability. Let's examine a few of these.

The "strict laboratory conditions" established by Puthoff and Targ have come under severe criticism by scientists and magicians who have been able to duplicate Geller's psychic feats using conventional trickery and have explained plausible workarounds for the "controls" that the experimenters put in place.

Subsequent analysis of Puthoff and Targ's research methodology and experimental procedures demonstrates a shocking lack of standards. For instance, Geller's confederate Shippi Shtrang was almost always present with either Uri or the experimenters.[33] The notion that Shtrang may have worked as an accomplice in a magic routine seems not to have occurred to either of the researchers. In every case in which Geller claimed to have demonstrated his abilities, the same outcome could be reached by a skilled magician employing a few simple techniques.

Another example of problems with the project's "strict protocols" and "rigorous standards" was discovered in the sealed room, which wasn't actually sealed. Instead, in order to get cables in for the electroencephalograph

(EEG) tests, a square hole was cut in the steel wall and the space around it was plugged up with gauze. There were reports of gauze being found about the floor after a session when Geller was "psychically" receiving images. In this specific case it was after a drawing of grapes was received.[34] Contrary to the two scientists' descriptions of their protocols, things were not quite as rigorous as they may have suggested.

There are many other examples of lax standards. The subjects weren't chosen at random but were self-selected. SRI researchers would receive unsolicited phone calls from people who claimed to have psychic abilities. They also seem to have chosen subjects based on how much they liked them personally. The experimenters would encourage the subjects, or "assume that these experiments were going to be successful." According to Puthoff and Targ, they did this because it apparently impacted the outcome of psychic success rates if the audience was supportive and enthusiastic.

At the start of the SRI investigation, Randi offered his services to Targ and Puthoff, but they were uninterested. Randi was a magician. What could he possibly contribute to the research program? As Randi explains:

> No matter how well-educated, alert, well-meaning, or astute men of science are, they are certainly no match for a competent magician — fooling people is his stock-in-trade. The only persons the conjuror has difficulty with are the feeble-minded, since they are incapable of following the carefully calculated sensory and psychological cues that make his deceptions possible. Wherever there is any possibility of human intervention, in the form of chicanery, being an element in any experimental process, an experienced conjuror must be called in. And not just any conjuror, but one whose speciality is just that particular brand of chicanery. A common error among laymen is that one who possesses some magical trick apparatus, or who knows a few sleights, is a magician. That is like saying that a man who owns a scalpel and knows where the brain is located is a neurosurgeon.[35]

If there was even the slightest hint of success, the CIA had compelling reasons to continue the project. So why did they put an end to the research?

As the CIA review of Stargate makes clear, they didn't come up with anything useful:

> The foregoing observations provide a compelling argument against continuation of the program within the intelligence community. Even though a statistically significant effect has been observed in the laboratory, it remains unclear whether the existence of a paranormal phenomenon, remote viewing, has been demonstrated. The laboratory studies do not provide evidence regarding the sources or origins of the phenomenon, nor do they address an important methodological issue of inter-judge reliability.
>
> Further, even if it could be demonstrated unequivocally that a paranormal phenomenon occurs under the conditions present in the laboratory paradigm, these conditions have limited applicability and utility for intelligence gathering operations. For example, the nature of remote viewing targets are vastly dissimilar, as are the specific tasks required of the remote viewers. Most importantly, the information provided by remote viewing is vague and ambiguous, making it difficult if not impossible, for the technique to yield information of sufficient quality and accuracy for actionable intelligence. Thus, we conclude that continued use of remote viewing in intelligence gathering operations is not warranted.[36]

The KGB, despite any disinformation campaigns to the contrary, were also unable to produce any obvious psychics with the ability to infiltrate or disrupt America's military might. There exists footage of Nina Kulagina (their own version of Uri Geller) making things on a table move without touching them. But like the SRI, CIA, and DIA, or the Army, the KGB didn't manage to demonstrate that actual psychic abilities existed, let alone harness them. Similar results to those produced by Puthoff and Targ have not been reproduced in any rigorous research lab where the possibility of cheating was eliminated. When more stringent controls than those that existed at SRI were put in place the "psychic" abilities of "sensitives" went back to the levels expected by mere chance. A related issue emerges when we note that the James Randi Foundation has for a long time made available a prize of $1 million to anyone who can successfully prove these types of abilities.[37] The hitch is that the panel of judges is made up of magicians, and if they can figure it out, then the contestants don't get the money. Many have tried, but so far the prize remains unclaimed.

HOW FOLK PSYCHOLOGY DECEIVES US ALL

There are many morals that can be drawn from how Puthoff and Targ were taken in by a trickster. How was it that two top-notch PhDs in physics, who knew how to perform experiments, could not see what was self-evident for a stage magician without an advanced degree?

Many wonderful examples from the field of perceptual psychology and related fields demonstrate how our sense experience of the world and related psychological mechanisms like memory are not as reliable as many of us folk psychologists imagine. We will provide just two; we hope these will stand as representative of how unreliable our cognition and our perception can be. One example comes from the field of perceptual psychology, the other from research on memory.

The premise of folk psychology is that we would obviously notice something strange or out of place if we were looking right at it. Presumably this is also what Puthoff and Targ believed. If Geller were doing a trick, the two researchers would spot it. However, there is evidence that this is not the case.

In their remarkable experiment to test our ability to see the unexpected, Christopher Chabris and Daniel Simons made a video of a group of people passing a ball. There have since been many iterations of this experiment with subtle differences in each, but the basics are as follows. Half of the players are dressed in white T-shirts, the other half in black T-shirts. There are also a few basketballs, perhaps two or three. Participants who watch the video are asked to count the number of times players in the white T-shirts pass the basketball and to ignore all the passes made by players in the black T-shirts.

As with many psychology experiments, the setup communicated to the participants is not the whole story. The real question of the study was not whether observers could correctly count how many times players in white T-shirts passed a ball but whether they noticed a person in a gorilla suit walk into the middle of the group, look *directly at the camera*, beat her chest, and walk away.

As the authors write, "Almost everyone has the intuition that the answer is 'yes, of course I would [notice the gorilla].' How could something so obvious go completely unnoticed? But when we did this experiment at Harvard University several years ago, we found that *half* of the people who watched the video and counted the passes missed the gorilla."[38]

Half of the participants in the study did *not* "see" the gorilla that was directly in front of them, even while looking at the spot. To confirm that participants were looking in the correct direction (that is, directly at the gorilla) subsequent versions of this experiment used a device to track where the observers were looking. When told what had happened and asked to watch the film again, everyone saw it. But the point is that most of us *assume* that we would see it, whereas in reality half of us miss it. Importantly, there seems to be no correlation between intelligence or education and the likelihood of seeing the gorilla.

It turns out that looking is insufficient for noticing even large unexpected things in your field of vision. The missing element is attention. The experimenters cleverly provided an activity that absorbed a lot of cognitive capacity, and so there was not enough left over to pay attention to the unexpected. We don't see only with our eyes; we require our mind's participation.

Of course, the connection to magic at this point is obvious. Magicians are acutely aware of how to misdirect attention so that the key elements, which often happen right in front of the audience, are simply not noticed. There's a saying among magicians: The first time you do a trick it is performance, the second time it's pedagogy. When people don't know what to look for, they can be fooled. But the more you see the same trick, the more you start looking in the "wrong" (or perhaps right) places, and you learn how it's actually done. Magicians direct our attention, but we're generally unaware that this is happening. In fact, many of us try to focus especially hard to discover how the trick is done. And while we are focused right where the magicians want us to focus, we manage to miss the metaphorical gorilla right in front of our eyes.

We don't necessarily see big unexpected things right in front of us, and this is true even when a skilled con artist isn't deliberately hacking our perceptual system. However, this is only part of the reality illusion. As Macknik and Martinez-Conde note, "The spooky truth is that your brain constructs reality, visual and otherwise."[39] They continue, "Perception is not a process of passive absorption but of active construction."[40] We may miss something right in front of us, and we may also misremember significant events. It turns out that sometimes our memories of events are almost entirely fiction.

We have all had our memory fail us. We lose our car keys or phone. Someone introduces themself and we forget their name as soon as they've said it. After a night of too much drinking, we may discover disconcerting gaps in our recollection of the party. And no one remembers important events from early in life. Despite such lapses, memory feels pretty reliable. It is the central component of our lived biographies, our sense of self, without which we would not be who we are.

While we have all had memory issues at one time or another, there are certain life events that we will never forget. These are what memory researchers dub the "flashbulb" events. Monumental historical occurrences where you remember exactly where you were. Weddings, or funerals, or that day you met that famous person or discovered you had won the lottery. These memories are etched into our minds like words carved onto a stone: unmovable, unchangeable, and reliable.

But are they?

Memory researchers disagree. Elizabeth Loftus, a prominent American psychologist, conducted an experiment in which participants were shown videos of simulated car crashes. Later, asked to recount what had happened, they confused whether there was a yield sign or a stop sign. They got wrong whether the cars were speeding or not, which car hit which, whether there were any injuries, and if they were suffered by children or adults.[41] In a U.S. Army study, subjects who were torture victims were often unable to identify their assailant even though they had spent half an hour or more in a highly charged emotional setting with them.

The problem here is the gulf between an intuitive sense of how our memories work and how our cognition actually performs this function. Folk psychology depicts memory as a kind of video file stored in a memory bank. When we want to remember, we search our storage bank until we find the "file" we want. Our mind presses play, and our little homunculus watches the playback. But this is not how psychologists who study memory understand our capacity.

Memory seems to work less like a playable video and more like a live performance that needs to be recreated every time we want to remember something. Instead of accessing an unchanging file, we have actors and a script and re-enact the scene over and over. But over the years our script has been damaged by wear. Some of the blurry bits have been amended with edits. These edits can be made by ourselves, but also by others. The actors do not stay the same. As in a real stage performance, sometimes actors are replaced, and it turns out that some actors are better in some roles than others. Sometimes lines originally uttered by one are given to another. And as with a play that has not been recorded, we don't have access to the earlier versions. Each time we stage the play in our mind, it feels as though it hasn't changed; it's only when we obtain an objective reference for the earliest memories that we can compare how far the new performance has drifted off the original script.

Three findings need to be highlighted. First, memories change over time, even in important aspects. Second, the change is imperceptible by the subjects themselves. Unless shown direct evidence to the contrary, we believe that our memories are for the most part stable and relatively accurate recollections of an event. And third, the new, altered memories feel as accurate and real to us as the initial ones.

The research on memory is both surprising and consistent. We simply do not remember the way we think we do, and memories are not as reliable as we assume. We can and often do get key pieces of the story wrong.

MAGIC AND CONSPIRACY FALSE POSITIVES

Incorrect conspiracy theories often have some evidence to support them. People who believe in them are are not necessarily just making stuff up. The SRI researchers had a certain type of personal and experiential evidence. They set up experiments to test a psychic, and that psychic passed the tests. It is understandable that these researchers thought that they had stumbled upon the discovery of a lifetime. They had evidence, after all! But as our analogy with magic tricks demonstrates, first-person evidence, the evidence of our senses, is liable to provide us with incorrect descriptions of the world. A few conclusions follow.

First, when we encounter a conspiracy theory that turns out to be incorrect, we may be convinced by the claims because we are unable to explain what happened without recourse to the conspiratorial interpretation. Here is the first place where the analogy to magic is useful. Many magic tricks at first defy explanation. However, this fact by itself should not convince us that magic is anything more than trickery. The same applies to outlandish conspiracy theories. Just because we are at present unable to explain why something happened the way it did should not seduce us into assuming that therefore the conspiracy must be the correct explanation. No matter how many magic tricks we see, even amazing ones that we cannot duplicate or explain, we should not believe that physics-defying magic is real. We need to bring that same skepticism and commitment to a rational, materialist scientific worldview to our investigations of conspiracies.

Second, as with magic tricks, one reason we are fooled by erroneous conspiracy theories is that we are making assumptions about the world that we are unaware we are making; we tend to also assume that our perceptions can be trusted and our memories are pretty good, neither of which is correct. Evidence from the fields of psychology dedicated to awareness, attention, memory, and perception tells us that our minds are constantly taking shortcuts that magicians and con artists can hack. The same is true of conspiracies that turn out to be false. A conspiracy influencer may point out that the Apollo 11 flag waved on the moon, despite there being no atmosphere on the moon, and if we were to fact-check this claim, we'd discover that it's true. But this is only convincing because we are assuming there can be only one cause for the flag to wave, when in fact an astronaut is moving the flagpole, which would also cause the flag to wave. We've made an assumption that's just not correct.

Third, first-person evidence is not by itself good proof. It can be useful supporting evidence, but too often our encounters with false conspiracy theories occur when we meet a true believer who has had an incredible experience. We are then left with an uncomfortable choice: believe either that the person is lying or that the conspiracy is true. However, there is at least one more alternative: It is very possible for someone to have had an amazing experience and to have interpreted this experience incorrectly.

And fourth, it turns out that false conspiracies can be (and often are) supported by intelligent, well-meaning people who are highly educated. The credentials of the claimant, in and of themselves, do not make the conspiracy more or less plausible. Unless their education is *directly* related to the topic under consideration, the fact that someone has a PhD, or is a patent holder or is famous or rich or charming or all of these together, does not mean we should be seduced into believing that their interpretation of their own experiences is any better than anyone else's. The fact that Harold Puthoff had a PhD in physics, wrote physics textbooks, had patents related to lasers, and worked at a prestigious research institution does not in any way make him qualified to carry out tests in the domain of psychology, sociology, or the paranormal. The world of conspiracy theories is replete with highly educated experts in domains not relevant to the conspiracy, whose education is regarded by other nonexperts as somehow relevant to determining the validity of the conspiracy. The Amaz!ng Randi was the expert who was able to unmask Geller when the two physicists and the CIA were fooled.

2

CHAOS AND CAUSATION — IS THE ILLUMINATI BEHIND EVERYTHING?

UNDERSTANDING OUR WORLD

At its core, every conspiracy theory is an attempt to explain the way things are. We might want to know why a famous person was killed, or why an unusual natural disaster or weather event occurred, or why the prices at our local supermarket have gone up, and conspiracy theories can offer satisfying (if often inaccurate) explanations for those or any other odd or alarming situation that arises.

Because conspiracy theories are explanations, they are a form of analysis known as **causal reasoning**, one of the key methods with which we try to make sense of the world around us. To understand how crucial this form of thinking is, and what some of its limitations are, we need to examine the concept of causation itself.

The idea of causality is so fundamental to the way we see reality that we often don't even notice that we're using it. But every one of our decisions is ultimately based on the idea that choosing a course of action will change the eventual result, hopefully to a result that we would prefer. We choose to take a drink of water because we believe it will cause us to become less thirsty. We put on a light jacket because we believe that it will cause us to become less chilly. We go to the gym to work out believing that it will cause us to become healthier (or look better).

Not only do we use causal reasoning to make decisions on what we should do, we use it to make sense of the things that happen around us and to predict what might happen next. My car's engine stopped because I ran out of gas, so if I fill the tank back up it will run again. You caught a cold because you were in an elevator with a person who was sneezing and coughing, and if you gargle with salt water your throat will feel better. My favourite team was scored on because I wasn't wearing my lucky hat, and if I put that hat on my team will win. My cow died because the old woman across the street is a witch, and if we set her on fire then the livestock will stop dying. My politician lost the election because there was widespread voting fraud.

Causal reasoning is something we are constantly doing, but that doesn't necessarily mean that we're good at it. As we'll see, causation is a complicated concept that is easy to get wrong, and there are many errors and fallacies that are easy to fall prey to. In addition, the complex and chaotic world we live in makes it harder for us to know for sure what, exactly, the cause of an event was.

DIFFERENT KINDS OF CAUSES

Part of the problem with the way we think about causation is that there is more than one kind of cause. For example, a person might say something like "Cigarettes don't cause cancer. After all, I smoke, and I don't have cancer. And other people *don't* smoke, and they *do* have cancer. The whole thing is just a big conspiracy by the doctors and the researchers who are trying to profit from raising money."

And this hypothetical person may be partially correct. There are plenty of smokers without cancer, and plenty of non-smokers with cancer. Does this mean that there is no causal relationship between smoking and cancer?

The issue here is that there are several different kinds of "cause" being used in this one short example. When we don't separate them, it can create confusion. And, of course, whenever there is confusion, false conspiracy theories — like the idea that researchers are lying about smoking and cancer — can easily find their way in.

One kind of causal relationship is called **necessary cause**. What this means is that, in order for an effect to occur (we'll call this effect "Y") a specific cause (which we'll call "X") needs to be present. Without X, Y *can't occur.* For example, a person needs oxygen in order to live. A computer needs a power source in order to turn on. A student needs to enrol in a course in order to pass that course.

In each of these examples, the effect (Y) can't happen unless the cause (X) is present. However, the other thing these examples all have in common is that in none of these situations does the presence of cause X *guarantee* that Y will occur. A person might have access to oxygen and still die from decapitation. A computer might have access to power but not turn on due to a hardware problem. A student may have enrolled in a course but completed none of the work. These examples demonstrate *necessary* causes, but not *sufficient* causes.

A **sufficient cause** is when the presence of cause X *guarantees* that effect Y will occur. For example, cutting off a person's head guarantees that they will die. Throwing an unprotected chicken egg off a 10-storey building onto cement guarantees that it will break. Finishing with 65 percent in a course that requires at least 50 percent to pass guarantees that you will pass the course. Unlike the necessary cause examples, these sufficient causes are enough to make sure that the effect definitely happens. Also unlike the necessary cause examples, none of these sufficient cause examples are *required* in order for the effect to occur. Cutting off someone's head will guarantee that they die, but you don't need to cut off their head to kill them. There are many, many other ways.

And so, returning to our cigarette and cancer example, we can start to see where the mistake has been made. When the person says that they smoke and don't have cancer, they are establishing that smoking is not a *sufficient* cause of cancer. Smoking a cigarette is not enough to guarantee that someone develops cancer. When the person says that other people don't smoke and still get cancer, they are establishing that smoking is not a *necessary* cause of cancer. You don't need to smoke a cigarette in order to get cancer. Does this mean that smoking is not a cause of cancer?

No, because there is a third causal relationship: **contributory cause**. This refers to a situation in which the presence of cause X isn't required for effect Y to occur, and it doesn't guarantee that effect Y occurs; however, cause X does increase the likelihood of effect Y occurring. Studying for a test doesn't guarantee that a student will pass the test, and plenty of students don't study at all and still pass. Eating healthy and exercising doesn't guarantee a long life, and people live long lives without doing either of those things. Neither of those are necessary or sufficient causes, but both of them increase the likelihood of the effect. Studying contributes to the likelihood of passing, and living healthy contributes to the likelihood of living a long life. In the same way, smoking cigarettes increases the likelihood of developing certain cancers[42] and is therefore still a cause of cancer.

Confusing sufficient, necessary, and contributory causation is a common mistake and, as shown in the cigarette example, can become a contributory cause of believing false conspiracy theories. On the other hand, an understanding of these different relationships can help us to break down, analyze, and think more clearly about conspiracy claims.

CAUSAL REASONING AND THE TWIN TOWERS

Let's look at a quick example of how these ideas can be used to help us think more clearly and thoroughly about conspiracy theories. One of the most common claims about the collapse of the World Trade Center towers on September 11, 2001, is that "jet fuel can't melt steel beams." This sentence is part of a larger argument that looks something like this: The fires in the WTC towers were allegedly started by jet fuel, but jet fuel doesn't burn at a temperature hot enough to melt steel beams. In order for the WTC towers to collapse, the supporting steel beams must have melted. Therefore, explosives must have been placed in the towers to bring them down, and therefore it must have been an inside job.

This argument is a series of causal claims:

1. Jet fuel doesn't burn at a temperature *sufficient* to melt steel beams.
2. It was *necessary* for the steel beams of the structures to melt in order for the buildings to collapse the way they did.
3. Therefore, it was *necessary* for there to have been explosive devices placed in the buildings.

This argument appears fairly strong at first glance. After all, jet fuel burns at about 1200 degrees Celsius (2200 degrees Fahrenheit) and steel melts at a much higher 1510 degrees Celsius (2750 degrees Fahrenheit).[43] However, there is a counter-argument:

1. For the structures to have weakened enough to collapse, it isn't *necessary* for the steel to have melted.
2. It was *sufficient* for the steel beams to have weakened.
3. Steel beams lose approximately half of their structural strength at 600 degrees Celsius (1100 degrees Fahrenheit).
4. Jet fuel and the secondary fires caused by the explosions burned at a heat that was *sufficient* to weaken the steel beams by 50 percent.[44]

While this short counter-argument alone is unlikely to convince anyone that 9/11 was not an inside job, it does illustrate how a more nuanced and complete understanding of claims based on causal relationships can be helpful when one is trying to weigh evidence and come to a reasonable conclusion.

SOME CLASSIC CAUSAL REASONING ERRORS

In addition to the errors that can emerge from a misunderstanding of these three kinds of causal relationships, there are other causal reasoning mistakes that are extremely easy for us to make. One of the most common ones is confusing causation with correlation, and there is a very famous example that is often used to illustrate this error: If you look at a chart that describes the number of North American deaths by drowning during the year, you will see that it is relatively low at the beginning and the end of the calendar year and then peaks in the middle of the year. If you look at a similar graph of ice cream sales, you will see an almost identical pattern emerge. Does this mean that eating ice cream is a contributory cause of drowning? Or, weirder still, that people drowning is a contributory cause of other people buying more ice cream?

Of course, the answer is no to both of these questions. There is a correlation between drownings and ice cream sales (they both change in a similar way at a similar time), but that doesn't mean there must be a causal relationship between the two. Instead, there is another variable at play — the fact that it gets warmer in North America in the middle of the year. When it's warmer, more people swim. When it's warmer, more people eat ice cream. But ice cream and drowning are not causally related. Causation requires correlation, but *correlation does not necessarily imply causation.*

It's very easy for this error to transfer to the world of conspiracy theory. As we have discussed earlier, we are very good at finding patterns in the world around us. For example, if you look at American tea consumption and the number of Americans killed in lawn mower accidents between 2005 and 2009 (as Tyler Vigen does in his 2015 book *Spurious Correlations*), then you will see an extremely strong correlation between the two.[45] Unlike the ice cream and drowning example, in which the heat of summer is the shared cause, there is no obvious third variable that would affect both of those rates. And because our brains want to find meaning in the world, a person coming across this data could easily jump to the conclusion that there must be a causal relationship between these two phenomena. Perhaps the government (or some secret group that controls the government) is putting something in tea that is making people drowsy when they smell freshly cut grass so that the population is reduced through frequent lawn mower accidents? It's the perfect plan.

Another causal reasoning error we frequently make is the source not only of many false conspiracy beliefs but of superstitions in general. If a soccer player puts on her socks inside out by accident and then plays an unusually good game afterwards, she may come to the conclusion that it was the inside-out socks that must have resulted in the good game. From then on, she'll always put on her socks inside out before a game. This form of thinking is called **post hoc ergo propter hoc**, which is Latin for "after this, therefore because of this." When one event closely follows another event, we have a tendency to assume the first event must have caused the second one.

Of course, there is a temporal aspect to a causal relationship. For something to have a causal impact on something else, it must have happened earlier than the effect (at least, according to conventional concepts of time). However, that doesn't mean that anything that happened before something else must have had a direct causal impact on it.

Because of this common error, it's understandable why some people became concerned that the MMR (measles, mumps, rubella) vaccine might be responsible for their child developing autism spectrum disorder (ASD). They saw their child receive the vaccine, and then months or years later they saw their child develop the symptoms of ASD. However, multiple large studies have found no correlation between the vaccine and ASD (and hence, no causation either).[46] The reason that ASD symptoms show up after the vaccine is simply that the age at which children typically receive the vaccine is earlier than the age at which ASD symptoms start to show up. Just because one thing happens before another thing doesn't mean the first thing caused the second; by this logic, we could say learning long division causes puberty because we generally learn long division in school before puberty kicks in.

One of the most famous examples of post hoc ergo propter hoc reasoning was a result of the Zapruder film of the assassination of John F. Kennedy. Moments before the shots that strike Kennedy in the shoulder and head are fired, a man can been seen opening an umbrella (it wasn't raining). When people watched the footage and saw the umbrella opening, many concluded that this "Umbrella Man" must have been involved in some way with the assassination, and that the opening of the umbrella must have contributed to the killing. Some argued that the opening of the umbrella was a signal to a hidden assassin, while others claimed that the umbrella itself must have been the murder weapon: "The system is based on launching devices of various types, used to launch a self-propelled, rocket-like dart, or flechette. The flechette can carry either a paralyzing or fatal poison. The flechette itself is very simple. It is about the same size and looks like the tip of a large chicken feather . . . The launching devices developed by Mr. Charles Senseney at Fort Detrick, Maryland for the CIA included a cane, a fountain pen, soda straws, and an umbrella. The umbrella was used to shoot President Kennedy."[47]

In 1978, the Umbrella Man (Steven Witt) appeared before the House Assassinations Committee to explain himself, and he brought his umbrella with him. As it turned out, Witt had brought the umbrella to the Kennedy motorcade as a kind of protest. The idea was that Neville Chamberlain (the British Prime Minister often disparaged for trying to appease Adolf Hitler before World War II) was associated with having a black umbrella, and President Kennedy's father had supported Chamberlain. It was an obscure symbolic act, not an elaborate assassination method.[48]

The mistakes we make when trying to locate the causes of effects can lead us to believe in false conspiracy-based explanations, and so it's crucial that we understand the complexity and nuances of causal reasoning, and the common errors to which we often fall prey. But there is a larger issue with our desire to find causes, and it has to do not with the habits of our minds but with the complexity of the external world.

CHAOS

In the winter of 1961, a mathematician named Edward Lorenz was working on a computer. He had created a program that would, if you entered all the relevant data, simulate weather systems and make forecasts for days or even weeks into the future. Weather may be complicated, but it is still subject to the laws of physics, and by the early 1960s, computing power had gotten to the point where computers could perform large, complicated tasks.

Lorenz put in all his data points and ran the program. The computer crunched the numbers and spit out a prediction for how the weather would look for the next few weeks. Lorenz then repeated the process with the same data, which should have resulted in the same outcome. However, the second time he ran the numbers, the end result was an entirely different weather system that looked nothing like the original. Lorenz was baffled by this situation, until he realized what had happened. In the original run, one of the initial parameters had been set at .506127, but the second time, that same parameter had been set to .506, with the last three decimal places omitted.[49]

The difference between .506127 and .506 is extremely minor — imagine if you told someone it was 27 degrees outside, and they corrected you and stated that it was actually 27.000127 degrees. For Lorenz, the implication of this experiment (which he then repeated several times with similar results) was that perfectly accurate long-range weather forecasting was likely to be impossible. The tiniest change in the initial conditions of a system would end up having a massively outsized effect on the eventual outcome. The way this has often been represented (and one of the ways in which Lorenz himself described it in a 1972 talk) is that a butterfly flapping its wings in one part of the world could eventually impact a large weather event in another part of the world.[50]

While it sounds far-fetched at first, the mechanisms behind the "butterfly effect" are reasonable and intuitive. A famous proverb that predates Lorenz's work by at least three centuries provides a poetic way of understanding the role tiny changes can have on eventual outcomes:

For want of a nail the shoe was lost
For want of a shoe the horse was lost
For want of a horse the rider was lost
For want of a rider the message was lost
For want of a message the battle was lost
For want of a battle the kingdom was lost
And all for the want of a horseshoe nail

The initial condition is a lost nail — something tiny and insignificant — and the eventual outcome is the loss of a kingdom. It is important to note that the lost nail (or the butterfly flap) is not a *sufficient* cause to create the eventual outcome. In the case of the hypothetical lost kingdom, there would have been many, many other factors, both large and small, that would have played a role in the kingdom's collapse. But that fact doesn't disprove the butterfly effect, it reinforces it. It is not just the one flap, or the one nail that shifts what happens, it is the collection of *all* the butterflies (and moths, and breezes, and sneezes, etc.) or *all* the lost nails that plays a role in generating the complex, chaotic systems that surround us.

It is also important to note that while tiny changes in initial conditions can have an outsized impact on eventual outcomes, that doesn't mean that we can successfully manipulate eventual outcomes the way we would like. There are too many tiny little components for anyone to ever grasp the entire chaotic system.

The authors once interviewed a woman who was almost killed in a car crash. Her car spun out of control and was headed for the edge of a high cliff when it struck a large tree and came to a stop. There are countless factors that would have played a contributory role in both the crash and the survival — the condition of the car's brakes, the training of the driver, the amount of sleep she had gotten the previous day, the time other people on the road had set their alarm clocks that morning, the weather (and all the butterfly flaps that had affected it), and every decision that the woman had made that had led her life up to that moment in time.

One of the factors that played a role in her survival had happened perhaps a hundred years earlier. A seed fell off a nearby tree and was carried by a light breeze over to a particular spot on the ground. A combination of light rain and sunshine allowed the seed to germinate and grow, and over the next century the seed would have turned into a sapling and then into a tree strong enough to prevent a car from driving off a cliff. If a person had been there when that seed fell, and felt the light breeze that slightly changed its location, there would have been no way for them to realize that in a hundred years the light breeze that they had just felt would contribute to saving the life of a woman who hadn't even been born yet.

CHAOS AND CONSPIRACY CLAIMS

When we consider whether a conspiracy claim is accurate or not, one of the things we should always think about is this concept of chaos. This is because conspiracy claims make the argument that a group was secretly in control (or had undue influence over) the outcome of a situation. However, as we know from chaos theory, it is almost impossible for anyone to have enough information about a complicated situation to be able to predict it fully and accurately. And if prediction is impossible, how could control be possible?

For an example of this, we can look at one of the most popular conspiracy claims: Princess Diana was murdered by the royal family, and the "accident" that occurred in the tunnel under the Seine in 1997 was actually engineered and deliberate.

At first glance, this claim sounds reasonable. The British royal family is extremely wealthy, powerful, and connected. Diana had very publicly separated from her husband, the future King Charles, in 1992 and divorced him in 1996.[51] The entire affair was a black eye for the royals, and Diana stayed in the public eye with charity work and an active personal life.

When Diana died, there was an immense outpouring of grief for a beloved public figure. Mixed into that grief was the belief by many that her death was actually an assassination — in a 2004 survey, more than one-quarter of British people said they believed the car crash had been deliberately planned.[52] Mohamed al-Fayed — the father of Dodi Fayed, Diana's boyfriend at the time, who was also killed in the crash — argued, "I'm certain 100 percent that a leading member of the royal family has planned that and that the whole plot was executed on his order with the help of members of MI6."[53]

However, when we apply chaos theory to the events of August 31, 1997, the idea that the entire thing was a royal conspiracy becomes harder to believe.

The crash occurred under the Pont de l'Alma tunnel, in the heart of Paris, between the Champs-Elysées and the Eiffel Tower. Tens of thousands of people would have been going about their evenings in the area, and it would have been impossible for even the British royal family to have had control over everything that was happening. Maybe you want to funnel Diana's car into a specific tunnel, but a tourist from Spain has just broken down in their Fiat, causing a traffic snarl. Maybe the streets are crowded with aggressive sightseers, which convinces Diana to stay at the hotel rather than going out. Maybe the car that you have sabotaged to cause a crash is blocked in by angry cab drivers who are on strike and picketing out in front of the hotel. Maybe it starts to rain.

In addition, any potential conspirators would have been scrambling to adjust their elaborate plans to respond to last-minute decisions and changes in plans that Diana and Dodi Fayed were making. The British embassy was unaware that Diana and Fayed were planning on flying to Paris that day. Even Diana's own personal bodyguards had only learned of the plan the previous evening.[54]

Any sort of elaborate assassination plan taking place in this context would have needed to take into account all sorts of contingencies that no one could reasonably be able to predict. Of course, this doesn't mean that Diana's death definitely wasn't a planned murder. But it does mean that when we are weighing evidence regarding whether we should believe a conspiracy claim, we need to consider the difficulties that chaos poses to any attempt at control.

The official findings of the exhaustive 871-page Operation Paget inquiry report into the death of Diana concluded that her death was not caused by an assassination conspiracy, and two French reports found that the death was an accident. John Stevens, who led the Paget inquiry, stated: "Our conclusion is that, on the evidence available at this time, there was no conspiracy to murder any of the occupants of the car. This was a tragic accident . . . A crash of this nature is similar to a major crash of an airliner. There is a long chain of events. Take out any link of that chain and this would not have happened."[55]

Rather than an orchestrated event in which each piece was part of a perfectly organized and controlled symphony, the Paget report describes a series of errors, coincidences, poor choices (particularly by the driver,

Henri Paul, who had been drinking before the crash and had high levels of alcohol in his system), and bad luck that resulted in Diana's death. Similarly, a 2007 coroner's inquest into the crash concluded that it had been caused by a combination of alcohol, speed, and the irresponsible actions of the paparazzi who had been chasing Diana's car through the streets of Paris.[56]

Here is an example of a tiny event having a potentially large impact in the story of Diana's death: According to the Paget report, a month before the crash, Diana chose to kiss Dodi Fayed while on his father's yacht, and a paparazzo named Mario Brenna was able to capture the moment on film. Brenna was able to sell that photograph for over £1 million, which then generated a lot of excitement among paparazzi and provided a strong economic incentive to get more photographs of the couple. This eventually contributed to the frenzy of photographers chasing the couple through the streets of Paris, which contributed to the crash and Diana's death.[57] None of that could have been predicted by Diana when she chose to kiss Fayed that day, but such is the nature of chaos.

A CHAOTIC CASE STUDY: THE ILLUMINATI PLOTS TO TAKE OVER THE WORLD

Chaos theory is something that we need to take into consideration when we examine any specific conspiracy claim. It is even more important when we are considering a conspiracist worldview stating that *everything* that happens in the world is the result of an all-powerful secret group manipulating the economy, politics, the weather, and culture from behind the scenes — or, to put it another way, that sinister manipulation by a secret group is a sufficient cause to explain events in the world. There are many versions of this worldview; sometimes they involve shapeshifting reptilians, or Freemasons, or some other cabal of puppeteers. One of the longest-lived versions, and one of the most influential, is the idea that everything that happens in our world is under the control of a group called the Illuminati. It's worthwhile to do a brief summary of this conspiracist claim to see how chaos theory applies to and impacts the reasoning behind it.

It's helpful to think of the Illuminati as being two things, not just one. There was the radical revolutionary group that called themselves "The Illuminati" that briefly emerged in Bavaria in the late 18th century, and then there's the shadowy group that has been built up in the public's imagination in the centuries since the collapse of the Bavarian Illuminati. They are related, but they are not the same thing.

The Bavarian Illuminati was the brainchild of Adam Weishaupt, a politics professor at the University of Ingolstadt at a time when his nation was still heavily influenced by tradition, represented by the royal family and the church.[58] In particular, Weishaupt had a grudge against the Jesuits, whom he considered his personal enemies and the enemies of humanity in general. Weishaupt and a select number of Bavarian academics and intellectuals wanted to create a secret order in which radical and revolutionary ideas could form and circulate, with the end goal of completely upending the old systems and replacing them with a philosophy entirely based on reason and science. The leaders of the Illuminati claimed the group would take on the "enemies of reason and humanity."

Rather than an immediate and violent revolution, Weishaupt and his fellow Illuminati had a different plan in mind. Since there was already a secret society operating in Europe (the Freemasons), the Illuminati would infiltrate Masonic lodges and slowly, like a spider wasp egg hatching in a paralyzed spider abdomen, consume and replace the members of the Masons with Illuminati. While Weishaupt held the Masons in some contempt, he realized that he could adopt some of their organization, traditions, and rituals in order to give his own brand-new group more of a sense of history and heft. It was this desire that led Weishaupt to select the name "Illuminati" for the air of mystery and ancient mysticism it carried (replacing an earlier and sillier draft: "The Order of the Perfectibilists"). While allegedly valuing reason and truth, Weishaupt also took active measures to try to convince new recruits that his young organization was actually an ancient order.

Weishaupt's Illuminati philosophy didn't totally originate with him but drew from contemporary English and French philosophers of liberty, as well as the ancient Greeks. However the ideas were extreme and revolutionary for the time. As described by anti-Illuminati historian John Robison in his 1797 book *Proofs of a Conspiracy*, "They accounted all princes usurpers and tyrants, and all privileged laws as their abettors . . . they meant to abolish the laws which protected property accumulated by long-continued and successful industry; and to prevent for the future any such accumulation. They intended to establish universal liberty and equality, the imprescriptible rights of man . . . and out all religion and ordinary morality, and even to break the bonds of domestic life, by destroying the veneration for marriage vows, and by taking the education out of the hands of the parents."

While Robison was clearly horrified at the goals of the Illuminati, he did report them accurately. Weishaupt intended on breaking the institutions of his society (including royalty, capitalism, nationalism, and religion) because he thought that they all interfered with human happiness and human progress.

The Rise and Fall (and Rise) of the Illuminati

After a few slow years, Weishaupt's group was reasonably successful in recruiting, including some high-ranking members of the nobility. However, while Weishaupt had made lofty and ambitious plans, the execution of those plans was anything but smooth. There were problems with competing esoteric secret society organizations such as the Rosicrucians, who were in favour of religion whereas the Illuminati wanted to dismantle it. The Rosicrucians had also made some headway in recruiting powerful members who started publicly denouncing the Illuminati as a dangerously revolutionary and atheistic movement.

There were internal struggles as well, since the sort of people who have an inflated enough ego that permits them to think they can reshape the entire world rarely get along well with each other. Some of the key leaders of the Illuminati (such as Weishaupt, Franz von Zwack, and Adolph Knigge) had serious fallings-out and actively started to undermine and sabotage one another.

To make things worse, the success that Weishaupt had in recruiting new members meant that there were now more people who could reveal the Illuminati secrets that Weishaupt was trying to keep. The Bavarian government became increasingly aware of the rumours and whispers that were circulating about a threat to their power, but it was allegedly a moment of unpredictable chaos that would provide the authorities with the evidence they wanted to shut down the organization. According to historian Leopold Engel, on July 10, 1785, an Illuminatus named Jacob Lang was couriering Illuminati material when he was struck by lightning. Lang was killed, and the documents were found concealed in his clothing. The Bavarian authorities seized the documents and raided Lang's home to gather more evidence.

After this, the authorities were able to start tracking down key Illuminati members, and after Zwack's home was also raided, the Bavarian government ordered the immediate dissolution of any and all secret societies in the nation. Many more Illuminati members were arrested and interrogated. Weishaupt fled the country and faded into obscurity, and the Bavarian Illuminati came to an abrupt end, after less than a decade of existence.[59]

However, just as the Illuminati was waning as an actual political force, the myth of the Illuminati was on the rise, thanks to historical events. In 1789, a short four years after the Illuminati was revealed and destroyed in Bavaria, all of French society would be in upheaval as revolution swept across the nation.

It's easy to see why someone already frightened of what had almost happened in Bavaria might look at the French Revolution and see Illuminati fingerprints. Two of the main targets of the Revolution — the royal family and the clergy — were also two of Weishaupt's main targets. The French Revolution happened only a few years after Weishaupt's attempts to take over his own nation. And the shocking violence that would eventually dominate the movement, including the decapitation of King Louis XVI and his queen, Marie Antoinette, led some to believe that there must have been, as a necessary cause, some kind of evil master manipulator behind the scenes, pulling the strings on the hands that dropped the guillotine blade.

The fear that spread through Europe during and after the French Revolution allowed the Illuminati to be reborn — not as an actual group, but as a boogeyman that could be used to explain the rapid changes that were occurring. In 1793, an article in the *Vienna Journal* noted that yes, the terrible living conditions of the French lower classes, the financial chaos caused by government mismanagement of the economy, the despotic rule of the French nobility, and the hypocritical behaviour of church leaders were all contributory factors that made revolution more likely, but there still must have been a hidden necessary cause to light the fire: the Illuminati. John Robison came to the same conclusion in *Proofs of a Conspiracy*, which was widely read and even made it to the newly formed United States of America, where it inspired the anti-Illuminati sermons of Jedidiah Morse. Morse argued that the Illuminati, having succeeded in France, had turned their evil eyes on the USA. In a move that would be echoed by Senator Joseph McCarthy a century and a half later, Morse claimed to have a list of over a hundred Illuminati who had already infiltrated the Masonic lodges in Virginia.[60] These sermons from an influential preacher would help spread the fear of the Illuminati to the "New World."

What was missing in all of this speculation was any hard evidence linking the Illuminati to the revolutionary fervour that seized France at the end of the 19th century. As well, there were enough contributory causes — financial, social, historical, and cultural — that a hidden secret group wasn't necessary. In addition, some of the contributory causes dated back hundreds of years, and some of the events that triggered the Revolution (such as the terrible weather, including a massive hailstorm, that destroyed much of the crops in 1789 and contributed to a serious famine) would have been impossible to predict, let alone control.[61] The Revolution wasn't simply one event, but countless smaller events spread out over many years.

The idea that, since the French Revolution occurred *after* the formation of the Bavarian Illuminati, the Illuminati must have *caused* the French Revolution is another classic example of post hoc ergo propter hoc. Weishaupt was influenced by many of the same ideas and theorists that drove the architects of the Revolution, and many of those theorists who influenced the Revolution were home-grown French philosophers and European Enlightenment thinkers, not Bavarian conspirators.

The Illuminati Continued

Robison's work was highly influential to another book that brought the Illuminati panic into the 20th century — Nesta Webster's *World Revolution: The Plot Against Civilization,* published in 1921. In addition to blaming the Illuminati for the French Revolution, Webster had a more recent revolution in which to see Illuminati manipulation — the Russian Revolution of 1917.

Webster was also heavily influenced by another text that had emerged in 1903. *The Protocols of the Meetings of the Learned Elders of Zion* was a forgery, assembled by plagiarizing earlier bits of propaganda and some works of outright fiction,[62] that showed up in pre-Revolution Russia and claimed to be the authentic plan of a secret Jewish cabal to take over the world. Even though Weishaupt and his fellow Illuminati leaders were not Jewish, and the leaders of the French Revolution were not Jewish, and the leaders of the Russian Revolution were overtly atheist, Webster's fervent antisemitism drove her to a singular Jewish conspiracy behind all those events.[63] After publishing several influential antisemitic and anti-Illuminati books, Webster followed up with her 1926 work *The Need for Fascism in Great Britain*. This demonstrates both the motivation behind Webster's claims and one of the possible dangerous political end results of Webster's brand of scapegoating and fear-mongering.

In the middle of the 20th century, a Canadian naval officer added another element to Webster's Illuminati speculation. While the Illuminati hypothesis had always been **Manichean** — the Illuminati were seen as an evil group that were carrying out evil deeds for purely evil ends — William Guy Carr upped the Manichean ante by positioning at the head of the Illuminati none other than Satan himself.

Carr adopted Robison's claim that the Illuminati had been behind the French Revolution, and Webster's claim that a secret contingent of Jewish conspirators was behind the Illuminati.[64] However, Carr argued that ultimately the World Revolutionary Movement (WRM) ushering in the New World Order (NWO) was Luciferian. Carr claimed that Weishaupt himself was influenced by Satan to form the Illuminati. Satan came to Earth, took the form of Weishaupt's sister-in-law, seduced him, and then blackmailed him into carrying out the Luciferian plan.[65]

Carr's reasoning behind all of this sheds some light into the conspiratorial mindset and brings us back to psychology and causal reasoning again. While in a hospital room with a broken back in 1943, Carr started reading the Bible. He began to see patterns between his interpretation of Biblical prophecies and 20th-century events, leading him to assume that the necessary cause of all earthly matters must be supernatural:

> Ever since that day I have been convinced that what the vast majority of people call "accidents" or mere coincidence, are in reality "Acts of God" . . . Further study convinced me that in the Bible was to be found the "key" which would unlock the mystery which surrounds what so many authors have referred to in the past as The Secret Power which rules from BEHIND the scenes of ALL governments and causes them

> to adopt policies which ultimately lead to their own destruction . . . Satanism is the manual of action which puts the Luciferian conspiracy into effect on this earth.

Our capacity for patternicity; the fear caused by unpredictable and alarming world events; our dislike of chaos and coincidence — these make a potent cocktail for conspiracism.

By the midpoint of the 20th century, thanks to writers such as Webster and Carr, the myth of the Illuminati was not only alive and well but had mutated into a form that Weishaupt wouldn't have recognized as anything to do with his original plan for a secret society.

Enter the Scammers

After the 1960s, many people in North America were looking for a causal explanation for another revolution — not a solely political one this time but a cultural one. Pop culture had undergone a radical change in a short period of time, and the "hippie" movement had frightened the establishment and people with tidy haircuts. The Manson Family murders had confirmed to some that the entire counterculture movement was a clear and present danger to the fabric of society. Opportunistic scammers offered simplistic causal explanations for these societal shifts.

Some of these scammers even claimed to be reformed members of the Illuminati. Mike Warnke, for example, built himself an entire career on the claim that he was a reformed Satanist with contacts in the Illuminati. Drawing heavily on the work of Carr,[66] Warnke offered a causal explanation for all the frightening events of the 1960s: "The year 1965 overall seemed to be a downward turning point for the entire world — for mankind. It was about then that the sale of narcotics suddenly accelerated, the flower children blossomed from out of nowhere, restlessness manifested itself in hundreds of senseless acts all over the planet, rock music hypnotized, blanked-out thinking, and stirred confused youth to defiance of old values and traditions. Evil seemed to be afoot on Planet Earth."[67]

Warnke's explanation was that all of this, and more, was caused not by complex social, economic, and cultural factors but by the Satanic Illuminati. Warnke's books and speaking tours sold well, and he made many appearances on mainstream television shows in the 1980s.[68] He would continue to spread his claims for over 20 years before two evangelical reporters wrote an exposé in 1993 titled *Selling Satan: The Evangelical Media and the Mike Warnke Scandal* that revealed the false biography and lies Warnke had been peddling.

Another scammer named John Todd spread a similar tale among evangelical churches in the 1970s. Claiming to come from the Collins family of witches (not an historical lineage, but instead a fictional family taken from the 1960s television show *Dark Shadows*), Todd told listeners that, before he had seen the error of his ways and reformed, he had witnessed how the Satanic Illuminati (an idea taken from Carr and Warnke) used the evil magical knowledge from an occult bible titled the *Necromonicon* (an idea taken from the horror writer H.P. Lovecraft, although Todd was accidentally mispronouncing "Necro*nom*icon") to put Satanic messages into all popular music, including Christian rock.[69] In 1984 and again in 1987, Todd was convicted of sexual assault. He died in prison in 2007, but not before claiming that he had returned to his witchy ways.[70]

From Robison, through Webster, Carr, Warnke, and Todd, and up to our current crop of paranoid spokespeople, many have claimed to provide a hidden necessary cause behind the tumult and turmoil that every generation finds itself living through. Weishaupt's Bavarian Illuminati is long gone, but the spectre of the Illuminati still haunts our thinking and the zeitgeist.

CHAOS AND ORDER

Humans want to understand the world they find themselves in. This is made more difficult by the nature of the world, which is complex, chaotic, and often appears frustratingly random. We use cause-and-effect reasoning to try to make some sense of things, and this form of reasoning can be highly effective when used properly.

It is also very easy to use it improperly and fall into fallacies and errors of judgment. Conspiratorial thinking is an example of misused causal reasoning. **Paranoid spokesmen** are all too eager to take advantage of this to sell us a seductive, although inaccurate, worldview, which claims to explain everything for us in a tidy little container.

Conspiratorial causal relations that involve secret societies who have complete control over politics, society, and the economy (but for some reason still have to remain hidden in the shadows) don't take into account the chaotic nature of history. Because of the butterfly effect, large complex systems are almost impossible to predict. If prediction is difficult, complete control becomes basically impossible.

However, there is a causal relationship that needs to be addressed regarding these totalist explanations. The work of Nesta Webster was a contributory cause of the antisemitic violence that swept through Europe in the middle of the 20th century. The demonic stories told by Carr, Warnke, and Todd were contributory causes of the Satanic Panic, which led to dozens of false arrests and convictions in the 1980s. When we are tempted into simplistic causal explanations, we often look for terrible remedies for them. Conspiracism can be a contributory cause of great harm in the world.

3

BELONGING BEFORE BELIEF — WHAT'S ANIMATING THE ANTI-VAX COMMUNITY

Why would someone believe a conspiracy theory which can conclusively be demonstrated to be incorrect? Why might someone believe a conspiracy that could harm them or their loved ones? In the previous two chapters we have provided two different answers to that question: Sometimes we believe incorrect theories about the world because we make a mistake in interpreting our sense experiences. That's what happened to the SRI researchers examining Uri Geller. Or we may believe an incorrect theory because we make a mistake in reasoning, such as confusing one type of cause for another, as in the claim that "the heat from burning jet fuel isn't sufficient to melt steal beams, but steel beams must necessarily melt for the Twin Towers to collapse." But sometimes, our beliefs function as social glue, something that connects us to our communities.

Human beings are social creatures by nature. This is not a question of personal preference but a fact of our evolutionary history. Even the loners among us are fundamentally social. There's evidence for this from our closest relatives in the animal kingdom: chimpanzees and the bonobo, which are highly social, living in groups and relying on their community's support for survival. Like our primate cousins, we need each other for almost everything we do. We need each other to help raise our young. We need each other to hunt, build shelters, and keep watch over our community. Being part of a group is essential to our existence and our survival.

Our emotions and mental states are part of this evolutionary story. From an evolutionary perspective, emotions and mental states have a purpose. They motivate us to do the things that will keep us alive and reproducing. Eating when we are hungry feels great for a reason. It is nature's way of motivating us to do what's needed so we stay alive. Just imagine what would happen to humanity if staying in one place and starving to death felt amazing. Our brains are set up to reward us when we do actions that are beneficial for our survival. Eating, sleeping, and having sex all feel good for that reason. And since having a community is essential to survival, we get rewarded for having one, fitting in with one, and going along with one.

An example is seen when people are forcibly removed from almost all social contact, such as in solitary confinement in prison. There is a reason why, under international law, solitary confinement is illegal. The Nelson Mandela Rules for the Treatment of Prisoners outline the UN's position on solitary confinement, defined as "the confinement of prisoners for 22 hours or more a day without meaningful human contact. Prolonged solitary confinement shall refer to solitary confinement for a time period in excess of 15 consecutive days."[71] Rule 43 equates solitary confinement with torture:

> In no circumstances may restrictions or disciplinary sanctions amount to torture or other cruel, inhuman or degrading treatment or punishment. The following practices, in particular, shall be prohibited:
>
> (a) Indefinite solitary confinement;
> (b) Prolonged solitary confinement.[72]

But why? Because taking people away from others is deeply harmful to their well-being. The Vera Institute of Justice, a non-profit research organization that focuses on American prison reform, notes, "Solitary confinement can lead to serious and lasting psychological damage." And: "In New York State, the rate of suicide was more than 5x higher for people in solitary confinement than in the general prison population between 2015 and 2019."[73] Solitary confinement is an extreme case, but its impact demonstrates that we are constitutively social.

Because we are social, our brains reward us when we go along with the group. We will often do so for no other reason than that they are the group and we want to fit in. This can have hilarious and tragic consequences. A well-known hidden-camera TV gag shows the funnier side of our conformist nature. Imagine an elevator in which a group of actors are all facing the back of the elevator instead of the way people usually do it, facing the doors. Now an unsuspecting person not in on the joke enters the elevator. They face the doors as they normally would when they enter. But seeing everyone facing the other way, will they turn around and do what the group does? Often yes. We tend to "go along to get along," as the saying goes. It's funny when the group is doing something silly, and even more so when we can watch it unfold on TV. It's not at all funny when the group is doing something terrible. In many cases many of us will go along with groups even when they turn violent and predatory — a theme we will explore more on our chapter on moral panics.

In 1951, social psychologist Solomon Asch conducted a famous study on conformity.[74] The subject of the study was placed in a group of other participants who were secretly collaborating with the experimenter. The group was presented with a card showing a line and another card showing three comparison lines. Everyone was asked to answer a simple question out loud: Which of the comparison lines was the same length as the line on the first card? The study contained no optical illusion or other trick; there was an obvious correct answer. The participants collaborating with the experimenter all gave the same wrong answer. The test subject was always the last to speak — after hearing everyone else give the wrong answer. The question Asch posed was: Would the test subjects assert their individuality and provide the correct answer, contrary to the group's opinion? Or would they conform with the group despite all the evidence to the contrary? The results varied depending on the version of the experiment, but between one-third and three-quarters of the subjects conformed with the majority. They gave a clearly incorrect answer in order to fit in.

A couple of factors of Asch's experiment are worth pointing out. The collaborating participants and the test subject didn't know each other. And yet, despite this, the group exerted a pressure to fit in. Further, when asked why they had conformed with the group and given the wrong answer, subjects gave a number of interesting responses. One typical answer was that the subjects knew that the group was wrong but that they didn't want to stand out. Another common answer was that perhaps the group knew more than the individual and it would be best to trust the group over one's own interpretation of reality. This is a point we will develop below.

What is remarkable about Asch's experiment is that the correct answer is obvious. How much stronger are conformist group dynamics in situations where there is no obvious right answer? Take fashion, for instance. We tend to wear what the members of our group wear because they are wearing it. Or what about truth claims about the world that are much more difficult to establish than the length of a line relative to other lines? What if my group believes that this religion is better than that one, or this political tradition is more realistic than another?

This is not to say that we are mere automatons. Even Asch's experiment did not manage total conformity under ideal experimental conditions. And when there was even one dissenter in the group of confederates, it often emboldened the test subjects to voice their own opinions that ran contrary to the majority. Nonetheless, group dynamics are a powerful force, and going against the group is far more the exception than the rule.

Our need for community can trump our need for correct factual descriptions of reality, especially if the two are in conflict. An important consequence of this idea is that it can shed light on why obviously incorrect conspiratorial beliefs are so hard to debunk. It is not always about the factual content of the conspiracy theory. What sometimes matters more is the social function that the conspiracy theory serves in connecting us to other people. And when we try to debunk a conspiracy focusing just on the facts, we miss how threatening this can be. If changing our beliefs will negatively impact our connection to our community, then the strategic choice is often not to change them.

"FUNCTIONALISM" — OR WHY IT'S BETTER TO HAVE FRIENDS THAN BE RIGHT

Let us develop the idea mentioned above about the justifications we make when going along with the group. To many of us, it seems like our decisions are our own. I choose to stand up for the national anthem, or to wear a certain outfit, or to believe in that religion. It really feels like these are my own choices. But what if this is an illusion? The premise we develop below is that social conformity acts like an invisible force, and this force often accounts for what is motivating in decision making. The stories I tell myself about why I wore this or believe that are retrospective justifications, which often erroneously foreground my autonomy from the collective. These insights about group conformity, developed by social psychologists like Asch from the 1950s to the present, are to some extent echoed by early theories in sociology as well. These sociological theories shed light on how entire belief systems and worldviews can be part of the process of group identity formation and expression.

Intellectually speaking, Western Europe was an exciting place in the 18th and 19th centuries. Lots of new ways of understanding and interacting with the world were emerging. Among the many new areas of interest was the study of society itself. The social sciences, which emerged as distinct fields of inquiry during this time, started examining things like the economy and how large groups of people behave. Early social theorists were interested in phenomena that are true of all human cultures, and what these might reveal about human nature. For example, all human communities use language, and theorists wondered if there might be something universal that could be said about human language. Is there anything that is true of all languages, despite their differences in grammar and syntax?

They also wondered about religion. What is true of all human religions? Are there underlying themes, ideas, or functions that pertain to all of them? In trying to solve this riddle, Émile Durkheim, one of the founders of sociology and anthropology, developed an idea known as **functionalism**. Durkheim imagined that society could be broken down into **social institutions** that serve particular social functions. What is the function of religion? Durkheim argued that it was to unite communities. Although we are social animals, living with other people can be annoying and difficult, and social tensions do arise. That's where religion comes in, says Durkheim. Getting together with other people and performing prescribed rituals makes us feel good because we are affirming our connection to other members of a group.

Take, for example, sporting events. When you go to the stadium to cheer on your team, you don't know most of the other people there. Besides cheering for the same team, there may be very little that you have in common. The fans of a sports team are diverse in terms of age, religious beliefs, levels of income, friend groups, and interests. It's not out of the question that the person who cut you off on the highway last week and for whom you had a few choice words is now a fellow fan sitting a few rows away. A special social magic happens when we all sing the songs associated with our team. We *feel* that we're in it together. We *feel it in our bones* that we are united against the evil foe that is the other team and its fans.

A basketball game and Sunday morning mass are nothing alike in their content, but Durkheim would argue that these social formations fulfill a similar *social function*: They rely on communal ritual activity to generate a sense of community. The function of religious narratives and symbolism is to motivate us to engage in this socially productive behaviour. Underneath the varying beliefs that differentiate one religion from another are the uniting rituals that all religions engage in, and these generate a sense of community. This idea of generating and maintaining a sense of community is embedded in the very word *religion*. Its Latin root word, *religare*, means "to tie together."

Beliefs are important for individual practitioners of a religion, but that shouldn't cloud our perspective as analysts. What we are after is different. When examining religions, or any ideological system, we don't just ask whether a specific theology is the best description of reality. That is a question for individual believers. Rather, we want to know what this system of thought is doing for the community. When I chant at a sports event or sing in a religious ceremony, I don't think to myself, "I'm doing this to reaffirm my allegiance to the group." Rather, I think things like "My team is the best!" Or "My religion is the right one and I'm doing the right thing." Durkheim realized that these are the stories we tell ourselves to make sense of the underlying social function we necessarily need to participate in as social creatures. From this functionalist perspective, the narrative content of the stories is less central to the analysis than what they help us accomplish.

If beliefs can be understood as serving to establish and reaffirm community ties, then it becomes apparent that the narrative content of any belief system is of secondary importance. If the belief system gets us to reaffirm our social ties, then it works, regardless of how accurate a description of reality it provides. Remember the subjects in Asch's experiment? The reasons they gave for why they went along with the group supported the underlying social function of group cohesion.

From this functionalist perspective, we can also explain why irrational beliefs are hard to dislodge. Beliefs are not always arrived at after deliberation about the facts at hand. They can function as the glue that binds us to our group. Beliefs unite nations, sports fans, religions, and conspiratorial communities. Incorrect conspiratorial beliefs are not necessarily more irrational than many other beliefs, and they are just as intractable for the same reasons. Like other belief systems, conspiracy theories can function to tie a group together.

Armed with an understanding of the role of group dynamics in shaping our beliefs, we turn to a historical example in which people's access to their community was threatened. Most conspiracy theories are not accompanied by massive world-changing events like a global pandemic. However, because of its extreme impact on our lives, the global pandemic in relation to the anti-vax conspiracy theory more clearly expresses underlying dynamics that are also at play in other conspiratorial communities but often in a far more muted way.

From the functionalist perspective, which assumes that beliefs are the mechanisms that bind us to our communities, some ideas espoused by the anti-vax movement start to make a lot more sense. According to the consensus opinion of epidemiologists at the time, the lockdowns were necessary, but they prevented people from being together. Since community is (often) more important than being right, the loss of access to our communities was a threat. Conspiracy theories about lying or misguided experts emerged as a narrative that functioned to protect access to community.

The anti-vax community had a strategic advantage during the lockdowns because its ideology allowed people to remain in physical contact. Being a member of that community was therefore self-reinforcing. They formed communities in the real world, not just in the virtual space to which many others had confined themselves, as they met to protest the lockdowns and other health measures.

A SHORT OVERVIEW OF THE LONG HISTORY OF ANTI-VAX

The interesting thing about the COVID-19 vaccine scare is that aside from its connection to a new virus, almost nothing else about it was new. This generally holds true for erroneous conspiracy narratives. While the subject might appear new, the narratives often recycle the same stories and the same worries. For example, there are multiple versions of the conspiracy theory that the development of the 5G network was in some way related to the COVID-19 pandemic. In one version, COVID-19 was caused by the introduction of the 5G internet network: Either the rollout of the 5G network weakened the human immune system, making us more vulnerable to catching the virus, or the virus is transmitted through 5G networks.[75] This seemed like a new idea, but there was an earlier version: When the 4G network was rolled out, it was linked to swine flu. And 3G was connected to SARS.[76] As our chapters on subtext and on aliens make clear, conspiracy theories are often updated rather than invented out of nothing, and anti-vaxxers have been around for a surprisingly long time.

The first outcry about public health measures and vaccines started in 1853, following the first compulsory vaccination act of Great Britain. When that act was expanded in 1867, a group of anti-vaxxers mobilized in the city of Leicester, England, organizing huge protests. In 1885, between 80,000 and 100,000 people took to the streets in the "Great Demonstration" against mandatory vaccination.[77] The Anti-Vaccination League, as they called themselves, expanded, and, by the 1880s, there was an energized and active anti-vaccine movement spreading beyond Leicester.[78] The Anti-Vaccination League of New York City was founded in 1885[79] to challenge new vaccine legislation in the United States.[80]

Unfortunately, worries about vaccine safety occasionally had a basis in fact. In the Cutter Incident of 1955, over 250 cases of polio were attributed to the live polio virus being included in the production of the vaccine.[81] But despite mistakes related to vaccines, and despite the fact that there are rare but serious side effects that can emerge with any vaccine, getting vaccinated is almost always safer than being exposed to a virus without being vaccinated.[82]

As Heidi J. Larson shows in her excellent study *Stuck: How Vaccine Rumors Spread and Why They Don't Go Away*, many major public health vaccine drives have been accompanied by a hesitant or downright hostile movement against them. Vaccine scares have re-emerged every so often, and the reasons people give for their skepticism are recycled as well. In the 1885 demonstration, one sign read "Keep your children's blood pure." Sterilization has been another consistent worry about what the vaccines are really doing to people.[83] Hesitancy and resistance have been part of the story of vaccines from the beginning.

The modern history of the anti-vax movement did not start with gastroenterologist Dr. Andrew Wakefield, but he did play a pivotal role in the mainstream worry about vaccine safety, and his credentials added credibility to the movement. In 1998, Wakefield published a paper in *The Lancet*, a leading British medical journal, in which he (and co-authors) claimed that there was a link between the MMR vaccine and autism. In the minds of many parents, Wakefield's article and his subsequent activism established a clear causal relationship.[84] The link was further strengthened in some parents' minds by personal experience, because the vaccine tended to be administered around the same time that autism becomes apparent in children and is diagnosed.[85]

Larson notes that Wakefield's theory has been so successful in part because it emerged at the beginning of the internet age, allowing his conspiracy theory to spread faster than previously possible. "The production, reproduction, and rapid spread of vaccine anxieties went viral as never before, and Wakefield gave them a story to tell and a meme to share. 'Vaccines cause autism' was simple, repeatable confirmation of a brewing anxiety. And it easily fit in a character limited Tweet. Even more compelling, although Twitter [now X] allowed 140 characters initially, the average tweet was 34 characters. When Twitter doubled the permitted length to 280 characters, the average length dropped to 33 characters. Short Tweets get more traction. Wakefield's meme fit the formula."[86]

Wakefield's study has been thoroughly debunked. The CDC states that "Fact: Many carefully performed scientific studies have found no link between MMR vaccine and autism."[87] In 2010, *The Lancet* retracted Wakefield's article, and Wakefield was stripped of his medical license as a result of "serious professional misconduct."[88] As vaccinologist Paul Offit put it, this scandal is "one of the biggest frauds in the world."[89] Wakefield's entirely erroneous theory nonetheless caused many parents around the world to decide against vaccinating their children. As Larson notes, "Despite an abundance of evidence to the contrary, perceptions about the risk of autism still persist, with 75% of parents surveyed reporting autism concerns."[90]

On the American anti-vax website Children's Health Defense,[91] there are many examples that show Wakefield's key ideas are still front and centre.

"Thimerosal in Vaccines May Contribute to Autism Severity, New Analysis Shows,"[92] and "'An Encouraging Sign': 60% of Pregnant Women and Young Mothers May Delay or Refuse Routine Vaccines for Kids."[93]

Together with Wakefield's activism, other cases of vaccine hesitancy and skepticism have kept the issue in the media spotlight. In 2009, for example, activists in India petitioned to have the human papilloma virus (HPV) vaccine program stopped citing safety concerns.[94] Similarly, in 2013, as Larson notes, "the Japanese government suspended their 'proactive' recommendation of HPV vaccination in response to public pressure."[95] In 2015, Ebola vaccination trials were suspended in Ghana because of public fears the vaccine would actually spread the disease. And then an entirely unprecedented event supercharged the anti-vax movement.

COVID-19 AND THE LONELINESS EPIDEMIC

On December 12, 2019, a number of patients in the Chinese city of Wuhan had a new "pneumonia-like" illness that seemed resistant to standard treatments.[96] By March 11, 2020, with "more than 118,000 cases in 114 countries and 4,291 deaths" the World Health Organization (WHO) declared the disease a global pandemic.[97] It was the novel coronavirus, or more commonly, COVID-19. There have been other global pandemics in this century, including H1N1 in 2009, polio in 2014, Ebola also in 2014, Zika in 2016, and again Ebola in 2019.[98] What was different about COVID-19 was the number of countries it impacted and the unprecedented public health responses enacted to try to mitigate the threat.[99]

The public health responses to the COVID-19 pandemic were meant to slow the spread of the disease. They included travel restrictions, monitoring of travellers, social-distancing measures, quarantines, school closures, limiting social gatherings and cancelling public events, work-from-home protocols, increased testing, suggesting masks be worn in public places, among other impositions on people's daily lives.[100] Perhaps the most novel and impactful of these were the social-distancing measures, specifically the lockdowns.

As an article in *Science Progress* reported, "The global lockdown is a unique phenomenon prompted by the desire to protect lives from the ravaging pandemic. The lockdown was adopted on two fronts, namely, domestic and international. Domestically, the government restricted people's movement and instructed confinement to homes, thus limiting if not entirely halting the daily interactions between humans. On the other hand, countries locked down national borders, restricting the movement of people and goods, thus hampering the economic and human relations that had previously existed among countries."[101]

Not all countries enacted the same measures, nor did they enact them at the same time. A few, including Sweden and Taiwan, bucked the global trend and didn't require lockdowns at all.[102] Also, within a single country, responses could vary from one jurisdiction to another. Unquestionably, for many people around the world, the public health measures meant to stop the spread of the disease had major impacts on all aspects of their lives. An early WHO review of the lockdown notes: "these measures can have a profound negative impact on individuals, communities, and societies by bringing social and economic life to a near stop. Such measures disproportionately affect disadvantaged groups, including people in poverty, migrants, internally displaced people and refugees, who most often live in overcrowded and under resourced settings, and depend on daily labour for subsistence."[103] For some, the impacts could be existential. "Without the means to earn an income during lockdowns, many are unable to feed themselves and their families. For most, no income means no food, or, at best, less food and less nutritious food."[104] There were other unintended consequences of the lockdowns as well, with regards to mental health, risks to people in abusive domestic situations, addictions, and much more.

These desperate measures to slow the spread of the contagion came at the cost of creating an entirely different pandemic, one of loneliness. Like the biological pandemic, the pandemic of loneliness hit people with varying levels of severity. While anyone could contract COVID-19, some populations were more vulnerable to having serious complications than others; similarly, while everyone suffered from the social-distancing policies, especially the lockdowns, many folks were literally alone. They lived on their own, and when the lockdowns were imposed, they lost all access to their social world.

But even for those who were not part of a vulnerable population, the lockdowns were arduous. In this social context, the anti-vax movement gained new strength. Not all skeptics of the public health measures were anti-vaxxers — the movement was much more diverse than that — but the political momentum that gathered strength in response to the public health measures does represent an evolution of the earlier vaccine resisters. Larson notes that a "persistent theme found historically and today is the libertarian position that vaccine programs represent government over-reach."[105] This position remains a consistent refrain of those who resent social-distancing measures, travel restrictions, "vaccine passports," and other instances of state authority. While the movement is admittedly about more than just vaccines, vaccines remain a lightning rod.

TheyLied.ca is a Canada-based website that emerged during the COVID-19 pandemic and is representative of the diversity and tone of contemporary anti-vax sites.[106] A large portion of the site is dedicated to the public health responses to COVID-19, such as masking. But the site also includes posts about vaccines in general as well as other health topics like alternative treatments for cancer.

TheyLied.ca, Children's Health Defense, and similar websites present a mixture of half-truths and outright wrong theories as medical fact. For instance, TheyLied.ca claims, "No matter the quality, no matter the compliance, masks are entirely ineffective at preventing transmission or infection,"[107] whereas the website for the Centers for Disease Control and Prevention (CDC), an evidence-based, high-quality public health resource, reads, "When worn by a person who has a virus, masks can reduce the chances they spread it to others. Masks can also protect wearers from inhaling germs; this type of protection typically comes from better fitting masks (for example, N95 or KN95 respirators)."[108]

Sites like TheyLied.ca also tend to play fast and loose with the idea of "expertise." On Children's Health Defense, many posts are written by people with advanced degrees, including PhDs. At first glance, it would appear that these sites are doing their due diligence by relying on experts, but few of the writers have degrees in medicine, public health, or related fields. They may be educated, but they are not experts in the topics on which they are holding forth and they rarely acknowledge the consensus view of the medical community. Non-experts on a given subject are not in a position to evaluate disagreements between experts. The best we can do is try and find consensus, or at least a majority opinion among experts, and go with that. That's why sites like those of WHO or CDC are superior in the quality of information they provide. They present the up-to-date majority view of medical experts from around the world. And, to combat the incorrect information on conspiracy-theory sites, they have produced fact sheets predicated on the best available medical evidence.[109]

THE PERFECT STORM

There are many reasons why someone might believe something untrue. The centrality of community is just one of them. When it comes to vaccines in particular, there are additional factors that account for why the topic distresses some people so much.

The first is a type of cognitive bias: the **omission bias**. Omission bias refers to the fact that people feel they are more responsible for the consequences of their actions than for the consequences of their inaction. That is, if I choose to do something and as a result something bad happens, I will tend to see it as being my fault. By contrast, if I don't do something and something bad happens, well, that's just the way things are. You can't control everything.

When it comes to vaccines, this bias is a problem. Vaccines are amazingly effective, but you don't notice when they work. In fact, the effectiveness of vaccines accounts for part of the skepticism. "Why do we need all these vaccines?" is a common question on anti-vax sites like TheyLied.ca. This seems reasonable because when vaccines work, we don't notice. By contrast, if someone does get the vaccine and then gets complications from that vaccine, omission bias suggests that they might be liable to blame themselves. This is even more true if the person in the example is making decisions for loved ones. If they take their young child to get vaccinated and the child is harmed, they may blame themselves for that harm.

Another reason why vaccines in particular can seem frightening is how we conceive of risk. For a look at how fear colours our perception of risk, it is worth turning to Peter Sandman's work. Sandman is one of the founders of the field of crisis communication. He got his start as a reporter during the Three Mile Island nuclear disaster in Pennsylvania in March 1979. Sandman realized that there had been two meltdowns: one in the nuclear reactor itself and the other in the communication about it. This experience led him to focus his PhD on communication strategies during crisis situations. Among other ideas, Sandman developed a taxonomy of perceived threats. Why does a society develop an emotional overreaction to certain dangers but not to others? Why, for instance, do people seem far less concerned about car fatalities than they do about hydroelectric towers near schools? There is little to no evidence that electromagnetic fields from hydro towers harm kids, but lots of evidence that cars do. Yet it is much easier to mobilize a community to prevent the construction of new towers than it is to get them to curb dangerous traffic.

One of Sandman's central insights is that risk refers to two distinct ideas. When experts use the term *risk*, they are usually talking about statistically significant dangers that can impact populations, but the public are sensitive to emotionally potent stories that often do not match any statistically significant threat. To help clarify what's going on, Sandman introduces two concepts to distinguish between what we might mean by *risk*. The first is *hazard*, referring to the statistical significance of threats to a population. The second is *outrage*. Outrage is how the public feels about any given hazard.

Outrage is the *emotional* response the public has to a perceived threat. It is the sense a political community develops that "something must be done about this." When we read news stories about a dog biting a small child, our response tends to be outrage. We experience an emotionally potent reaction to a story that doesn't necessarily mirror a genuine threat to our collective safety. Do unleashed dogs near children really constitute a danger? To answer that, we would need longitudinal data, not the moral indignation generated by a personal tragedy. Is it something policy makers need to address by changing bylaws or enacting other measures? Experts may weigh in with their statistics about the hazards of dog bites. But this will often go ignored, much to the bemusement of experts, because it does not address the emotional content of compelling stories.

Sandman makes an interesting observation in his book *Responding to Community Outrage*:

> If you took a long list of hazards and rank-ordered them by something such as expected annual mortality (how many people they kill in a good year) and then rank-ordered the same list by how upsetting the various risks are to people, the correlation between the two rank ordered would be

> approximately .2 . . . In other words, the risks that kill people and the risks that upset them are completely different. There are risks that upset millions of people even though they are not killing very many. And there are risks that kill millions of people without upsetting very many.[110]

This insight helps shed light on what's going on with the worry about vaccines. It turns out that there are predictors that indicate when outrage becomes especially inflamed. Sandman suggests that "at least 35 variables . . . show up as components of outrage."[111] Here is a list of the 12 most common:

1. Is it voluntary or coerced?
2. It is natural or industrial?
3. Is it familiar or exotic?
4. Is it not memorable or memorable?
5. Is it not dreaded or dreaded?
6. Is it chronic or catastrophic?
7. Is it knowable or not knowable?
8. Is it controlled by me or by others?
9. Is it fair or unfair?
10. Is it morally irrelevant or morally relevant?
11. Can I trust you or not?
12. Is the process responsive or unresponsive?

Many of the COVID-19 public health measures fell into a category that tends to produce outrage. The public health measures were felt to be coercive (1). The vaccine was an industrial product, not made by nature (2). The virus seemed exotic (from China) not familiar (like the common flu) (3). The public health measures were controlled by others (8). The impact of the lockdowns was unevenly distributed and therefore felt unfair (9). The process was unresponsive to public concerns (12).

If we focus on the emotional and communal aspects of the *function* of ideas and belief systems, the reaction to the public health measures during COVID-19, especially the vaccines and the lockdowns, we are able to explain more clearly why conspiracy theories arise and persist.

HOW TO MAKE ENEMIES AND ALIENATE PEOPLE

To keep ourselves safe, we need to investigate the content of belief systems. This book provides strategies for discovering which ideas are more reliable and, therefore, more trustworthy. But we need to remember that beliefs are not just descriptions of the world. Belief systems are social. They connect us to our communities, and our communities deeply impact what and how we believe.

People who believe in incorrect theories are not stupid. Dr. Kary Mullis won the Nobel Prize for chemistry in 1993. He also espoused erroneous theories about climate change and believed that there was no link between HIV and AIDS. Sir Isaac Newton believed in alchemy. Aristotle thought that light objects fall slower than heavy ones. It is incorrect to dismiss people who believe in demonstrably wrong theories as doing so because they are unintelligent.

And disparaging people's intelligence also has the consequence of alienating them from our community. We will not change anyone's mind by belittling their ideas and focusing on how factually wrong they are. We only serve to drive them away, potentially into the arms of groups that further encourage harmful or incorrect beliefs.

Let's imagine the following example. The COVID-19 lockdowns have begun. A person, let's call her Kate, lives alone. Kate is generally well informed about world events. She has a mix of friends with different political beliefs. Because of the lockdowns, she has been spending more time online. She starts seeing some posts that are skeptical of the effectiveness of the lockdowns and other public health measures, like masking. Kate isn't enjoying being stuck at home alone. She's bored and annoyed.

Kate has no specialized knowledge in fields like epidemiology or public health, but being curious and open-minded, she does what many of us might do in her situation. She phones her friends and family to ask what they think.

At this point, one of two things may happen. Kate may discover that despite some minor differences, she lives in an ideologically homogenous community. All her trusted friends and family members agree that the public health measures are necessary (or, conversely, unnecessary). Kate may decide that she has learned enough and that she'll go along with her group. The arbitrary nature of how our beliefs emerge is worth noting. It is often a matter of happenstance (place and time of birth, social status of one's parents, etc.) that determine our community. And this in turn can directly impact what we come to believe. Often, we believe something because our friends and family do, and not, as we might imagine, as the result of deliberate reflection.

But let's consider a situation in which there's some disagreement between her friends and family. As Kate workshops the idea that perhaps the public health measures are unnecessary, she discovers two distinct reactions. One group seems tolerant, friendly, and open-minded, taking her concerns seriously. The other group by contrast seems quite hostile. They are dismissive of her worries and make her feel stupid for having asked her questions. Without knowing more, which group do you think Kate will end up spending more time with? Like Kate, many of us make our decisions in this way. We don't just want to "have access" to a community. If we don't feel valued, respected, and understood by one group, whereas another makes us feel good about ourselves, then we often gravitate towards the latter group, directly impacting what we end up believing. Not because we have fact-checked and vetted both sides, but because one side seems welcoming and the other doesn't.

Unfortunately, these two groups really did emerge during the pandemic. And it was often the anti-vaxxers who were tolerant and welcoming, while the "mainstream" and their experts were often seen as condescending, dismissive, and unfriendly.[112] No one likes being told that they are wrong, having their concerns dismissed, or being made to look foolish. The social dimension of belief systems illustrates that our relationship to our community can be the force that makes one belief seem more plausible than another.

4

THE INFORMATION ECOSYSTEM — THE EVOLVING FEMA DEATH CAMP CONSPIRACY

SCREENED

For most of our existence, human beings have used their senses to gather information about their immediate surroundings. Any image we saw through our eyes, or sound we heard through our ears, was caused by something that was reasonably close to us and could possibly have an impact on our safety. A person could see to the horizon (about five kilometres away) or hear distant thunder (from about 30 kilometres away). However, within the last 200 years, communication technologies such as the radio and the television have extended our eyes and ears, allowing humans to see and hear things from thousands of miles away, and to perceive images and sounds that have nothing to do with their immediate reality. At the start of the 21st century, the smart phone put that ability into the pockets and hands of millions of people, fundamentally changing our relationship to communication and reality and in so doing changing the human being itself.

Just because our phones are not physically attached to our bodies does not mean that they are not a part of us. As you read this sentence, how far away from your phone are you? Within earshot? Within arm's reach? It's increasingly possible that you are reading this sentence *on* your phone or a similar gadget. Our digital devices should, at this point, be considered an extension of ourselves. In 1968, the Canadian theorist Marshall McLuhan argued in *War and Peace in the Global Village* that "the computer is by all odds the most extraordinary of all the technological clothing ever devised by man, since it is the extension of our central nervous system," and over 40 years later it makes more sense to refer to it as an appendage that is part of us, rather than clothing that we can take off. But this appendage, rather than giving you information about your immediate surroundings, is linked to the largest information system ever devised by humans. And billions of other human minds are connected to it as well — interacting with and influencing each other as they spread their ideas. We are in an idea orgy.

The smartphone presents the user with a screen on which to experience ideas. At first glance, it would seem that the average person has far greater access to information today than at any time in human civilization: The sum of humanity's knowledge is waiting to be viewed on the screen that is almost always within our arm's reach. However, it's important to consider the idea of the "screen" and remember that it has two completely opposite meanings. To "screen" something might mean that you are showing or displaying it, the way that a movie is screened. But it might also mean that something is being hidden or concealed, the way that a lowered curtain might screen the stage from the audience. And so, the question becomes: Do our devices screen reality *for* us, or screen reality *from* us?

REALITY AND INFORMATION

Of course, "reality" is something over which philosophers have struggled for thousands of years; their speculations include Plato's allegory of the cave and the Gnostic belief that the world as we know it is nothing more than an illusion question whether we know we're not simply dreaming or hallucinating when we think we are experiencing an external truth.

This ambivalence towards the idea of reality is understandable; as we have seen in earlier chapters, the tools we use to perceive and interpret reality are flawed at best and misleading at worst. Our senses can be fooled, our memories are unreliable, our beliefs shape our experiences, and as social animals we are extremely susceptible to being influenced by the people around us. Despite that, we can use careful empiricism and observation to try to gather data and get our flawed and misleading subjective perceptions *closer* to the objective and external reality that is collectively experienced and shared by all the other flawed and misled conscious beings within it. Without at least a little agreement between individuals about some of the facts and truths based on this shared reality, cooperation, understanding, and interactions become extremely difficult, if not impossible.

We need a word to describe ideas, concepts, facts, and data that get us closer to this truth. We'll use the word **information** for this purpose. In this context, *information* refers to reliable and accurate ideas that are based on observation and expertise. Of course, knowing the absolute truth may be too lofty a goal to try to reach, but information at least gets us a little closer to it and further from confusion, inaccuracy, and deception. If you asked someone for directions to a location, and they gave you clear, correct, and verifiable instructions on how to get there, then they would have given you information.

On the other hand, the person you asked might be mistaken. Maybe they honestly thought they knew the way but were thinking of a different location, or had gotten some of their instructions mixed up. In this case, the other person meant well and believed they were speaking the truth, but regardless of their good intentions, their instructions led you in the wrong direction. We call this kind of sincerely given but honestly *mis*taken idea **misinformation**.

But what if the person knows the way to the location but they don't want you to get there? Instead of accurate facts, this person is providing you with deliberately misleading advice to send you astray. And because they know they're lying, they can twist the instructions around so you end up someplace inconvenient or even dangerous. You are no longer going where *you* want to go, you are going where *they* wanted to send you. We call this deliberate and deceptive manipulation **disinformation**.

INFORMATION, MISINFORMATION, AND DISINFORMATION

The COVID-19 crisis provided us with plenty of examples of all three kinds of idea organisms. When recognized experts in the field of immunology and biology warned the public that there were rare but serious potential side effects that a person could experience after taking one of the COVID-19 vaccines, that was an example of information. It was based on the most accurate knowledge we had at the time, filtered through experts, and delivered in a way that was meant to inform and caution.

On the other hand, in the early days of the pandemic (before reliable knowledge could be acquired through observation and testing), many people, including recognized experts in their fields, got things wrong. For example, for the first few months, experts recommended the use of gloves rather than face masks to help stop the spread of the virus. Once the data gathered became more robust, experts changed their opinions on this, and the importance of masks was stressed, while the effectiveness of gloves was questioned.[113] The early recommendation to use gloves wasn't a deliberate lie; it was an error based on incomplete knowledge. An argument could be made that experts shouldn't have been making recommendations before enough data were in, but the errors were not deliberate attempts to manipulate through lies. The glove recommendation was an example of *mis*information. Of course, misinformation is still harmful. It led people to take actions that they mistakenly thought would protect them, and the false sensation of safety provided by the gloves could have possibly encouraged people to take more risks, resulting in more people becoming infected. In addition, once the recommendations changed, many people were understandably suspicious of the experts and the governments — having just been wrong about gloves, they were probably still wrong about wearing masks. And some people saw a sinister conspiracy.

For an example of *dis*information, we can again look to what happened once vaccines were available. In November 2020, when the AstraZeneca COVID-19 vaccine was about to be introduced worldwide, memes showed up targeting Facebook and Instagram users in India and Latin America. These memes claimed that the AstraZeneca vaccine was going to have a terrible (and ridiculous) side-effect: turning the people who used it into chimpanzees.[114]

The best kind of disinformation is that which contains some truth within its lies, and even in this absurd example there is a small amount of accuracy to which the inaccuracies can cling. The likely reason that the claim was made that users of the vaccine would turn specifically into chimpanzees (rather than armadillos or lungfish) is that a chimpanzee adenovirus (artificially mutated to prevent it from growing in human cells) was employed in the creation and production of the vaccine.[115] But this doesn't mean that the vaccine would therefore turn its users *into* chimpanzees any more than the use of chicken eggs in the production of the influenza vaccine means that the flu shot turns its users into poultry.

The memes appeared to be organic, which is to say that they were disguised as posts by concerned users who had come across articles and petitions online and wanted to spread that information to other users in order to warn them. However, this was in fact an organized disinformation campaign originating from Fazze, a Russian subsidiary of a U.K.-based marketing firm. Fazze had been commissioned specifically to target and discredit the AstraZeneca vaccine using fake social media accounts to circulate memes, and by paying established influencers to promote and push those memes.[116] What's harder to trace is the original source that hired the firm to conduct the campaign, and why they did so.

The Fazze memes can be considered disinformation rather than misinformation for a few key reasons, and these have to do with the origin of the untruths and the motivation behind them. Although misinformation can have harmful consequences, those harmful consequences are not the *purpose* of the misinformation. In this case, the harmful effects — the discrediting of a potentially useful vaccine and the generation of general distrust in populations — *were* the purpose. The marketing firm was fully aware that the memes were untrue; rather than making a mistake, they were deliberately promoting lies. Misinformation is authentic but incorrect. Disinformation is inauthentic, incorrect, and deliberately manipulative.

To understand how these three varieties of organisms circulate, we need to examine the virtual ecosystem they inhabit. An extremely useful concept in understanding the relationship between organisms and their environments is the theory of evolution.

THE ARMS RACE OF EVOLUTION

The theory of evolution explains why we see such an incredible variety of animals and plants in the world, and it describes the method through which species emerge, adapt, and become extinct. It is also helps us understand the ecology of information viruses.

From a biological perspective, success can be measured by the degree to which a species reproduces. Traits possessed by the members of a species may be more or less well adapted to the current environment, and that degree of suitability will help determine who survives and reproduces and who does not. The individuals who reproduce will, through genetics, pass on their successful traits to their offspring. The individuals who are less well adapted are more likely to die off before reproducing, and so those undesirable traits are less likely to be passed to the next generation. A species composed of individuals who are a good fit for their environment is a species that is more likely to survive, while a species composed of individuals who are a poor fit is more likely to go extinct.[117]

In the idea world, success can be measured in the same way. A successful idea organism is one that passes rapidly from host to host, and one that is spread by each host to the most other people. In nature, this process is achieved through natural and sexual selection and mating to produce offspring, and in the idea world this process is achieved when a meme, story, post, tweet, or photo is shared through social media or email. Just as in the natural world there is only so much food, space, and resources to go around, there is only so much virtual room in the zeitgeist. Many social media platforms have a built-in algorithm that prioritizes content based on how many shares or likes it gets, and any content that isn't shared or liked quickly fades from view into obscurity — the meme version of extinction.

A successful idea organism, on the other hand, can have a long virtual life. Success breeds success, as any meme or tweet that starts to gain traction will be featured longer in the social media spotlight, thereby giving it more opportunity to spread to new hosts, allowing the data lifecycle to continue. An extremely successful idea organism might even spread all the way to conventional media sources — newspapers or news channels — exposing itself to millions of potential new hosts.

A biological organism may have any number of traits that make that individual better adapted to its environment. A rabbit with slightly longer ears might be able to hear predators coming from farther away, giving it more time to escape or hide. A rabbit with extremely long ears might trip over them, slowing that individual down and making it more likely to get eaten and fail to reproduce and pass on its traits to the next generation.

When we look at the plant or animal kingdom, we are seeing which traits have been the most successful in allowing the individuals that possess them to survive in their environments, whether that's the bottom of the sea floor or under the desert sun.

So what are the traits that encourage the spread of idea organisms through the virtual ecosystem? And which idea organisms have an evolutionary advantage?

HOW TO SURVIVE AND REPRODUCE AS A DATA ORGANISM

Before we begin, we should consider the limits of our knowledge and understanding. Despite what we know about biological evolution, we are unable to predict with certainty what animals might look like a million years from now. This is because all sorts of things could happen in the natural environment that we can't predict, and those unexpected events would have a strong impact on the process of natural selection, as new situations may require different characteristics and strategies.

The virtual world changes much faster than the natural one, so it's even more difficult to predict future trends. But we can make some observations about the general qualities that might help an information organism survive, at least in our present situation.

Let's first consider brevity. Long explanations and arguments can allow for a greater understanding of subject matter, a more thorough examination of the context and implications of a claim, and a more careful exploration of counterarguments, but they also take more time to get through. There is a reason that the abbreviation *TLDR* exists: people didn't want to bother taking the time to write out the words *too long, didn't read*. This is because social media tends to be wide and shallow rather than narrow and deep. In other words, social media encourages people to skim across the surface of a wide number of subjects, rather than taking a deep dive into any particular one. The platform X, for example, demands by its very programming that data are packaged in short blasts. We become accustomed to these short blasts, and once we have been conditioned to receiving many short collections of data, it becomes a burden to have to spend longer than a few minutes to finish something. If information is presented in meme form, it takes even less of our time and attention (and also provides less context, depth, and soundness of argument).

This doesn't mean that no long-form content is shared. Many people watch online videos well over 60 minutes in length or share long articles. However, in the virtual ecosystem, short content has an evolutionary advantage — it's much easier for a 10-second TikTok video to reach millions of eyes than it is for an hour-long podcast to reach the same number of ears.

Because nuance and complexity take time to express, memes, tweets, and posts tend towards the more polemical. And this sort of content has another advantage. What is more likely to generate a response — a careful, cautious, and well-researched position, or a hot take? If someone agrees with an extreme position, they are more likely to forward it or repost it, causing it to spread to more hosts. If someone strongly disagrees with it, they are still more likely to interact with it in some way, such as posting a response or forwarding it, in order to generate more outrage and heat.

This helps us to understand why, according to a 2018 study by three MIT scholars, fake news posts on Twitter were 70 percent more likely to be retweeted than true stories, and true stories took six times as long to reach 1,500 people as false stories did.[118]

Truth has a disadvantage in the virtual ecosystem. A false story can be tailored to appeal to people's confirmation biases. A false story can be made deliberately short, new, and shocking — all qualities that work well in the digital environment. A true story often has the liability of requiring context, being complex, and not being totally satisfactory to any one particular ideology or worldview. Conspiracy theories in particular can do extremely well, as they can be specifically engineered for the moment, or simply mutate and evolve in a way that appeals to prejudices and biases, or capitalize on the particular fears circulating in the zeitgeist and provide us with a satisfying scapegoat on which to attach our fears and hatreds.

CASE STUDY: THE FEMA DEATH CAMP CONSPIRACY

In the natural ecosystem, environmental changes can be catastrophic to the survival of a species unless that species has the ability to adapt to them. A classic example of this is the peppered moth of England, a species that is ordinarily light in colour with small dark spots and flecks on its wings, but very occasionally is dark with light spots instead. Before the industrial revolution, peppered moths lived on light-coloured trees and rocks with small dark spots of lichen on them, so the light-coloured moths blended in with their environment, making them harder for birds to find and eat. However, during the industrial revolution, the moths' trees and rocks were covered in soot, making the light-coloured moths stand out to predators. Within 50 years of this environmental change, the population of peppered moths changed from light to dark as the light-coloured ones were picked off before they could reproduce and the previously rare dark varieties fit in well with the new environment, survived, reproduced, and passed their characteristics on to their offspring.[119] To the outside observer, it might appear that individual moths changed colours. However, what was occurring was a population-level shift in the colours through the process of natural selection.

Idea organisms also need to adapt to changing environments to ensure they are reproduced and passed on in their virtual ecosystem. For an example of how this occurs, we can look at a disinformation organism that emerged online in 2007: the Georgia Coffins photo.

First, we need to look at the environment this organism came from. The Federal Emergency Management Agency (FEMA), part of the American Department of Homeland Security, was founded in 1979 to deal with disaster recovery. Almost immediately, some people were suspicious of this new branch of the government — specifically, many thought there were secret plans to create enormous concentration camps to imprison a large percentage of the American population.

There was some irony in these conspiracy theories in that there had been plans drawn up by the U.S. Army in the 1950s, '60s and '70s for mass detention of American citizens, but while the American concentration camp conspiracy theories were for the most part circulating in right-wing circles, the actual U.S. Army plans were mostly designed with left-wing protestors in mind.[120] In 1979, a tape recording and a pamphlet by Texan William Pabst, both titled *Concentration Camp Plans for U.S. Citizens*, became extremely influential in right-wing conspiracy circles. Pabst didn't point the finger at the newly founded FEMA, but within a few years, FEMA featured heavily in conspiracy theories that built on Pabst's original work.[121]

By the 1990s, the idea that FEMA was planning some sort of shadowy manipulation of the American population that would result in mass incarceration or even extermination was common enough in conspiracy circles that it was a plot point in the 1998 film *The X Files*. FEMA offices tightened up their security out of concerns that believers in the FEMA concentration camp plot might be inspired by the film to physically attack the agency.[122]

This is the historical context in which the Georgia Coffins photo emerged.[123] The environment in which it emerged was the internet — first on blogs and as a part of viral emails being passed around by individuals, and then eventually on social media sites once they arrived on the scene in the mid-2000s.

The photo itself is unexceptional, even uninteresting. On what appears to be a winter day, a person, their face covered by the hood of their parka, stands in a field, surrounded by large rectangular plastic bins, lifting the lid of the bin in front of them. At first glance, there doesn't seem to be much reason for anyone to pass this along or post it; it doesn't appear to be a data organism that will do particularly well.

But it isn't the image itself; it's the interpretation of the image that made this data organism survive. Emails and blog posts featuring this dull photo described what was supposedly happening: This photo had been taken at a facility that contained more than 500,000 coffins — evidence that evil forces within the American government were preparing a man-made disaster or pandemic. As one version (posted to paranoid spokesman Alex Jones's website in 2008) stated:

> Yep, these are cheap plastic coffins. Hundreds of thousands of them. Don't believe it? Why coffins? Why in the middle of Georgia? Well, apparently the Government is expecting a half million people to die relatively soon, and the Atlanta Airport is a major airline traffic hub, probably the biggest in the country, which means Georgia is a prime base to conduct military operations and coordination. It is also the home of the CDC, the Center [*sic*] for Disease Control. I don't want to alarm anyone, but usually you don't buy 500,000 plastic coffins "just in case something happens," you buy them because you know something is going to happen. These air tight seal

> [*sic*] containers would be perfect to bury victims of plague or biological warfare in, wouldn't they?

This organism was successful enough that, for a few months, simply entering *Madison, Georgia,* as a search query in Google would bring up coffin conspiracies on the first page of results, and entering the same query into YouTube would feature related videos.

As usual, the truth was far less interesting than the conspiracy theory. The photograph was of a storage facility run by Vantage Products Corporation — manufacturers of coffin liners. About 50,000 (not 500,000) of the items were kept in a field near the factory. But any information organism about this photograph ("a coffin liner supply company is storing coffin liners") is at a significant evolutionary disadvantage to any disinformation organisms ("the government is going to murder hundreds of thousands of people and bury the bodies in these cheap coffins"). The disinformation is shocking, frightening, disturbing, and interesting. The information is dull and uninteresting. The disinformation organism reproduced wildly over the internet, while the information organism floundered on a few news articles that few people read and even fewer forwarded or posted.

However, while the Georgia Coffins organism did very well at first, due to its novelty and shocking content, novelty by definition is not a characteristic that lasts for a long time. The organism would need to change if it was going to remain successful in the data ecosystem. Fortunately (for the organism, at least) it was able to mutate into two separate organisms, each of which was well suited for its environment.

The first significant mutation adapted to a specific historical event. In 2014, there was a great deal of concern in the United States about the possibility of an Ebola outbreak showing up in America.[124] The Georgia Coffins meme was a perfect fit for this environment, and all that needed to be done was to change the wording in the disinformation to indicate that the Obama government was expecting millions to die of Ebola. In its slightly altered form, the organism once again spread through social media, forwarded by angry and frightened users.

The right-wing conspiracy sphere was particularly suspicious of President Barack Obama (or Barack *Hussein* Obama, as the paranoid spokesmen would almost always stress), and there was another version of the Georgia Coffins organism that took advantage of this suspicion. Around the same time as the Ebola rumour was spreading, the old FEMA death camp conspiracy developed new life. Memes were circulating that showed images of the camps themselves, footage of the fleet of trains that would be used as part of a forced mass relocation, and a photograph of what was claimed to be 500,000 cheap plastic coffins that would be used to bury anyone who tried to resist the Obama government. The photos of the "camps" were real photographs but had been taken at North Korean detention facilities; the train footage was stolen from a documentary about a train maintenance yard; and the evidence for the 500,000 coffins was, of course, the Georgia Coffins photograph.[125] Because of the deliberately misattributed sources of this "evidence," we know that the people who originally assembled these disinformation memes would have been fully aware that they were lying.

By 2017, the environment had changed again. The Ebola scare had faded from the American public's imagination, and President Obama had been replaced by President Donald Trump. Now neither variant of the Georgia Coffins organism was suitable for its ecosystem. Rather than simply fading into obscurity (meme extinction), the organism changed again and re-emerged in 2020, when the COVID-19 outbreak occurred. Now, old footage of the coffin liner storage facility was reintroduced on Facebook as evidence not that an Ebola outbreak was imminent or FEMA had built death camps, but that COVID-19 was a planned pandemic.[126]

Because disinformation is not beholden to the truth, it is more flexible and adaptable. The truth is stable, but disinformation can shift to take any form that is useful at the time — even when it contradicts an earlier form of itself. The Georgia Coffins organism is a clear example of this, since depending on what was happening at the time, the photograph could be attached to disinformation about FEMA, Obama, Ebola, COVID-19, or anything else on the front burner in the conspiracy community.

INFLUENCING THE INFLUENCERS

Of course, disinformation organisms don't create or modify themselves (although AI is likely being employed to modify them). And while natural selection is a useful model for illustrating how different organisms succeed or fail in the idea ecosystem, it doesn't describe how the content for these organisms is created, or the motivations of their creators.

Sometimes the motivations are clear. Some people and organizations have an interest in manipulating populations, and disinformation campaigns are a useful tool. The FBI had large and wildly unethical disinformation programs (such as COINTELPRO) for decades. The Russian intelligence agencies have several units devoted to exporting disinformation to interfere with other nations.[127] There are also non-state organizations that have an interest in using disinformation to manipulate — if a tobacco company is worried about information coming out concerning the dangers of cigarettes, for example, they could try to flood the zone with lies and manipulations. As Lee McIntyre writes in his book *On Disinformation:*

> Modern science denial began on December 15, 1953, when the heads of four of the largest US tobacco companies gathered at the Plaza Hotel in New York City, along with a public relations specialist to advise them on what to do about a forthcoming scientific study that drew a link between cigarette smoking and lung cancer. His advice? Fight the science. Take out full-page ads in American newspapers. Hire your own scientists to create an alternative narrative. Reach out to newspaper and magazine journalists, editors, and publishers to get them to tell "both sides" of the smoking controversy. Lean heavily on the idea that this is an open scientific debate where nothing has yet been "proven." The goal: to get the public to question the truth about something that scientists didn't really question . . . The tobacco companies rode that wave of doubt for the next forty years as they continued to profit.[128]

This is a classic illustration of the way that deliberate disinformation is employed by state or corporate actors to benefit one party. But there is a stranger way that disinformation ends up introduced into the idea ecosystem, and that is when individual social media influencers are conditioned into producing it.

The concept of conditioning comes from the psychological school of behaviourism, rooted in the work of people such as Ivan Pavlov and B.F. Skinner. The claim made by adherents to this theory is that human behaviour is driven by associating actions with pleasure and pain. Actions that produce pleasure or reduce our pain are actions we will likely adopt, whereas actions that increase our pain or decrease our pleasure we will likely avoid, sometimes even without consciously knowing why we are doing so.

This idea is helpful in trying to understand the phenomenon of influencers changing their content to become more and more radical (often specifically conspiracy-related) and less reasonable and reality-based as they become more popular. There are many examples of this, from social media celebrities such as "wellness" gurus[129] to famous public academics.[130]

As we have already seen, disinformation has an evolutionary advantage in its ecosystem. And because creators are rewarded for having content that promotes engagement, and because conspiracy-related disinformation content is shocking, novel, short, simple, and extreme, it does well in its environment. Therefore, there is incentive to start creating conspiracy-related disinformation content.

In addition, influencers are given almost instant feedback that shows them how their content is doing with their followers, in the form of likes, reposts, forwards, and comment section engagement. As well as the ego boost that comes from seeing a post do well, there are often financial incentives to gather more views and clicks. A large audience might be parlayed into a lucrative deal with a sponsor, or give an influencer the ability to have paid ads placed before their videos. Some social media platforms have a direct payment program, in which influencers are paid a small amount of money for each view their posts receive.

Imagine there is an influencer who has an interest in history and often posts content featuring odd but established facts and trivia about various historical periods. One day, they post something a little more conspiratorial: the claim that the *Titanic* didn't really sink, and instead it was the re-badged and damaged sister ship the *Olympic* that hit the iceberg. Being a more controversial claim, the post generates more controversy, including an argument in the comment section among followers of the influencer. Because of this increased engagement, the algorithm of the platform starts pushing and promoting the post, which causes it to be seen more often by more users.

This in turn increases the action on the message board, which results in a feedback loop of increased engagement leading to more prominence, which leads to increased engagement, which leads to more prominence, and so on. People who agree with the post repost it because it supports their beliefs, while those who disagree also repost it in order to criticize or mock it. But it doesn't matter what the motivations are behind the reproduction of the post; the only thing that matters is that it is being reproduced.

Because this post (with the sort of inaccurate but brief and shocking content that has an evolutionary advantage in its ecosystem) results in more attention and clout for the influencer, and since attention and clout are the most valuable resources in social media, the influencer will be conditioned through positive reinforcement to continue the behaviour of posting conspiratorial content. To avoid losing followers, the influencer will try to maintain or even intensify that content. In this way, the influencer influences their followers, but the followers condition the influencer through the immediate feedback allowed by the social media platform.

In addition, there is an arms race among influencers competing for the scarce resource of attention. If a second influencer posts something even more controversial and polarizing (for example, claiming that the Roman Empire didn't really exist),[131] then that post will generate even more heat and more attention. Because this claim has less evidence and is more ridiculous, people will rush to the comment section to debunk it. People will repost it to mock it. Mainstream media might even publish stories about how absurd it is. But rather than eliminating this new organism, all this heat results in the post thriving in its ecosystem and feeds it new minds to colonize. The first influencer must either compete, by making their own content more shocking, or fade into obscurity (data extinction). The end result of this arms race is a data ecosystem swarming with disinformation, which results in extremist views becoming more familiar, mainstream, and accepted by the population.

The social media platforms benefit from this arms race, since anything that drives up engagement allows the platform to raise more revenue, either by selling advertisement space, or by monetizing their users' personal information. Allowing disinformation has been a conscious business decision on the part of social media companies, despite the well-documented causal relationship between social media disinformation and extremist violence.[132]

DEFENDING OURSELVES IN A HOSTILE ENVIRONMENT

All of this means that what could theoretically have been used as the first line of defence against disinformation — the algorithms of the social media platforms — has instead acted as an incubator, ensuring that the most virulent ideas and claims reach the most eyes, regardless of the accuracy of the content.

Since we can't rely on the technology to protect us from itself, our first layer of defence has to be media literacy. Even a basic understanding offers some protection: understanding the difference between reporting and editorial, for example, or being able to evaluate expertise and credentials. Assessing the source of information before consuming that information can help protect people from the sort of hazardous misinformation and weaponized disinformation that is so prevalent in the virtual ecosystem.

But poor arguments can also come from quality sources, and some bad ideas and claims will be able to penetrate your first line of defence. Then you are forced to rely on your second line of defence: mental hygiene, the mind's version of the immune system. No, there aren't furious little white blood cells scrambling around your mind, looking for bad ideas and disinformation to eliminate. Instead, the mind must be inoculated with attitudes, skills, habits, and knowledge if it is going to interact with the data ecosystem.

Starting with attitudes — it's critical for our mental hygiene that we maintain philosophical humility and always consider the possibility that we could be incorrect about a position. As soon as certainty starts to set in, we become more vulnerable to confirmation bias and less able to critically evaluate our beliefs. And as difficult as it is to admit that we could be wrong, it is often even more difficult to consider that someone else's position may be correct, particularly in a highly partisan and confrontational environment. Years of fiercely fought and pointless message board flame wars filled with ad hominem attacks have helped to entrench the idea that we must live or die on the hills of our beliefs, that our identities depend on maintaining the positions that we have already adopted. We often see certainty in conviction as a sign of strength, but we would be better off as a society if we valorized uncertainty, inquiry, and the capacity to learn and change.

Once we have adopted our uncertain attitudes, we can then bring in critical thinking skills to dismantle claims into their individual parts, assess each part, reassemble what's left, and then evaluate the claim. As simple as it sounds, the ability to test the acceptability and relevance of premises and to test the sufficiency of claims is a powerful tool in identifying and eliminating potentially harmful idea organisms.

It is also important to have a solid foundation in general knowledge for two important reasons. Firstly, the more we know about something, the more we realize how much more there is to the topic that we *don't* know, which in turn helps with adopting the philosophical humility mentioned earlier.

Secondly, a person who doesn't have a solid grounding in history is in more danger of falling for a fallacious conspiracy claim. As we addressed earlier, the world is an extremely complicated and chaotic place, and we have the propensity to look for patterns that seem to help us to understand what is going on — even when the patterns we find are sometimes just illusions. Conspiracy theories have the strong and comforting appeal of superimposing order over the chaos that we are all surrounded by, changing coincidence and error into malicious intent and secret schemes by shadowy groups in complete control.

Inaccurate conspiracy claims are extremely flexible (a significant advantage of not being beholden to the truth), and they tend to take the shape of whatever information a person is missing. So the more accurate the background and context a person has access to, the smaller the missing pieces, and the less likely they will look to a conspiracy claim to fill that gap.

THE STATE OF THE IDEA ECOSYSTEM

An ironic tragedy in all of this is that there are people trained to help us analyze evidence, evaluate claims, provide context, etc. Those people are journalists. However, carefully fact-checked, well-written and -researched long-form newspaper stories can't compete in an ecosystem teeming with a non-stop parade of clickbait headlines and hot takes. Between 2004 and 2022, the time when social media sites were emerging and becoming dominant, the United States lost more than 25 percent of its newspapers.[133]

Of course, there were problems with the information we received from newspapers in the pre–social media era. Ownership and advertiser biases could dictate what information made it into a newspaper and shape how issues and stories were framed. Editorial control served as a filter, sifting through data to decide what reached the eyes of the reader. But in the social media age, survival of the fittest (as decided by algorithms) has replaced the editor as the filtering device.

Our new idea ecosystem is one in which disinformation has an evolutionary advantage over information, and since the corporations that operate the media platforms benefit from engagement, there is considerable disincentive for them to monitor or regulate disinformation. The arms race for views and reposts encourages more and more extreme content. As extreme content becomes more common, it also becomes more mainstream and acceptable.

Because of the accelerated development of communications technology, all these changes have happened too rapidly for legislation or education to keep up. A person born in North America in 1970 would have grown up with a phone at the end of a cord connected to the wall. A person born in 1990 would have been very familiar with the internet dial-up noise. A person born in 2010 would never have known a world without smartphones and wireless network connections. These rapidly changing conditions have provided us with countless opportunities and benefits. But disinformation organisms make up the bulk of the data in the virtual environment that we created and that is now in the process of creating us. We must remain constantly vigilant against these threats.

5

DISINFORMATION CAMPAIGNS — WHEN THE CONSPIRACY THEORY *IS* THE CONSPIRACY

THE DISINFORMATION VIRUS

As the HIV/AIDS epidemic exploded in the early 1980s, an ideological pathogen emerged almost simultaneously. A worry began to circulate that this new disease had been purposely engineered at Fort Detrick, Maryland, a U.S. military facility long suspected of engaging in biological warfare research.[134] The theory first appeared in the summer of 1983, when the English-language Indian newspaper the New Delhi *Patriot* published a letter from an "American scientist" who "wanted to remain anonymous," claiming that HIV/AIDS had been made in a U.S. lab. The article "AIDS May Invade India: Mystery Disease Caused by US Experiments," didn't pull any punches. The first two paragraphs summarize the main claims:

> AIDS, the deadly mysterious disease which has caused havoc in the US, is believed to be the result of the Pentagon's experiments to develop new and dangerous biological weapons.
>
> Now that these menacing experiments seem to have gone out of control, plans are being hatched to hastily transfer them from the US to other countries, primarily developing nations where governments are pliable to Washington's pressures and persuasions.[135]

The claim that the U.S. had created the HIV/AIDS pandemic was repeated by other news organizations outside the U.S., primarily but not exclusively in Africa and South America. By 1987, it had entered into the American mainstream media. On March 30, trusted news anchorman Dan Rather of CBS reported that the HIV/AIDS virus had "leaked from a U.S. Army laboratory conducting experiments into biological warfare."[136] By now, the original source of the message had been amplified by named medical experts. Rather cited the work of Dr. Jakob Segal, a retired professor and biophysicist at Berlin's Humboldt University, who was secretly employed by the East German intelligence service.

Dr. Segal, together with his wife, Dr. Lilli Segal, and colleague Dr. Ronald Dehmlow, published a report entitled "AIDS: Its Nature and Origin" which repeated the original claim that the disease was most likely "manufactured" by the U.S. and did not have natural causes.[137] According to Segal, there existed "circumstantial evidence" that HIV/AIDS was created at Fort Detrick in 1977 by combining two naturally occurring viruses, HTLV-1 and VISNA.

Some aspects of this theory seemed plausible, starting with Fort Detrick itself. According to the *Patriot*, "Fort Detrick is notorious as a place where biological weapons are being developed in laboratories and where in the past they were repeatedly tested at its proving grounds."[138] According to a State Department's report, there is some truth to this. "Between 1943 and 1969 Fort Detrick was the U.S. Army's biological warfare research and development centre."[139] And some worried that, as the *Patriot* article suggested, the research continued in secret after Richard Nixon publicly stated on Veterans Day in 1969 that biological weapons would be outlawed.

What about the *Patriot*'s claim in the same article that "in the 1950s and 1960s both the Pentagon and the CIA secretly tested new types of biological weapons in the densely-populated areas of the US and Canada, such as New York, Philadelphia, San Francisco and Winnipeg"? Operation Sea-Spray was not as far-reaching as the article suggests, but it is a documented case of the U.S. military testing a biological agent on unsuspecting inhabitants of San Francisco.[140] In Operation Sea-Spray, the U.S. Navy wanted to test if America was vulnerable to a biological weapons attack, releasing a biological agent in the Bay Area to see how far and fast it would spread. The substance they used was supposed to be inert, and for the most part it was, but residents of San Francisco were not informed that they were going to be (or had been) subjects of a biological weapons experiment, and there was at least one confirmed fatality related to the test. Operation Sea-Spray confirms the existence of U.S. biological weapons research, and so, maybe, the story in the *Patriot* is less of a stretch than it might at first appear.

Then there is the infamous example of the Tuskegee syphilis study. Starting in 1932, the United States Public Health Service studied the effects of syphilis when left untreated. The study lasted until 1972, and more than 100 men died, all African American. They had not been informed that they were part of a medical study, and they were purposely not given available treatments.[141] They simply served as human guinea pigs.

By the 1980s, revelations about the CIA's illegal MKUltra project, which included testing hallucinogenic drugs on unsuspecting American and Canadian civilians, had also come to light. The fact that the CIA targeted vulnerable members of society and experimented on them with potent and often dangerous drugs, in combination with psychiatric interventions that amounted to medical torture, came as a shock to many American (and Canadian) citizens. Victims of MKUltra, when they survived, often suffered debilitating health effects that lasted a lifetime. Operation Sea-Spray, the Tuskegee syphilis study, and MKUltra all really happened. They are actual top-down government conspiracies the likes of which are usually reserved for horror films.

The "CIA created HIV/AIDS" theory has also been absorbed into popular culture. In 2005, hip-hop artist Kanye West, in his song "Heard 'Em Say," said, "And I know the government administer AIDS." In a *Rolling Stone* article, he repeated the claim, adding, "My parents taught me that AIDS was a man-made disease designed to get rid of the undesirable people."[142] He is not alone in thinking this.

However, we have strong evidence that these claims were actually part of a Soviet disinformation campaign mounted for the sole purpose of convincing American civilians to distrust their espionage and military branches. As early as 1987, the U.S. State Department released *Soviet Influence Activities: A Report on Active Measures and Propaganda, 1986–1987*, which detailed most of what was known about how the lie was generated and disseminated.[143]

According to Soviet defector Ilya Dzhirkvelov, a former KGB officer, the New Delhi *Patriot* was a Soviet mouthpiece set up in 1962 by the KGB,[144] and its purpose was to publish Soviet disinformation.[145] In fact, each of the newspapers that initially parroted the claims from the "American scientist" were either Soviet fronts or located within the Soviet Union. After the appearance of a Soviet article making the same claims and citing the *Patriot* as a source, a "Public Affairs Officer at the U.S. Embassy in New Delhi met with the editor of the *Patriot* and asked if such a [story] had ever appeared in his publication. The editor said he could not recall having published anything on the subject that Soviet media were attributing to his paper."[146]

This was all part of Operation Denver or, as it is more commonly known by the KGB designation, Operation INFEKTION. Operation INFEKTION was perhaps the Soviet Union's most successful disinformation campaign. As the 1987 State Department report notes, its purposes were to:

- Discredit the United States and generate anti-American sentiment abroad;
- Reinforce longstanding false Soviet propaganda charges of U.S. biological warfare activities and counter U.S. reports of Soviet violations of the 1925 Geneva Protocol on Chemical Weapons and the 1972 Biological Weapons Convention;
- Undermine U.S. defense arrangements with allied countries and create pressures for the removal of U.S. military facilities overseas by [l]inking the spread of AIDS to the presence of U.S. Armed Forces personnel stationed abroad; and
- Discourage contacts with Americans (including tourists, diplomats and businesspeople) by demonstrating to Soviet citizens that American imperialism is responsible for a frightening disease that has made its way into the U.S.S.R. and Eastern Europe.[147]

Disinformation is itself a conspiracy, and it bolsters already existing conspiracy theories. And disinformation can reduce our collective trust in those institutions meant to protect us. "The media is lying to us!" and "You can't trust what the government tells you!" and "Scientists are just saying what they are told to say!" are some of the understandable reactions of a society awash in disinformation.

A SHORT HISTORY OF DISINFORMATION

Disinformation has the advantage of being one of the cheapest methods of interfering with a political enemy. The modern invention of disinformation is credited to Joseph Stalin. The following story is perhaps apocryphal, but even if it is not true, Stalin thought it was — it describes the purpose of disinformation perfectly.

In 1938, CBS Radio broadcast Orson Welles's *The War of the Worlds*. The radio drama took the form of news reports from around the U.S. on an apparent alien invasion. Although the audience was informed at the start of the program that it was fictional, some who tuned in late apparently took it as a real news broadcast, and a mass panic ensued. Or so it has been reported — but in fact there is considerable doubt.[148] A few people were temporarily confused, and there were a few reports of minor injuries, but the panic was probably not as massive as has since been claimed.

That question is almost beside the point, though, since Joseph Stalin believed that the radio play did unleash a panic. This triggered an insight: You can damage your political enemy just as effectively with words as you can with soldiers and spies. Narratives can sow panic and fear, and they are much cheaper and easier than troops and espionage agencies. If you can get your enemies to believe things that you want them to, then you often don't need the soldiers and spies. Thus the modern concept of dezinformatsiya was born.

The KGB in the former Soviet Union were true masters of disinformation, as the HIV/AIDS campaign demonstrates. The KGB's term for the political use of disinformation was *active measures* and, as the scholar of Soviet disinformation Thomas Rid explains, the goal of active measures is to confuse and distract a political enemy, including their population. In his helpful book *Active Measures: The Secret History of Disinformation and Political Warfare*, Rid provides a three-pronged definition:

> First, and most important, active measures are not spontaneous lies by politicians, but the methodical output of large bureaucracies. Disinformation was, and in many ways continues to be, the domain of intelligence agencies — professionally run, continually improved, and usually employed against foreign adversaries. Second, all active measures contain an element of disinformation: content may be forged, sourcing doctored, the method of acquisition covered; influence agents and cutouts may pretend to be something they are not, and online accounts involved in the surfacing or amplification of an operation may be inauthentic. Third, an active measure is always directed toward an end, usually to weaken the targeted adversary. The means may vary: creating division between allied nations, driving wedges between ethnic groups, creating friction between individuals in a group or party, undermining the trust specific groups in a society have in its institutions.[149]

If the enemy is distracted, they may begin to focus their attention on the wrong targets. Or, sensing that information is not trustworthy, they may retreat from the political arena entirely because "it's all lies anyway." Either way, mission accomplished. When disinformation works, the political enemy wastes valuable resources on ineffectual or even counterproductive measures.

The raw materials for political disinformation are existing social and political tensions found within any community. These tensions may be related to class, gender, race, ethnicity, or any other demographic or historical factor. But it is difficult to measure the success of any disinformation campaign. Is the conflict we are seeing the result of the disinformation campaign, or is it happening organically within that political community? Or perhaps some combination of both?

In the "CIA created HIV/AIDS" disinformation campaign, the KGB played upon pre-existing tensions within America, specifically the fears among homosexual and racialized minorities, both of which have long-standing experiences of persecution at the hands of mainstream Americans and the institutions that serve them. The campaign also played upon a fear that the government was willing to play fast and loose with the health of Americans, especially if they were of an "undesirable" group. The KGB did not generate these tensions, but it used the fear already present in these marginalized communities.

Below we'll give two examples, Operation Neptune and Field Manual 30-31B, which both focus on the KGB's use of disinformation against the U.S. and its allies. Then we'll present two more recent examples, which introduce other non-state actors known to be operating in the disinformation space.

OPERATION NEPTUNE

One of the tensions in 1960s postwar Germany was the continued presence of former Nazi collaborators, sympathizers, and authority figures. This is a common problem after any regime change: Leaders of a disgraced government may be replaced, but civilian supporters are much more difficult to find, and they usually make up a significant portion of society. After Germany capitulated in May of 1945, the remaining high-ranking Nazi leaders were rounded up and put on trial, and those found guilty were executed or sometimes incarcerated. But the lower-level Nazis, as well as regular civilians who had supported the regime, remained free German citizens, and the new generation of Germans was coming to terms with this. Nazism had lost all credibility, and most people would not avow allegiance to the disgraced party and its horrendous history, but there remained many secret Nazis who were in some way sympathetic to the previous regime, still living, working, and occupying positions of authority in the country, including doctors, lawyers, judges, police officers, military officers, and clergy. Germany of the 1960s had a Nazi problem.

This problem was exploited by Eastern European secret service agencies, invented by their Soviet KGB masters, in order to humiliate the German government and, by extension, the U.S. and the West generally, and to pursue more specific political aims, such as preventing trade negotiation deemed unfavourable to the Kremlin. They would accomplish this by fabricating associations between the new crop of German politicians and the disgraced Nazi regime. Even the mere suggestion that someone was sympathetic to the former Nazi Party was often enough to derail their political career, and, if nothing else, to have prospective political allies think twice about making common cause with them.

The following story is a remarkable case of disinformation that typifies many of the cloak-and-dagger espionage campaigns of the Cold War. It was first described by former Czech spy Ladislav Bittman after he defected to the West. In the 1960s, an urban legend was circulating that held that there existed undiscovered treasure troves of Nazi gold. The idea was that since the Nazis had looted much of the wealth of Jewish families, some of that loot had been buried by individual Nazis as the war was turning against them, to be kept safe until afterward. But what if a Nazi had buried some gold but then got themselves shot, and now this treasure was just waiting to be discovered? It was not totally implausible.

Using this urban legend as the foundational myth, Bittman suggested to the KGB and the Czechoslovakian secret service (the StB) that they orchestrate a made-for-TV event where some Czech divers would "discover" what looked like Nazi gold chests in a Bohemian lake, except the treasure chests would contain not gold but Nazi documents. Within mountains of genuine Nazi documents would be a few well-placed forgeries suggesting that certain current German politicians had in some way been collaborating with the Nazis.

One night, Bittman and two others took a boat out into Devil's Lake, near the German-Czech border, and submerged two chests, which had been artificially aged. Once the chests were confirmed to be in the correct location, Bittman informed the local TV crew that he and a few other "researchers" had discovered what they thought was the location of Nazi gold and that they would be recovering the chests the next day. Czech TV together with Bittman and two divers went out into the lake and dove down. They eventually emerged triumphant with the two chests, which they then handed over to the Soviets for inspection.

All this was just the set-up. The real disinformation campaign then took place over the next decade. Anytime a West German politician began engaging in trade negotiations deemed unfavourable to the Soviets, compromising information about key politicians would emerge suggesting they had collaborated with the Nazis or participated in war crimes. Sometimes this information would be passed along through diplomatic channels. Sometimes the compromising information was sent directly to Jewish community centres. Any skeptical questions that might arise about why this information was only now coming to light could be explained away by an operation like this one. Often, newspapers would publish the slander. And the population would predictably react with horror. "Why are we negotiating with a Nazi?" was an expected response. Sometimes these stories managed to actually derail the trade negotiations, scoring a win for Soviet disinformation. But even if the trade talks continued, a sense of distrust was nonetheless generated.

FIELD MANUAL 30-31B

The overarching goal of Soviet disinformation was to harm America. This notion of harm included undermining America's standing among its allies. Was America a safe and helpful geopolitical partner? What if American intelligence agencies engaged in secret and dangerous activities that could destabilize domestic politics? Given the very real history of American involvement abroad, this was not a baseless worry. Enter the case of Field Manual 30-31B, which was to embarrass the U.S. on the global stage and make citizens of allied countries suspicious of the Americans.

The U.S. Army issues field manuals (FM) to its soldiers, numbered to indicate the specific area of focus. "The 30s series was focused on military intelligence."[150] Lessons learned in the Vietnam War, for example, would be included in subsequent field manuals to aid soldiers entering a similar battlefield.

The KGB was aware of the existence of these field manuals and decided to create a forgery. Department A, the department within the KGB primarily responsible for disinformation campaigns, generated an unusually good forgery known as FM 30-31B, the *B* indicating that this was a supplement to the existing field manual. The idea was a stroke of cynical political genius. The main premise of the forged field manual was that secret American military units were behind political (often communist) insurgencies in allied countries. As Rid explains, "The disinformation artists of Service A effectively managed to redefine far-left, anti-American militants as American puppets, creating a self-radicalizing, positive feedback loop: violently resisting American power would only prove the strength of American power, and thus trigger more violent resistance."

The argument went like this: According to the forged document, America's allies were not taking communist insurgencies seriously enough, so undercover American military operatives should stage fraudulent insurgencies within allied countries. They were to cause havoc and mayhem to convince the allied governments to adopt more aggressive anti-communist stances; if communists were seen to be blowing things up and harming citizens, governments of the affected countries would start to take the "communist threat" more seriously. The U.S., the manual suggested, wanted to make sure that their allies were as anti-communist as they were.

The real intention was to make the ideas in this disinformation campaign public, thereby suggesting that domestic insurgencies were actually American operations aimed at destabilizing domestic politics. The implication was clear: America is not a safe or trustworthy political ally.

When internal political tensions arose in countries strategically allied with the U.S., Field Manual 30-31B would mysteriously surface in domestic publications. This happened a number of times in the 1970s. For instance, in 1974, when Turkey invaded Cyprus, a bout of domestic violence erupted. FM 30-31B was secretly sent to the publisher of *Baris*, a Turkish magazine. The editors of these papers took the document to be an actual training manual for the U.S. military and proceeded to publish damning sections, which left many readers with the distinct impression that the political tensions unfolding in Turkey were actually the result of a U.S. operation. The effect was to slow or completely derail political collaboration.

This happened more than once. The manual surfaced in a Philippine publication in 1976 as the U.S. was increasing its military presence in the country. In 1978, the manual was published in Spain as the country was deciding whether or not to become a member state of NATO, the military alliance directly at odds with the Soviet Union and its Warsaw Pact. But perhaps the most notorious example is when the field manual was used in Italy in 1978, when Red Brigade terrorists abducted Aldo Moro, the head of Italy's conservative party. As this genuine communist insurgency was taking place, Field Manual 30-31B surfaced once again. As Rid explains, "to many Italians, the field manual finally offered documentary evidence of a spy plot. The Milan-based weekly *L'Europeo*, left-leaning and often sharply critical of the United States, published detailed experts and pictures of the forged documents that the magazine's editors considered 'absolutely authentic.'"

When disinformation and conspiracy theories intertwine, the result is a tangled mess that is almost impossible to disentangle.

2016 U.S. ELECTION

The above examples all come from the Cold War and were operations directed by the Soviet Union against America or NATO allies. But disinformation did not die with the collapse of the Soviet Union. In the age of social media, it is even more prevalent and sophisticated. The Soviet examples from the '60s to the '80s provide the basic template, a template in analog. Today, disinformation has entered the digital age. The strategies have become more specific to niche audiences. Hackers and private data mining companies are involved, and they use social media sites and bots to push their messages. But the underlying strategy is the same: confuse and distract a political enemy to gain some sort of strategic advantage.

The U.S. election of 2016 is a great example. What was especially strange is that there were a number of separate disinformation campaigns.[151] At least two were foreign, run by post-Soviet Russian military intelligence, and the other was (sort of) domestic, employing the use of a British social media–based data mining company. Having focused so much on Russia, it might be a nice break to look at how private intelligence companies have also gotten into the game of misleading voters and changing elections by spreading lies and half-truths.

Cambridge Analytica was a private data mining company based in England that provided its services to political parties hoping to win elections. Cambridge Analytica (henceforth CA) has been implicated in swaying (and perhaps winning) elections in Brazil, Kenya, and may have helped Brexiteers quit the European Union, as well as swaying opinion on important topics in China and India. Our focus, however, is what happened in the United States leading up to the first Trump victory.

The story started sometime in 2014, when CA partnered with researcher Aleksandr Kogan, a lecturer at Cambridge University and researcher in psychology. Kogan used Facebook to create a survey. The survey seemed innocuous enough. It looked a lot like other Facebook surveys floating around the platform at that time, but there was an important difference. To complete this survey, users needed to log into their Facebook account. In the process, they apparently agreed to share their data with the researcher, who was actually subcontracted by CA. Users shared not only their own data but also the data of many (if not all) of their Facebook friends.

From the roughly 270,000 who participated in the survey, Kogan and CA harvested the data of approximately 87 million Facebook users. This data was compiled with likes, shares, location, and personal pictures to create a psychometric model of potential voters. This allowed them to create a vast psychological profile that would help CA micro-target personalized ads to Americans with the aim of influencing how they would vote in the upcoming election.

Why was the hiring of election consultants in this situation problematic? The practice is common and acceptable in democratic elections. But there's a catch. In most countries, when a party creates an advertisement, they need to make it clear that this is a sponsored election ad, they must show who paid for the ad, and the claims in the ad need to be legitimate. Ads are not allowed to slander an opponent.

In an undercover story aired in 2018 by Channel 4 News in the U.K., executives at CA provided startling insights into election messaging in a digital age. In a meeting with a putative Sri Lankan candidate, then–managing director Mark Turnbull said that election messages "Don't need to be true. They just need to be believed."[152] He also stated, "It's no good fighting elections on facts. What matters are hopes and fears."[153] Indeed, this is very much how the messaging during the 2016 election campaign was organized. The private data of millions was harvested without their permission and then used to create a psychological profile focusing mostly on their fears. These profiles were then used to craft bespoke messages, often totally untrue, articulating fears that were central to the target's political identity.

During the 2016 election, CA created ads specifically for subsets of the electorate claiming that Hillary Clinton "is a crook," that she was in some way responsible for the attacks on U.S. facilities that happened in Benghazi, or that her policies were hurting voters more than Trump's policies were. It was classic disinformation, but this time personalized to voters' individual concerns and interests.

Disinformation has not gone away with the Cold War, it has just become more bespoke and tailored.

CLIMATEGATE

In a catastrophic example of disinformation campaigns created by corporations, Big Oil managed to slow or reverse important policies meant to mitigate the climate crisis. The *Guardian* explains, "The fossil fuel industry has perpetrated a multi-decade, multibillion dollar disinformation, propaganda and lobbying campaign to delay climate action by confusing the public and policymakers about the climate crisis and its solutions."[154]

There exists a trove of publicly available internal oil company documents demonstrating that Big Oil has known for decades that its products are harmful to the environment.[155] Already in 1959, Edward Teller, famous for his research into atomic weapons, gave a talk to oil and gas executives explaining how their products were related to the greenhouse effect.[156] In the 1960s, various oil and gas companies conducted their own internal research to investigate the climatic impact of their products. A study conducted by the American Petroleum Institute in 1965 found that "carbon dioxide is being added to the earth's atmosphere by the burning of coal, oil, and natural gas at such a rate that by the year 2000 the heat balance will be so modified as possibly to cause marked changes in climate beyond local or even national efforts. . . . The pollution from internal combustion engines is so serious, and is growing so fast, that an alternative nonpolluting means of powering automobiles, buses, and trucks is likely to become a national necessity."[157]

A 1979 Exxon study notes that "nevertheless, recognizing the uncertainty, there is a possibility that an atmospheric CO_2 buildup will cause adverse environmental effects in enough areas of the world to consider limiting the future use of fossil fuels as major energy sources." Geoff Dembicki notes in his book *The Petroleum Papers*, "As far back as the late 1960s, Imperial Oil had begun to realize that public concern about the pollution its products caused was a growing corporate risk."[158]

Many other examples demonstrate beyond reasonable doubt that by the 1970s, oil and gas executives knew that their products could cause serious environmental harm, a potential threat to the industry's bottom line. But what to do? Taking a leaf out of Big Tobacco's response to the science demonstrating a link between smoking and serious health risks, Big Oil began its own disinformation campaign.[159] This was a coordinated response to public pressure and focused on undermining the public's perception about the consensus among scientists that petroleum products have adverse environmental impacts. The campaign didn't need to convince everyone. It merely needed to make a minority of voters skeptical about the need for immediate action.

As a leaked internal memo notes,[160] the disinformation campaign will have achieved its goal when:

- Average citizens "understand" (recognize) uncertainties in climate science;
- recognition of uncertainties becomes part of the "conventional wisdom";
- media "understands" (recognizes) uncertainties in climate science;
- media coverage reflects balance on climate science and recognition of the validity of viewpoints that challenge the current "conventional wisdom";
- industry senior leadership understands uncertainties in climate science, making them stronger ambassadors to those who shape climate policy;
- those promoting the Kyoto treaty on the basis of extant science appear to be out of touch with reality.

Through advertising, cherry-picking experts willing to toe the line, organizing climate conferences, generating fake grassroots organizations, and bombarding media outlets with contrary "facts" to the emerging climate consensus,[161] they created a counter-narrative to the consensus view that global warming is generated by humans.

The Cato Institute is a right-wing political think tank co-founded in 1977 by Charles Koch, co-owner of Koch Industries and a major player in the Alberta oil sands. He gave the institute $20 million in seed money, and by the 1990s, Cato was well known for spreading climate disinformation. In 1991, for example, Cato hosted a conference titled Global Environmental Crises: Science or Politics? The blurb for the conference flyer, written by climate contrarian Professor Richard S. Lindzen, provides us with the tone of the conference: "The notion that global warming is a fact and will be catastrophic is drilled into people to the point where it seems surprising that anyone would question it, and yet, underlying it is very little evidence at all." Of course, his claim was clearly disputed by the industry's own scientists and their studies from decades before.

Patrick Michaels's presentation "The Political Science of Global Warming" is of particular interest. Michaels had run an experimental media campaign a few months prior to the conference with the aim of convincing Americans in three test communities that global warming wasn't real."[162] His work was funded by utility companies masquerading as a grassroots organization, the Informed Citizens for the Environment. Pretending to be a real grassroots organization is a disinformation practice known as **astroturfing**.

As Dembicki explains in *The Petroleum Papers*, "That was the message Michaels delivered to the Koch-backed Cato Institute conference, which took place only a month after his work on the Informed Citizens for the Environment campaign. It was still early days in the climate debate, but Koch Industries had already settled on an effective strategy. Getting a credentialed scientist to poke holes in the rapidly strengthening scientific consensus was a useful way to distract people's attention from the real interests that were threatened by governments taking action on the crisis."[163]

This strategy of using credentialed academics and think tanks to confuse the public about the consensus opinion has been going on for decades. Climate skepticism is far higher today than it was in the 1980s.

A pivotal event that supercharged climate skepticism is known as Climategate. In November 2009, hacked emails from climate scientists were purposely released in a way that made it look like scientists were faking their data. Taking a lesson directly from the KGB, these emails were strategically leaked just before a major climate summit in December of that same year in Copenhagen.

The hack led to the scientists being the subject of a dozen investigations lasting over two years in both the U.S. and U.K. No wrongdoing was found. The effect of the leak, however, was to significantly weaken the resolutions that came out of Copenhagen.

MANUFACTURING CONFUSION

Even under ideal circumstances, the quality of information we tend to get from corporate news media is not great. Often, news about the social and political world is not based on what is most vital for us to know as citizens and voters, but on what keeps our interest longest and leads to more engagement. This means that a lot of our news is more like infotainment: seemingly relevant information about the world that is of little value when we are trying to make informed political decisions.

Our data is bought and used not just by those trying to sell us their products but also by private disinformation companies like CA, foreign intelligence agencies, and multi-billion-dollar corporations. Our media is undermined by thousands of domestic and foreign agents active across dozens of governmental and private agencies, all working to influence our perception of our political reality.

When analyzing the sociopolitical world, we need to keep the role of conspiracy theories in the service of disinformation front and centre. We assume that there is a mainstream account of events that represents the most commonly held belief and repeats the official story. Within that paradigm, the conspiracy theory is disruptive; it is reasoning from below, critical of the mainstream account and of mainstream authority. But there's another side to the story — sometimes conspiracies are created by people in power in order to confuse an issue and keep us from making necessary changes or particular choices. When we believe we have discovered some disruptive truth, such as "the CIA created HIV/AIDS to further marginalize racialized and stigmatized peoples in the U.S.," we may simply have fallen for someone else's power play. Sometimes the conspiracy theory *is* the conspiracy.

6

MORAL PANICS — THREE WITCH HUNTS AND THE CONSEQUENCES OF BAD INFORMATION

Sometime in 2019, my (Lee's) nine-year-old daughter came home from school quite upset. When I asked her what was wrong, she told me that her teacher had warned her about a video depicting a scary monster that could harm her. I didn't really understand, so I dug a bit further. In speaking to other parents, I discovered that there was a YouTube video which depicted a grotesque mannequin-type doll-monster with a giant unnatural grin and unctuous long black hair, which apparently was encouraging young kids like my daughter to engage in self-harm, even to the point of taking their own life. And then, as was reported by the *Buenos Aires Times*, a 12-year-old girl did take her own life.[164]

When I discovered what was happening, I started seeing red. This was exactly the type of situation some moronic internet troll would create, I thought. Other parents were furious as well. We started to organize. First, we started to talk to school authorities. We began asking questions about the type of access our kids had to the internet at school. Weren't they being supervised? Could they access YouTube and other sites unchaperoned? Shouldn't these videos be pulled from the internet? Maybe YouTube or Google could help? We went to parent-teacher nights to complain about the lax safety standards at our school. The same thing was happening in other schools and in other cities, and in other countries. The Momo Challenge, as it was known, was a global affair.

The interesting thing about this event is that although my daughter was scared, she hadn't actually seen the video. What she knew was that there was a "monster" who would scare kids into hurting themselves. It turns out that the teachers who had given this general warning to the students hadn't seen the video either. And when I tried to search it on YouTube, I came up empty. The video simply didn't exist. It never had.

The entire thing was a hoax. What actually happened was that, sometime in 2018, comments on the WhatsApp messaging service, and later on YouTube, started to emerge warning about a video that was seducing teenagers to self-harm, and reports from South America indicated that teenagers were hurting themselves as a result. The *Buenos Aires Times* article cited above, from July 25, 2018, read "Police Suspect 12-Year-Old Girl's Suicide Linked to WhatsApp Terror Game Momo." On August 2, 2018, Fox News ran a headline reading "Sinister Momo 'Suicide Challenge' Sparks Fear as It Spreads on WhatsApp."[165] By 2019, we even had Kim Kardashian warning parents about the dangers of the Momo Challenge.[166]

Eventually the hoax was exposed. As the *Skeptical Inquirer* noted, the Momo Challenge was a repackaged version of the Blue Whale Challenge, a similar internet hoax. And as with the Momo Challenge, warnings were issued to parents and teachers to be alert and aware. An example of a warning one might receive reads: "The Blue Whale 'suicide game' is believed to be a hidden online social media group with its main aim to encourage our children to kill themselves. Within the group daily tasks are assigned to members who have to do different tasks for 50 days. They include self-harming, watching horror movies and waking up at unusual hours, but these gradually get more extreme. But on the 50th day, the controlling manipulators behind the game reportedly instruct the youngsters to commit suicide. Please share and warn all other parents of the dangers of this game."[167] At the peak of the panic, police forces in France, Canada, Germany, Spain, and the U.S., among many other countries, were issuing public warnings similar to the one above.

While the Momo Challenge itself was a hoax, the reactions to the hoax were very real. We were all caught up in what the sociologist Stanley Cohen calls a "moral panic," namely a public overreaction to a perceived social threat, when a social majority believes that there is a minority in their midst working against the interests of the community — think witches, communists, drug dealers, or cult leaders. The panic is described as *moral* because it's seen to emerge from bad people doing bad things. It's described as a *panic* because the threat is wildly overestimated or entirely fictitious and the solutions suggested to deal with it are overreactions, cures that are worse than the disease. As a public overreaction to a perceived conspiracy, moral panics are often considered a subgenre of conspiracy theories

In the previous two chapters we examined the forces that impact the type and quality of information we have access to, and we investigated what is popular and why. In this chapter, we want to show the consequences of relying on dubious information.

HOW TO MAKE A MORAL PANIC

Cohen developed the theory of moral panics by examining an event that occurred in his home country of England in the mid-1960s, known as the Mods and Rockers scare. In the warmer months, domestic tourists in Great Britain have always flocked to beachside towns such as Brighton, Clacton, or Margate for a little rest and relaxation. But in 1964, things apparently turned sour.

> Easter 1964 was worse than usual. It was cold and wet, and in fact Easter Sunday was the coldest for eighty years. The shopkeepers and stall owners were irritated by the lack of business and the young people had their own boredom and irritation fanned by rumours of café owners and barmen refusing to serve some of them. A few groups started scuffling on the pavements and throwing stones at each other. The Mods and Rockers factions — a division initially based on clothing and life styles, later rigidified, but at that time not fully established — started separating out. Those on bikes and scooters roared up and down, windows were broken and some beach huts were wrecked and one boy fired a starting pistol in the air. The vast number of people crowding into the streets, the noise, everyone's general irritation and the actions of an unprepared and undermanned police force had the effect of making the two days unpleasant, oppressive and sometimes frightening.[168]

What followed that initial event (what we will later term *impact*) was perhaps predictable. Cohen notes that *every major newspaper* ran headline stories with titles like "Day of Terror by Scooter Groups" and "Youngsters Beat Up Town" or "Wild Ones Invade Seaside — 97 Arrests." It was admittedly a slow news day. Newspaper pictures also emerged showing gangs of hooligans throwing trash cans, lawn chairs, and beer bottles at each other. Stories were written about families choosing to stay home rather than risk being caught up in the mayhem. The *Daily Express* paints the scene: "There was Dad asleep in a deckchair and Mum making sandcastles with the children when the 1964 boys took over the beaches at Margate and Brighton yesterday and smeared the traditional postcard scene with blood and violence." Why would anyone want a piece of that "holiday"?

Not long after the first reports started covering this phenomenon, the public began calling for action. Local authorities were petitioned to get the matter under control. More police should be engaged in crowd control duties. Punishments for offenders should be strict and ruthless. "Zero tolerance for violence" was the maxim.

But like the Momo Challenge, the Mods and Rockers clash was mostly an invention of the press. The boredom and irritatation of the young people in Clacton echoed that of their peers in Margate and Brighton on Easter Sunday. While they were up to some mischief, it was not the organized mass riot that the newspapers were peddling. The distortion was an example of "exaggerating grossly the seriousness of the events, in terms of criteria and the amount and effects of any damage or violence." For instance, the claim that the Mods and Rockers were causing massive property damage was rebuffed by the deputy publicity manager of Margate, who said that the 50 broken deck chairs was not much more than happened on any given holiday weekend. The same is true of the claims of arrests, violence, the groups' intentions, their social status, and their motivations.

The Mods and Rockers scare, just like the Momo Challenge, was a moral panic. The social majority of England (parents, authority figures, the elderly, basically anyone not a mod or rocker) began believing that there was a subgroup in their midst (dangerous and violent teenagers with too much time on their hands) who were actively threatening the safety of that majority.

Relying on established theories in disaster research, Cohen went on to describe the stages, "a sequential model," a community goes through when a moral panic develops: 1. Warning; 2. Threat; 3. Impact; 4. Inventory; 5. Rescue; 6. Remedy; and 7. Recovery. While not every moral panic necessarily contains all of these stages, all moral panics show evidence of some. The stages are helpful for recognizing a given event as a moral panic, and it's worth investigating what each stage entails.

Warning

The model was originally developed to explain reactions to environmental disasters. The warning is when the public is made aware that something could go wrong. A geologist might start to worry that a volcano in our vicinity might erupt in the next few months or years. In the Mods and Rockers example, there may have been opinion pieces on the wayward drift of the young today, and a general decline in "standards and morals." In the case of the Momo challenge, the warning came in the form of reports of the dangers of internet trolls, internet predation on kids, and the like. The warning sets the stage of social preparedness. Something somewhere may be going wrong at some point.

Threat

At this point, the danger is closer in proximity, either temporally or physically. In the example of the volcano, we may start seeing smoke. Primed by the initial warning, we're starting to become concerned about the possibility of an impending calamity. The sense of approximation does not need to be as literal as seeing the smoke on a volcano. The media often informs the public of threats not immediately visible. I may live too far away from the volcano to actually see the smoke, but may nonetheless be impacted by an eruption. The media does the work of informing us of threats that we may not perceive directly but which nonetheless can threaten us directly. Sometimes the warning and the threat occur almost simultaneously.

Impact

The disaster has struck. The volcano has erupted and casualties abound. For most of the modern world this will be entirely relayed by the media. 9/11 is an event almost everyone experienced entirely on television. And in the case of the Mods and Rockers, the impact stage was when the newspapers started to blare their headlines about mobs of rival gangs marauding the streets of holiday resorts in England. For me, the impact came when my daughter told me about the Momo Challenge.

Inventory

During this phase, the disaster is conceptually organized. It is a phase during which "rumours and ambiguous perceptions become the basis for interpreting the situation." Where has it happened? What is the extent and how many have been impacted? When a volcano erupts, we eventually learn about the death toll, the extent of the territories affected, and initial estimates of the cost of the damage. In the Mods and Rockers example, this is when most of Britain first learned of the complexities of the various youth subgroups, their animosity, and their propensity for violence. We learn where the social disaster is taking place (Brighton, Clacton, Margrave). It is in this phase that Cohen notes a decided "exaggeration and distortion" in the reports, or a distinct "over-reporting" of the events.

Rescue

We have now tipped into another dimension of the moral panic. Authority figures get involved. In a natural disaster, this is the moment of rescue. Firefighters, paramedics, and the military may arrive and begin their work. In the moral panic, authority figures begin to enact policies meant to immediately ameliorate the situation. During the Mods and Rockers scare, "suspicious" young people were turned away at the train stations, more police were seen on the beaches, young people already in holiday towns were stopped and questioned, and barricades were erected.

Remedy

This stage is like rescue but more deliberate and long-lasting, and it often spurs changes that remain in place after the initial emergency. In the realm of natural disaster, this is the phase when we begin to plan early warning systems, change the school curriculum to include emergency drills, and enact other policy changes. During a moral panic, this often results in changes to the penal system, to censorship, or the like.

Recovery

In both natural and moral disasters, this is the period during which normalcy is restored. We will see below that this period in a moral panic is often accompanied by a type of social amnesia. And while some sense of normalcy is re-established, the moral panic has often changed society at a structural level. Policies established during the panic are often left in place, and if they eventually are repealed, it can take a long time.

FOLK DEVILS

Another element that Cohen notes as part and parcel of a moral panic is the belief in an evil agent behind it all. In every moral panic, we assume that there is someone or some group to blame. This makes the moral panic quite different from a natural disaster. We assume that this agent is evil as opposed to misguided or deluded. "They," whoever they may be, have made a choice to do evil. Cohen calls this agent a **folk devil**.

It is worth noting that this folk devil label is usually assigned to a disenfranchised subset of the community. The role of folk devil has often been thrust upon women, the poor, immigrants, racialized people, and/or religious or ethnic minorities. Once the nefarious agent is socially identified, they tend to be spoken of in hyperbolic terms: "They hate our freedom," "They are in league with Satan," "They are moral degenerates."

Cohen also notes the recursive nature of the panic. As stories are reported, they function almost as a template for those not yet part of it. Amazingly, the fictitious animosity between the "original" Mods and Rockers was taken very seriously by subsequent British youths, who were not themselves part of the initial "unrest." That is, they believed the reports as much as anyone. And later in the '60s, there were actually more organized altercations between members of the two subcultures who relied on the reported events of '64 as a guide for how to behave.

Let's now turn to three famous examples of moral panics in American history. In some sense they are all witch hunts, and by examining them, we will better see the evolution of the moral panic.

SALEM

The Salem Witch Trials is perhaps the most famous instance of a moral panic. Salem is worth studying because it took place well before the existence of mass media, and it functions as a template for many subsequent panics. This fact was noted by President Harry Truman, Arthur Miller, and others during the Red Scare of the 1950s.

The Salem panic began in the Winter of 1692. It lasted less than a year, and by the end of it, the small Massachusetts community had executed 19 people and two dogs for witchcraft.[169] How did a dull little town fall victim to the hysterical fever that led them to turn on their neighbours and friends? Using Cohen's model, we can trace the development of this all-too-common social phenomenon.

The warning phase had been going on for decades. The residents of Salem, Massachusetts, were three generations away from the "pilgrims." The pilgrims, the grandparents of the Salem town folk of 1692, were self-selected religious radicals who left England in despair at being unable to rid the English church of its Catholic vestiges. They had immigrated to America to create a religious utopia, the City on a Hill.

But everyone could see that Salem was not the Protestant utopia that the Puritans had wanted to create. It was a cold, dull place where the residents toiled from sun up to sun down. Drinking was about the only release available to the community members, and drink they did. Another activity people tend to engage in when trying to have a nice time led to unwanted and unexpected pregnancies. Servants would run away with the stable hands, and people would show up to church too drunk to stay awake during service. With all this misbehaving about, the central theme of sermons for years had been a warning. Specifically, God was displeased and would soon unleash a well-deserved and necessary correction.

The threat emerged early in the years of 1692 at the house of the local parish priest, Samuel Parris, who had children of his own and was also caring for his orphaned niece. It was she, 11-year-old Abigail Williams, who first showed signs of being a victim of witchcraft. She would experience bouts of hysterical laughter, spasms, fits, and what was known as "paroxysms." She would complain of being pinched, bitten, or pricked, although no evidence of physical trauma could be found. Soon after, one of Parris's own daughters,

Elizabeth, also showed signs of being a victim of witchcraft. Quickly thereafter the "infection" of witchcraft spread among the girls' friends and acquaintances. Ann Putnam was the next to be afflicted, followed by Mercy Lewis, the servant at her house. Then Mary Walcott, Annie's best friend. And on it went.

It is worth noting that the first people to be "afflicted by witchcraft" were roughly of similar age and spent a lot of time together. Their affliction did not become a matter for the community while it was contained to the Parris household and the girls' small circle of friends. For it to grow into a larger phenomenon, another element was needed.

It was Samuel Parris's neighbour, Mary Sibley, who ensured that the afflicted girls would be the talk of the town. Sibley took the role that the media would come to play in later panics. While Samuel was away with his wife, Sibley who was looking after the Parris children, decided to counteract the witches' works with a bit of counter-magic. She baked a "witch cake" meant to remove the curse from the girls and also identify their assailants. The girls started to name names. At that point the "threat" had been positively identified for the community, and what had been a relatively private matter became a subject of great interest for the rest of Salem. As Parris himself stated in a rather prescient insight, "By this means, the devil has been raised among us." Not the biblical Devil, as Parris probably meant, but the folk devil of Cohen's theory.

The girls began by accusing three people, our folk devils. One was a Parris household slave, a racialized woman named Tituba. Another was the vagrant, Sarah Good. And once accused, Sarah Good accused Sarah Osborne, a proud woman known to have "loose morals" because she took lovers. The event had transcended from a few girls in and around the Parris household to a community affair, and as is typical, the mantle of folk devil was thrust upon those in the community least able to defend themselves. The first people to be accused of witchcraft are an enslaved person of colour, a homeless woman, and an unmarried poor woman.

The impact and the inventory in Salem took place at the same time. As the first accusations became known, the town realized it was already in a disaster (impact) while simultaneously trying to figure out who was to blame (inventory). Courts were brought into being to discover which members of the community were on which side. While Sarah Good and

Sarah Osborne both vehemently denied any complicity, Tituba "confessed" to everything and embellished the story with fabulous tales of midnight flights with other community members to the witches' Sabbath. A flurry of accusations followed. To name but a few: March 12, Martha Corey is accused; March 19, Rebecca Nurse; March 23, the five-year-old daughter of Sarah Good; April 3, Sarah Cloyce. And it just kept going. What we know as the Salem Witch Scare was out of control between the months of May and September. Around 144 to 185 were named, 55 people confessed, and 19 were executed, or "hanged by the neck until . . . dead."

The summer marks the rescue phase. Authority figures called into action to help save the community now get to work in earnest. People are put to death. The girls and others continue to accuse, and the trials continue unabated until September. Finally, by October there comes a decree from the local magistrate that there shall be no new witch trials, and any trials that occur are for those who have already been accused. While more people are convicted of witchcraft, there are no more executions. The remaining "witches" have their sentences commuted, and by January of 1693 the panic is over, the trials ended for good.

Salem was the first big witch scare in the U.S., but it was far from the last. Another equally famous one happened at the dawn of the Cold War, and this time the media was heavily involved.

THE RED SCARE

For American anti-communists, 1949 was a bad year. China, one of the oldest civilizations in the world, had just "fallen" to communism. This was also the year that the Soviets developed their own nuclear bomb, and according to analysts at the time, they managed it between three and 10 years ahead of schedule.[170] By 1949, some of the worst aspects of Stalinism had become known in the West. The Soviet Union was not a workers' paradise brought to earth but rather a totalitarian regime replete with political prisons, show trials, pervasive fear, manufactured famine, and a complete lack of political accountability or freedoms. Communism was deeply feared, and all the while it was seemingly scoring massive victories throughout the world. It was in this political milieu that one of the largest secular witch hunts of modern times was born: the Red Scare.[171] More accurately, the second Red Scare: The first happened in America shortly after the successful communist revolution in Russia.

Taking full advantage of these political worries was a junior Republican senator from Wisconsin, whose very name would soon become synonymous with modern-day witch trials. In the 1950s, Joseph McCarthy made a remarkable discovery: Moral panics can do wonders for a fledgling political career. The Salem Witch Trials were an example of a naive moral panic because the leaders themselves believed in the existence of witches in the community. However, Senator McCarthy knew full well that what he was saying was mostly untrue, but he said it anyway because it benefited him politically.

As he ascended the steps onto the stage of the Lincoln Memorial dinner, on February 9, 1950, McCarthy had two speeches in his pocket and was still unsure which one he'd deliver. One was about housing for the elderly; the other would begin a fire-and-brimstone moral panic. What followed was one of the most important speeches in American political history, now referred to as the "enemies within" speech. Brandishing a piece of paper (which was actually his other speech), Joseph McCarthy claimed to hold evidence of 205 active communist members working at the State Department. While the warnings about communism, communist infiltration, and the dangers of Stalin had preceded McCarthy by at least a decade, it was McCarthy who really brought them forth as a distinct contemporary threat.

Newspapers quickly repeated McCarthy's characterization of the unseen threat in America's midst, and he was said to be both delighted and surprised by this result. Like a prospector looking for oil, McCarthy had fortuitously struck a vein of fear in America's consciousness, the best find for an aspiring demagogue.

It is worth looking at the very first person who McCarthy charged with being a communist, Dorothy Kenyon. Kenyon was a former municipal judge who had belonged to a variety of civil liberty and social justice organizations. McCarthy argued these were *all* front organizations for Soviet communism. Stating "the Communist activities of Miss Kenyon are not only deep-rooted but extend back through the years. Her sponsorship of the doctrines and philosophy of this ruthless and Godless organization is not new."

It turned out, however, that McCarthy was unable to establish that any of the 28 organizations he accused was actually a front for Soviet communism, or that Kenyon herself was a communist. When it became evident that he had overreached, he didn't even bother to show up on the day she defended herself and simply moved on to his next (hopefully more promising) target.

Other victims of McCarthy's accusations didn't come out of the affair nearly as well as Kenyon did. Raymond Kaplan was a radio engineer for *Voice of America* who had also worked on a radio transmitter project with MIT, which McCarthy claimed was sabotaging America's propaganda war with the Soviet Union. Among McCarthy's accusations was that the locations chosen for the radio towers were purposely disadvantageous, and so the engineers, like Kaplan, who worked on this project must be sympathizers of the Soviet system. Kaplan was called before the hearings and accused of placing the towers in suboptimal locations. On his way home from the hearings, he threw himself in front of a truck and died. A note to his wife found in his pocket stated that he didn't want the accusation to besmirch his young family.

Not only were Kenyon, Kaplan, and the many others called before the hearings not spies, they were often patriots in the best sense of the word. They worked hard to make their country better. For their efforts, they were singled out and harassed, and many came to great harm.

The rescue is the stage when authority figures come and fix the problems the disaster has wrought. During the Red Scare, ever more restrictive policies that counteracted the letter and spirit of the U.S. Constitution (particularly the Fourth Amendment) were enacted. It was at this phase of the panic that the famous words forever associated with the Red Scare were uttered: "Are you now or have you ever been a member of the Communist Party?" It's worth noting that the Communist Party was (and still is) a legal entity in the U.S., and membership was by no means equivalent to supporting the Soviet Union, Soviet-style Marxism, or Stalin. But in a state of fear, these objections all fell by the wayside.

The Red Scare ended much like Salem did, not with a bang but with a whimper. Joseph McCarthy overreached. The end began with the so-called Army-McCarthy hearings. President Eisenhower, who was severely critical of McCarthy, had suggested they be televised so that the public could see his tactics live and not just read about them in sympathetic news outlets. In the hearings, which were previously open only to reporters, the public saw an often drunk McCarthy bullying young soldiers with baseless accusations.

They did not like what they saw, and the tide of public opinion turned against McCarthy.

Interestingly, though the media is often in part responsible for creating moral panics, it may also be the solution. Salem ended after news reports and an open letter published in a newspaper spotlighted what was happening. When the Army hearings were televised, people could finally see McCarthy's antics themselves.

Perhaps the end was most succinctly enunciated by Senator Joseph Welch in his now infamous rebuttal to one of McCarthy's baseless accusations: "Have you no sense of decency, sir, at long last? Have you left no sense of decency?" This summarized how most people had come to feel about McCarthy, even those who agreed with his initial assessment that communism presented an internal political danger. McCarthy lost his remaining supporters in the Senate, and on December 2, 1954, the Senate voted to censure him by a vote of 67 to 22.

While the Red Scare ended with the Army-McCarthy hearings, and while McCarthy himself passed away at just 48 years old, the Red Scare cast a long shadow into the second half of the 20th century. Some of the accused lost everything. For many, the damage caused to their reputations meant setbacks that took years if not decades to correct.

THE SATANIC PANIC

Alas, witch hunts — the classic moral panic — are not a phenomenon of the distant past. They have continued well into modern times. They emerge in both secular and religious guises. A startling modern example began in 1983, at the McMartin preschool in Manhattan Beach, California. It was part of a widespread phenomenon of the 1980s known today as the Satanic Panic.

Many warnings set the stage for the Satanic Panic. An important one was the publication of *Michelle Remembers*, written by psychiatrist Lawrence Pazder. In this bestselling book, Pazder relied on the defunct psychological technique of recovering repressed memories. By hypnotizing his subject, he claimed to have discovered a network of organized Satanic abuse. This and similar influences functioned to alert society of a general threat on the horizon.[172]

At McMartin, the impact began when a mother of one of the children accused a preschool worker of having sexually abused her son. However, the claims of this mother, who had a history of psychiatric illness related to delusions, were highly implausible.[173] She suggested the abuse took place in underground tunnels with flying witches and slaughtered animals, all apparently part of a Satanic ritual. The specific allegations, including that the accuser had jabbed her son's eyes with scissors, could not be corroborated with any physical evidence, and the mother provided none herself. She also accused another of the preschool workers of having ritually murdered a baby.[174] But no tunnels or animal or human remains were found in police raids following the accusations. There was nothing.

Nonetheless, the police sent a letter to the parents of the daycare children. It read: "Our investigation indicates that possible criminal acts include oral sex, fondling of genitals, buttock or chest areas and sodomy, possibly committed under the pretense of 'taking the child's temperature.' Also, photos may have been taken of the children without their clothing. Any information from your child regarding having ever observed Ray Buckey to leave a classroom alone with a child during any nap period, or if they have ever observed Ray Buckey tie up a child, is important."

Of course other parents started checking in with their children. Child psychologists were brought in to conduct their own investigation using psychological techniques now deemed suspect. Many of the children were coerced into agreeing with the accusers. As a *New York Times* journalist who reviewed the files put it, "The children quickly recognized that the only way their interview was going to end was to tell the psychologists what they wanted to hear."[175] In fact, the interviews were so coercive that the McMartin case is partly responsible for the implementation of stricter standards to be applied when it came to how children were to be interviewed.[176] However, at the time, the doctrine that "children don't lie" was the default assumption of police, courts, and other professionals directly involved in this case.

The fear that Satanists were running preschools in order to ritually molest and even murder children was not contained to the McMartin preschool. It spread like a contagion, inflamed by the mass media. Soon, other preschools became suspect. The Jordan, Minnesota, daycare case erupted shortly after. Both cases went to court, and not one of the accused was found guilty.

Despite the lack of physical evidence and the outrageous nature of the claims, this incident became a national sensation. The media had a field day. During this impact/inventory period, we saw distinct exaggeration and distortion in the news reports and general over-reporting. It began with a report by KABC in Los Angeles. But others soon got in on the act. Phil Donahue and *20/20* helped mainstream the accusations, and so did NPR's *The Morning Edition.* Conservative and religiously focused news outlets spent an especially long time discussing the matter, as it confirmed their worries about America's spiritual decline.

In 1988, then–talk show presenter Geraldo Rivera dedicated a two-hour-long special to the dangers of Satanism in America. NBC's "Devil Worship: Exposing Satan's Underground" contained a segment that focused on the McMartin preschool incident and the worried parents.[177] He provided a lurid narrative about how heavy metal music was full of Satanic innuendo meant to seduce children into worshiping the Devil. In his introductory remarks he stated, "Whether Satan exists is a question of belief, but what is beyond doubt is that Satanism exists." But there was virtually no evidence of any organized Satanic movement, especially not one that was abducting, abusing, and murdering kids.[178]

As the panic spread, "right-thinking people" came in to help with the rescue phase. Self-proclaimed experts on Satanism weighed in on the dangers. Ted Gunderson, a former FBI official, claimed that 4,000 children were ritually murdered in the U.S. annually.[179] In response to this new and dangerous threat, parents and church groups started hosting information sessions to help spread the word of the danger.

As the 1990s dawned and the McMartin trials ended without any convictions, the panic died down and eventually disappeared. But some of the structural changes to society remained, and many people caught up in the panic had their lives and reputations ruined. The McMartin preschool was shut down. The owners went into hiding. Others were handed long jail sentences for crimes they most certainly did not commit. But those who fanned the flames of the panic moved on to new causes.

A MODERN PERIL

As Cohen demonstrates, moral panics are not the aberrations of history that we sometimes assume them to be. Rather, they are part of any modern political community.

> Societies appear to be subject, every now and then, to periods of moral panic. A condition, episode, person or group of persons emerges to become defined as a threat to societal values and interests; its nature is presented in a stylized and stereotypical fashion by the mass media; the moral barricades are manned by editors, bishops, politicians and other right-thinking people; socially accredited experts pronounce their diagnoses and solutions; ways of coping are evolved or (more often) resorted to; the condition then disappears, submerges or deteriorates and becomes more visible.[180]

The United States has had dozens of moral panics just in the 20th century. Some were more severe, all-encompassing and longer-lasting than others, but all follow essentially the same pattern outlined by Cohen. The allegations sometimes contain some (often small) kernel of truth, yet the panic does nothing to solve any real problem. McCarthy did not find a single spy, but he did ruin many lives. A moral panic erupted after the terror attacks of 9/11, attacks that were real and alarming. But the anti-Muslim panic associated with those attacks did nothing to make the world safer.

As suggested at the beginning of this chapter, moral panics are often creations of the media, arising when we rely on short, sensationalist, unvetted information that plays on our fears. The news media of 1950s America did a lot to spread the worry that communists had infiltrated American political and military institutions. McCarthy set it in motion, but the media ran with it. The Satanic Panic was boosted by reputable mainstream outlets. In both the Red Scare and the Satanic Panic, none of the accusations were true. And yet a panic ensued because segments of the population were convinced that a conspiracy was taking place in their midst. That's the real-world impact of bad information.

7

GOOD AND EVIL — QANON VS. THE SINISTER CABAL

THE IMPLICIT INGREDIENT

If you're baking a conspiracy theory, several ingredients are necessary. More than one person must be involved (or there would be no one to conspire with), and it needs to be secret (or the planning wouldn't be conspiring). However, these characteristics alone aren't sufficient for something to be considered a conspiracy. For example, if a group of friends planned a surprise birthday for another friend, or if two neighbours decided to shovel an elderly person's sidewalk during a snowstorm without telling them first, that would be an example of more than one person planning something together in secret. Yet we would not consider either of these scenarios a conspiracy. Something important is missing from those examples: There is nothing sinister or malicious about them. The concept of evil is a crucial element to our understanding and normal use of the term *conspiracy.*

This might seem obvious enough to almost be not worth mentioning. But the ingredient of evil is a complicated addition to a recipe, and it deserves some closer analysis. So what do we mean when we say something is *evil*?

Do we mean that the *consequences* of an action are harmful and destructive? Certainly, someone might refer to a terrorist attack or the bombing of a city full of civilians as evil. Or are we saying the *motivations* behind an action are wicked and hateful? In that case, the evil isn't a description of the act itself, but of the qualities of the person or people who carried out the act.

Does evil depend on one's perspective, or is there an absolute yardstick that we can use to measure it? If it's a matter of perspective, then it's relative. To understand the concept of relativity, imagine two people drifting in space towards each other. The first person might have the belief that they are the one standing still in space, and it's the other person that's moving. The other person might think the exact same thing. When we say *relative*, we mean that no absolute statements can be made, only subjective perspectives are possible.

There is a saying often used to support the idea that evil is a relative concept: "One person's terrorist is another person's freedom fighter." Depending on the position and perspective of the person making the assessment, a person carrying out a violent act might be seen as either evil or virtuous. Conversely, if evil isn't dependent on the perspective of the observer but is a judgment that can be made accurately and objectively regardless of the positions of the people involved, then it is *absolute*, rather than relative. It exists outside of the subjective experiences of the individual (a terrorist would be a terrorist regardless of what perspective you were coming from).

Does evil originate in the world of human choices, or is evil an external force that operates through humans? If evil is an earthly concept, then we are the ones who bring it into the world through our decisions and actions. In that case, a world without humans is also a world without evil. If evil is an external cosmic force that exists independently of humans, then humans are simply vessels for that force, portals through which the force of evil can impact the external world.

Depending on which definition you are using, the answer could be yes to any of these questions. Philosophers and theologians have disagreed and continue to disagree about the nature of evil. To try to make things clearer, we need a definition of evil that helps us to understand conspiracy theories, conspiracy thinking, and conspiracism.

Since evil is such a slippery, contentious, and complicated concept, rather than trying to come up with one definition that serves our purposes, we'll be using two related but separate concepts: badness and evil. For our purposes, we're going to use *badness* to refer to an earthly product of human actions, whereas *evil* indicates a motivation for action that has its origins in an epic cosmic battle between two eternal forces. As we'll see, the distinction is crucial when it comes to our understanding of conspiracy theories.

AN UNDERSTANDING OF BADNESS

Let's start with an examination of badness, which we're defining as intensely harmful consequences resulting from deliberate action or deliberate inaction. Our definition of badness will state that it is relative — people committing bad acts frequently, through elaborate justification and rationalization, consider themselves to be heroes rather than villains. For example, the firebombing by American forces of Tokyo in March of 1945 likely killed over 100,000 civilians.[181] By any standard, the deliberate fiery death of innocent people is a bad act. However, the architects of that bombing campaign would have believed that they were doing something necessary to the war effort.

There is nothing supernatural about the category of badness; it is simply the result of human choices. Those choices may be understood as having complex historical, economic, sociological, or psychological causes, but they don't require the intervention of a deity or a cosmic force as a motivation. They don't need a villain doing evil things simply for the sake of evil.

Because the explanation for this kind of badness involves human-built structures (such as war, the economy, politics, law, etc.), it is unnecessary that the people who are behind bad acts are themselves bad by nature. There have been many famous social science experiments over the years whose findings support this idea. For example, in an experiment by Stanley Milgram, participants were asked to help researchers test the effects of punishment on learning. To do this, the participant (the "teacher") was asked to provide pairs of words to another participant (the "learner") who was hooked up to an electric shock generator. When the learner repeated a word pair incorrectly, the teacher was asked to push a switch that delivered a shock to the learner, and then turn the intensity of the machine up for the next incorrect answer.[182]

After a few incorrect answers, the shock machine would be turned up to a point where the learner would be complaining, then screaming, then pleading for the experiment to stop. If the teacher displayed any hesitancy about continuing, the man running the experiment would tell the teacher that "the experiment requires that you continue" or "you have no other choice, you *must* go on," or other variations of those lines.

After the dial was turned up to 330 volts, the learner (who had complained of having a bad heart) would make no noise at all and cease answering questions. Of course, the learner wasn't really dead — they weren't even really being shocked. The "learners" were in on the experiment, which was designed to see if normal, everyday people could be convinced to perform a bad act simply by placing them in a situation in which an authority told them to. What percentage of the population would be obedient to the point of murder?

After running the experiment, Milgram argued: "A commonly offered explanation is that those who shocked the victim at the most severe level were monsters, the sadistic fringe of society. But if one considers that almost two-thirds of the participants fall into the category of 'obedient' subjects, and that they represented ordinary people drawn from working, managerial, and professional classes, the argument becomes very shaky . . . This is, perhaps, the most fundamental lesson of our study: ordinary people, simply doing their jobs, and without any particular hostility on their part, can become agents in a terrible destructive process."[183]

There are plenty of other less unusual examples of this sort of structural badness. When we buy clothing for a cheap price that we know is only possible through the inhuman working conditions of the people who made it, or we support or ignore policies that result in massive environmental degradation, or justify mass murder for political or patriotic reasons, we are participating in badness. We may have no conscious bad intent and yet participate in a destructive structure that results in badness.

Using this definition of badness, no supernatural force is required to motivate people to cause terrible harm. No sinister hidden group is needed to inflict unimaginable destruction and suffering on the world — we everyday ordinary people can manage it perfectly well on our own.

AN UNDERSTANDING OF EVIL

Now let's define evil. As noted in the first part of the chapter, we're using *evil* to refer to motivations, not consequences. The idea of evil is absolute, not relative. And evil is a force that exists in the universe and operates through people who have been seduced by evil (and possibly through other non-human entities such as demons and aliens).

In the modern Western world, evil is associated with one figure in particular — Satan (a.k.a. Lucifer, a.k.a. Beelzebub, a.k.a. the Enemy, a.k.a. the Devil). In contrast to the divine goodness manifested in the Christian world by God, Satan is the cause of sin, temptation, suffering, conflict, and violence in the world. To refer to an action as Satanic is to classify it as sinister, destructive, corrupting, diabolical behaviour. However, despite the oversized presence Satan has in modern culture's imagination, Satan doesn't appear much in the Old Testament of the Bible.

In Genesis 3, a serpent in the Garden of Eden tempts Eve to eat the fruit from the tree of knowledge of good and evil, and this being is often said to be Satan. However, nothing in the text supports that interpretation. On the contrary, the way that God curses the snake (and the snake's offspring) in Genesis 3:14–15 to crawl on its belly, have its head stepped on, and bite humans on the ankle strongly suggests that the snake in the Garden of Eden was actually meant to be a snake, rather than Satan.

In Numbers 22:22, God sends down one of His angels to carry out one of His tasks by interfering with a disobedient man named Balaam, and the name given to the angel in the original Hebrew was Satan, referring to the concept of an adversary. In this context, the angel was an adversary to Balaam's progress (hence the name), but only at the direct request of God. There is nothing in this passage that would associate the Satan of that passage with our modern understanding of the Devil.

Satan is featured more prominently, and even has a speaking role, in the book of Job. However, similar to the role of the Satan in Numbers, the Satan in the book of Job is clearly working for God and doing His bidding. God mentions that his servant Job is a good and decent man who is blameless, and who shuns evil. This Satan points out that this might be because Job is a fortunate man who has been treated well by God, and if Job's fortunes changed, so would his attitude towards God. God then instructs Satan to go to Earth and do terrible things to him, to see if Job will maintain his upright ways. Job then suffers all manner of terrible things, including the loss of his livestock, the burning of his fields, the death of all of his children, and the loss of his health. However, he doesn't lose his faith. Then God appears to Job to tell him that His ways are too vast and mysterious for Job to understand. Job accepts this answer for his misfortunes.

The book of Job exists in part as an answer to the question: Why do bad things happen to good people? But the answer provided here does little to inspire the conspiracist mind. While there is a deliberate agent controlling the disasters and misfortunes that befall Job (always a key aspect of conspiracism), that deliberate agent is God, and He is doing so for the purposes of a greater plan that Job is too small to grasp the meaning or purpose of. The acceptance of and trust in secret plans is certainly not an easy fit with a conspiracist mindset, in which secret plans are not to be trusted and instead must be exposed (and possibly interrupted).

In the New Testament Gospels, the figure of Satan begins to more closely resemble the modern concept of the Devil. In the books of Mark and Matthew, demonic spirits (representatives of evil) who have possessed people are driven out by Jesus. In the account in Mark, the demon yells out, "Have you come to destroy us?" and Jesus commands the demon to be silent, suggesting that no negotiation or parley with this enemy is possible or useful (there's no bargaining with evil). At this point in the Bible, Satan is clearly in opposition to Jesus and tries to tempt Jesus in the wilderness to use his powers to make food to eat. Jesus refuses, and the Devil is driven away. In these passages, we see a very different Satan than the one we encountered in the Old Testament. Now, Satan isn't an adversary in the employ of God, acting as a kind of prosecutor. Instead, the New Testament Satan is a manifestation of evil, attempting to corrupt and infect the world. This version of Satan is much more relevant to our understanding of conspiracism. With this new version of the Devil, unfortunate events are not necessarily part of a larger plan of which we can have no understanding, but instead can be the work of a hostile actor actively working against that which is good and just. In short, it can be the work of evil.

THE MANICHEAN WORLDVIEW

To help us define the way we are using this term a little more carefully, there is another term that we need to examine first: *Manichean*. In the early centuries of Christianity, before the Catholic church established the rules and doctrines that would become the official canon, there was a wide variety of sects and groups. Each had its own ideas regarding the nature of the universe and the relationship between God and humans, and these were very different than what was proposed in the writings of St. Paul. Old ideas were interacting with new ones, and the wide variety of cultures and belief systems in the area guaranteed a diverse collection of interpretations. The Gnostics, for example, had a radical reinterpretation of the stories of the Old Testament that transformed the God of Genesis into Yaldabaoth — the actual source of evil in the world, who was only masquerading as the true God.[184] And in the third century CE, the Manicheans blended Christianity with Persian beliefs to come up with an understanding of the presence of misfortune and suffering in the world.

Whereas Job was told that the reasons for his agonies were too large for him to understand, and part of a greater plan, the Manicheans saw a world caught in an eternal and cosmic conflict between good and evil. Rather than one all-powerful being in charge of all things, the world was being fought over by two separate but equally powerful rulers, one light (God) and one dark (Satan).[185] This was the explanation for why terrible things happened to undeserving people, for why sometimes earthquakes and storms devastated entire communities, and why humans often behaved poorly or violently towards other humans — these were all manifestations of evil in the world.

When we refer to *Manichean*, we aren't talking about the actual religion; the name lives on as a description of a binary system in which opposing forces of light and darkness are in a perpetual state of struggle against each other. Of course, the actual Manichean religion was far more complex and nuanced than this simplistic black-and-white worldview.

Historian Richard Hofstadter explains the modern conspiratorial Manichean perspective: "The distinguishing thing about the paranoid style is not that its exponents see conspiracies or plots here and there in history, but that they regard a 'vast' or 'gigantic' conspiracy, set in motion by demonic forces of almost transcendent power, and what is felt to be needed to defeat it is not the usual methods of political give-and-take, but an all-out crusade."[186]

Hofstadter gives several examples of this conspiratorial Manichean view: In a 1798 sermon, a preacher warned of the danger to the Christian religion from the Illuminati, stating, "These impious conspirators and philosophists have completely effected their purposes in a large portion of Europe, and boast of their means of accomplishing their plans in all parts of Christendom . . ." In the 1850s, a Texas newspaper printed an editorial about how the Pope and the royal families of Europe were plotting the destruction of the government of the United States, and how the "infectious venom" of Catholicism had already infected the White House. In the 1890s, the American Populist Party claimed that a sinister global cabal of gold manipulators was orchestrating world events in order to keep the honest farmers down, arguing that "every device of treachery, every resource of statecraft, and every artifice known to the secret cabals of the international gold ring are being used to deal a blow to the prosperity of the people and the financial and commercial independence of the country."[187] When Hofstadter was writing his essay "The Paranoid Style in American Politics" in the mid-1960s, the Manichean battle was between the capitalist West and the communist Soviet Union. At first glance, this economics-based conflict seems purely secular, missing out on the "demonic" aspect that drives a Manichean worldview, but there was a spiritual aspect to the Cold War. In an attempt to lean into the binary division between the two sides by stressing the difference in the God-fearing West and the atheist Communist Bloc, the Eisenhower government added "In God We Trust" to paper money, and "under God" to the Pledge of Allegiance.[188]

It can't be denied that, during the second half of the 20th century, the Soviet Union was a geopolitical threat to the United States, and to other nations as well. The danger of nuclear war wasn't the imagination of paranoid minds, nor were the tanks that rolled into Prague in 1968. In all of Hofstadter's examples, there is "truth and reality."[189] But Hofstadter stresses the absolutist and apocalyptic framework in which these fears are expressed. It isn't simply that there is a threat. The actions of these groups aren't simply badness, the groups themselves are *evil.* Using the example of the American Anti-Mason movement of the 1820s, Hofstadter writes: "Anti-Masons were not content simply to say that secret societies were rather a bad idea. David Bernard, in the standard handbook of anti-Masonic materials, *Light on Masonry*, declared that Freemasonry was the most dangerous institution that was ever imposed on man, 'an engine of Satan . . . dark, unfruitful, selfish, demoralizing, blasphemous, murderous, anti-republican and anti-Christian.'"[190]

It is extremely tempting to frame a conflict in this manner for four main reasons.

Firstly, it ups the stakes to an absurd extent, since the outcome of the conflict determines whether good or evil triumphs. These increased stakes provide tremendous motivation to those with a Manichean worldview, since nothing is as important as the result of this war. Hofstadter notes this first seductive aspect:

> As a member of the avant-garde who is capable of perceiving the conspiracy before it is fully obvious to an as yet unaroused public, the paranoid is a militant leader. He does not see social conflict as something to be mediated and compromised . . . since what is at stake is always a conflict between absolute good and absolute evil, the quality need is not a willingness to compromise but the will to fight things out to a finish. Nothing but complete victory will do. Since the enemy is thought of as being totally evil and totally unappeasable, he must be totally eliminated.[191]

Just as the demon exorcised by Jesus in the Gospel of Mark can't be reasoned with, the evil faced by the conspiracist is an unredeemable corruptive force that seeks the elimination of everything good and pure.

Secondly, buying into a Manichean system transforms the entire world into a massive battleground, and in the fog of war generated on a battleground, you can't necessarily trust the information you're given. Maybe the mainstream media are actually agents of evil. Maybe "experts" are spreading the disinformation required by their demonic masters to undermine the forces of good. This is tempting because it allows us to exercise confirmation bias by giving us an excuse to ignore any data that contradict our own beliefs.

Thirdly, psychologists have argued that humans prefer that large, dramatic events have large, dramatic causes behind them, rather than randomness and chaos.[192] The Manichean worldview leans into this tendency by making everything a part of a large epic struggle. As discussed in chapter 2, in times of struggle, we are more likely to make connections that aren't really there. The overly simplistic structure provided by a dualistic, black-and-white conflict can be, counterintuitively, soothing to us. Political science professor Michael Barkun argues: "In an odd way, the conspiracy theorist's view is both frightening and reassuring. It is frightening because it magnifies the power of evil, leading in some cases to an outright dualism in which light and darkness struggle for cosmic supremacy. At the same time, however, it is reassuring, for it promises a world that is meaningful rather than arbitrary. Not only are events nonrandom, but the clear identification of evil gives the conspiracist a definable enemy against which to struggle, endowing life with purpose."[193]

Barkun points out that, unlike the structural explanation of badness we examined earlier, a Manichean view of evil lends itself well to conspiracism. Barkun notes that the Manichean worldview encourages three principles that fertilize the conspiracy theory mindset: nothing happens by accident, nothing is as it seems, and everything is connected.[194]

Fourthly, if you see yourself as part of a binary system in a battle against evil, then by definition anything you do must therefore be for the purposes of good. Whatever means (tactics, strategies, techniques) you employ in this battle are justified by the ends (the triumphing of good over evil). We have many examples of where this sort of reasoning can lead. Many of the actual conspiracies of the 20th century (MKUltra, COINTELPRO, etc.) resulted in undeniable and extensive badness. However, because they were all done during the Manichean Cold War, that badness was excused by the people and organizations carrying them out as necessary to fight evil. The lack of nuance encouraged by this belief system amplifies the threat posed by the opposing side while minimizing or ignoring the harm done by the home team.

MODERN MANICHEAN CONSPIRACY MOVEMENTS

The examples Hofstadter provides of this binary worldview demonstrate how easily this perspective can be used to rationalize terrible actions and harmful consequences. However, his examples all still have one foot (or at least a toe) in the world of reality. There really was an 18th-century Illuminati attempting to take over Europe. Royal families and religious institutions really do have an impact on the lives of everyday people. Wealthy investors have manipulated economies, and the Soviet Union really was a clear and present danger.

But several modern examples of Manichean conspiracist movements have much less grounding in truth. One useful example emerges in the United States in the 1990s out of a widespread financial scam that had people sending money wrapped in tinfoil through the mail.

In 1994, Clyde Hood was an electrician in his 60s living in Mattoon, Illinois, who suddenly had a lot of money — millions of dollars — to spend and hand out to his friends. He started buying collectible cars and travelling the world. What was his secret? According to Hood, he had received divine revealed knowledge. God had spoken to him and told him to start an investment firm named Omega Trust and Trading that allowed average, everyday people to gain access to a top secret elite financial system. The plan was simple — since only the super-wealthy could buy into this system, he would take smaller investments from a large number of people, consolidate all of their investments into one large sum, and then use that sum to buy in. He promised his investors that he would be able to turn $100 into $12.5 million in just three years.[195]

Of course, almost none of Hood's more than 10,000 "investors" received even their initial investment back, let alone millions of dollars. There was no secret financial system. And yet, despite the lack of success, people continued to send money to Hood. The money was wrapped in tinfoil to prevent dark forces from intercepting it. Hood had aimed his scheme specifically at evangelical Christian communities,[196] which were primed to accept his Manichean description of the evil forces trying to prevent Omega Trust from fulfilling its promise to investors. One of the thought-terminating clichés used by Hood to convince his religious targets to continue to send him money was "Keep the Lord's warehouse full,"[197] reinforcing the idea that this was a battle between good and evil, and that good needed cash. The Manichean aspect of the Omega Trust scam provided an explanation to Hood's victims as to why their investments hadn't paid off as promised. It wasn't because Hood was a crook, it was because dark forces were mobilizing, secret, and sinister.

After six years and over $12 million of scammed money, Hood and several of his compatriots were arrested. During the trial, Hood admitted that the entire thing had been a long con.[198] Federal authorities seized Hood's assets and set up a fund to help Hood's victims recoup some of their losses, but of the thousands of victims, fewer than 400 people came forward — possibly due to embarrassment, but perhaps because the sunk cost fallacy was preventing them from even acknowledging, despite overwhelming evidence, that they had been scammed at all. Some of Hood's victims even showed up outside the courtroom where Hood was being sentenced to show their support for the man who had swindled them out of their money.[199] Some blamed the evil shapeshifting lizard people that controlled the government for Hood's arrest.[200]

One of Hood's victims took his Manichean money con and ran with it. A resident of Washington State named Shaini Goodwin had sent some foil-wrapped money to Hood in 1998, and after the scam fell apart and Hood was convicted, Goodwin started posting messages to New Age spirituality message boards under the name Dove of Oneness, claiming that she had secret information about the imminent Omega payoff. She also requested donations to continue providing this vital intelligence to her followers. However, after a few years of maintaining her public faith in Omega, Goodwin developed her own Manichean conspiracy. In her version, there was a war between the *white knights* and the *dark agenda*. The white knights had forced the American government (which was under the control of the dark agenda) to pass a bill called NESARA, which stood for National Economic Stabilization and Recovery Act. This bill would remove all personal credit card debt, eliminate income tax and the IRS, and make Goodwin's believers extremely wealthy.[201] As the conspiracy spread, and more people started following Goodwin, she started promising more benefits of NESARA that were just around the corner, including a cure for cancer (that the dark forces were withholding for evil purposes), 90 percent reductions in retail prices, and increased Social Security payments.[202]

The people falling for Goodwin's pitch did so in part because of financial desperation (which is why promises to erase credit card debt and mortgage payments were featured so prominently in Goodwin's claims). Unlike NESARA itself, the desperation felt by its believers was very real. The explanation of the real causes of this desperation would be extremely complicated, having to do with the restructuring of the post-industrial economy, the impact of globalization, banking regulations, demographic changes, tax structures, international trade agreements, changes in workforce demands, and countless other variables. A simple explanation — even an inaccurate one — can be very tempting to people trying to find a reason for their struggles. It's understandable that people bought what Goodwin was selling them.

However, the problem with buying into an inaccurate belief system is that reality has no obligation to conform to people's hopes. Just as the Omega Trust never paid off, the implementation of NESARA never seemed to arrive. But because it was part of a greater Manichean battle between the light and the dark, believers could point to any world event as an explanation for the delay. Goodwin argued, for example, that the September

11 attacks were engineered to prevent the Federal Reserve from putting NESARA into effect.[203]

Just as the Omega Trust scam outlived Hood and evolved into NESARA, so too did NESARA outlive Goodwin (who died in 2010) and become part of a larger meta-conspiracy that would again argue that the world was being fought over by two opposite forces, one good and one evil. That meta-conspiracy is QAnon.

THE WHITE HATS VS. THE BLACK HATS

The QAnon conspiracy belief provides one of the clearest examples of the seductive nature of a Manichean worldview.

As we will discuss again later in the book in the chapter on cognitive dissonance, the poster known as Q first showed up on online message boards making predictions that didn't come true. But regardless of the specific and wildly varying and contradictory claims Q made, one theme ran through all of them: There was an epic battle between good (represented by President Donald J. Trump, who had sacrificed everything in order to bring Christianity, justice, and prosperity back to the United States) and the forces of evil (a rotating cast of characters that could include anyone useful to the narrative, but who were all meant to be Satanic cannibalistic child abusers). In Q drop 4941, on October 30, 2020, Q reposted the entirety of a letter written by Archbishop Carlo Maria Viganò to President Trump. The second paragraph of the letter read: "This historical moment sees the forces of Evil aligned in a battle without quarter against the forces of Good; forces of Evil that appear powerful and organized as they oppose the children of Light, who are disoriented and disorganized, abandoned by their temporal and spiritual leaders."[204] This is a textbook description of the binary Manichean conspiracist view, one that Q was, by reposting the letter, supporting and endorsing.

QAnon was an open-source conspiracy theory — Q would write cryptic posts, and then the Anons (people who followed the Q posts) would try to understand and expand on them. As a form of shorthand, the Anons started referencing the forces of good within the QAnon belief system as the *white hats* and the forces of evil as the *black hats*, in a reference to the simplistic and dualistic morality of old Westerns. In Q drop 4960, on November 7,

2022, Q made a direct reference to the white hats, writing, "Watch carefully. White hats have secured many systems, but problems still remain."[205]

To explore whether QAnon is a Manichean movement, we can apply our four seductive aspects to see if they hold true. An epic battle between good and evil has as its goal the control of the entire world. Do those raised stakes provide immense motivation to the believers of Q? Yes. The Anons who pore over every Q drop and spend hours listening to Q interpreters have done so at a great cost to themselves — broken friendships, estranged families, and the immense opportunity cost of the time spent trying to parse their way through the labyrinthine rabbit hole of the Q conspiracy.

Journalist Mike Rothschild describes the effects of their devotion: "Many profess to spending their every waking hour entirely ensconced in 'research' — rereading Q drops, watching Q videos, listening to Q podcasts and livestreams, and 'digging' to find the connections at which Q only hints. And they confess that they have trouble sleeping when they're not researching. They profess their lack of enjoyment at things they used to love. And they discard anything that doesn't confirm the conspiracy theory."[206] And why wouldn't they? What else could be going on in their life that is as important as the fate of the entire world?

The last sentence in that Rothschild quote leads to the next seductive aspect of Manichean thinking: that in the fog of war generated by the epic battle between good and evil, you must be hypervigilant about not being tricked by incorrect misinformation or deliberate disinformation from the enemy. Unfortunately, because of our tendencies towards confirmation bias, this can mean that the more bought in we are to a worldview, the more vulnerable we are to manipulation by those agents who play into our biases. We can see this in the tremendous variety of outlandish claims that have circulated through the QAnon community — not directly through the Q drops themselves, but through the Q influencers who tell their followers that conventional media and experts are part of the evil agenda, and that only the influencers can truly be trusted. This is how hundreds of Q followers descended on Dallas, Texas, in November of 2021: An influencer who called himself Negative 48 in online forums (actual name Michael Protzman) had told them that he had decoded the Q drops, done a little numerology, and calculated that both John F. Kennedy and John F. Kennedy Jr. were still alive and would be showing up on Dealey Plaza on November 2. The mainstream media would tell you that JFK Sr. was killed in Dallas in 1963 and that JFK Jr. was killed in a plane crash in 1999, but because the mainstream media is a tool of evil, nothing that they say needs to be believed. This frees up a lot of space for new beliefs, and conspiracist influencers are quick to try to fill up that space with their predictions and speculations. Ultimately, neither JFK nor his son showed up, but many of the believers (ignoring the evil media and listening to the good influencers) remained waiting in the plaza for weeks afterwards.[207]

The third seductive aspect is that the Manichean worldview provides a comforting appeal to our desire for large, dramatic events to have large, dramatic, and *deliberate* causes. After a few years lurking in dusty online forums, the QAnon movement fully emerged into the population in 2020, at a time when people were frightened, confused, angry, and frustrated about both the COVID-19 pandemic and the official government response to it. QAnon provided a storyline that, as inaccurate as its predictions were, provided a satisfying explanation to many people who felt their own lives were spinning out of control due to unimaginably vast and obscure forces.

The fourth seductive aspect is the justification of carrying out bad acts in order to fight evil. We have plenty of examples of how Manichean beliefs can contribute to this, from the over 20,000 people murdered in European witch hunts of the 16th and 17th centuries[208] to the American Red Scare trials of the 1950s, to the Chinese Cultural Revolution of the 1960s and '70s, to the invasion of Iraq by American forces in 2003 to combat the "Axis of Evil." Shaini Goodwin may have called herself the Dove of Oneness, but she also fed into her followers' thirst for blood and vengeance, celebrating in a blog post the death of "100,000 bankers"[209] (like most of her claims, this one was not based in reality).

And at the heart of the QAnon movement is a similar bloodlust. Many influencers post lists of specific public figures that should/will be executed. And at the heart of the entire movement is a promise — that a "storm" will come and violently wash away evil using any means necessary. We'll talk more about this storm in the next chapter on millenarianism.

LOOKING FOR EVIL

The 20th century was rich in horror. From the opening genocides carried out by the German state against the Herero people and the Turkish state against the Armenian people, to the Rwandan genocide against the Tutsi as the millennium neared, there was no shortage of human-caused atrocity.

The Holocaust in the early 1940s was a study in industrialized mass murder. Germany, a thoroughly modern country, with safeguards such as an independent judicial system and a free press, had fallen into a racist and fascist regime. Millions of humans were brutally murdered in a twisted attempt to "purify" the German race by eliminating "undesirable" members, which included Jewish people, Romani people, people with mental and physical disabilities, people who had anti-fascist views, and people who today would be considered part of the LGBTQ+ community. The levels of cruelty were unimaginable. It is understandable that someone confronted by this would look to evil, as we have defined it above, as the only possible explanation.

It is very tempting to look to that kind of evil as an explanation of the pain and suffering in the world. It's tidy, and to a degree it shifts responsibility away from ourselves. But the truth is rarely tidy, and the responsibility for the harm that we bring into the world lies with us. Regardless of the degree of badness (and as humans we have achieved a very high degree of badness), there are earthly explanations. And when we go looking for evil, not only can we miss the badness right in front of us, we can — in our zeal and certainty — bring about more badness. In the next chapter, we'll examine another aspect of the conspiracist Manichean worldview as we ask the question: When people believe evil is the cause of suffering, how do they alleviate it? The answer to this question shows one of the dangers of Manichean thinking.

8

CONSPIRACY AND MILLENARIANISM — THE DANGERS OF APOCALYPTIC CULTS

THE CONSPIRATORIAL WORLD

The world that we see through conspiratorial goggles is a terrifying one: Few things happen by chance or coincidence. Evil forces behind the scenes are pulling strings and manipulating the economy, world events, the weather, and pop culture for their own evil purposes. Nothing mainstream can be trusted, since mass media exists only to lull the sheeple into a false reality. No plot is too absurd, no secret plan too sinister.

Because of the mass illusion that deceives most of the population, those in the know are badly outnumbered. To make things worse, they are mocked publicly for trying to free their fellow people from the flickering shadows of the cave. The people that the conspiracist is trying to save are instead holding fast to the poisonous simulation that the evil forces are using to placate and immobilize them.

From a conspiracist perspective, what can be done to make our situation better? Since the mainstream systems and structures surrounding us are part of the evil cabal's plans, the conventional avenues for enacting changes in a democratic society (running for office, voting, advocating for incremental changes in policies and laws) are just window dressing with no real effect in the battle between good and evil. No ordinary solution will have an impact on a cosmic battle.

A more epic and cosmic remedy is required. And, for the conspiratorial mind, a more epic and cosmic remedy is provided.

BACK TO GOOD AND EVIL

While the term *Manichean* is used to describe the dualistic model of good vs. evil, the idea that the world is caught up in the tensions between two opposing forces predates the Manicheans. It is one of the earliest worldviews we can find in human civilization. For example, the ancient Egyptians had a belief system that was centred around Ra, the sun god. Ra was considered wise, just, and incorruptible. Ra was the personification of a concept known as ma'at, which referred to order, righteousness, and justice. Later, Ma'at would be the name of a goddess, who is sometimes referenced as Ra's daughter.[210]

But it was obvious to the ancient Egyptians that the world was not an ordered, righteous, or just place. There were constant dangers: floods, invasions, civil unrest, animal attacks, and famine. There must be an opposing force introducing these elements into Ra's world. That force was called isfet, embodied by the evil serpent god Apophis. This evil force gained prominence in ancient Egyptian culture during the First Intermediate Period (around 2100 BC), at a time of great turmoil and loss of stability in Egyptian society. While Ra was wise and trustworthy, Apophis was chaotic and violent. Lacking sense organs, Apophis couldn't see or hear and was incapable of speech. Instead, the serpent screamed in darkness while trying to prevent the sun from coming up each morning. The rhythms of night and day, weather, and eclipses all provided evidence for the epic struggle between the forces of ma'at and isfet, and it was the duty of each Egyptian to act in such a way that contributed to the stability of the Egyptian state (thereby preventing Apophis from defeating Ra and causing isfet to overcome ma'at). Notes have been discovered in graves of ancient Egyptians in which it is explained that the person in the grave devoted their life to contributing to ma'at and therefore qualified for a comfortable place in the afterlife.

Other ancient cultures, such as the Mesopotamians and the Vedic Indians, had similar dualistic battles as part of their belief systems. But somewhere between 1500 and 600 BC (scholars differ on this point), a new belief system emerged that added a new element to this dualistic struggle — the idea that a reckoning would inevitably come and defeat evil for good. This new belief system was based on the works of the Iranian prophet Zarathustra (aka Zoroaster) who founded the religion Zoroastrianism.[211]

THE END OF THE WORLD

Zoroastrianism, like the belief systems of the ancient Egyptians, Mesopotamians, and Vedic Indians, proposed a dualistic worldview in which there was an epic battle between two opposing sides. In the case of the Zoroastrians, the side of good was referred to as asha, while the opposite side was known as druj. The concept of asha contained the ideas of rightness, proper rituals and behaviour, truth, and order. Druj, meaning "falseness" or "the lie," was the negation of all of those. Asha was personified in the godly figure of Ahura Mazda, while druj was represented by the demonic figure Angra Mainyu.

According to Zoroastrianism, while a person was alive, their actions could either promote asha and support the efforts of Ahura Mazda, or they could promote druj and assist the evil plans of Angra Mainyu. When a person dies, regardless of their sex or their class, their soul is sent to a bridge over an abyss. The people whose actions were more in line with asha cross over into heaven, whereas those whose actions contributed more to druj are plunged into the netherworld to be tormented and tortured.

Zarathustra's writings depicted a time of struggle, in which violence against and persecution of Zarathustra's people were endemic. But this struggle was not an eternal aspect of the world. There was hope on the horizon. There was an event that linear time was moving towards, an event that would perfect the world, eliminate druj forever, and bring about a final judgment. This event was called Frashokereti, or the "making wonderful." During Frashokereti, every soul who had ever existed would return to take part in a massive tribunal, and each person would be confronted with their actions and given their final judgment. The hills and mountains would melt, causing immense rivers of molten lava to run across the landscape, which everyone would be required to walk through. To the people who were in line with asha, the lava would feel no more intense than a nice warm bath, while those judged to be wicked would be burned into oblivion. Then, with the evil finally purged from the world, the righteous (both the dead and the still living) would be returned to a perfect earth: "The 'making wonderful' will indeed change everything. What lies ahead, at the end of time, is a state from which every imperfection will have been eliminated; a world where everyone will live forever in a peace that nothing could disturb; an eternity when history will have ceased and nothing more can happen; a changeless realm, over which the supreme god will reign with an authority which will be unchallenged for evermore."

Remember that description of an event that will "change everything." As we'll see, it repeated many times in many different guises throughout history, in both religious and secular forms. The idea that an event like this is just around the corner has become known as **millennialism** or **millenarianism** because of the version from the book of Revelation in the New Testament. Regardless of the origin, there are a few characteristics that any millenarianist belief possesses: A miraculous event will forever transform the world, after which good will triumph and evil will be vanquished, and the entire community of believers will benefit, rather than just a single person.[212]

THE OLD AND NEW TESTAMENTS

While Frashokereti was one of the earliest examples of the expectation of a great transformative purging event freeing people from difficult conditions, it certainly wouldn't be the last. The Old Testament has passages that suggest at such an event. In the book of Daniel, a potentially prophetic dream is described in which four beasts (representing world powers) would be defeated by a messianic figure, after which that messiah would rule over a just and abundant kingdom. Norman Cohn, a historian of apocalyptic movements, identifies the key themes in the story:

> Already here one can recognize the central phantasy . . . The world is dominated by an evil, tyrannous power of boundless destructiveness — a power moreover which is imagined not as simply human but as demonic. The tyranny of that power will become more and more outrageous, the sufferings of the victims more and more intolerable — until suddenly the

> hour will strike when the Saints of God are able to rise up and overthrow it. Then the Saints themselves, the chosen, holy people who hitherto have groaned under the oppressor's heel, shall in their turn inherit dominion over the whole earth.[213]

Much of the Old Testament features the struggles faced by the Israelites, and the stories in Daniel (and other books that include prophecies, such as Ezekiel and Isaiah) provide comfort to the reader, letting them know that the difficult times they might be facing will eventually be overcome. In Jewish literature from the first century CE, such as the books of Enoch, Isaac, and Ezra, there was a more explicit movement towards the idea that the appearance of the messiah would bring about 1,000 years of peace and prosperity.[214]

Christianity also developed the millenarian idea that the world would soon be perfected and evil eradicated. But for those early Christians, this was not something that would happen sometime in the distant future. In the book of Matthew, Jesus is reported to have said: "Assuredly, I say to you, there are some standing here who shall not taste death till they see the Son of Man coming in His Kingdom." While this line is of course open to various interpretations, it seems to suggest that Jesus was promising a great change in the world within the lifespan of at least some of the people listening to him.

A passage in 1 Thessalonians, attributed to Paul, one of the most influential figures in the formation of the early Christian church, says: "We who are alive, who are left until the coming of the Lord, will not precede those who have fallen asleep. For the Lord himself will descend from heaven with a cry of command, with the voice of an archangel, and with the sound of the trumpet of God. And the dead in Christ will rise first. Then we who are alive, who are left, will be caught up together with them in the clouds to meet the Lord in the air, and so we will always be with the Lord."

Again, while the passage has many possible interpretations, the phrase "we who are alive" suggests that Paul (like Jesus before him) was arguing that this event would happen during the lifetime of himself and others who were alive as he was writing the words. It's also worth noting that this description of the end of days differs from the ones provided in the Old Testament. While the Old Testament predictions concerned what would happen to the political situation on earth (to human bodies), Paul's description involves a transformation in the spirit world (to human souls). Both earthly transformations and spiritual transformations would be part of the apocalyptic narrative going forward, as we'll see in some of our later examples.

THE BOOK OF REVELATION

Arguably the most influential part of the Bible on millenarian beliefs is (appropriately) the final part — the book of Revelation. Written in the first century CE in a poetic and descriptive manner, the book describes a situation that has been variously interpreted by scholars and other readers as occurring in the author's past, present, and future (or a combination of all three). The situation described in Revelation includes the lead-up to the final epic battle between the forces of good and evil, the battle itself, and its aftermath.

The book of Revelation is a letter written by an early Christian who goes by the name John, and it is written for the congregations of seven early Christian churches. It is a kind of writing known as an *apocalypse* (from the Greek word apokalypsis), which means *unveiling* or *uncovering*.[215] And, according to John, what was unveiled was a vision in which Jesus explains to him how God's plan is to be fulfilled.

First, Satan (in the form of a great red dragon with seven heads) knocks the stars from the sky with his massive tail. Then Satan attempts to eat the newborn baby of a "woman clothed with the sun with the moon under her feet," but the child is saved by God, and the woman flees into the wilderness. An epic battle begins in heaven between the Satan-dragon and God's angels. Satan and his demons lose the battle and are cast down to earth, whereupon he continues his pursuit of the woman clothed with the sun, who has been given a pair of eagle's wings to help her escape. Satan becomes furious and wages war against the rest of her offspring.

After Satan is thrown from the heavenly realm to ours, he summons two terrible beasts — one from the sea, and one from the bowels of the earth.

The metaphorical nature of the book of Revelation is what gives it so much of its rhetorical power; the images (dragons, monsters, violence, fire, etc.) are vivid and startling, which makes them memorable. However, this also means that the work must be analyzed, and since so few people are familiar with the book's historical context, our own context is often superimposed over top. Modern-day people become convinced that this 2,000-year-old piece of writing must be about *us* and our modern situation. From a historical perspective, the woman and her children represent the Christian messiah and his followers, the pursuing of the woman by the dragon likely represents persecution of the early Christian church, and the terrible beasts are almost certainly a reference to the military and economic might of the Roman Empire (the superpower with which the author John would have been most familiar).[216] However, the description could apply to any superpower, past, present, or future.

Now trapped on earth, the beasts are joined by a figure known as "the false prophet," and they raise an army to fight against the true believers. To combat them, Jesus returns on a white horse to lead his followers. A massive battle is joined in Armageddon (likely referring to the ancient Palestinian city of Megiddo), and the beasts and the false prophet are defeated, captured, and thrown into a lake of fire.[217] The humans who supported them are butchered, and their corpses are torn apart by birds. Anyone who has received the mark of the false prophet (666) on their hands or foreheads will receive eternal torment.

Finally, Satan himself (representing all evil, misfortune, and injustice) is banished for 1,000 years, during which time anyone who stayed true to their Christian beliefs is rewarded for their faith, including the executed martyrs, who are resurrected and returned to the earthly paradise. During that millennium, the world is ruled by Jesus Christ and his supporters. Finally, after his exile, Satan returns with an army composed of the enemies of Christianity, who are then destroyed by heavenly fire. The Last Judgment follows, and it is similar to the Zoroastrian Frashokereti: Anyone whose name does not appear on the "roll of the living" is thrown into a lake of fire forever. After this, time has reached its end, and history has been completed.[218]

The book of Revelation illustrates many of the key attributes of millenarian beliefs. There is a cosmic Manichean battle between good and evil, with people divided on either side. The ones who side with good are persecuted but eventually victorious. There is a predestined conclusion that all of history is inexorably moving towards, and there are signs and symbols that can be deciphered as guideposts to show how far along we are in the process. There is a tension between the ideal world that we are meant to live in and the corrupted world of today. There are personifications of good and evil (in the forms of a messiah and a false prophet). There is a battle, and a purifying moment in which the evil is burned away (often, and in this case, literally). Then, those who held fast to their beliefs are rewarded and can live in an unchanging paradise for the rest of time. We will see these attributes repeated in many movements throughout history, including some modern versions.

MILLENARIAN BELIEF IN ACTION

Regardless of whether we are talking about a religious system or a pop culture extended universe, we refer to the "official" story as **canon**. People within any group of believers will have different perspectives, but canon is a top-down decision on what should be accepted and what shouldn't. The creation of canon within any organization is a complicated procedure that involves in-fighting, arguments, and politics. It is also a process that remains ongoing throughout the existence of any belief system.

By the fifth century CE, the Catholic church was well into the process of creating its canon, and one of the most influential figures was the Roman philosopher Augustine of Hippo. In his work *The City of God*, written in the early fifth century, Augustine established several key concepts that would enter the Catholic canon, including ideas about good and evil, demons, morality, the afterlife, and the role of the church in politics. Augustine also addressed the meaning of the book of Revelation, arguing that it was not meant to be taken literally as millenarian map to the end of the world, but instead should be taken as a metaphorical description of the spiritual battle between good and evil. In 431, the church declared millenarian beliefs as superstitious and incorrect.[219]

However, although canon is generally shaped from the top down by the leaders, belief systems can develop differently in the population. Millenarian beliefs are very tempting, since they promise control and order in the world and give people hope that the difficult times they are living through will not last forever. Since there is rarely a shortage of difficult times, there is rarely a shortage of millenarian beliefs, and rarely a shortage of people claiming to be messianic figures to capitalize on those beliefs.

Éon de l'Étoile was a 12th-century French noble who proclaimed himself Son of God and built up a violent following of supporters who moved from province to province causing chaos and death. While Éon's horde benefited materially from the destruction through looting and theft, the alleged justification for the killing was the belief that the victims were on the side of the Antichrist and Satan. Their deaths were necessary to bring about the Millennium.

When Éon was finally taken prisoner by authorities, he argued that he would not be judged. Rather, he was the one who had come to bring about the final judgment. But instead of this occurring, he was starved to death in a prison cell, and his most fervent followers were burned at the stake, crying out for the world to end as they were led to their deaths.

Similar arguments were made during the Crusades to justify massacres of people who practiced Islam or Judaism. As Norman Cohn writes, "In the eyes of the crusading *pauperes* the smiting of the Moslems and the Jews was to be the first act in that final battle which . . . was to culminate in the smiting of the Prince of Evil himself. Above these desperate hordes, as they moved about their work of massacre, there loomed the figure of Antichrist."[220]

The violent imagery of the book of Revelation was inflicted in real life on communities that were thought to be standing in the way of the realization of the glorious Millennium. Even clearly immoral acts (robbery, murder, sexual assault, etc.), if they were done for the alleged purpose of bringing about the End of Days, could be considered not only guiltless but holy.

Because of the importance of vaguely defined figures who played vital roles in Revelation, it was common for people to see contemporary figures in those roles. For example, the 13th-century Holy Roman Emperor Frederick II of what is now called Germany appeared to many German believers to fulfill the characteristics of the messiah who would bring about the End Times and usher in the millennium. But to many Italian believers, he appeared to possess qualities that would suggest he was, in fact, the Antichrist. When Frederick II died in 1250 without revealing himself as either the messiah *or* the Antichrist, believers on both sides were disappointed. This disappointment made believers more vulnerable to being scammed when, around 1280, a man claimed to be the resurrected body of Frederick II. The man gathered a following and demanded that King Rudolf recognize his legitimacy, but instead the king had the man burnt at the stake. The imposter went to his fiery death promising to return in three days, and another man in another area of Germany did come forward claiming to be the resurrected body of the resurrected body of Frederick II. He was also executed. All these claims and executions resulted in the spread of the belief in Frederick's resurrection — rumours of which continued into the 14th century.

It's important to note here that people who hold millenarian beliefs don't always just sit back and wait for the apocalypse to happen. They don't even sit passively and look for signs to help them predict the date when it will happen. Often, people will take deliberate action with the goal of *bringing about* the end of the world. For an example of this, we can look to what happened in the German town of Münster in the mid-16th century.

MÜNSTER AND THE LAST DAYS

At the beginning of 1534, a Dutch baker named Jan Matthys arrived in Münster. By that point, Christianity in Western Europe had split into Catholicism and Protestantism, and Protestantism itself had split into several different sects. Matthys belonged to the Anabaptist movement (a radical subdivision of Protestantism) and argued to the people of the town that the machinery of the Millennium had to be oiled with the blood of the unrighteous. His ideas caught on in Münster, particularly as he argued that the town would become the centre of the apocalyptic events, and Anabaptists from hundreds of miles around relocated there for a front-row seat to the End Times.[221] The people of Münster may have been more receptive to Matthys's message because of local economic and political strife, as well as increased crop failures and the recent outbreak of the Black Death.[222]

Once he had influence over the town, Matthys advised executing all the non-Anabaptists to purify Münster in preparation for the events of the book of Revelation, but he was convinced to allow them to be expelled from the town instead. Sensing a threat to his power, Prince-Bishop Franz von Waldeck ordered Münster to be surrounded by troops and sieged until the Anabaptist rebellion was crushed. Meanwhile, inside the city walls the apocalyptic rebels prepared for war, and some who spoke out against Matthys were publicly murdered.

In a situation like this, it is reasonable to ask a question: Does the leader of the movement really believe in their own message, or are they simply lying in order to manipulate a population? There are plenty of historical examples of each, and some that are a combination of the two. In the case of Matthys, it is likely that he believed his own messianic claims, as after a prophetic dream in which he saw himself leading a small group of fighters to defeat the bishop's army and break the siege, he attempted to do just that and was instead butchered by the mercenaries waiting outside the city walls.

Rather than abandoning the apocalyptic beliefs, the people of Münster replaced Matthys with his apprentice Jan Bockelson, who became an even more extreme apocalyptic messiah than Matthys. He ran through the city naked in a religious fervour before falling into a prophetic trance to determine what course the city should take. Under the rule of Bockelson, the sieged city passed radical new laws to help bring about the End Times, including establishing mandatory polygamy and making the punishment for any insubordination death. A massive throne was erected in the marketplace, and Bockelson would sit on it, dressed in the finest robes and jewelry, to pass new city ordinances. However, living conditions in the blockaded city were becoming increasingly grim, to the point that the citizens of Münster were forced to eat rats, mice, and human corpses to survive.[223] Bockelson promised his beleaguered followers that salvation would arrive by Easter or he would allow himself to be burned in the public square. When Easter came and went without salvation appearing, Bockelson claimed that the salvation had been a spiritual, rather than a physical one. He claimed that God would turn the stones in the city to bread, which also didn't happen.

In June 1535, the bishop's soldiers were able to enter the city and massacre the remaining Anabaptists. Bockelson was captured and held in chains, and then eventually tortured to death with red-hot irons. The End Times remained elusive.

20TH-CENTURY SECULAR MILLENARIAN MOVEMENTS

The first half of the 20th century saw the birth of two of the most destructive ideologies in human history: Nazism and Soviet communism. While the two movements were diametrically opposed in some ways, they shared body counts in the millions of humans, and each of them derived energy and justification from millenarianism.

As we have seen, there was already a centuries-rich history of millenarianism in Germany before the Nazis emerged as a political force in the 1930s. However, unlike those earlier millenarian movements, Nazism wasn't overtly Christian. While the Nazis did use some Christian imagery and language to help manipulate a population that was still attached to traditional religion, the ideology drew from many different sources, including occult and esoteric beliefs such as the existence of Atlantis and other lost civilizations, to create a new form of spirituality based on force and violence.[224]

While the lines of Christian Manicheanism were drawn in the cosmic battle between God and Satan, Nazi Manicheanism drew its lines based on unscientific concepts of "purity of race." On one side, the "Aryan race" (based on flawed misunderstandings of genetics and mythology) represented the elect who would transform the world into a paradise, and the evil to be eliminated included anyone who didn't fit into that artificial and absurd category.[225] This worldview was reinforced by the spread of books such as *The Protocols of the Elders of Zion*.[226] It was literally a millennial movement, as can be seen clearly in a *New York Times* newspaper article from September 5, 1934, that reported, "Chancellor Adolf Hitler today proclaimed the arrival of the Nazi millennium, predicting that the next 1,000 years would not witness another revolution in Germany . . . 'National socialism as a world philosophy is not only the expression of a political system and reform of the State, but also of a reshaping of personal, communal and cultural life,' he asserted."[227]

The moment that would bring on this millennium involved both the burning of books to rid the society of impure ideas and beliefs, and the burning of millions of humans to rid the world of the corrupting influence of impure humanity. Rather than lasting 1,000 years, however, the Nazi millennium was reduced to rubble in less than a dozen years.

Lasting a few decades longer was Soviet communism. While Nazism still had some lingering superstitious aspects, Soviet communism was firmly and resolutely atheist in its outlook, but it looked towards a Marxist utopian millennium in which the New Soviet Man would emerge with "nerves of steel" and "muscles like iron nails" and total dedication to the reproduction of the socialist Soviet state.[228] It wasn't a supernatural being guiding the Soviets to their earthly paradise, but instead a force of history as promised by Marx and Engels. It wasn't just the communists who had an economic-based millennium to look towards, of course. After the collapse of the Soviet Union in 1991, there were influential thinkers in the capitalist West who argued that the apparent end of the Cold War represented the beginning of a capitalist millennium. Francis Fukuyama, in his book *The End of History and the Last Man*, wrote:

> What we may be witnessing is not just the end of the Cold War, or the passing of a particular period of postwar history, but the end of history as such: that is, the end point of mankind's ideological evolution and the universalization of Western liberal democracy as the final form of human government. This is not to say that there will no longer be events to fill the pages of *Foreign Affairs* yearly summaries of international relations, for the victory of liberalism has occurred primarily in the realm of ideas or consciousness and is as yet incomplete in the real or material world. But there are powerful reasons for believing that it is the ideal that will govern the material world *in the long run.*[229]

Fukuyama's prediction proved no more accurate than any of the millennial predictions that had come before it.

NEW RELIGIOUS MOVEMENTS AND MILLENARIANISM

Many modern conspiracy theories have drawn from millenarian traditions. However, unlike political ideologies and organized religions, which draw from canonical texts and sometimes centuries of tradition, New Religious Movements (NRMs, sometimes referred to as cults) don't have long histories to which to conform, and so are more flexible and fluid. This can be seen in the millenarian aspects of NRMs, which can combine supernatural and secular concepts into a complex and sometimes even contradictory belief system.

The Church Universal and Triumphant (CUT) combined the theosophical writings of 19th-century occultist Helena Blavatsky (who wrote about lost continents, hidden enlightened masters, and revealed knowledge), the Bible, and UFO beliefs. The leader of the movement, Elizabeth Clare

Prophet, declared that there was an epic struggle between good and evil (represented in this case by the "Capitalist-Communist Conspiracy" and the Illuminati) and that the world would end in a nuclear war. However, the members of CUT would survive the firestorm in bunkers and emerge into a new world. In March 1993, thousands of CUT believers, many of whom had given their life savings to the group in order to fund the construction of the shelters, fled underground to wait out the imminent apocalypse. The apocalypse did not arrive, and the CUT members emerged back out into the same world again.[230]

Other groups take a more active role in the end of the world. A tragic example of this is a movement led by Bonnie Nettles and Marshall Applewhite in the U.S. in the '70s. Human Individual Metamorphosis, or HIM, was another combination of biblical, theosophical, New Age, and UFO-related beliefs. These belief systems are all different, and in some cases contradictory, but they overlap in the idea that this world has a veil that separates us from a greater truth — whether that truth is about a prophecy, an ascension to a greater consciousness, or aliens.

Drawing from the book of Revelation, Nettles and Applewhite declared themselves to be the witnesses referenced in Revelation 11:3 who would be granted heavenly authority to prophesy for 1,260 days. Their prophecy was a millenarian one: The earth was about to be "recycled" so that the corruption and evil could be eliminated and replaced with a new Eden.[231] Only those who followed the words of Nettles and Applewhite would be spared this imminent catastrophe by being rescued in a flying saucer sent by evolved humanoid aliens. Government officials and scientists worldwide knew the truth about all of this but were keeping it from the public out of fear that people wouldn't be able to handle it.[232]

After several failed prophecies about when the flying saucer would arrive, and after Nettles died of cancer and was not (as promised) resurrected three days later, the group largely maintained their faith.[233] In March 1997, with the group now renamed Heaven's Gate, 39 members (identically dressed in what they called their away team uniforms) took their own lives through a combination of drug overdose and asphyxiation. Most of the dead members left video recordings expressing how excited they were to be escaping the tainted earth and their bodily prisons by evolving and reincarnating to the next spiritual level.[234]

While the members of Heaven's Gate tried to purify earthly corruption from within by shedding their earthly forms, two years earlier, in Japan, the group Aum Shinrikyō had attempted to purify earthly corruption from without by actively bringing about the apocalypse.

Led by self-proclaimed guru Shōkō Asahara (born Chizuo Matsumoto), Aum Shinrikyō had an apocalyptic belief system that drew from the book of Revelation, Hinduism, Buddhism, Zoroastrianism, the French prophet Nostradamus, and even Japanese manga such as the animated television series *Space Battleship Yamato*.[235] However, unlike CUT, who were waiting for the purifying moment to occur, and Heaven's Gate, who attempted to purify themselves through the destruction of their own bodies, Aum Shinrikyō planned to purify the rest of the world in a fiery act of destruction. This attitude of taking a more active role in the end times is known as *forcing the end*.[236] Asahara promoted a Manichean battle between good (followers of Asahara — or to be more specific, only Asahara himself and his clones) and evil (Freemasons, secret Jewish cabals, and the CIA).[237] Aum's apocalypse was to be a nuclear Armageddon that would cleanse the Earth of the impure through radioactive fire, and it would be brought about by Aum itself. Under Asahara's orders, his scientists manufactured and stockpiled chemical and biological weapons and were working towards the ultimate goal of creating nuclear arms.[238]

The justification for the annihilation of most of the life on Earth was a religious one. Based on a radical interpretation of the Buddhist concept of phowa, a ritual used in some Buddhist traditions to transfer the consciousness of a dying person to the afterlife, Asahara argued that the elimination of the impure masses was a kind of mercy killing, preventing the accumulation of bad karma that would be inevitable in a world dominated by evil.[239] In other words, the Manichean and millenarian beliefs of Asahara were used to justify mass murder.

Aum didn't succeed in producing and deploying nuclear weapons, although they did launch deadly attacks using sarin gas on a residential neighbourhood in 1994 and the Tokyo subway system in 1995 that resulted in 20 fatalities and thousands of injuries. They attempted to release anthrax and botulinum toxin several times. All for the purpose of forcing the End Times into existence.[240]

CONSPIRACISM AND MILLENARIANISM

Not every conspiracy theory involves millenarian beliefs, and not all millenarian beliefs are conspiratorial. However, all-encompassing conspiracist worldviews that involve a Manichean system of good and evil lend themselves to millenarianism, since evil can't be defeated through conventional means.

For example, the NESARA movement we discussed in the previous chapter includes a millenarian aspect, in that believers are awaiting a moment when NESARA is enacted, resulting in a complete overturning of the old system and the dawning of a new age, free from credit card debt, financial manipulation and exploitation, poverty, and even physical illness.

The QAnon belief system demonstrates the clearest example of the relationship between conspiracism and millenarianism, as well as the clearest example of the potential consequences of this relationship. The moment of "making wonderful" for the QAnon community is the Storm, and like many millenarian events, it is predicted to purify the world of evil through an act of extreme violence.

As discussed earlier in the book, the QAnon movement is a Manichean belief system in which the good is represented by the American military, which arranged to have Donald Trump elected in the 2016 election in order to start a series of events that would lead to the extermination of evil, in the form of Democratic politicians, Hollywood celebrities, and wealthy Jewish families (all of whom are secretly cannibalistic Satanist child abusers).[241] On October 5, 2017, during a photo op at the White House, President Trump stood alongside several military commanders. While posing for pictures, Trump said to the press: "You guys know what this represents? Maybe it's the calm before the storm." When asked by the press what he meant by that remark, Trump refused to provide an answer. Political analysts speculated that it was a reference to an upcoming war with North Korea, or perhaps Iran.[242]

After the cryptic comments, an anonymous commenter on the 4chan message board started predicting Hillary Clinton's imminent arrest in a thread titled "Calm Before the Storm." The list of people who were about to be arrested started to swell, aided both by vague posts by Q and by the legions of Q followers and influencers. The Storm began to take shape as an event in a series of posts in November 2017:

> My fellow Americans, over the course of the next several days you will undoubtedly realize that we are taking back our great country (the land of the free) from the evil tyrants that wish to do us harm and destroy the last remaining refuge of shining light . . . Public riots are being organized in serious numbers in an effort to prevent the arrest and capture of more senior public officials. On POTUS' order, a state of temporary military control will be actioned and special ops carried out. False leaks have been made to retain several within the confines of the United States to prevent extradition and special operator necessity. Rest assured, the safety and well-being of every man, woman, and child of this country is being exhausted in full. However, the atmosphere within the country will unfortunately be divided as so many have fallen for the corrupt and evil narrative that has long been broadcast. We will be initiating the Emergency Broadcast System . . . during this time in an effort to provide a direct message (avoiding the fake news) to all citizens. Organizations and/or people that wish to do us harm during this time will be met with swift fury — certain laws have been pre-lifted to provide our great military the necessary authority to handle and conduct these operations (at home and abroad) . . . It is time to take back our country and make America great again. Let us salute and pray for the brave men and women in uniform who will undertake this assignment to bring forth peace, unity, and return power to the people.[243]

Rather than a choir of angels, or a blast from heavenly horns, the Storm would be heralded by an announcement from the Emergency Broadcast System (a system that had been replaced by the Emergency Alert System in 1997).[244] This would begin the systematic elimination, through public executions, of the cannibal cabal that had corrupted the world.

Pivotal to the concept of the Storm, and limiting the time period in which it could occur, was the need for Donald Trump to be commander-in-chief. When Trump lost the 2020 presidential election, there was a crisis among believers in the Storm. This contributed to the events of January 6, 2020, when thousands of supporters of Donald Trump (many of whom were wearing Q T-shirts and carrying Q flags) attempted to force the end by storming the Capitol Building to prevent the entirely symbolic vote count that would establish Joe Biden as the new president. When that was unsuccessful, a rumour began circulating in the Q community that Biden had to be sworn in *before* the storm could start, and so, seconds after his inauguration on January 20, 2020, he (and the rest of the evil cabal) would be taken into custody. When that didn't happen either, the Q community started claiming that the "real" inauguration wasn't on January 20 at all, but on March 4.[245] March 4 also came and went without Trump returning to power, and without the Storm washing away evil and ushering in a golden age that would feature a Great Awakening of the masses. Over 30 million Americans[246] were forced to confront a difficult discrepancy between what they believed was supposed to happen and what they witnessed with their own eyes.

Even after Trump was re-elected in 2024, the promised millenarian moment of the Storm did not arrive. On the contrary, many conspiratorial influencers were surprised and disappointed when, in the summer of 2025, the Trump administration asserted that the billionaire child trafficker Jeffrey Epstein had died by his own hand and had not been murdered, as many people believed, and that there was no client list of famous people that could serve as a guidebook for rounding up the evil ones in the first wave of the Storm.[247]

THE END OF DAYS

We live in a flawed world in which the distribution of punishment and reward often appears random and arbitrary, and justice is hard to come by. This makes it tempting to believe in a system in which, regardless of how things are going, there is a secret plan, made by people or beings far wiser and more powerful than us, that ensures good triumphs and evil is vanquished.

The tendencies that contribute to a conspiratorial mindset — including patternicity and Manichean thinking — all make it more likely that a person is tempted by the seduction of millenarianism. The agents behind the plan (messiahs, gods, aliens, gurus) and the content of the millenarian moment (fire, flood, mass murder, flying saucer, rapture) may differ, but the underlying drive for a world that makes sense remains the same.

As seen in the example of Heaven's Gate, millenarian thinking can pose a danger to the believers themselves, and as seen in the examples of Aum Shinrikyō, Nazi Germany, and Stalinist Russia, it can pose a clear and present danger to society in general.

There is another serious consequence of millenarian thinking. Throughout history, countless movements have predicted a moment in which everything would change: The old world would burn away and be replaced by a paradise. One thing they all have in common is that, at least so far, every one of them has been incorrect. What happens to a person when their most cherished beliefs don't match up with what they see? To answer that question, we'll need to look at the concept of cognitive dissonance.

9

COGNITIVE DISSONANCE — WHAT HAPPENS WHEN THE FLYING SAUCER DOESN'T LAND

INTRODUCTION TO DISSONANCE

If someone is sure they will be saved by a flying saucer while the world drowns in a flood. what happens to them when neither of those things occurs? What happens to a group of researchers when their theory doesn't match up to their observations?

We are flawed beings existing in a messy world. There is a complicated and often inconsistent relationship between our perceptions, our beliefs, our knowledge, and our actions. For example, Caleb might observe the way that pigs behave, and from those observations form the very reasonable belief that pigs are intelligent, sentient beings that can feel pain. He might also have the knowledge that pigs are butchered in slaughterhouses, which would certainly *cause* them great pain. He might also have the belief that causing pain in a sentient animal is wrong. He might also find ham delicious and might often eat bacon. His action of eating bacon doesn't comfortably sit with his beliefs regarding pigs and pain and his knowledge of slaughterhouses. So what is he supposed to do about this inconsistency?

If we had direct access to reality, and our actions were completely in line with our beliefs, we wouldn't encounter this sort of problem. Instead, our senses would give us an unfiltered and unbiased understanding of the world, free of the sorts of distortions that we have discussed in other chapters. We would then build accurate knowledge from these clear perceptions and form beliefs based on that factually correct knowledge. Our actions would then be perfectly in line with our beliefs, which would have a strong foundation of authentic knowledge, which would be drawn from our crystal-clear perceptions of the world.

This isn't what we do, of course. Instead, as we have discussed in earlier chapters, our perceptions are greatly influenced by our beliefs. What we *expect* to see changes what we *do* see. Our knowledge is incomplete and biased, based on flawed perceptions of an external world that often resists our attempts to understand it. And rather than letting our beliefs drive our actions, we sometimes tailor our beliefs to fit in better with the actions we have already taken so that we can retroactively justify them.

But there is a psychological price that we must pay for all of these cognitive shenanigans. When our perceptions, beliefs, knowledge, and/or actions are internally inconsistent, we may experience a condition known as **cognitive dissonance**. This concept was pioneered by the controversial American social psychologist Leon Festinger in the 1950s.

CONSONANCE AND DISSONANCE

Here's how dissonance works. According to Festinger, our individual thoughts and experiences are either relevant to each other or irrelevant to each other.[248] Angela's experience that she enjoys chocolate ice cream, for example, isn't relevant to her belief that JFK was assassinated by the CIA. Eating ice cream has nothing to do with presidential assassinations. But her experience of enjoying ice cream *is* relevant to her action of buying ice cream at the store, because enjoying ice cream is what motivates that action. Her experience in this case lines up with her behaviour. Meanwhile, her knowledge that too much sugar is bad for a person's health is relevant to but *inconsistent with* her action of buying ice cream. It's relevant because ice cream contains a lot of sugar, but inconsistent because she is making a choice that her own knowledge would suggest she shouldn't make.

When thoughts and experiences are relevant to each other, they are forced to be in relation with each other. There are two ways in which they can be in relation: They can be either internally consistent or internally inconsistent. If they are consistent, there's no problem. They line up appropriately with each other, and it is a simple matter to keep both of them in your mind at the same time without friction. For example, Angela's experience of enjoying ice cream matches up very well with her action of purchasing ice cream at the store. Why is she buying it? Because she enjoys the taste of it. There is no contradiction there, or inconsistency. When we see this trouble-free consistency, we say that these thoughts or actions are in **consonance**, like two musical notes that harmonize. For example, Afsana's heliocentric belief that the world is a sphere that spins on its axis and orbits the sun is in consonance with her knowledge that there are different time zones around the world, since that is exactly what's predicted by the hypothesis that the world is a spinning sphere that only faces the sun on one half at any given moment. When Afsana stands at the edge of the ocean and watches a ship dip down below the horizon, that observation is in consonance with her belief that the Earth's surface is curved. No tension there.

However, the same can't be said of Angela's action of buying ice cream and her knowledge that too much sugar is bad for a person. Here there is an inconsistency — why should she be buying and consuming something that she knows is bad for her? Dentist bills are expensive. Ice cream contains lots of calories that she would be better off getting from foods with more nutritional value. When we encounter this sort of friction, we say that these thoughts or actions are in *dissonance*. For example, Melanie's geocentric belief that the world is flat is in dissonance with her knowledge that there are different time zones around the world, since the flat world hypothesis doesn't predict that there should be time zones and has a lot of difficulty explaining it. When Melanie stands beside Afsana by the ocean and watches the same ship dip down below the horizon, that observation is an uncomfortable one for Melanie. Why should the bottom of the ship be concealed by the water while the top of the ship is still visible? That doesn't fit in with Melanie's idea of a flat Earth.

Festinger argues that this experience of dissonance is unpleasant.[249] It's a sensation that encourages the person experiencing it to take action to reduce or eliminate it — just as the unpleasant experience of thirst encourages a person to drink water. A thirsty person will take a drink, but what will the person in a state of cognitive dissonance do? If we were completely rational creatures, we would adjust our perceptions, beliefs, and actions so that they were in greater consonance with each other and with our experiences.

After thinking about time zones and watching a ship sink down over the horizon, Melanie *should* reconsider her belief in the flat Earth and change her belief system to one that is in greater consonance with her knowledge and observations. However, as we have seen repeatedly, that isn't necessarily how we roll. And there are several reasons why.

SUNK COST FALLACY

Part of the reason why we don't simply change our beliefs when we encounter dissonance has to do with how we react to the concept of investment. Let's look at an example from the world of finance.

Imagine Jeremy has invested $10,000 in a stock in the hopes that it'll go up and make him a tidy profit. However, as the weeks go by, he sees in the newspaper that the stock price is starting to fall. His $10,000 initial investment is now only worth $9,000. All signs suggest the stock is going to fall even more — should he bail out and recoup what's left of his investment?

While that might be the financially prudent thing to do, we often pay more attention to what we have already put into something than to what we stand to lose by staying in it. Rather than thinking "I should get out so I can at least keep the $9,000 I have left," Jeremy thinks, "I can't bail out now — if I do, then I've lost $1,000." He's trying to protect his lost $1,000 instead of his remaining $9,000, even though $9,000 is obviously more important to protect than $1,000.

And it might not just be the financial loss that Jeremy's worried about. He might have even more invested in that stock than he realizes — including some of his self-image. If he thinks of himself as a savvy investor, or if he bragged to other people that he was going to make a fortune on this stock, or if he got into an argument about it with another investor whom he considers to be less intelligent than he is, then it isn't just money that he stands to lose. He's also going to lose face.

If Jeremy stands by his bad bet because of what he has already invested in it, rather than getting out because of what he can still salvage, he has fallen victim to the **sunk cost fallacy**.

Now, let's apply this to a conspiracy theory example. Melanie doesn't just believe in the idea that the world is flat; she is part of a community of people who believe the world is flat, and this community forms a significant portion of her social group. She has devoted hundreds of hours to watching videos promoting Flat Earth theory. Her belief has alienated her from non-believers, and she has lost some friends and family members over it. She has argued with people about the shape of the world, and some of those arguments have become quite heated and emotional.

As Melanie watches that ship disappear over the horizon, she has a lot invested in her Flat Earth belief. If she bails out now, she might lose a lot of her social group that believes in the flat Earth. This is particularly important, since she has already lost a lot of people from her social group that *don't* believe in the flat Earth. If she lets go of her Flat Earth belief, all those hours spent watching Flat Earth videos would change from being valuable and educational time well spent to being a complete waste. Those angry, heated arguments would be lost, and she would have to admit to people who mocked her for her beliefs that they were right and she was wrong. Rather than seeing herself as a shrewd customer who sees the truth that most people miss, she would have to see herself as someone who became caught up in a ridiculous belief system.

That is a lot of powerful motivation to not change her beliefs. But when faced with obviously dissonant information, how can a person avoid changing their minds?

HOW WE AVOID DISSONANCE

There are two main strategies that we employ when we're trying to minimize dissonance. We can seek out consonant information, or we can avoid dissonant information.

In the case of Melanie trying to protect her sunk cost in the Flat Earth theory, after watching the ship dip down below the horizon she could seek the company of her fellow believers. By surrounding herself with people who share her belief, she strengthens her confidence in that belief through the **bandwagon effect**. After all, if other people believe it, it must be correct. They might also be able to provide her with a justification for the dissonant observation. Maybe large bodies of water curve light, which only makes it *appear* that the ship was slipping below the horizon. Maybe the ship was sinking. The explanations might sound weak, but they don't have to bear up under scrutiny if they aren't being scrutinized.

In addition, by immersing herself in a community of like-believers, Melanie is less likely to come across other dissonant information, since the other believers will also be trying to minimize their own dissonance.

Using a combination of various motivated reasoning techniques — for example, *avoidance* or *biased* assimilation — a person can minimize the dissonance they experience when they face a contradiction. Melanie could simply go out of her way to avoid encountering information that doesn't sit well with her beliefs, but if she does encounter threatening information that causes dissonance, she could interpret it in such a way that it isn't as challenging. Let's say she comes across a NASA photograph of the Earth taken from space, and she reads that it's a composite image, put together from many other images. Rather than thinking "that's so the photograph will look more attractive and presentable," she could think "that's because NASA needs to use photo trickery to try to hide the fact that the Earth is flat."

And, if these sorts of strategies aren't enough and it becomes absolutely necessary, we can change our beliefs and actions to become consonant with new observations or knowledge. But what about when the contradiction is so glaringly obvious and unavoidable that these techniques won't work, *and* the belief being challenged is so fundamental to our identity that to change it is inconceivable? To answer that question, Festinger explored some case studies.

To find the right combination of sincerely held beliefs coming up against demonstrably dissonant observations, Festinger examined examples of failed prophecies.

A **prophecy** is different than a guess or a prediction. A guess is just idle speculation that isn't based on much more than a hunch or a hope. A person doesn't have much invested in a guess, and when a guess turns out to be wrong, there's no reason to do any deep soul searching. A prediction is more careful and considered than a guess, and it is normally based on observed patterns and known facts that are then extrapolated into the future. However, when a prediction turns out to be wrong, it's a fairly simple matter to tell yourself that you didn't have all the facts, or that there was some unexpected variable that changed the outcome that you were expecting.

A prophecy is a very different thing. Whereas a guess comes from a hunch and a prediction comes from observation and analysis, a prophecy comes from **revealed knowledge**.

A person making a prediction may claim to have keen insight or a strong grasp of the situation. But a prophet is making a much weightier claim — that they have received knowledge directly from some sort of supernatural and all-knowing entity (a god, alien being, ghost, spirit, etc.). The prophet claims to be a vessel or conduit through which the divine knowledge can make its way out into the mundane world. And that knowledge, like the being that has communicated it to the prophet, must be perfect (although it can sometimes be open to interpretation).

An incorrect guess can be brushed off, and an incorrect prediction may be professionally or personally embarrassing but not catastrophic, but an incorrect prophecy suggests that the person who made it is a false prophet. This is certainly a problem for the prophet, but also for the prophet's followers, who likely have a great deal of sunk cost invested in the prophet's claims.

Finding examples of failed prophecies wasn't difficult for Festinger and his colleagues. The 15th and 16th centuries are filled with them — many of them apocalyptic or messianic visions that didn't come true. However, Festinger wanted more modern examples so that the researchers could have more confidence in the accuracy of the reporting. One famous example of a more modern failed prophecy comes from 19th-century America — the Millerites and the "Great Disappointment."

THE GREAT DISAPPOINTMENT

In New York State, a preacher named William Miller, after a close reading of the book of Daniel, had concluded that the end of the world prophesized in the Bible could possibly occur sometime between March 21, 1843, and March 21, 1844. By 1833, Miller was regularly preaching in several towns, had done a few speaking tours, and had published his views on the end of the world in a series of articles in a local newspaper. Baptist leaders, recognizing his increasingly widespread popularity, ordained Miller an officially licensed preacher. This backing from an authority allowed him more opportunities for speaking tours. He travelled back and forth across the northeast of the United States, spreading the good news about the imminent destruction of the world. By 1836, 42 ministers had signed an endorsement of Miller and his eschatological views. And Miller's number of converts kept increasing until they numbered more than 50,000.[250] A name was coined for them: Millerites.[251]

A considerable amount of mockery of this new movement was published in the mainstream media. Newspapers in Boston and New York printed articles and editorials attacking Miller's ideas and making fun of Miller's followers. But the Millerites were undaunted and continued to prepare for the end of the world.[252] This shouldn't be a surprise — when someone is publicly ridiculed, it just adds to the sunk cost of their belief. And the greater the sunk cost, the lower the chance that a person will admit that they were wrong.

The final doomsday date was rapidly approaching, and excitement was building. And, as you would expect from a movement this large that contained so many different humans, that excitement manifested itself in a number of ways. On the spiritual side, there was a massive outpouring of prophesying, speaking in tongues, claimed miracles, faith healing, etc. Even Reverend Miller himself was a little taken aback by this outpouring of fervour, writing in a letter that "my heart was deeply pained during my tour to see in some few of my former friends a proneness to wild and foolish extremes and vain delusions, such as working miracles, discerning of spirits, vague and loose views on sanctification, etc."[253]

Clearly, people were extremely invested in the belief system. And after the March 21, 1844, date passed without the world ending, the Millerites did not abandon their beliefs; they doubled down. They proselytized more; Miller travelled and preached more; the Millerite presses started working around the clock to push out more material. By August of that year a leading Millerite (not Miller himself but preacher named Samuel Snow) had decided on a new doomsday: October 22, 1844.[254]

Many Millerites had to make difficult choices regarding their careers and livelihoods. Even something as simple as harvesting your crops could be seen as a sign that your faith was wobbly, since why would you be gathering food for a winter that you were certain would never arrive? This was the dilemma faced by a Millerite in New Hampshire named Leonard Hastings. He had planted a field of potatoes that would help him and his family survive until the following spring. But since all those potatoes were destined to be burned up in flames with the rest of the world, what was the point of harvesting them? Hastings did what many Millerites did, and left the potatoes in the ground to rot.[255]

Hastings was not unusual among the Millerites for this behaviour, as believers sold their property for a fraction of what it was worth, gave away their possessions, or simply abandoned their homes and shops.[256]

Unfortunately for those who had sacrificed so much, just as March 21 had ended without the world burning, October 22 came and went uneventfully. The world did not end. Instead, that day would come to be known as "the Great Disappointment."

As you would expect within such a large movement, there was a variety of reactions to this very public failure of the prophecy. Tens of thousands of Miller's followers gave up on their beliefs — some rejoined mainstream churches, and some just gave up on organized religion altogether.[257] Hundreds more believed that the prophecy was correct but the date was just wrong — this group continued to wait for the fire they knew was just around the corner. But others reinterpreted the meaning of the prophecy. They maintained that something incredibly significant *had* occurred — except it hadn't occurred on earth but in the heavens.[258]

From this event, and a few similar ones from earlier in history, Festinger built up a series of conditions in which the disconfirmation of a belief would result in an increased conviction in the belief rather than an abandonment of it. In other words, if the following five things are true, a person is more likely to double down on a failed belief system than to abandon it:

1. The belief must be held with deep conviction and have some relevance to the behaviours and actions of the believer.
2. The believer must have committed some sort of action based on their belief that would be difficult or impossible to undo.
3. The belief must be rooted enough in the real world that it's possible for events to confirm or refute the belief.
4. Some undeniable and unambiguous evidence that refutes the belief must occur, and the believer must be aware of this evidence.
5. The believer must have social support from a community of like-minded believers who are going through the same thing. An isolated believer would likely be forced into abandoning their belief due to the massive degree of cognitive dissonance caused by the public refutation of the belief, but a community of believers could support each other and themselves.[259]

It is that last condition that results in the increased proselytizing. According to Festinger, because a community of believers is crucial to lessen the cognitive dissonance created by the refutation, there is pressure to try to expand that community during moments of crises of faith. As Festinger writes: "If more and more people can be persuaded that the system of belief is correct, then clearly it must, after all, *be* correct."[260] If Festinger is correct, this in an alarming bit of news. Not only will people with unsupported views hold on to those views, even when faced with evidence to the contrary, but they will become even more fervent and active in those views. However, as we will see, the truth (as always) is more complicated than that.

WHEN PROPHECY FAILS

Festinger wasn't satisfied with a historical analysis; he wanted to test his hypothesis out in the field. And in 1954 he got his chance, when he saw a local Chicago newspaper story headlined "Prophecy from Planet Clarion Call to City: Flee That Flood. It'll Swamp Us on December 21, Outer Space Tells Suburbanite."

The suburbanite in question was a former Scientologist named Dorothy Martin, who by using the technique of "automatic reading" — in which a person allegedly channels another entity through their own arm to write out messages from that entity — had contacted beings from outer space. These beings had become concerned about the state of things on Earth, due to the recent increase in atomic testing. Apparently, they had had their own cold war on their planet, which was named Car: Their evil Luciferian scientists had invented something called alcetopes, which were basically nuclear bombs. Car had been destroyed by these devices, but the good people of the light had left the evil scientists to their fiery doom and escaped to the planet Clarion. And now they were sending Dorothy Martin a message that Earth was going to be flooded on December 21, 1954. However, it wasn't all doom and gloom, because they also promised that a flying saucer would land on Earth before the destruction to allow Martin and her fellow believers to escape to Clarion.[261]

Martin had told some fellow UFO enthusiasts about her message, and a small group of believers had started to form, using Martin's house as their meeting place. At its largest, her group had a few dozen members. Included in that group were Dr. Festinger, three of his colleagues, and two grad students, all pretending to be believers.

As far as proper study protocols go, this was wildly improper, and the methodology of this study has been rightly criticized. By pretending to agree with the beliefs of the group, the researchers strengthened and supported the beliefs of the other group members. This means it's impossible to know how the subjects of the study would have behaved if the researchers had not been involved, which means that this can't be considered a proper experiment. By not identifying themselves as researchers, they created very serious issues of informed consent. In 2025, new evidence emerged that the researchers had played much more active roles in shaping and even causing some of the vents chronicled in When Prophecy Fails than had been previously acknowledged.[262] Therefore, like other flawed "experiments" such as the Stanford Prison Experiment, this study should be viewed more as an illustration of the concept, rather than evidence for the concept.

In the months leading up to the predicted apocalypse, the group in general and Dorothy Martin in particular were not overly active in promoting their beliefs or attempting to gather new members; part of their belief system included the idea that people who were meant to find the group would be guided there by alien forces. However, as the deadline approached, the stakes were raised for several of the group members. One man, Dr. Charles Laughead, lost his job the Michigan State College Hospital after his participation in the group became public. Another member — identified only as Kitty in the study — said: "I have to believe the flood is coming on the 21st because I've spent nearly all of my money. I quit my job, I quit school, and my apartment costs me $100 a month. I have to believe."

This set of beliefs conformed to three of the five items on the list that Festinger and his colleagues had developed. The belief was sincere, had inspired actions that had a real effect, and involved predictions about the real world that could be verified or falsified. All that was left to see was whether the predictions would come true or not.

As the date drew nearer, the group waited anxiously for news regarding their flying saucer rescue. Dorothy Martin received a phone call on December 17, just four days away from doomsday, in which someone who identified himself as "Captain Video" stated that he was a representative from Clarion, and that the group would be picked up that afternoon at four p.m. This caused a frenzy in activity in the house, as a previous automatic writing message had informed the group that no metal of any kind was to be allowed on the spacecraft, so the believers spent the early afternoon removing all of their zippers, clasps, buttons, bobby pins, and belt buckles. And when four o'clock arrived, the group was standing in the kitchen with their coats, ready to be picked up.

By 5:30 they were back in the living room again, with their coats hung back on the coat racks and their minds deep in a state of dissonance. However, the group was able to justify the non-event by deciding that the whole thing had just been a drill, to practise for the real saucer evacuation. Three days later, Martin received another message announcing that the departure would be that day, and the group sat around until midnight. After nothing happened again, Dr. Laughead spoke to one of the undercover observers and said: "I've had to go a long way. I've given up just about everything. I've cut every tie. I've burned every bridge. I've turned my back on the world. I can't afford to doubt. I have to believe. And there isn't any other truth . . . I can't afford to doubt. I won't doubt even if we have to make an announcement to the press tomorrow and admit we were wrong. You're having your period of doubt now, but hang on boy, hang on. This is a tough time but we know that the boys upstairs are taking care of us." It must be noted, though, that this response from Laughead was prompted by one of the researchers, who had asked Laughead for help restoring his "faith" after the saucer hadn't shown up.[263]

Finally, at 4:45 a.m., Dorothy Martin received an inspiring message from the planet Clarion. Because of the love and light demonstrated by their little group, doomsday had been called off and the world had been spared destruction.

Now the fourth and fifth conditions had been met — undeniable and unambiguous evidence had been presented that the prophecy had not come to pass, and a group of like-minded individuals was experiencing similar cognitive dissonance. And, as Festinger and his colleagues had hypothesized, the group became more outspoken and started to court the press more often after the prophecy had failed, even going so far as to hold a Christmas sing-along in front of Martin's house on December 24 and telling the press that they expected a man from Clarion to attend.

However, there have been legitimate criticisms of Festinger's conclusions. *When Prophecy Fails* only follows the group subjects for a few months after the public sing-along, and there is no evidence that most of them held on to their beliefs longer than that. Even in that short amount of time, the peripheral members of the group who weren't staying at the Martin house drifted away from the rest, and the more recently someone had joined, the more likely it was that they left. On the other hand, as we'll examine later in the chapter, Martin herself dove further into the world of aliens and conspiracism.

While the Martin case became famous in social psychology circles, as a study it was fatally flawed. But the concept of cognitive dissonance has been further explored by other researchers in more controlled settings.[264] Since the publication of Festinger's contested work, there have been other case studies and experiments to test the results of cognitive dissonance on belief. There have been mixed results (some confirming the predictions of the theory, and others going against it) which is not surprising. Humans beings are a complicated bunch, and any theory which claims to predict what will always happen can never take into account the complexities and specificities of the situation and the people in it. Even Festinger backed away from the certainty of his claims regarding how people respond to dissonance, admitting that "There are many factors affecting people's behavior, attitudes, and opinions about which the theory of dissonance has nothing to say."[265] It is not the influence on a person's actions and behaviours, it is one of many potential influences on a person's actions and behaviours.

MORE FAILED PROPHECIES

The concept may shed some insight into the QAnon movement, which has featured many, many failed prophecies and predictions. Q started wrong right from the beginning — the first ever official Q drop stated that "HRC extradition already in motion effective yesterday with several countries in case of cross border run."[266] Q drop 2 said that "HRC detained, not arrested (yet)" and said that there would be "massive riots organized in defiance and others fleeing the US." The "HRC" in these posts is Hillary Rodham Clinton, and she was neither detained nor arrested as promised by Q. The next 60 or so drops carried on in a similar fashion, with similar accuracy. After that, the drops would become less specific and more cryptic.

But even as the Q posts became less eager to prophesize, the Q community at large continued making predictions, and by the end of 2021, there had been several high-profile failed predictions. Leading up to the presidential inauguration, a ton of chatter on message boards and comment sections stated that Biden would be arrested right before or immediately after he was sworn in. There was the failed prediction that Trump would return to office on March 4. A Q influencer who goes by the handle Juan O Savin — and who hinted that he is secretly JFK Jr. but is actually an insurance investigator from the Seattle area named Wayne Willott[267] — told people they could bet everything they had that on April 1 Trump would be marched back into the White House by the U.S. military. None of this occurred, of course, and 2022 dawned with Biden still in the White House. Every time one of these prophecies failed, a mixture of disbelief, confusion, anger, and rationalization flooded the message boards. Many people said they looked foolish or even crazy to their families or co-workers. There were also supportive messages and thought-terminating clichés such as "trust the plan," "this is 5D chess," and "God always wins." While they may seem empty of actual content, such slogans serve to interrupt any train of thought that may lead to dissonance. And a small percentage of cynical replies would mock those clichés as "hopium" or "copium" — a portmanteau of *hope* or *cope* with *opium*.

Our modern information ecosystem ensures that the fifth condition of Festinger's list is always met — people can always, regardless of the belief system, find an online community to help them through moments of cognitive dissonance that might otherwise shake their certainties. In addition, plenty of agents and organizations are actively promoting disinformation for their own financial or political benefit, and they help us hold on to flawed, inaccurate, and dangerous beliefs. If Festinger's hypothesis holds true, then optimistic predictions that movements such as QAnon will falter after failed prophecies are flawed and inaccurate. We should be expecting instead the movement to become more fervent and active.

But there is another important part to the cognitive dissonance picture, and to understand it, we should quickly examine the 2012 work of Wood, Douglas, and Sutton[268] and the 2015 work of Irwin, Dagnall, and Drinkwater.[269] According to both studies, people often believe a collection of conspiracy theories that can't all be true, as they are mutually contradictory or logically incompatible. For example, the more a person believes that Osama bin Laden was already dead when U.S. special forces raided his compound, the more they also believe that bin Laden is actually still alive. Obviously those two claims can't logically both be accurate, but people are able to hold both ideas in their heads at once.

A lot of ink has been spilled trying to understand this phenomenon. Susmito Rittik argued that a strong positive correlation exists between belief inconsistency and religious commitment — that full commitment to a faith-based idea that will occasionally possess contradictions requires a degree of comfort with holding on to inconsistent concepts.[270] Barron, Morgan, Towell, Altemeyer, and Swami claimed that there is a mental illness present in the conspiratorial mind, arguing that this comfort with logical inconsistency demonstrates schizotypal personality attributes.[271] But of course, not everyone who believes in multiple inconsistent conspiracy claims is religious, and not everyone who believes multiple conspiracy claims has a mental illness.

Festinger argued that some people just appear to have a greater tolerance for cognitive dissonance, arguing that "for some people dissonance is an extremely painful and intolerable thing, while there are others who seem to be able to tolerate a large amount of dissonance."[272] However, the relationship a person's tolerance to dissonance has to their conspiratorial beliefs is a complicated one.

DISSONANCE AND CONSPIRACY THINKING

It's fairly straightforward to predict how a large tolerance for dissonance could make a person more likely to accept demonstrably false conspiracy claims. Any false conspiracy claim, such as the belief in a flat Earth, is going to run counter to almost all the data a person will encounter. Being comfortable with that contradiction would allow a person to hold on to their beliefs, even in the face of overwhelming evidence to the contrary.

But Festinger argues that there is also a danger in having a low tolerance for dissonance. Because people tend to be more inclined to protect their ideas than to change them, a person who finds it very unpleasant to be presented with information that contradicts their beliefs will likely try whatever it takes in order to reduce that dissonance while maintaining their beliefs, including doubling down on those beliefs, adding new false beliefs to support the previous threatened beliefs, and isolating themselves from anyone who might challenge their beliefs. Festinger proposes that this situation might cause a person to become even more entrenched in their beliefs.[273]

For example, let's return to the UFO group that Festinger studied in the 1950s. Their beliefs were very clearly and publicly contradicted by the undeniable fact that the world didn't end. Dorothy Martin, the spiritual leader of the group, was in danger of being committed to a mental institution if she stayed in the area — there had already been an attempt to institutionalize her fellow group member Dr. Charles Laughead.[274]

Rather than abandoning her beliefs, Dorothy Martin dove deeper into them. She fled to Arizona in early 1955, where she met alleged alien contactee George Hunt Williamson. Williamson claimed to be able to communicate with aliens through the use of a Ouija board and had been helping to publish a magazine titled *Valor*, which had both occult and fascist leanings. By now, Martin had changed her name to Sister Thedra. Thedra, Williamson, and Dr. and Mrs. Laughead then moved to Peru together to seek out the ascended masters of the "Great White Brotherhood." By the 1980s, Thedra had ended up in Northern California, where she helped publish antisemitic rants about the UN and *The Protocols of the Elders of Zion* channelled through Doris Ekker, an alleged medium who claimed to be in touch with the commander-in-chief of the Pleiades sector of the Intergalactic Federation Fleet.[275]

The brush with cognitive dissonance that Sister Thedra experienced in the 1950s led her to seek out more and more extreme versions of her belief system. Unfortunately, this is not an unusual story arc for people who have gotten swept up in conspiracism. People who feel as though they have been rejected by mainstream society can take refuge in other rejected knowledge systems rather than embracing the mainstream belief that they feel they have been rejected by.[276] People who feel persecuted can sometimes use that feeling as motivation to take a heroic stand.

If critics of *When Prophecy Fails* are correct, and Festinger and his co-researchers actively manipulated Martin's group to produce the results they wanted, then in an odd and inadvertent way that also supports Festinger's claim. Faced with the cognitive dissonance of their theory of cognitive dissonance not being confirmed, the researchers doubled down and compromised their professional ethics to engineer the observations they want to protect their beliefs, and in doing so reduce their own dissonance.

THE IMPORTANCE OF CHANGING OUR MINDS

As thinking beings, we prefer that our beliefs, actions, and experience not be contradictory. But this doesn't mean that the uncomfortable experience of cognitive dissonance always acts as a kind of braking system that keeps us from falling too far into a rabbit hole. As we have seen, sometimes it creates the paradoxical situation that our challenged belief systems are reinforced or even intensified. We can end up doubling down on foolishness and nonsense, trying to protect the ideas we already have, rather than being committed to figuring out what the truth actually is. Many a person has held on to a false conspiracy theory despite incontrovertible evidence to the contrary because of the sunk cost they have invested in it, but this can lead to much greater costs later to their social life, financial situation, and physical and mental health.

But the fact that Festinger's theory hasn't proven airtight provides us with reason to be optimistic. While it's possible a person will be drawn further into a failed belief, it is also possible that someone can emerge from one. As human beings we can have both the capacity of rationality and the courage it takes to confront the implications of that rationality. It can help lead us back out of a belief system that threatens to consume us, particularly when other people close to us give us the grace to back away from that system without giving into the temptation of mockery or telling us, "I told you so!"

We shouldn't shy away from information that causes dissonance with our beliefs. Instead, we should be willing to accept that our ideas may be incorrect. When we receive accurate data that doesn't fit well with our beliefs, rather than doubling down, we should do the difficult but vital work of asking ourselves whether our beliefs fit well with reality. Reality has no obligation to conform to what we want to believe.

10

CONSPIRACISM VS. FALSIFIABILITY — WHY A FLAT EARTH NEEDS A FAKE MOON LANDING

WHY SCIENCE WORKS

For thousands of years, humans have wondered about the world they inhabit and have come up with countless ingenious but wrong theories to explain various natural phenomena. Aristotle, for example, developed a theory of gravity by positing that heavy things enjoyed being on the ground, in part because they are lazy. If you lifted something up, it would struggle to regain its natural position on the floor. Hence, heavy things fall down.[277] For many thinkers over the centuries, it was obvious that the solar system revolved around the Earth, and silly to imagine that it could be the opposite.[278] They even provided rather coherent explanations for their theories, citing for instance that if the world were in motion there'd be a terrible wind which would blow everything off. Apparently, the ancient Egyptians did not think that the brain had any function, so they removed it during the mummification process. Pre-modern European medical theory held that disease was caused by too much mucus, or blood or bile, which gave rise to the famous "cure" of bleeding with leeches.

What unites all of these examples is that from today's perspective they are patently wrong. Today we know that there is a force of nature we call gravity that all physical objects exert and are subject to. We know that most of the observable motion in the sky is due to the Earth's motion, not the stars'. We know that the brain is not just useful but vital. All this knowledge has been bestowed on us by the mysterious and remarkable mode of inquiry known as science.

Exactly what science is and how it functions is a more interesting philosophical question than we often presume. For instance, the ontological status of scientific discoveries is hotly debated among philosophers of science. Does science discover actual truths about the universe or merely a useful manner of speaking and conceptualizing natural phenomena? Many of us are tempted to say that science discovers truth, but if that is the case, what do we call previous scientific theories that turned out to be wrong in light of later scientific discoveries? Was Newton simply wrong when he "discovered gravity"? Einsteinian theory would suggest he was. But it feels strange to say that Newton was just plain wrong.

Maybe science is "just" a way of speaking of the natural world, providing us with conceptual models to manipulate it the way we want. The sociologist and philosopher of science Thomas Kuhn asked this question in his groundbreaking book *The Structure of Scientific Revolutions* when he pondered whether we may "have to relinquish the notion, explicit or implicit, that changes of paradigm carry scientists and those who learn from them closer and closer to the truth."[279] Newtonian physics is a powerful theory since it can be applied in most cases with accurate results. Maybe the fact that it works matters more than a philosophical question of "truth." Newton's theory was good enough to be used by the Apollo engineers to get people to the moon and back. Engineers don't build bridges that are "true" but "merely" build bridges that work. Maybe that's good enough.

The question of how and why science works is worth exploring because it will inform how we should approach our investigations into conspiracy theories. What makes scientific inquiry different from other ways of knowing? What is it about science that makes it such a powerful tool to explain natural phenomena? The answers to these questions will help to develop our method of inquiry into conspiracies.

Some philosophical concepts are buried within any scientific enterprise, and the concept of falsifiability is of particular importance. Amazingly, a lot of these ideas were articulated in the Western intellectual tradition hundreds if not thousands of years before the field of scientific inquiry took form. In a sense, they are unprovable philosophical tenets which make science possible. It is also worth noting that the philosophy of science, like any academic field, is not monolithic. Different thinkers will have different lists of key concepts that make science a unique discipline. And even when they agree on some of the core ideas, they may be at odds when ranking their importance.

Nature is the object of scientific inquiry. Science asks and answers questions about nature. Natural effects must be described by way of natural causes. The project of science excludes from the outset the supernatural, the metaphysical, and the theological. There can be no supernatural explanation that enters any part of the investigation. If we wanted to explain why a volcano erupts, we are prohibited from relying on God, a supernatural entity, as an explanation. Science does not make any claims to explain all of reality. Its scope is bounded by nature. Whether the natural is all that there is in reality is not a question that science can answer. That is a question for philosophy, or theology, or something besides.

Another aspect of science is the need to create a theory that relies on reasonable logical relationships to explain the effect under investigation. Other appeals to truth, such as authority, are not permitted. Science can be disruptive because it upends established views of how the world is thought to work. If the theory can relate a series of natural causes to effects that clearly explain the phenomenon under investigation more reasonably than any other theory, it should be regarded as the best explanation. No matter who developed the theory, and no matter how eminent the scientists are that disagree with the theory, reason, not authority, should be the final judge of what is the best scientific description. This is how it should work. In the real world, of course, power relations do come into it.

Two ideas introduce limits to our understanding of what constitutes a scientific theory: We assume that the effect is due to a natural cause and that nature is a closed system. We must develop a theory within these constraints.

Let us say we are wondering about why the sun rises in the morning, or why the stars at night seem to move around as though circling a point in the sky. The ancient Greeks, like many other ancient cultures, had a myth to explain it. They suggested that the god Helios drove a chariot across the sky every day. This chariot was the sun, and Helios was able to drive it because he was a god. The extent to which this myth was believed by ancient Greeks as a literal explanation is debatable.[280] There were probably various relationships to this story, ranging from faith in its literal truth to perception of it as mere metaphor. The story does not play by the rules of science. It introduces a non-natural entity, a god, to do the heavy lifting in explaining a natural event.

The ancient Greeks also produced science-like explanations. They were renowned astronomers,[281] and one theory they developed was that the Earth was surrounded by concentric spheres that revolved around it. Each shell or layer was separated from another shell by some distance. The Earth remained stationary in the centre of this model. The various spheres each contained different heavenly bodies. One contained the moon; another, the sun; others, planets; another, stars.

This theory is more scientific than the myth since there is no recourse to the supernatural. It explains observable nature by positing a natural theory of the universe. Why does the sun seem to rise? It does so because it is contained within a sphere which revolves around a stationary Earth. This is also why the stars seem to rotate around a point in the sky, and why the moon has phases. Like any good scientific theory, it explains many things at once. It does not rely on a god to do any of the work but explains nature with more nature.

In science, whenever possible, theories should be testable. If we have developed a causal explanation for something, we want to confirm whether it is correct by reproducing the effect through an experiment.

FALSIFIABILITY

The pillars of scientific reasoning are:

1. All natural effects have a natural cause;
2. the universe is a closed system;
3. science develops theories about nature;
4. these theories of nature must be testable.

These pillars served well enough for the first few hundred years of scientific inquiry. But there was one element of the program that had yet to be articulated. This was rectified by the philosopher of science Karl Popper, who pointed out that scientific questions must be posed in such a way as to be falsifiable. That is, it must be possible for a statement to be proven wrong if it is to qualify as a scientific statement. As Popper writes in *The Logic of Scientific Discovery*, "It must be possible for an empirical scientific system to be refuted by experience."[282] And he provides a helpful little example: "The statement, 'It will rain or not rain tomorrow' will not be regarded as empirical, simply because it cannot be refuted; whereas the statement, 'It will rain here tomorrow' will be regarded as empirical."[283]

The geocentric model of the solar system is a scientific statement that also conforms to the notion of falsifiability. To state that the Earth is stationary and that the sun and stars perform the motion that we experience with our senses does qualify as a testable hypothesis that can be proven correct or incorrect. It passes the falsifiability claim. By contrast, a claim that we all live in a computer-generated reality in which super-intelligent overlords have concocted a hoax universe, and everything we experience is a computer-simulated illusion, is not falsifiable. This is conspiracism. There can be no piece of evidence that would demonstrate that the world we are experiencing is actually the real world and not a computer-simulated illusion.

AS IN SCIENCE, SO TOO IN SOCIAL SCIENCE

When investigating conspiracy theories, it is useful to make the same assumptions about the world that we make in scientific inquiries. Just like with science, there are fundamental principles about the world that we cannot prove but need to assume. Specifically we assume that: 1) the social and political world does not also contain the supernatural; 2) claims in the social and political world must be based on verifiable evidence that is reasonably related to the inquiry at hand; and 3) a conspiracy theory must be stated in such a way that it can, at least in principle, be falsifiable.

We have already dealt with assumptions one and two elsewhere in this book. Below we focus on the concept of falsifiability.

On the surface, the claim that secret societies like the Freemasons or the Illuminati rule the world is falsifiable. According to this idea, all world events are orchestrated by a cabal of influential agents working behind the scenes. The American Revolution has been attributed to the work of Freemasons, and this claim is falsifiable.[284] We can examine the historical record and discover how many revolutionaries in the American colonies were Freemasons. It turns out, most of them were, which seems to make the case. However, on further examination it turns out that most of the opponents of the American Revolution were also Freemasons. Most of the middle and upper classes of society in both Britain and America were Freemasons, including the King of England! It does not follow, then, that the American Revolution was executed according to the secret plans of the Freemasons, since proponents and opponents alike were Freemasons. This is the power of falsifiability.

However, we may encounter a rejoinder which casts us into the murky world of conspiracism. Conspiracists claim that pro-Revolutionary and anti-Revolutionary Freemasons were all working according to a yet greater and more mysterious secret plan. The conspiratorial idea is no longer subject to historical facts. The assumption is that the Freemasons (or the secret society of your choice) are society's actual power brokers, and any counterclaim is always met with the charge that "well, that's what they want you to believe."

The central problem with conspiracism is that these systems of belief are not falsifiable. They break Popper's final rule of how scientific inquiry functions and, by extension, also how social scientific inquiry works. If we want to know something like "Are secret societies determining all major world events?" we need to phrase our question in a way that it can be tested and therefore shown to be false. If we do not, we have opened the door to a dangerous line of reasoning, liable to trap us in systems of thought from which escape is almost impossible.

To make this danger as clear as we can, it is worth noting that there exist belief systems specifically designed to trap us, such as those constructed by religious cults that aim to exploit their members. The theologies of these cults evince thought loops, reinforced with the already mentioned thought-terminating cliché, in which all counterclaims are rationalized in a way that reenforces the cult's ideologies and power structure. Doubt is often characterized as a dangerous force in these belief systems. In science and social science, by contrast, progress had been made by theorists who doubted what stood as established dogma for the previous generation. A new recruit into a cult might be told that, as they move forward with their spiritual progress, friends and family may become jealous and want to remove them from their new-found community. As they become more invested in a belief system that is clearly harmful, their family might in fact want to get involved. At this point, the thought-terminating cliché undermines all attempts to help the recruit break out of their toxic community.

These types of non-falsifiable thought traps exist all over the place. Cults are but one example. Toxic personal relationships often work like this, as do financial scams or medical grifts. To protect against these thought loops, it is important to maintain the concept of falsifiability so we can think clearly about these claims and escape from ideas that are obviously wrong but are nonetheless self-reinforcing.

THE WORLD OF THE FLAT EARTHERS

One might be forgiven for thinking that the Flat Earth theory is a holdover from some archaic age in which people actually believed the Earth to be a flat disc, but the history of Flat Earthers is more recent than one might expect.

Some of the best arguments for a spherical Earth were presented in the ancient world.[285] For instance, a ship does not suddenly disappear from sight when sailing away but rather seems to "sink." First the hull is lost, then part of the mast, and finally it is gone. Much the way it would look if it were sailing out of view on a ball-like surface. Ancient people used this to argue for a spherical Earth.

Or, what about the fact that a sundial at the same time of day is in a slightly different position in one city compared to another? This was first noticed by the Greek philosopher Eratosthenes, who discovered that on the summer solstice the sun was directly overhead in Athens but not in Aswan, roughly 800 kilometres away. The easiest way to make sense of this is to assume that the Earth is a sphere. Eratosthenes even went on to calculate the size of the spherical Earth, coming to an answer that is remarkably close to the one that modern science has discovered.[286]

The ancients had many other good reasons for suggesting that Earth was a sphere. All the other celestial bodies are spheres, so why not also the Earth? Then there are the observations made during an eclipse. Two ancient Greek philosophers, Empedoclese and Anaximander, offered the following argument: Why is the shadow on the moon circular when the Earth passes between it and the sun? It is clearly the Earth's shadow. Why is it curved if the Earth isn't curved? Answer: The Earth *is* a sphere.[287]

It is simply not true that all premodern people believed that the Earth was flat until "Christopher Columbus sailed the ocean blue" and "discovered" that it was a globe. Many people knew it was a globe thousands of years before Christopher Columbus or Ferdinand Magellan were born.

But ancients also presented interesting arguments against a spherical Earth, reasonable objections before much was known about the nature of space, the force of gravity, and other more recent discoveries. If the Earth is round, why don't we all fall off the sides? In light of our understanding of gravity, this question seems quaint, but it was a reasonable question when the law of gravity was unknown. Remember that gravity was first theorized by Sir Isaac Newton in 1666. A related question: If the Earth is round and spinning, why is it that if someone jumps, they land roughly in the same place and not a significant distance away as the Earth moves rapidly below them?

Circumnavigation of the Earth was another type of proof that came later in the history of the Western intellectual tradition. Christopher Columbus apparently didn't believe that the Earth was a flat disc. He believed it was a sphere. But he didn't tell his crew where he intended to go because he was worried that they believed they'd fall off the edge. The first actual circumnavigation that took place was in 1522, when Magellan took a three-year detour and accidentally went around the whole world. This added more fuel to the argument that the Earth was a sphere.

However, until modern photography, much of the evidence for a spherical world was less tangible than it would later become. Once flight was invented, it was easy to effectively experience the curvature of the Earth. And although by the era of space travel most people knew the Earth was a sphere, the startling "blue marble" picture sent back from the Apollo 17 lunar lander was definitive proof for non-scientists that we do indeed live on a very large ball.

Weirdly, as the scientific evidence for a spherical Earth became overwhelming, the origins of a modern Flat Earth movement were starting to take root. The movement can be traced back to the 1800s and the publication of Samuel Rowbotham's pamphlet entitled *Zetetic Astronomy: Earth Not a Globe*. Writing under the pseudonym Parallax, Rowbotham argues that the Earth is a flat disc with one "pole" in the middle, encircled by continents and ocean and then another "pole" that is actually a wall of ice preventing everything from falling off the sides.[288] Others began to proselytize his theory in their turn. William Carpenter, for instance, published *Theoretical Astronomy Examined and Exposed* in 1864, and in 1893 Lady Elizabeth Blount founded the Zetetic Society. In 1956, Samuel Shenton created the Flat Earth Society, which continues today. Among the prominent members are Mark Sargent, one of the most vocal proponents in the Flat Earth movement and the subject of the Netflix documentary *Behind the Curve* (2018).

What is also strange about the Flat Earth theory is how remarkably falsifiable it is. Its claims can be tested by armchair scientists without much expense or experience. The Bedford Level experiment, for example, can be done at home with some basic tools. It was actually first conducted by Rowbotham, and it accounts for some of the Flat Earthers' initial success in convincing people there might be something to this idea.[289]

In Cambridgeshire, England, there exists a 34-kilometre-long shallow canal — long enough to help us see the curvature of the Earth. Still water is flat; it is basically level. If the Earth is a sphere, and if we look over a level canal of any significant distance, the curvature of the Earth should cause the water level to appear to descend relative to the point of observation.

The first iteration of the experiment evokes the ancients' question of why the ship doesn't just get smaller but seems to disappear in stages, starting with the hull. Rowbotham had a friend row a small boat with a flag attached to the back, starting at Welches Dam and proceeding to a point six miles (about 9.5 km) away known as Welney Bridge. Rowbotham got into the canal and watched his friend with a good telescope. If the Earth is a sphere and his friend travelled far enough, he would appear to descend out of view, starting with the flag on his boat. But it did not vanish. Rowbotham believed he had falsified the theory that Earth is spherical. The only alternative, he thought, was a flat Earth.

Rowbotham then conducted another experiment. This is the most famous version. He planted a row of flags along the same stretch of the canal at intervals of one mile, five feet above the surface of the water. He then looked through a telescope aimed horizontally with the tops of each flag. But the final few flags did not descend "into" the water. They remained "absolutely horizontal."

Much of the first half of *Zetetic Astronomy* is given over to experiments like this. Rowbotham then goes on to develop his theory of a disc-shaped Earth, described above.

Rowbotham's experiments are of interest because they were performed in the spirit of science. They attempt to explain nature in terms of more nature. The theory relies on experiments that are repeatable; it is premised on a coherent and falsifiable theory about the way the world works.

There was, of course, a mistake in Rowbotham's methods, which was quickly discovered by Alfred Russell Wallace in 1870. The missing element that Rowbotham did not take into account was the refraction of light due to the atmosphere. Based only on the curvature of the Earth, objects 35 kilometres away should not be entirely visible. However, atmospheric refraction "curves" light around the globe, making things that should have disappeared visible. Atmospheric refraction is more prevalent close to the Earth than higher up, making Rowbotham's experiment at the water's level particularly subject to it. The Bedford Level experiment was repeated by Wallace, but he took the issue of atmospheric refraction into account. When refraction is added in, the Bedford Level experiment actually supports the description of a curved Earth.

Based simply on Rowbotham's experiments, the worry that the science about the shape of the Earth might be wrong is not a conspiracy theory. The Flat Earth theory becomes a conspiracy theory once we assume that the truth is being purposely hidden. As a Flat Earth Society website explains:

> There is no Flat Earth Conspiracy. NASA is not hiding the shape of the Earth from anyone. The purpose of NASA is not to "hide the shape of the earth" or "trick people into thinking it's round" or anything of the sort.
>
> There is a Space Travel Conspiracy. The purpose of NASA is to fake the concept of space travel to further America's militaristic dominance of space. That was the purpose of NASA's creation from the very start: To put ICBMs and other weapons into space (or at least appear to). The motto "Scientific exploration of new frontiers for all mankind" was nothing more than a front.[290]

MOON LANDING "HOAX"

Zetetic Astronomy was first published in the second half of the 19th century, already quite late for anyone to take the Flat Earth idea seriously; by then, the evidence for a spherical Earth was overwhelming. Even so, Rowbotham's experiments might have been convincing for some, partially because the undeveloped state of technical experimentation still allowed for incorrect ideas to pass for coherent explanations. But then humanity invented flight, and satellites, and space travel.

So, one might ask: What about all the evidence from the moon landing, the International Space Station, planes, and satellites that prove the Earth is a sphere? It is a bad sign when a conspiracy theory such as "the Earth is flat" requires another conspiracy for its support. The more conspiracies are needed to support the initial theory, the more dubious it becomes. When confronted with evidence from the moon landing, including pictures that the Earth is actually a sphere, contemporary Flat Earthers argue that the moon landing was faked.

Like the Flat Earth theory, the moon landing conspiracy lists a set of claims that supposedly demonstrate that the landing never took place.[291] A famous one is the fact that, in video footage, the American flag planted on the lunar surface is waving. Since the moon does not have an atmosphere, the video simply could not have been shot on the moon; it must have been shot on Earth. The usual location given is the desert surrounding Area 51 (Groom Lake), a secret military base in Nevada. A Hollywood studio has also been suggested.

Why are no stars visible in either the still photographs or the video recordings? Flat Earthers claim that, because stars would give away the actual location of the site of the false moon landing, the film footage was edited before being released to the public.

There's also the claim that the footage shows multiple light sources, suggesting it was shot not on the moon but on Earth; you can clearly see astronauts on the lunar surface, even when they are standing in shadows. This apparently demonstrates that they are on a movie set. And what about the shadows — of various rocks, the flagpole, the lunar lander, and astronauts — that seem to go all over the place? If the only light source on the moon is the sun, then they should be pointing in the same direction. They are not, and this proves that multiple light sources were used.

There are donuts of radioactive death surrounding the Earth, known as the Van Allen belts. It is not possible to pass through those without receiving a lethal dose of radiation, and since the astronauts are still alive, they could not possibly have travelled to the moon.

There are many more claims besides these, and some of the ones listed might seem disturbingly convincing. But not to worry. All of them have been thoroughly examined, fact-checked, and debunked.[292] Let us begin with the flag.

This claim makes a logical error of the "single cause." Just because flags wave on Earth because of wind doesn't mean that they cannot wave for another reason. The lunar flag is not like a terrestrial flag. It had a metal rod that ran along the top to prevent it from drooping.[293] The moon landing was a big media event showing the world that the United States could keep pace with the Soviet Union in the space race. Having a clearly visible American flag on the moon amounted to "flipping the bird" to the Soviets. As Neil Armstrong worked the flagpole into the ground, he had to twist left and right. This momentum travelled up the flagpole and was expressed as movement in the "waving" flag. The moon is in a vacuum, which made the flag wave even more than it would on Earth, because there was no friction to slow it down.[294]

It is not surprising to anyone who has taken nighttime photographs that the stars are not visible in the published pictures. Even with today's technology, it is difficult to capture any celestial object without extremely long exposure times. The astronauts were not trying to take pictures of the stars. They were taking pictures of each other, the lunar surface, and the lunar lander. If they had taken pictures of the stars, the white objects in the foreground would have been overexposed.

The fact that the astronauts are visible even when they are in the shadows has to do with the fact that they are on the moon and not on Earth. The surface of the moon is covered in a light-coloured dust-like material known as regolith. It is composed mostly of broken rocks and other lunar debris. An important aspect of regolith is that it is more reflective than most of the Earth's surfaces, way more than terrestrial soil and most ground cover on Earth.[295]

Using the moon landing conspiracy theory to bolster the Flat Earth conspiracy theory demonstrates the need for the concept of falsifiability. When we encounter the moon landing hoax conspiracy theory or the Flat Earth conspiracy theory as a *falsifiable* set of claims, we can easily disprove that both are incorrect theories of reality. The moon landing really did happen, and the Earth is really a sphere. However, when we encounter these conspiracy theories as conspiracism, in which all evidence is turned into more evidence for the conspiracy, we have entered the realm of a self-protecting thought loop. As we suggested earlier, when there is an a priori commitment to a set of claims, the facts are not what are important.

IN THE SPIRIT OF SCIENTIFIC INQUIRY — THE METHOD IN ACTION

What we want to take away from the above is a commitment to the scientific spirit and its application to questions in the social world. Many explanations of the world were once good science but turned out to be wrong. The theory of phlogiston is one such example. As European science was starting to develop, some early chemists hypothesized that some matter had a combustible element within it, which they called phlogiston. This was one among a number of competing theories about how and why things caught on fire; the discovery of oxygen and its role in combustion was still a few hundred years away. When the theory of phlogiston was developed, it played by the rules of science. It used nature to describe nature, in this case a supposed element responsible for fire. It relied on the assumption that nature is a closed system. It made falsifiable statements about the world. Eventually, all chemists moved on to new ways of describing the underlying chemical mechanics of combustion. The theory of phlogiston became unscientific and had to be dropped.

We need to do the same, no matter how personally attached we might be to a certain way of viewing the world. Almost always, ontologies represent ideological communities in which we find friends and meaning. Nonetheless, we must proceed in the spirit of science. If our claims about the world are put in falsifiable ways, and they are shown to be false, we must be ruthless and jettison them.

This approach puts certain limits on our thinking. Like a natural scientist investigating an unusual natural phenomenon, when we investigate a potential conspiracy theory, we assume that there is a non-mystical, non-supernatural explanation. No matter how strange and unusual the data, we begin with the assumption that it is either natural or that it is human-generated. There is no recourse to super natural beings like demons pulling the mystical wool over our eyes. Second, whenever possible, we must put our ideas into a testable form. And we must be honestly willing to have our hypothesis proven wrong. No recourse to conspiracism allowed. In fact, we should (ideally) welcome the challenge to have our hypothesis tested by skeptical analysts. If there's a real conspiracy, it will withstand the test. All real conspiracies have.

What will emerge from this approach is that real conspiracies tend to have certain "marks." MKUltra, the CIA's illegal mind control project, has these marks. CIA records show it actually happened, and these documents can be verified by experts who know what to look for in CIA documents and can spot forgeries. The CIA documents about MKUltra are now accessible through the CIA website. There is even a (sort of) apology by the CIA. Furthermore, the victims of these experiments all have similar stories, and these stories check out in terms of hospital records, what they can recall of their experiences, who the staff at the institutions were, and the like. Some of these victims have filed lawsuits and won, which is not something that happens if the conspiracy is based on fraudulent or dubious claims.

Contrast this with the Flat Earth conspiracy. There is no documented evidence that makes any sense that suggests that the Earth is flat. There is also no coherent reason why a secret society would go to all the trouble of convincing the world's population that it is a sphere when it is flat. The claims, when put in a falsifiable form, are easily falsified, and not just by scientists. They can be falsified by people at home. The conspiracy asks one to believe that there exists a hidden global political body that is ruling all the world and disguising the truth about everything, despite the fact that there is no historical precedent for the existence of anything remotely like this. Many governments have tried to become all-powerful and control the ideas of their citizens. At best, these efforts are a partial success. Usually they fail miserably.

We can prove the moon landings happened without going to the moon, we can disprove the Flat Earth theory in our own backyards, and we can escape the self-sustaining thought loops that keep us stuck believing things that are not true.

11

TEXT, CONTEXT, AND SUBTEXT — READING BETWEEN THE LINES OF THE CATTLE MUTILATION CONSPIRACY

THE FLEA IN THE CAPSULE

In the 1980s, a story started to spread through Moscow. After decades of being kept out by the Iron Curtain of the Cold War, American products were starting to show up on the tables of black-market sellers. Some of the most popular items being sold illegally were American blue jeans.

But rumours started to spread about the dangers posed by those garments. Apparently, Americans had secretly sewn a small glass capsule into the seams of the jeans before smuggling them into the USSR. When the unsuspecting Soviet buyer put them on for the first time, that capsule would break and release its contents. And those contents, according to the rumour, were fleas infected with syphilis.

The fleas (being fleas) would then bite the legs of the person who had put on the American pants. That person would unknowingly become infected with syphilis, which they would spread to anyone they had sex with, who would then spread it to anyone *they* had sex with, and so on. The black market American blue jeans were clearly a public health menace.

However, there was a problem with these rumours — they weren't true. American blue jeans *were* showing up along with other bootlegged and smuggled Western goods, but they didn't contain secret glass capsules in their seams. The entire story doesn't hold up well to even a short examination, as there are some fairly obvious questions that could be raised to challenge the details. How difficult would it be to trap a flea in a small glass capsule? How long could a flea stay alive in that airtight space? Could you infect a flea with syphilis? Could a person contract syphilis from a flea bite? The answers to these questions are: very, not long, no, and no.

This conspiracy theory, like many others, was false. However, that doesn't mean there is no truth to be found in it. While accurate information about conspiracies, such as MKUltra, COINTELPRO, Sea-Spray, and others, can obviously teach us valuable lessons about historical events, false conspiracy theories are also useful to study if we are looking for truth. We won't find it in the **text** of the theory, but if we examine the **context**, we can uncover truths about its **subtext**. Or, to put it another way, the story itself is a lie, but by looking at the background from which that lie emerged, and the situation in which it circulated, we can learn something about the society that believed that lie.

The text of this particular false conspiracy theory we have already gone over — that Americans are putting syphilitic fleas in glass capsules in black market jeans. There isn't much there to go on, so in order to read between the lines we require more information. To get this information, we need to start with the context.

LOCATING A STORY IN TIME AND SPACE

Because this is a story that takes place in the 1980s, and because it takes place in the Soviet Union, we can safely assume some aspect of it will have to do with the Cold War — particularly since the villain in the story is the United States. This means that part of the context of this claim is that it takes place during a time in which the USSR and the USA were locked in an ideological battle between communism and capitalism.

However, the two countries were unable to fight directly, since they each had nuclear weapons. The very appropriate acronym MAD (for Mutually Assured Destruction) described the situation — if one side used nuclear warheads against the other, the other would reply with some of their own. It was impossible for one side to destroy the other without being destroyed themselves, and it was extremely dangerous even to have a fight with non-nuclear weapons, since if one side started to lose a conventional conflict, they would almost certainly turn to atomic fission weapons as a desperate last resort.

This meant that, throughout the Cold War, the two sides had to come up with odd and unorthodox methods of fighting. The American military and spy agencies attempted to fight the Soviets with mind control programs employing hallucinogens and hypnosis (MKUltra), psychics and fortune tellers (Stargate), and even modern art (the Congress for Cultural Freedom). And because even remote possibilities were considered, plans were drawn up to conscript insects as tiny Cold War soldiers.

Weaponized insects have a history that goes back thousands of years, and many ancient civilizations used wasps, scorpions, bees, or fleas to fight their enemies.[296] But deliberate biological warfare using a bug as a vector of disease also has a long and disturbing history. During the 1930s in Japan, Unit 731 was formed to study biological weapons and carried out lethal experiments on unwilling subjects. The information gathered by Unit 731 would eventually be used against Chinese citizens when Japan dropped bombs loaded with plague-ridden fleas. Russian civilians were also experimented on during the program.[297]

Some of the doctors who authorized and carried out those experiments, including the head of the program, Dr. Shirō Ishii, would be officially pardoned for their atrocities by the American government after the war ended, since the information those doctors had uncovered was considered important for the new conflict against the Soviet Union. Only a few years later, during the Korean War, North Korea and China publicly accused the American government of using the data they had received from Unit 731 and dropping infected insects and bugs to try to cause plague and epidemics within the North Korean population, although the U.S. denied the accusations. Despite the denials, the American government (along with Canadian researchers) had been working in the late 1940s on a method through which hundreds of thousands of disease-infected flies could be placed inside a bomb. In the mid-1950s, the American government launched Operation Big Itch to test the feasibility of using fleas as tiny plague-filled assassins.

This is only one part of the context required to understand the blue jeans conspiracy theory. Understanding a little bit of the history of bugs as weapons — particularly during the Cold War — demonstrates why it would not be much of a leap of faith to believe that there were American fleas infiltrating Soviet society. But another piece of the historical picture needs to be addressed. This story came out in the mid-1980s, when the Soviet Union was on its last legs, with only a few years left before the communist empire would collapse.

Because of MAD, outright physical invasion by the USA of the USSR (or vice versa) was almost impossible. Rather than simply occupying the territory of the enemy, the two sides of the Cold War were interested in invading the hearts and minds of the enemy's citizens. Instead of trucks full of soldiers and tanks, ideas and ideology would sneak across the border and open up new fronts in the battle — turning members of the enemy into sympathetic assets. Both the USA and the USSR were worried about ideological infiltration, and with the Soviets in a weakened position in the mid-1980s, they were even more concerned.

This brief contextual examination is useful for the next step in the analysis of this conspiracy theory — reading the subtext.

WHY SYPHILIS?

To get context, we can look at the work of journalists and historians. Subtext is a trickier matter, and requires us to ask how the context tells us the hidden truth of that text.

The text is the conspiracy theory about syphilitic fleas in glass capsules sewn into jeans. The context is the Cold War, and the final years of the USSR. What is the subtext? Since this story isn't true, why did someone write and spread it? Why were people quick to believe it? What truths can we learn from this lie?

A good place to start are those parts of the text that make the least sense. Why syphilis? Plague would have been more practical (both as a weapon and as a disease that could be spread by fleas). Unlike accurate information, which has the disadvantage of having to stick closely to real life, an invented story like this one can be engineered to deliver the specific message the author wants to get across. Syphilis is a sexually transmitted disease, which means two things that are relevant here: It spreads quietly and insidiously through a population, and there is a stigma attached that is often associated with immorality. In this story, it isn't just that there is a disease that is being spread through the Soviet population; the author of this story wants to communicate that there is an insidious *moral* threat endangering the soul of the nation.

Why blue jeans? It would be far more destructive and less needlessly complicated to poison grain or taint a water supply with a biological agent. This is where the subtext starts to become clear. The blue jeans don't make sense because in this story they represent something else: capitalism in general and American culture in particular. At a time in which the Soviet system was failing, the fear that America might invade — not with an army, but with consumer goods — was rising. The purpose of this false conspiracy theory is to scare people away from American culture as personified by that most American piece of clothing — blue jeans. It is a threat to the spiritual and moral health of the Soviet nation.

WHAT LIES BENEATH THE OCEAN

To better understand the difference between text, context, and subtext, it helps to look at something a little less convoluted than conspiracy theory. To that end, popular movies can provide a useful opportunity.

The classic 1954 Japanese film *Gojira* (known in North America as *Godzilla*) is an excellent example. The text is borderline ridiculous — a giant lizard wakes up and crawls out of the Pacific Ocean to devastate the country of Japan, stomping on Tokyo and sending the population fleeing. However, a closer look at the text reveals some key information that will help us understand the subtext, once we have also looked at the context in which the movie was written.

An obvious clue as to the true meaning of the film shows up early and often. The event that wakes Gojira is an H-bomb test in the Pacific. Comments are made throughout the film about the dangers of nuclear power, as Gojira doesn't just crush and burn the areas he attacks — he also leaves them bathed in deadly radiation. There are scenes in which doctors pass Geiger counters over dying children and the needles spike.

A theme that runs through the entire film is the double-edged sword of technological advancement. In addition to the new bomb that wakes Gojira up, one of the main characters is a scientist who has developed another terrible weapon — the "Oxygen Destroyer." When used in a body of water, it vaporizes and eliminates all nearby life.[298]

In the end, the scientist reluctantly agrees to use his weapon to destroy Gojira, but deliberately kills himself with the device at the same time. The film ends sombrely, not triumphantly.

The context of the film also helps illuminate the subtext. *Gojira* was filmed in 1954 and was written only a few months after the *Daigo Fukuryū Maru* incident, in which an American H-bomb test accidentally irradiated a Japanese fishing vessel. Many of the sailors on that ship developed radiation sickness after being "dusted by the ashes of death," as the Japanese press put it.[299] Coming less than a decade after the nuclear destruction of Hiroshima and Nagasaki, the incident sparked debate in Japan about the risks of nuclear power. However, that debate was a careful one. The postwar American military occupation had ended only two years earlier, in 1952, and during that occupation it was illegal to publish anything critical of nuclear power.[300] The scenes of destruction, death, and burning buildings in *Gojira* would have looked very familiar to Japanese audiences. The American firebombing campaign devastated Tokyo and many other major cities. But by having the destruction come at the scaly hands of a giant monster rather than American bombers, the filmmakers were able to get away with much more than they would have otherwise. By framing the ethical debate about the fictional Oxygen Destroyer rather than the H-bomb, the characters in the film could point out the moral issues of nuclear power without naming it directly. Even the way Gojira looked was influenced by the destruction of Nagasaki and Hiroshima — the rough and bumpy skin of the monster was meant to resemble the scars suffered by survivors of the atomic blasts.[301]

The subtext in *Gojira* is clear (although less clear for American audiences of the time, since the English version removed 20 minutes of film, including anything that suggested nuclear power might not be completely positive).[302] However, finding subtext in films is not always so clear-cut, and sometimes there are competing subtextual interpretations of the same text.

WHAT'S HIDING IN THE BASEMENT

In 1956, the film *Invasion of the Body Snatchers* was released, based on a novel published two years earlier.[303] The text of both is almost identical. In the small American town of Santa Mira, something strange and insidious is happening. The main character, physician Miles Bennell, notices that many of his patients are suffering from the same apparent delusion — that the people around them aren't *really* who they say they are. They may look the same and sound the same, but they are different in some fundamental and terrifying way. Bennell thinks it must be some sort of mass hysteria infecting the town, but later on discovers a strange body growing in a giant peapod in the basement of a friend, and the truth becomes clear: The town is being infiltrated by an alien force that is systematically replacing the population with evil doubles. Bennell and his girlfriend, Becky, try to get help, but everywhere they turn, the townsfolk have already been replaced by podpeople. Eventually Becky succumbs to exhaustion and falls asleep and is also snatched and replaced, leaving Bennell to stagger alone out into traffic, desperately trying to warn everyone about the secret invasion happening under everyone's noses.

According to the author of the book, Jack Finney, no subtext was intended; it was just meant to be a spooky story. However, because of the context in which the film emerged, people have found plenty of subtextual interpretations.

Both the novel and the movie versions came out in the mid-1950s, a frightening time for the American population. The Cold War was less than a decade old at that point, but already complete nuclear annihilation was on the table; the Soviets had detonated their first atomic bomb in 1949. In addition to the physical threat posed by the USSR, Americans were concerned about the ideological threat of communism sneaking into the minds of the population. To sharpen the dread even more, China had just turned communist, and it was one of the most populous nations on Earth. Several high-level spies had been arrested, sparking concern that others were still hiding in the hallways of power.

But by the time the movie came out in 1956, it wasn't just communism that was striking fear into the American populace but the *fear of the fear* of communism. Senator Joseph McCarthy had fired up his anti-communist witch trials, and many innocent people had gotten caught up in them, having their lives ruined in the process. Paranoia was becoming overwhelming, and people reacted by throwing around accusations with reckless abandon.

Because of this historical context, there were several apparently contradictory subtextual interpretations of the text of the film. Some looked at the podpeople, with their communal impulses and plans and their lack of individualism, and saw a metaphor for the dangers of communism sneaking into small-town communities. Maybe your neighbour or even someone in your family picks up a pro-communist pamphlet. Maybe they start attending pro-communist meetings. Maybe the police chief gets convinced to become a Red, or the mayor. Maybe the entire town will fall under the hypnotic spell of Soviet ideology, and the country could be taken without a single shot being fired.

On the other hand, some looked at the same text and read a seemingly different subtext. The way that the podpeople, once they had the numbers, turned on and mindlessly persecuted the rest of the citizens of Santa Mira without mercy appeared to mirror the way that McCarthy and his kind operated. They turned neighbours against neighbours and family members against family members in their single-minded pursuit of rooting out any opinions or beliefs that didn't conform to their narrow definition of what it meant to be an American. Maybe the podpeople weren't the accused communists; maybe they were the fanatic witch-hunters making the accusations.

While these two interpretations may seem at odds, they are actually based in the same fear: the dangers of groupthink and rigid conformity in a society. Regardless of whether the podpeople represent communists or anti-communists or some other group, it is the danger in unquestioning and uncritical devotion to an ideology (regardless of its specific content) that the film uses to such great effect.

While movies are helpful to illustrate the relationships between text, context, and subtext, there are obviously some important differences between films and conspiracy theories. Few people believe movies are real, whereas false conspiracy theories are presented as true, and many people believe them. To examine a kind of story that more closely resembles a false conspiracy theory, we should look to the form of folklore known as the urban legend.

THE HOOK ON THE DOOR HANDLE

The urban legend is a very specific form of storytelling. Its settings tend to be normal, everyday situations. The stories take place in contemporary times rather than ancient ones. They often have a grotesque element as a person is punished in some sort of terrible way for going against one of society's norms. And the most important aspect of the urban legend is that it is told as though it really happened, often to a "friend of a friend" of the storyteller.[304] In this way in particular, urban legends are like conspiracy theories. In addition, like conspiracy theories, they mutate through repetition to stay relevant by adapting to changing information ecosystems. And, in another parallel to conspiracy theories, while a small number of urban legends are true (like the story of the Halloween haunted house that accidentally used a real corpse as one of its decorations),[305] most are fictions passed off as truths. But we can still find truths within those fictions by understanding the context in which the fiction emerges and spreads and examining the subtext hidden in the text.

Often, the text of an urban legend will involve a person being punished, harmed, or embarrassed as the result of making the wrong decision. The context is often some sort of change occurring in the contemporary culture, and the subtext will often be that the change is unwelcome and should be stopped.

Here's a classic example from 1950s Middle America: A teenage couple parks their car at a romantic spot well known by locals as the best place to make out. To get his date in the mood, the boy turns on his car radio, but instead of music there's an urgent news announcement. A crazed killer has just escaped from a nearby mental institution and is on the loose. He is easy to identify, as he is missing his left hand. In its place is a hook. The girl, hearing the news, immediately asks to be driven home, but the boy insists on staying and getting a little action. The two argue back and forth for a while. The boy says that he can protect her if the killer comes by, and that they will be safe in the car. The girl argues that the killer could smash in the window and attack them. Finally, growing frustrated, the boy agrees to leave. He slams on the accelerator and drives away. After an awkward trip back to the girl's home, the boy parks out in front, gets out of the car, and walks to the passenger side to open the girl's door for her. He looks down at the door handle to see a bloody severed hook.[306]

The meaning here is obvious — the killer was about to open the door and attack the two teens, but when the boy drove off, it was torn off his arm. Had the teens stayed even a moment longer, they could have been injured or killed.

Like most urban legends, the text of this story isn't true (and the details don't make much sense). The context is the America of the 1950s, a time of social change. The specific social changes relevant to this story have to do with three of the main concepts in the text: teenagers, cars, and sex.

The "teenager" was still a fairly recent idea in the 1950s. Before World War II, while of course there were people between the ages of 13 and 19, there was barely any mention of teenagers as a distinct cultural group in the mainstream press. However, by 1953, FBI head J. Edgar Hoover was warning the nation that "the nation can expect an appalling increase in the number of teenagers in the years ahead."[307] This was a rapid change in the culture's attitude and attention, which was brought about by other changes in society, both economic and material.

From an economic perspective, the nation was becoming more industrialized, and the needs of the workforce were changing. Jobs required more years of training, and the number of people going to high school shot up dramatically. The postwar economic boom also meant that younger people had jobs and income, which in turn meant that marketers had a greater motivation to define, examine, and appeal to the teenager segment of the population. From a material perspective, cars were becoming more popular, more reliable, and more affordable. For the first time, young people were freed from their parents' homes and able to easily roam about. There had been fears of car-driven juvenile delinquency and shenanigans since the turn of the 20th century, but in the early 1950s, it reached a fever pitch.[308]

In particular, there was a fear that, given the relative privacy and independence that a car could provide, teenagers would be able to engage in risky and immoral (by the standards of the time, at least) sexual behaviours.

Given that context, the subtext of "The Hook" becomes clear. The main characters are teenagers, doing exactly the thing that was causing a moral panic — parking and making out. It's worth noting that in all the versions of this story, it's the boy who's interested in going further and the girl who is trying to fend off his advances and cool things down. The lesson here in the subtext is that it is the responsibility of the girl or woman to prevent sexual activity, since the boy or man will be unable to control himself. The hook-handed killer symbolically represents the consequences of the teenagers' actions (STDs, pregnancy, stigma, etc.) rather than the imaginary threat of literal hook-handed killers wandering the countryside. The subtextual purpose of the fictional story is to scare teenagers away from sexual activity, and to reinforce the pre-1950s conventions and norms.

Many urban legends share a similar conservative outlook towards social change. For example, in "The Hippie Babysitter," from the late 1960s, a couple leaves their baby with a cannabis-smoking babysitter. During their night out, they call home to see how things are going, and the hippie babysitter tells them that everything is fine, and she put the turkey in the oven. Realizing that they don't have a turkey at home, the couple rush home, only to find the stoned babysitter has baked their baby in the oven instead.[309]

However, other urban legends punish (or at least reprimand) the main character for failing to *keep up* with social change. In the classic story of "The Killer in the Back Seat," also from the 1960s, a woman is driving alone on a desolate stretch of road at night. She notices a car following her. It starts tailgating her and flashing its headlights. Frightened, she speeds up, but the other car keeps pace. Looking in the rear-view mirror, she sees the other driver's face. He is sometimes described as being "rough-looking"; in many variations of the tale he is a Black man. In either case, the sight of the other driver's face makes the woman even more frightened and more determined to get away.

Finally, after a long car chase, she pulls into her driveway and honks the horn. Her husband runs out of the house, and the other driver gets out of his car as well. The husband grabs the driver and demands an explanation, and the other driver reveals that he saw a man hiding in the woman's back seat and was simply trying to warn her about the danger. The couple opens the back door, and sure enough a murderer is hiding in the back seat.[310] In this example, the subtext is that character is at fault for holding on to her traditional biases at a time when society was starting to challenge some long-held prejudices.

When the text of urban legends is analyzed through a subtextual lens, the true but hidden meanings can become much clearer. The same is true of false conspiracy theories. By closely examining the text of a conspiracy claim and understanding the context in which that claim originated and circulated, we can learn a lot about the underlying subtext, which in turn can show us much about why human beings so frequently look for a conspiratorial explanation. As an example, let's look at one of the strangest and most disturbing conspiracy theories to emerge from the United States in the 1970s: the cattle mutilation epidemic.[311]

THE DEATH OF SNIPPY

On September 9, 1967, a Colorado rancher found her horse, which would later be referenced to in media reports as Snippy, dead on the ground near the edge of a clearing on her ranch. Strangely, the horse was intact except for its head, which had been stripped of all flesh and hide. The horse's organs were gone, except for the brain, and all fluids appeared to have been drained from the body.

What made the story creepier was that it took place in the context of a flying saucer flap. In the weeks leading up to the discovery of the horse, there had been several publicized sightings of UFOs in the area, and the media speculated that the two events might be linked in some way. Colorado papers featured headlines such as "UFOs Are Sighted in South Colorado," "Did Horse, 'Saucer' Tangle?" and "Flying Saucer Sought in Death of Horse." A pathologist and hematologist named Dr. John Altshuler was visiting the area and was asked by police to examine the horse corpse. Altshuler noted the lack of blood, the surgical cuts, and the way that it appeared that a high-tech laser had been used in the dissection. It should be noted, though, that Dr. Altshuler was nearby because he had read about the UFO sightings, and since he was a true believer in the extraterrestrial origin of UFOs, he wanted to experience them for himself. As such, Dr. Altshuler was already primed to see an alien hand at work in the odd state of the horse's corpse.

While much local buzz was generated by the story (mostly around the possibility of UFO involvement), it was an unusual tale rather than part of a larger phenomenon. However, this would change in 1973, when a series of cattle "mutilations" would spark a nationwide panic, eventually dragging the FBI and the federal government into the situation.

WAVE OF MUTILATION

From 1973 to 1980, there was a lot of press and a lot of concern from the public about what appeared to be a wave of strange cattle mutilations in the American Great Plains. Similar to the Snippy story, these "mutes" (as they came to be known) had some odd characteristics: The animals appeared to have been drained of all of their blood, they had very specific organs and body parts removed, and the work seemed to have a surgical quality that suggested professionals had been responsible. There were no tracks of any kind near the corpses, and the cows appeared to have died without struggling or fighting back in any way. This generated so much alarm and anxiety in the American population that in 1979, New Mexico senator (and former astronaut) Harrison Schmitt sponsored a cattle mutilation conference and demanded a federal investigation into the matter.

There were two official investigations, one by the Colorado Bureau of Investigation, and one by former FBI agent Ken Rommel. The CBI reported that, while it was possible that in a small percentage of the cases there *may* have been the use of sharp tools or instruments, for the most part both official investigations returned with the same conclusion: There was nothing particularly unusual about the deaths of the cattle or the state their bodies were found in. Rommel argued that "all of the mutilations investigated by me were caused by and totally consistent with what one would expect to find from normal predation, scavenger activity, and decomposition of a dead animal."[312] The missing organs were exactly the parts of a cow that one would expect scavengers to remove and eat, and the "missing" blood was actually just the result of normal coagulation during decomposition. Pathologists agreed with the official findings and pointed out that there was no shortage of reasons a cow might die while out on the plains: Lightning strikes, accidental poisoning, disease, heat, cold, dehydration, and dietary deficiencies all claimed the lives of hundreds of thousands of cattle every year.

In 1979, an anthropologist from the University of Arkansas performed an experiment in which the body of a young cow was left in a ravine and monitored. After only 30 hours, ordinary scavengers such as vultures, insects, and skunks had "mutilated" the carcass in exactly the same way as in the other cases, suggesting that no mysterious force was necessary to explain the state of the dead cattle.

Ultimately, nothing was suspicious about the deaths, but regardless of the official explanation, the phenomenon generated three distinct conspiracy hypotheses. None of them proved to be accurate, but we can gain some insight if we examine the text of each of them, the context in which they emerged, and the subtext behind them. The three hypotheses are:

1. The mutilations were part of a ritual by a well-funded and organized Satanic cult.
2. The mutilations were carried out by the American government as part of a top secret project.
3. The mutilations were part of an extraterrestrial experiment.[313]

We'll start with the Satanic cult.

THE DEVIL YOU KNOW

The text of the first hypothesis is as follows: A massive Satanic cult was operating within the United States and carrying out demonic and occult practices. The cattle were mutilated by this group. The purpose of the mutilation varied, according to which variation of the cult hypothesis you adhered to, but one of the main versions proposed that the cows were killed and drained of blood as part of a hallucinatory drug procedure. The cow would first be injected with PCP (a drug also known as angel dust). The cow would then be sacrificed, and the cult members would drink the PCP-infused cow blood for a strong mystic hallucinogenic experience. A black mass sex orgy would then follow as part of a Satanic ritual. As John Dunn, the president of the Oklahoma Cattlemen's Association, told the *New York Times* in 1975: "I think when all this thing shakes down, we'll find out it's cults . . . they begin killing them for the blood and sex organs and are probably saving up the stuff for their ceremonies on Easter."[314]

This Satanic cult apparently had wealthy and influential members, which is why they were able to carry off such a large operation, including the use of helicopters, without being caught or exposed. The goal of this group was to assassinate several American politicians, steal plutonium, build and set off a nuclear bomb in an American city, and begin a 1,000-year reign of darkness. A lot of this information came from a report written by a special agent from the Bureau of Alcohol, Tobacco, and Firearms named Donald Flickinger, who had gotten much of the information from a prison informant named Kenneth Bankston.

Examining the context of the Satanic cult hypothesis helps to understand it a little better. In the Western world, going back to at least the 15th century, there has been the fear that a hidden Satanic group was secretly manipulating things. Most of the descriptions in the text of the cattle mutilation cult hypothesis (secret Satanic groups, blood drinking, sacrifices, orgies) were present in beliefs that had already been circulating in the European population for hundreds of years. Even the very specific suspicion that cattle and other livestock were being harmed by a sinister collective has been in the culture for hundreds of years.[315] These fears helped drive the continental witch trials from the 1400s to the 1700s, resulting in thousands of deaths.[316] By the 1970s, there were no sanctioned witch trials in America, but the fear of a demonic cabal remained in the population. The events of the 1960s, in which conventional mores and attitudes had been shaken up by the rise of counterculture, caused an uneasiness in many that contributed to this fear. This was particularly true after the brutal 1968 Manson Family murders, in which several people were killed in an apparently sacrificial manner by a group that had fallen under the influence of a hippie guru. Cults, and the fear of cults, were becoming increasingly prominent in American society. When two dead calves were found in Lake Villa, Illinois, in 1975, police threw suspicion on a cult that had recently been recruiting members in Oregon, promising to take them on a flying saucer ride and to bring them to an evolutionary level above human.[317] That group would eventually become known as Heaven's Gate.[318] Moonies at the airport and Jonestown in the jungles of Guyana provided a public — and to many people alarming — face of New Religious Movements.

Of course, the Manson Family was hardly representative of the counterculture movement as a whole. There was no physical evidence for any elaborate PCP rituals being performed with sacrificed cattle. The Heaven's Gate cult had nothing to do with the deaths of calves in Illinois. And a lot of the Satanic cult panic was based on incorrect information. Kenneth Bankston — the prison informant feeding Agent Flickinger information about the massive Satanic cult — was making up stories to get a sweeter deal and to get moved to a lower-security jail (which he then escaped from). There had also been a number of Satanic cult "tell-all" exposé books published in the 1970s, such as Beatrice Sparks's *Jay's Journal*, which were actually works of fiction passed off as fact to generate more interest and sell more copies.

Based on this context, what can we surmise about the subtext of the Satanic cult conspiracy claim? Or, to put it another way, what real thing does the imagined Satanic cult represent?

Many Americans, particularly in the rural states in which this hypothesis was most common, saw their familiar and comfortable culture becoming less recognizable. The 1960s and early '70s were a time of accelerated change — in music, fashion, film, television, and politics. Short-haired crooners had been replaced by long-haired guitar-burners; gentle family sitcoms were being replaced by edgy and politically charged comedies. The baby boom generation born after World War II was just coming into their adulthood, meaning that the population leaned very young, which meant that this new cohort had an outsized impact on the culture and the society. There was an increased interest in religions and belief systems other than mainstream Protestant Christianity, and a growing appreciation for questioning traditions and conventional power structures.

Rapid social change can be a frightening thing for a population, and one of the main subtexts of the cult hypothesis is this fear of cultural change, represented in this case by an evil cabal deliberately eroding the social fabric of convention and decency and rebelling against mainstream religion and morality. The Satanism of the imagined cult is working in direct opposition to the mainstream Christianity that people took as the norm. While the text of this cult hypothesis is far-fetched and unsupported, the context in which it emerged helps us to understand the subtext that would have made this idea seem more possible to an audience already nervous and apprehensive about the changes in their culture.

BLACK HELICOPTERS

The cult hypothesis started to lose traction as the decade progressed. Despite the attention paid to the idea by law enforcement agencies, no evidence was forthcoming. And another aspect of the phenomenon made people less convinced that a cult was behind it. In part because of the lack of footprints and the remote locations of the cattle corpses, and in part because of an increased number of eyewitness accounts, in the mid-1970s increased attention was paid to the idea that helicopters were involved in the cattle mutilation (in particular, black unmarked helicopters). Considering the perceived scope of the cattle mutilation, people started to question whether even a well-supported cult would have the resources for a multi-state helicopter operation. But another organization *would* have the available resources: the American federal government.

As with the cult hypothesis, there were several versions of the claim that the mutilated cattle were part of a large federal government secret project. Some argued that the government was testing a new variant of VX nerve agent that would be effective only on people with an Asian background, to create a new weapon to use during the war in Vietnam, and the dead cows were test subjects for the experiments. Another version claimed that there had been a secret spill of chemical, biological, or nuclear waste, and the cows were being killed and dissected by a federal government agency to secretly survey and measure the impact. Regardless of the reason for the mutilations, all of the government-centred hypotheses proposed that the project was being hidden from the public and involved unmarked black helicopters.

Many ranchers and farmers had reported seeing such helicopters, and some even formed vigilante groups to fight back against them. This predictably resulted in several tense situations. An Iowa farmer claimed an unmarked helicopter had shot at him, and there were several recorded incidents of helicopters being fired upon. One Nebraska farmer shot a utility helicopter that was flying low over the ground to check power cables, and Nebraska National Guard helicopter pilots were instructed not to fly below 2,000 feet, to minimize the chances of being hit by gunfire.

While it may seem surprising at first that rumours of secret government experiments resulted in people firing on helicopters, when the context is considered, it becomes much less so. By the mid 1970s, several secret American government programs had come to light, and many of them were shocking and disturbing. The 1975 Church Committee was a Senate report on the CIA, FBI, NSA, and IRS that detailed many of the examples of gross overreach that had occurred, including assassination attempts of foreign leaders, MKUltra mind control experiments, and illegal FBI surveillance programs. By then, the public's trust in the federal government had already been eroded by the Nixon administration's Watergate scandal and reporting from Vietnam detailing war crimes and civilian deaths caused by American actions. It should be noted that, to the public, America's complex and troubling involvement in Vietnam was intrinsically tied in with the iconic image of low-flying helicopters.

There had also been scandals involving the American government and livestock. In 1968, during a nerve gas experiment at the Dugway Proving Ground in Utah, unexpected high winds dispersed nerve gas farther than intended, resulting in the deaths of over 6,000 sheep. The U.S. Army initially denied responsibility before later admitting to the mistake once evidence had been released to the public in the media. In 1976, dozens of horses were found dead at a drinking hole near the Dugway Proving Ground, and while the U.S. Army claimed they had ceased nerve gas testing, people were suspicious that the horses had been killed in another field test gone wrong.[319]

By the mid-1970s there had also been new revelations about secret government experiments carried out on large populations of civilians without their consent. These included information on the Tuskegee syphilis study, and Operation Sea-Spray, discussed in earlier chapters.[320]

There were also contextual reasons why farmers and ranchers in particular became sufficiently convinced of the federal government hypothesis to take violent action against helicopters. The cattle mutilation panic coincided with an economic slowdown that hit small farmers and ranchers hard and was made worse by actions at the federal level when, in 1973, the Nixon administration artificially capped the price of beef in an attempt to fight runaway inflation. As a result, ranchers held on to their cows rather than sending them to the slaughterhouse, in hopes that when the price cap was removed they could make more profit. This caused massive layoffs in the slaughterhouse and meatpacking industry, and when the cattle were finally sold, the meat was too fatty and undesirable. The resulting crash in the beef market became known as "the Wreck" and was catastrophic for small ranchers and farmers.

With this context in mind, the subtext of the secret government program hypothesis becomes very clear. The "black helicopters" and shadowy federal agents sneaking around mutilating cows represented a generalized loss of faith and trust in the government and an increased fear that the government was not concerned with the welfare of the rural citizens of the country.

Although this was a popular hypothesis, there was one question that seemed to undermine it. With all the resources available to the government (agents, helicopters, secret bases) why wouldn't they just have purchased cattle to experiment on in private in government installations, rather than using random cattle out in the middle of fields and attracting all sorts of unwelcome attention? For some, this was enough to convince them that a third hypothesis was the most likely: The cattle mutilations were the work of extraterrestrial beings.

ALIEN BUTCHERS

Even before the cattle mutilation phenomenon picked up speed in the 1970s, aliens were already in the mix. The owner of Snippy, the horse found "mutilated" in 1967, had proposed an extraterrestrial explanation. However, in the early 1970s, the Satanic cult hypothesis and secret government project hypothesis had more traction. It wasn't until the end of the decade that aliens returned as the main suspect.

Not surprisingly for a claim heavily tilted towards speculation, the alien cattle mutilation hypothesis came in many different versions. One of the most influential was circulated on May 25, 1980, on a Denver television station that aired a documentary by ufologist Linda Moulton Howe titled *A Strange Harvest*. The film was extremely light on physical evidence and relied instead on innuendo, interviews with people undergoing hypnosis, and psychic visions. The text of the claim is as follows: The cattle mutilations are caused by alien visitors in flying saucers. This is the reason there are no footprints around the corpses, and it explains how the mutilators can get to and from the sites without noise. The mutilations themselves are performed inside the flying saucers; thus the lack of blood at the mutilation sites. The American government is aware of the situation and perhaps even working *with* the aliens. In addition to mutilating cattle, the aliens occasionally abduct human beings, and the documentary featured a long interview between an alleged abductee and a hypnotist, who was able to extract (or implant) a story about being in a flying saucer and watching a cow mutilation take place. The mutilations are part of a larger alien project to test our soil, air, and water.

As disturbing as this all might sound, there is a twist in the text of this hypothesis. At the end of the documentary, Howe reads the writings of a psychic who had been using their "powers" to investigate the cattle mutilation phenomenon. According to the psychic, the purpose of the mutilation is to test a new miracle serum the aliens are developing in order to save their dying race. Once they have finished their work, and once they are certain we were worthy of it, the aliens will return to Earth, provide us with the serum, and humanity will share in the alien bounty.

As with the other two hypotheses, to make subtextual sense of the odd text of this claim, we need to examine the context in which it emerged. Almost from its advent in 1947, the flying saucer phenomenon had given rise to two main competing theories: one, that aliens were here to invade, and two, that aliens were here to protect us from ourselves. The idea that the American government knew more about UFOs than they were telling the public, and that there may be a threat to citizens from aliens, goes back to influential ufologists such as Major Donald Keyhoe, who in 1955 wrote *The Flying Saucer Conspiracy* to accuse the government in general and the Air Force in particular of covering up evidence about alien encounters. The idea that aliens were here to save us from ourselves was very common in the 1950s and early 1960s, with people such as George Adamski and George Van Tassel claiming to have met with spiritually evolved beings, often from Venus, who were concerned about earthlings' development of nuclear weapons. It's worth noting that in 1951, a very popular sci-fi film titled *The Day the Earth Stood Still* depicted a benevolent alien landing in a flying saucer with a warning about nuclear weapons, so before alleged contactees such as Adamski and Van Tassel claimed to have met with extra-terrestrials, the idea was already present in pop culture.

The alien hypothesis for the cattle mutilations drew from all these UFO influences, as well as other famous examples such as the alleged abduction and experimentation of Betty and Barney Hill in 1961. The subtext for the alien serum conspiracy theory is similar to the one shared by the 1950 abductees: the fear that humans, without help from "above," will behave in a way that will ensure their own destruction, coupled with the wish-fulfillment of imagining that an outside force will come and wave away the Earth's problems.

THE TRUTH IN THE FICTION

The cattle mutilation panic of the 1970s was an odd moment in history, but it gives us examples of text (the conspiracies themselves), context (the historical situation from which the conspiracy theories emerge), and subtext (what the conspiracy theories are really about).

While false conspiracy theories lead their believers further away from the truth, there is still much we can learn from studying them. By examining the social, political, economic, and historical context of a false conspiracy claim, we can learn about the worries, desires, prejudices, hatreds, and taboos of the society that created and circulated it.

The syphilitic fleas, Satanic cults, black helicopters, and alien cattle rustlers examined in this chapter may have been figments of people's imaginations, but the underlying fears and hopes that were concealed within them were based firmly in reality. False conspiracy theories betray aspects of the Zeitgeist that may otherwise be hidden. Understanding the subtext that fuels fictitious claims is crucial to understanding the motivations of the people who invent them, and the drives of the people who believe them. Ideas are three-dimensional — they have not only a surface but a far more complex interior that provides us with insight and knowledge into ourselves and society. Even when the lines are lies, there is still truth to be found between them.

12

ALIENS AND FLYING SAUCERS — UFOS AS CONTEMPORARY MYTHOLOGY

UFOS ARE REAL?

In July 2023, the world was captivated when a Pentagon insider revealed on live television and under oath that shadowy departments of the U.S. government, beyond the knowledge of elected representatives, had retrieved, stored, and reverse-engineered extraterrestrial alien spacecrafts. They were also in possession of "non-human biologics,"[321] which has been taken to mean an alien body or body part. The speaker was retired intelligence officer David Charles Grusch, who had last served at the rank of a "full bird colonel."[322] Mr. Grusch's testimony focused on his time at the All-domain Anomaly Resolution Office, also known as AARO. At AARO, it was his job to investigate unidentified flying objects inside American airspace. During this hearing, he was flanked on either side by former F-18 pilot Ryan Graves as well as retired commanding Navy officer and pilot David Fravor.[323]

In their testimony to the Subcommittee on National Security, the Border, and Foreign Affairs, the three men confirmed that (some parts of) the U.S. government know about the existence of extraterrestrial UFOs and are keeping their knowledge hidden from the public.

A brief note about terminology: Unidentified, potentially alien, spacecraft were first referred to as *flying saucers* or *flying discs*. These terms, however, quickly came to imply the "extraterrestrial hypothesis" (that the unidentified craft were piloted by extraterrestrials) and were replaced with the more neutral *UFO* (Unidentified Flying Object). Since the invention of the term, *UFO* too has become closely associated with the extraterrestrial hypothesis, and so it has been replaced at AARO and the Pentagon with *UAP*. This acronym first stood for Unidentified Aerial Phenomena, but that has now been updated to Unidentified *Anomalous* Phenomena, to broaden its scope. While the terms *UAP*, *UFO*, and *flying saucers* are still all in use, we will use *UFO*, as it is commonly understood and implies the extraterrestrial hypothesis, which is central to the conspiratorial dimension of these strange objects.

The two pilots, Graves and Fravor, testified to the anomalous reports from pilots who had encountered strange objects in the sky that seemed to move beyond any known "material science" that is currently available.[324] Fravor spoke about a personal encounter he had with an UFO, known as the Tic Tac.[325] It apparently flew in ways that he simply could not explain, and this was documented in video footage of the encounter.

The most astounding testimony fell to Grusch, who claimed that secret programs within the U.S. government deal with alien craft and alien technology and possess alien organic samples. He further claimed that there was a history of "reprisals" for anyone who had tried to come forward publicly to reveal the alien secret, ranging from demotion to "injury and harm."[326]

So do we now have convincing proof that the U.S. really is in possession of alien spacecraft they've been hiding from all of us? And if not, what explains this extraordinary testimony?

UFOS — A CONTEMPORARY MYTHOLOGY

As we argue below, the UFO phenomenon is a modern myth. This idea was suggested by Curtis Peebles in his book *Watch the Skies!*, which recounts the cultural history of UFOs. The UFO myth isn't really about flying saucers or aliens, it is about contemporary culture. Peebles explains that: "the flying saucer myth is a mirror to the events of postwar America — the paranoia of the 1950s, the social turmoil of the 1960s, the 'me generation' of the 1970s and the nihilism of the 1980s and the early 1990s. As the flying saucer myth entered popular culture, images and ideas were created which, in turn, shaped the flying saucer myth itself."[327]

The UFO myth has developed in stages over roughly the last 80 years. If you were to imagine an "alien" right now, you would not likely visualize it as depicted in American pop culture of the early 1950s. Back then, they were represented as humans, often from the planet Venus, who wore tight-fitting ski suits. The stories that we tell about aliens today did not spring ready-made out of a novel or someone's experiences with actual aliens. Rather there has been a long interaction between real world events and fiction that, together, have contributed content that developed our collective cultural understanding of UFOs and their pilots.

The UFO/alien myth emerged mostly in America, where real-world events inspired fictions that shaped the way that subsequent historical realities were interpreted. There exist three main sources for the modern UFO myth: misidentified secret government projects;[328] fictional narratives; and disinformation agents trying to confuse the public for money or political gain. We will explore examples of these three sources as contributing elements to the modern understanding of UFOs. The relationship between the myth and its sources is both progressive and iterative. Each step in that process changes how we understand and imagine UFOs and aliens.

To illustrate this, we start our story not at the beginning of the UFO phenomenon, but with an event that has become central to the modern understating of the UFO phenomenon.

THE ROSWELL INCIDENT

The story of the Roswell Incident goes as follows: one or more flying saucers crashed. A secret (a.k.a. "black") military organization swooped in and whisked everything away before people had a chance to take a good look. Nonetheless, numerous eyewitness reports became known. Because of these reports, we know that the U.S. government has been hiding the existence of aliens and using their technology for 80 years.[329]

First, it is important to note that some of this story *did* happen. Here's how an official Air Force report explains it: "When critically examined, the claims that the U.S. Army Air Forces recovered a flying saucer and alien crew in 1947, were found to be a compilation of many verifiable events. For the most part, the descriptions collected by UFO theorists were of actual operations and tests carried out by the U.S. Air Force in the 1950s."[330]

What really happened in Roswell in 1947? In the 1990s, the U.S. Air Force, in response to a General Accounting Office (GAO)[331] investigation, produced exhaustive reports of what took place that summer. The first of them, *The Roswell Report: Case Closed*,[332] was published in 1995. The next, published just over one year later, was titled *The Roswell Report: Fact vs Fiction in the New Mexico Desert*.[333]

Summarizing these sources, we know that early on June 14, 1947, some strange debris was found in the fields of W.W. Brazel, a farmer in Lincoln County, New Mexico. According to newspaper reports of the time, it consisted of a "bundle of tinfoil, broken wood beams, and rubber remnants of a balloon." UFO rumours (a.k.a. "UFO flap") was a new phenomenon, and Brazel hadn't heard of "flying discs." On July 5, he first learned of the phenomenon, and two days later, wondering if he might be in possession of one of these mysterious objects, headed to town to let local Sheriff George Wilcox know. Wilcox got in touch with Roswell Army Airfield (RAAF), and Major Jesse A. Marcel was assigned to the case. Marcel, together with a plainclothes officer and Brazel, went back to the ranch to pick up the rest of the debris. They returned it to Marcel's office to try to piece it together and determine what it might have been.[334]

Local newspapers generated some sensational headlines, taking full advantage of the popular interest in Kenneth Arnold's recent sighting of the first modern "flying saucers," which happened just a few weeks earlier. The *Roswell Daily Record* ran with "RAAF Captures Flying Saucer on Ranch in Roswell Region" and, the next day, "[General] Ramey Empties Roswell Saucer," accompanied by photos showing Major Marcel holding some of the debris. While the headlines were eye-catching, they do not support the claim that an alien craft landed or that any alien corpses were found at the crash site. Instead, they show the rather ordinary nature of the materials and suggest that it was probably a weather balloon that malfunctioned. Here is what the *Roswell Daily Record* had to say about what they found:

> When the debris was gathered up the tinfoil, paper, tape and sticks made a bundle about three feet long and 7 or 8 inches thick while the rubber made a bundle of about 18 or 20 inches long and about 8 inches thick. In all, he estimated, the entire lot would have weighed maybe five pounds. There was no sign

> of any metal in the area which might have been used for an engine and no sign of any propellers of any kind, although at least one paper fin had been glued onto some of the tinfoil. There were no words to be found anywhere on the instrument, although there were letters on some of the parts.[335]

There were a few early statements by officials that they had indeed recovered a "flying disc," but in the context of the materials that were actually found, this does not appear to refer to extraterrestrial intelligence and their equipment.

What had actually landed in Brazel's fields? According to now declassified reports by the Air Force and the CIA, it was most likely the remains of a high-altitude espionage balloon associated with Project Mogul tests. According to the Air Force report:

> Project MOGUL was a then-sensitive, classified project, whose purpose was to determine the state of Soviet nuclear weapons research . . .
>
> Upon review of the local newspaper photographs . . . and descriptions in popular books by individuals who supposedly handled the debris recovered on the ranch, Professor Moore opined that the material was most likely the shredded remains of a multi-neoprene balloon train with multiple radar reflectors . . .
>
> All available official materials, although they do not directly address Roswell *per se*, indicate that the most likely source of the wreckage recovered from the Brazel Ranch was from one of the Project MOGUL balloon trains. Although that project was Top Secret at the time, there was no specific indication found to indicate an official preplanned cover story was in place to explain an event such as that which ultimately happened.[336]

Air Force Brigadier General Roger Ramey gave a press conference that effectively ended interest and speculation on the matter. The materials found included tinfoil, wood, and "considerable" amounts of "scotch tape with flowers printed upon it."[337] Hardly the type of materials associated with an alien species coming to explore Earth. The story died a couple of days after it had begun. But it came back to life decades later with the publication of a number of interviews and books that cast the entire event in a new light. As the Air Force report notes, fictional narratives of the Roswell Incident that emerged decades later consolidated events that had been spread out over many years, depicting them as having occurred over just two or three days.[338]

But there is a second story that needs to be told first. It is a UFO hoax known as the Crash at Aztec. While the Roswell story initially died a few days after it started in 1947, a book emerged in 1950 that added much fuel to the Roswell fiction. *Behind the Flying Saucers*, by Frank Scully, recounts a UFO crash that supposedly occurred in 1948 in Aztec, New Mexico, from which alien bodies and alien technology were recovered. Unlike Roswell, this story stuck around for a couple of years until an intrepid reporter J.P. Cahn went through the bother of fact-checking all the claims. Cahn discovered that Scully was taken in by a scam and the authorities Scully cites in his book are fake. The "alien technology" was thin aluminum plates with no special properties. The scammer, Silas Newton, was later indicted on fraud for trying to sell an oil-finding invention that never found any oil.[339]

The Aztec crash story is important because of what happened a couple of decades later. In the late 1970s and into the early '80s, Major Jesse A. Marcel started making extraordinary claims about what had been found at Roswell: The materials were not of this world and likely had an extraterrestrial origin. His claims laid the ground for a number of soon-to-be-published sensationalist books about what purportedly happened there.[340]

The most famous of these books is *The Roswell Incident*, written by Charles Berlitz and William L. Moore. This work reimagines what happened at Roswell, merging some of the historical events with the claims in Scully's book. However, as the Air Force report notes, "What is uniquely lacking in the entire exploration and exploitation of the *Roswell Incident* is official positive documentary or physical evidence of any kind that supports the claims of those who allege that something unusual happened."[341] One of the co-authors, William L. Moore, would play a subsequent role in the evolution of the UFO myth when he perpetrated the Majestic 12 paper fraud.

Other works which continued to elaborate the myth include *The UFO Crash at Roswell*, *The Truth About the UFO Crash at Roswell*, and *The Roswell*

Report: A Historical Perspective. Films, "documentaries," and TV shows got in on the game. By the time the first episode of the TV conspiracy theory show *The X-Files* aired, the myth had been solidified. One episode opens with the crash at Roswell. There is an alien inside. It seems alive. David Duchovny's character, Fox Mulder, asks in a voiceover, "Are we truly alone? Or are we being lied to?"

ENTER THE MEN IN BLACK

Gray Barker was a mischievous salesman and jack of all trades back in the 1950s who liked pranking people, and he realized that the growing interest in UFOs might turn into a great opportunity to have some fun. His fun didn't take long to materialize, because his friend Albert K. Bender had just set up the International Flying Saucer Bureau (IFSB), which functioned as a citizen sleuth UFO investigations unit. Bender made Barker his lead investigator, and then Barker proceeded to prank Bender.

Barker pretended that as he started investigating, some shadowy FBI-like figures came by his house and told him to shut down his investigation. They seemed to have more information on Barker and his new organization than they should have. The whole thing was a joke at Bender's expense, but it contributed to the origins of the Men in Black theory, which supposes that members of secret government agencies silence those looking into UFOs. All of this is recounted in Barker's book *They Knew Too Much About Flying Saucers*, as well as the more interesting tell-all confession by John C. Sherwood, Barker's later protégé.[342]

ALTERNATIVE 3

We turn next to an obscure event in the evolution of the modern UFO myth, and although the story is less well known than Roswell, its impact on the UFO myth cannot be overstated. The British TV show *Alternative 3* contributed to the conspiratorial idea that secret government plots and disinformation programs operate right under our noses to secure the future for elites at the expense of the rest of us.

Alternative 3 was supposed to air on British television on April Fool's Day 1977 but was delayed because of a labour dispute. The original April

Fool's Day debut should have made the joke apparent. Nonetheless, when it finally did air on Anglia TV (now ITV) on June 20 as part of the *Science Report* program, most viewers did realize it was not to be taken seriously.

Alternative 3 was one of the first mockumentaries, a fictional comedy masquerading as a documentary. It depicts a reporter, Tim Brinton, investigating Britain's "brain drain," the phenomenon of scientists choosing to leave Great Britain for better research opportunities elsewhere. While researching this, Brinton discovers a weird mystery. The people he's after have not simply left the U.K.; they have actually disappeared. One person who was thought to have immigrated to Australia never got there. The reporter searches for others and discovers that they too have simply vanished.

His investigations seem to reveal a surprising and worrying truth. As "astronaut" Bob Grodin explains to Brinton, there exists a secret space program that preceded the well-known "official" Apollo space program that landed Neil Armstrong and Buzz Aldrin on the moon. This secret program accomplished a much earlier moon landing and even reached Mars, which was discovered to be habitable for humans and already to contain some form of life. What's more, this program was enacted as a strategy to save a small group of humanity from an inevitable catastrophic global climate collapse. Since the climate catastrophe could not be evaded, and since it would kill everyone on Earth, three alternatives were drafted to deal with this threat. The first was to use nuclear weapons to blast holes into the atmosphere and release the heat generated by global warming. The second entailed the creation of underground cities. But these "alternatives" were recognized as impractical and doomed to failure, and so a third alternative was developed: sending a group of humans to Mars to keep civilization going. This is why the scientists were disappearing. They were being drafted into a super-secret space program meant to save (some of) humanity.

Of course, the entire thing was an April Fool's gag. The credits at the end of the show make clear that each actor was portraying a character, not themself. The broadcast had some success, and it was later turned into a book with the same title, written by Leslie Watkins. And, really, that should be the end of the story of *Alternative 3*. Unfortunately, it was just the beginning.

While the original broadcast contained many clues that it was not a real documentary, a few people nonetheless took it seriously. But the real problem started with the publication of the book. Unlike the TV show, the book claims to be an honest work of non-fiction. In fact, the author suggests that the very fact that the original broadcast was claimed to be a hoax is proof that it must be taken seriously. Watkins writes: "Soon after transmission, Anglia's spin-doctors — presumably under pressure from governmental level — tried unsuccessfully to quell the furore by claiming it had all been a hoax."[343] This idea — that there is truth in fiction — is well-known within the world of UFO conspiracies and is referred to as *soft disclosure*. We humans, the theory goes, cannot handle the fact that there are other beings in the universe, and this truth needs to be spoon-fed to us slowly, and fiction is the best way to introduce unpalatable truths to the public. This concept undermines our collective understanding of truth by claiming that reality is fiction, and fiction is reality.

By the late 1980s, conspiracy theorists were taking *Alternative 3* seriously. They would often reference a "British documentary" as their source and would speak about three alternatives that an elite secret group of rulers relied upon to face the coming population and climate crises. This theory gained traction before the internet was easily accessible, and many people who cited the film had not actually seen it.

A number of influential authors also took up the Alternative 3 mythos. Among them were Preston B. Nichols and Peter Moon, who wrote about Alternative 3 in *The Montauk Project*, their 1992 book about time travel and secret U.S. experiments. In discussing the apparent silence of NASA on the finding of pyramids on Mars, a conspiracy theory put forward by filmmaker Richard Hoagland, Nichols and Moon write:

> Why would NASA assume such a stance about a subject that is so intriguing? The answer is perhaps explained by a book entitled *Alternative 3* by Leslie Watkins with David Ambrose and Christopher Miles. [Nichols and Moon are a little unclear about the actual authorship. Leslie Watkins wrote the book, whereas David Ambrose and Christopher Miles created the mocumentary. Neither Ambrose or Miles contributed to the book directly.] This book was based on a 1977 video that revealed a secret space program being run by an international conspiracy that included both the Russians and the United States. It is a fascinating account that includes astronauts

> breaking security, disappearing scientists, murder, and the establishment of slave societies on the moon and the planet Mars. The books claims that men actually landed on Mars as early as 1962.[344]

By this point, late-1970s farce had become early-1990s belief.

DOTY, BENNEWITZ, AND AIR FORCE DISINFORMATION

Paul Bennewitz was an electrical engineer with a PhD in physics and an interest in UFOs. He was a member of the Aerial Phenomena Research Organization (APRO), a citizen sleuth organization dedicated to examining UFO sightings.

Bennewitz claimed that he had recorded strange lights and radio signals around Kirtland Air Force Base and decided to let the Air Force know about it. Considering he had been able to discover these strange signals, perhaps others could as well, compromising national security. According to the book and documentary *Mirage Men*, he was put in touch with Special Agent Richard Doty.

The Air Force has always been worried about UFOs, sometimes because some members firmly believe in the extraterrestrial hypothesis. More often than not, however, it is because UFOs are often misidentified secret U.S. military projects. According to CIA historian Gerald K. Haines, "Over half of all UFO reports from the late 1950s through the 1960s were accounted for by manned reconnaissance flights (namely the U-2) over the United States."[345] Similarly, when researchers were searching for missing Mogul balloons, they would sometimes listen to UFO reports to track them.[346]

Apparently, Doty was assigned to Bennewitz, perhaps as part of an Air Force program to keep tabs on what the UFO community knew, or thought they knew, about UFOs. But according to the author of *Mirage Men*, Doty went further: He actively disinformed Bennewitz and, by extension, the larger UFO community. Whether his disinformation campaign was part of an Air Force project or whether Doty "went rogue" is a matter of debate. The deal was apparently simple: Bennewitz was to tell Doty what he knew, and Doty would supply him with "real and secret" information about what the government actually knew about UFOs, namely that elements within the government knew about aliens and were keeping their existence a secret. Doty's disinformation campaign was elaborate and long-lasting. Including setting up fake debris fields and providing secret documentation.[347]

Sometime in 1981, Doty met William L. Moore, the aforementioned co-author of *The Incident at Roswell*. What transpired next is detailed below.

THE MJ-12 PAPERS — WE KNOW THE GOVERNMENTS ARE IN ON IT

One of the problems that has befuddled believers in the extraterrestrial hypothesis is the lack of convincing evidence, especially physical evidence, such as an actual piece of alien technology made from alloys we have never produced and which our science is unable to explain. The next-best thing might be official records demonstrating that the government is in possession of alien craft. Despite the need for secrecy, government departments tend to keep extensive records, which allow later investigators to demonstrate wrongdoing.

During the 1980s, these sorts of secret official documents began to emerge. The following is from the FBI's own webpage: "In 1988, two FBI offices received similar versions of a memo titled 'Operation Majestic 12 . . .' claiming to be a highly classified government document. The memo appeared to be a briefing for newly-elected President Eisenhower on a secret committee created to exploit a recovery of an extra-terrestrial aircraft and cover-up this work from public examination."

The background to the FBI's report is as follows: Sometime in 1984, TV producer Jaime Shandera received a manila envelope without a return address, containing a canister of undeveloped film. Shandera and his friend William L. Moore, one of the *Incident at Roswell* co-authors, developed the film and discovered that it contained pictures of what appeared to be a secret document. Unsure of what they were holding, the two men decided not to publish the document until they could determine its authenticity. Throughout 1985, Moore, Shandera, and a third friend, Stanton Friedman, received more secret documents. Finally, during their own research at the National Archives, the three men discovered a misfiled memo addressed to General Nathan Twining that confirmed the authenticity of the documents they were being mailed. It is a memo written by Robert Cutler, an assistant to President Eisenhower.

In the Cutler-Twining memo, as it has since become known, Majestic 12 (aka MJ-12) is directly referenced. The three researchers now had the type of independent confirming evidence that they needed to authenticate the MJ-12 papers. They had managed to verify it through a misfiled memo in the National Archives. They concluded that they were sitting on one of the most important revelations in human history and had enough evidence to prove its validity, and so they released the documents to the public.

The documents were explosive. As the FBI noted, the papers comprise a briefing for incoming President Eisenhower. Such briefings are routine; incoming presidents need to be brought up to speed when they take office. Secrets kept from them while they were campaigning are suddenly things they need to know about. The MJ-12 inform the president of the existence of aliens, alien technology, and the recovery and retrieval operations for crashed discs like those found at Roswell. The document reads in part: "OPERATION MAJESTIC-12 is a TOP SECRET Research and Development Intelligence operation [illegible] and only to the President of the United States. Operations of the project are carried out under control of the Majestic-12 (Majic-12) Group which was established by special classified executive order of President Truman on 24 September, 1947, upon recommendation by Dr. Vannevar Bush and Secretary James Forrestal."[348]

These documents state that MJ-12's role is to deal with UFOs and aliens. They oversee the recovery of crashed UFOs, secreting them away to CIA bases, where the craft are examined and reverse-engineered. They are also in charge of a global cover-up to ensure that civilians remain in the dark.[349] The documents reference the Kenneth Arnold sightings as well as Roswell and note that aliens were found at the wreckage at Roswell: "In 07 July, 1947 a secret operation was begun to assure the recovery of the wreckage of this object for scientific study. During the course of this operation, aerial reconnaissance discovered that four humanlike beings had apparently ejected from the craft at the point it exploded."[350]

In 1988, in a made-for-TV special *UFO Cover-Up? Live!*, Moore and Shandera presented their documents. If people hadn't known about the MJ-12 conspiracy before, they certainly knew now. Just one year later, the television program *Unsolved Mysteries* aired an episode about Roswell in which the MJ-12 documents are directly cited.

The documents *look* official. Since this is potentially the best piece of existing evidence beyond an actual alien or UFO, a lot is riding on its validity. Renowned UFO researcher Philip J. Klass has looked at the MJ-12 documents carefully, and in what could best be described as an example of document forensics, he uncovered problems that shed serious doubt on their validity.

As Klass explains in his *Skeptical Inquirer* article "The New Bogus Majestic-12 Documents," if the MJ-12 documents are compared against actual formerly secret documents from the late 1940s, inconsistencies become readily apparent. One problem is with the formatting of the date. Above we read, "In 07 July, 1947," but in *all* verifiable official documents, a *0* never precedes the calendar date, nor is there a comma following the month. This is the sort of typographical mistake someone not familiar with the conventions of the time might make. There are other problems as well. Truman's signature on the briefing is totally identical to one from a different publicly available document, even including the scratch marks visible on the original document from which the signature had probably been copied. Roswell is referred to as "Air Base" when it should have been called "Air Field," not the kind of mistake an official document written at the time would contain. There are others, but the most damning issue is the raised letter *i*. Typewriters sometimes had one letter slightly out of alignment. In this case, the letter *i* was raised higher than the others, which turns out to be the case with Moore's own typewriter. It is also worth noting that Moore was behind the theory that the Roswell crash was of alien origin, something again noted in the MJ-12 papers.[351]

The Cutler-Twining memo had its own issues. The National Archives conducted a review and found that it was written on the wrong type of paper and was missing the watermark it should have had. Furthermore, General Cutler was out of the country at the time the memo was supposedly drafted.

The MJ-12 documents are fake, but they played their part in evolving the UFO myth. A common story that still circulates is that governments around the world know about aliens and are colluding to keep it a secret. A further development of this idea is that leaders have managed to orchestrate a side deal in which they and their loved ones will be saved while the rest of us end up as food or medicine for the alien invaders — what *Alternative 3* called "batch consignments."

JOHN LEAR AND HIS MENTEES

John Olsen Lear, son and heir of Learjet founder William Powell Lear, was interested in UFOs, and he believed the MJ-12 claims were real and the government was hiding alien spacecraft. In 1987 and again in 1988, Lear appeared on the TV show *Street Talk*, hosted by George Knapp, an investigative journalist and UFO believer, to discuss secret government knowledge of aliens and leaked documents. Lear went on to mentor two giants in the field of UFOs, William Cooper and purported Area 51 insider Bob Lazar, and Knapp would continue to influence the UFO myth well into the new millennium.

WILLIAM COOPER, THE GRAND SYNTHESIZER

A story as complex and multifaceted as the UFO saga needs to have its disparate threads tied together into a grand unified whole. The person who undertook this feat in the 1980s was William Cooper. Cooper's theories of aliens in cahoots with a secret geopolitical group, the New World Order, became the underlying script for 1990s alien conspiracies such as those shown in *The X-Files*.

Cooper's theories are vast, bringing together major tropes of various conspiratorial movements. In essence, Cooper suggested that there is abundant evidence of a secret world government. This government goes by many names and has many incarnations; the Bilderberger Group and the Illuminati are often mentioned. They are presumed to be the real power brokers behind the facade of democratic, communist, and fascist governments alike, the group that is truly in charge in every decade and in every country. Today this government is called the Deep State. According to this theory, they make the wars, and they end them. They created the drug epidemic in the 1980s in America in order to deliberately engineer a dependent class of workers. They synthesized HIV/AIDS as a method of population control, which became necessary after the somewhat predictable baby boom that followed the Second World War.

This secret all-powerful, world-governing society is also keeping the fact of alien existence hidden from elected representatives and from the public. Here is where Cooper's synthesizing powers really come into their own. He recounts events such as the Aztec New Mexico incident and Roswell and many others as the beginning of humanity's encounters with aliens. He traces many of the main events in the history of UFO lore, always siding with the interpretation that foregrounds the work of secret societies hiding extraterrestrials.

In his influential *Behold a Pale Horse* (1991), we can see Cooper actively synthesizing strands found in *Alternative 3* with the MJ-12 papers, black helicopters, and the fears of a secret society: "A symposium was held in 1957 which was attended by some of the great scientific minds then living. They reached the conclusion that by, or shortly after, the year 2000 the planet WOULD self-destruct due to increased population and man's exploitation of the environment WITHOUT ANY HELP FROM GOD OR THE ALIENS . . . By secret Executive order of President Eisenhower, the JASON Scholars were ordered to study this scenario and make recommendations from their findings. The JASON Society CONFIRMED the finding of the scientists and made three recommendations called ALTERNATIVES 1, 2 and 3."[352] It is worth noting that Cooper adds the real science advisory group the JASONS to that of Alternative 3.

Cooper continues: "Alternative 3 was to exploit the alien and conventional technology in order for a select few to leave the earth and establish colonies in outer space. I am not able to either confirm or deny the existence of 'batch consignments' of human slaves, which would be used for the manual labor as part of the plan. The Moon, code-named ADAM, was the object of primary interest, followed by the planet Mars, code-named EVE. I am now in possession of official NASA photographs of one of the moon bases. I believe that the Mars colony is also a reality."[353]

It is obvious that a good part of Cooper's theories is based on the MJ-12 documents hoax and the *Alternative 3* spoof. He insists any and all UFO landings happened just the way the most hyperbolic tellings suggest they did. He was mentored by John Lear and knew Bob Lazar. He corresponded with Gray Barker.

Finally, Cooper also claimed that animal mutilations, such as the cow mutilations of the late '70s, are evidence that the aliens are not keeping their word. They are abducting humans without bringing them back and are helping themselves to cattle beyond what they had agreed to.

While Cooper made a big splash in the conspiratorial underground world of the 1990s, his ideas have reached millions more by becoming one of the underlying narrative threads of *The X-Files*. Many who have never heard of Cooper are familiar with the theory that there is a "Deep State," made of shadowy unelected "politicians" who secretly know all about the aliens. They have built underground bases. They are deciding on batch consignments. They are making deals with the aliens, who nonetheless seem to be breaking treaties, abducting unsuspecting humans, and mutilating farm animals. It's a case of fiction imitating reality. But it works the other way around as well. As we enter into the 2020s, it is the thesis of the *X-Files* franchise that is aired in the House Select Committee on UAPs.

BIGELOW AND SKINWALKER RANCH

Like John Lear, Robert Bigelow is rich. And like Lear, he believes in UFOs as well as most other supernatural phenomena, including cryptids, ghosts, and interdimensional portals. In 1996, Bigelow bought a ranch in Utah that was supposedly a hotbed of paranormal activity, and he set up a research centre to study such activity, including UFO sightings. The National Institute for Discovery Science (NIDSci) employed part-time and full-time researchers, including journalist George Knapp, who lived on the ranch and documented any and all strange occurrences. Knapp and another NIDSci researcher, Colm Kelleher, went on to co-author a book about the ranch titled *Hunt for the Skinwalker*. Unfortunately, not much happened. Certainly not enough to convince a skeptic and apparently not even enough to keep Bigelow spending his personal money.

In 2005, Bigelow sold Skinwalker Ranch as it has since been called, to another rich UFO believer, Brandon Fugal. Fugal decided to bring in a television crew and some new high-profile researchers, including Travis Taylor. The TV show he helped create is called *The Secret of Skinwalker Ranch*, and at the time of writing, new installments are still forthcoming, all devoid of evidence that could support their UFO claims. The show continues to contribute to the evolving UFO mythology.[354]

THE "EXPLOSIVE INSIDER TESTIMONY" — DAVID GRUSCH AND THE STATE OF THE MYTH TODAY

When David Grusch began his testimony, two men were sitting behind him. A casual observer might be forgiven for assuming that these were members of the media or just curious spectators. To his left was a YouTube influencer and self-proclaimed UFO expert Jeremy Corbell. Behind Grusch to his right was none other than UFO-believing journalist George Knapp. Corbell, Knapp, and Travis Taylor are all friends of Grusch's, having met him at a UFO conference.

We know that Grusch is himself a believer in the extraterrestrial hypothesis, and that he is closely connected to some of the top players in the UFO field. This was the case years before his spectacular testimony, but most media reports of his testimony failed to notice any of these connections. It is important to situate Grusch within the pantheon of UFO believers and proselytizers. He is part of a cohort of Pentagon insiders who seem firmly convinced that UFOs are evidence for the extraterrestrial hypothesis. Or perhaps they have stumbled upon a great grift. UFO stories sell, especially the outrageous ones.

Grusch's testimony is problematic. Grusch claims that, as the MJ-12 documents suggest, there exists an "above" top secret program to recover crashed UFOs. Grusch received whistleblower protection so he could speak about it. However, Grusch, a former officer, also needed to get the Pentagon's permission to speak that day on Capitol Hill. This process is known as Prepublication Security Review,[355] and its purpose is to confirm that a government employee speaking about sensitive operations does not reveal any secrets. Grusch went through this review process and received the go-ahead. This can only mean that whatever Grusch revealed is *not* considered secret by the very departments he was accusing. Unless there is some super-complex double-bluff, the reason he was allowed to give testimony is that he was not revealing anything the Pentagon was worried about. Also, there don't seem to be any "reprisals" for having revealed "above top secret" information, which is something he claimed *did* happen to others who tried to come forward. Why not to Grusch?

Another problem with Grusch's testimony is that he had no evidence and relied solely on second-hand anecdotes. He had not seen any aliens — or, as he put it, "non-human biologics" — nor had he seen any alien spacecraft or alien technology that supposedly issued from these finds.

But what about the pilots who sat beside him and also testified? These pilots referred to videos captured by Navy F-18 jets, but these videos have been thoroughly debunked. One remarkable example is provided by Josh Semeter, director for space physics at Boston University, in a presentation organized by NASA on UAPs. Semeter analyzed a famous UFO video, known as "Go Fast," captured by F-18 pilots. The video appears to show an object zooming incredibly quickly near the surface of the ocean. The pilots can be heard exclaiming how remarkable it is. However, Semeter demonstrated that it was likely a piece of debris flying at windspeed, roughly 60 kilometres an hour. Most of the other videos have similarly mundane explanations. According to Grusch's boss at the time, then–AARO head Sean Kirkpatrick, somewhere on the order of 95 percent of the UFOs in the anomalous videos have been shown to be of terrestrial origin. The remaining 5 percent cannot be analyzed because of a lack of contextual data, not because they are too strange.

It is better to interpret Grusch's testimony as a statement of the contemporary understanding of the UFO myth. Grusch, George Knapp, Jeremy Corbell, Travis Taylor, and others have contributed to the main themes of the UFO story understood today — that UFOs are piloted by extraterrestrials. The MJ-12 conspiracy supplies us with the role the government plays, which is to keep this fact quiet and prevent the public from learning about it accidentally. Cooper contributes a right-wing skepticism of "The Government," while the folks from Skinwalker Ranch weave stories also found in Grusch's testimony about "interdimensional travel." The sinister tone of the presentation — "above secret" departments, "reprisals" against those who try to speak out, and a lone hero willing to risk it all — sounds a lot like a famous TV show from the '90s.

As is the case with previous installments of the UFO myth, from Roswell to the MJ-12 papers, the details that contextualize the testimony of Grusch will be forgotten. What will be remembered is that a Pentagon insider bravely came forward and revealed the truth to the world. He will be cited in years to come as providing conclusive evidence that aliens exist, fly UFOs, and constantly crash them when they arrive. Such is the power of myth.

CONCLUSION: EMPATHY IN AN AGE OF CONSPIRACY — THE GREAT SEATTLE WINDSHIELD EPIDEMIC

A CREEPING TERROR

In March 1954, something sinister was afoot in Washington State. It started in the smallest way imaginable (as sinister somethings often do) but would eventually grow into an epidemic of terror that would reach the highest levels of the American government.[356]

At first, it appeared that there was nothing much to it. A few people in the city of Bellingham had noticed that their car windshields had been damaged with small pits and chips. The police were notified, and they suspected local youths were probably responsible, using BB guns or slingshots to do the slight but irritating damage to the glass.

However, this hypothesis bumped up against the reality of the situation. For one thing, after the newspapers reported the damage, it started to spread quickly to the nearby communities of Sedro-Woolley and Mount Vernon. Not long after that, the island town of Anacortes was hit as well. The police set up roadblocks in the area and started to search cars for the sort of low-grade weaponry that could have caused the chips. Every car that tried to get over Deception Pass Bridge was closely inspected, as were the drivers and passengers. Despite this, the damage spread even further, and to a much more sensitive and secure location. The Whidbey Island Naval Air Station was hit, which resulted in dozens of Marines performing a detailed search of the base to try to find the culprits, to no avail. How was it possible that local vandals were able to move that quickly and effectively, even into high-security areas? There was no way that it could simply be the work of some lone-wolf hooligan — at the speed at which the damage was spreading, it would have to be an organized group secretly working together. In other words, if it was deliberately caused by the actions of people, it would have to be the result of a conspiracy. As one sheriff's deputy told a reporter, "This thing is far more than ordinary juvenile delinquency . . . it's a getting of revenge on society."

However, as the damage spread even further from Bellingham, other possibilities were considered. In areas where the incidents were more frequent, people noticed the presence of tiny, metallic-looking particles on the glass. Others found a strange ash-like substance clinging to the surface of the damaged windshields. Some suspected that there had been sand flea eggs in the material used to create the glass in the windshields, based on reports of drivers seeing specks that hatched before their eyes, causing the chip to happen as they watched.

There were even wilder hypotheses. Cosmic rays from space were blamed, as was a shift in the Earth's magnetic field. Aliens were suspected — maybe it was the residue from a passing flying saucer? Were tiny meteorites the culprits? Could it be that the air was filled with acid?

Eventually, one hypothesis started to get some traction. It was one of the most alarming ones — that the pits and chips in the windshields were an unforeseen consequence of the Castle Bravo hydrogen bomb test that had recently taken place at Bikini Atoll in the Pacific Ocean. By the time the windshield pitting epidemic had run its course, about 30 percent of people polled believed that this was the reason behind the phenomenon. That wasn't surprising — the test had been widely discussed in newspapers such as the *Seattle Daily Times*. The explosion was far larger than anticipated by the scientists who had created it — the largest explosion ever caused by humans. Headlines of the time, such as "3 H-Bomb Victims Face Death: Doctor Reports on Fishermen," "Witness Says: Hydrogen Test Out of Control," "Disaster Plan Result of H-Bomb Study," "AEC Discloses Blast amid Mounting Concern," and "Atomic Scare Ties Up Japanese Fishing Fleet," suggested to the public that something had gone seriously wrong. To a population for whom the destruction of Hiroshima and Nagasaki less than a decade earlier was still fresh in mind, this new weapon was understandably awe-inspiring and terrifying. If the physicists had badly miscalculated the size of the explosion of the bomb they were making, what else might they have gotten wrong? What other effects might the H-bomb have had?

Whatever was causing the phenomenon, it was clear that there was a pattern — it was heading straight for Seattle. On the evening of April 15, four chips were reported in the city. By the time the sun set over Seattle the next day, there were over 3,000 reports, and the populace was alarmed. Drivers reported watching the chips appear as if by magic as they drove through the streets. Police officers, dispatched to investigate newly formed chips in windshields, found chips in their own windshields as they reported to the scene. People were covering their cars in paper and cardboard, but to no avail. The pitting and chipping continued to spread through the city.

Facing a troubled and frightened city, Seattle mayor Allan Pomeroy sent a wire message to the White House and the governor of Washington: "What appeared to be a localized outbreak of vandalism in damaged auto windshields and windows in the northern part of Washington State has now spread throughout the Puget Sound area. Chemical analysis of mysterious powder adhering to damaged windshields and windows indicates the material may simply be spread by wind and not a police matter at all. Urge appropriate federal (and state) agencies be instructed to cooperate with local authorities on emergency basis."

Governor Arthur Langlie contacted the University of Washington, which assembled a team of researchers to investigate the situation. They ran experiments on glass, tried to replicate the chips using acid and resin, analyzed the pebbles and dust that people had sent in, and tested for radioactivity. The conclusion: None of the hypotheses that had been proposed was supported by evidence. The pits and chips were caused by the usual wear and tear that you would expect to see on any car. Other researchers, at the University of British Columbia, came to the same conclusion, stating that "mass hysteria is playing a big part in all these rumours . . . This is the time of year when dust, sand and bits of gravel begin to be thrown at cars from the car ahead. These particles naturally scratch windshields to some extent." The more miles on a car, the more likely it was to have pits and chips. Car lots with both new and used cars were used as field laboratories, and it turned out that the used cars had chips, and the new cars (which hadn't been driven on roads yet) didn't. The substance coating windshields was just the same coal dust that had been coating windshields for decades. There was an explanation for why it seemed as though the pits and chips were showing up all of a sudden: When people heard about the pitting phenomenon, they looked *at* their windshields instead of *through* them and noticed all sorts of things that had been there all along as if they had suddenly just appeared.

MAKING SENSE OF THINGS

It's often asked, "What sort of people believe in conspiracy theories?" And the answer is: people. Partly, as we have seen, this is because there are some genuine conspiracies. Some of the CIA mind control experiments, FBI surveillance overreach, and Russian disinformation campaigns sound as far-fetched as the false ones, and every time we learn about a true conspiracy, the rest of them become more plausible. Actual government activities such as the Tuskegee syphilis study, or the Watergate Hotel break-in, or the 2003 invasion of Iraq under the false pretense of weapons of mass destruction contribute to an understandable belief that some people in power are secretly manipulating and concealing things for sinister reasons.

But it is vital to ensure that healthy skepticism doesn't tip over into unhealthy paranoia. Throughout this book, we have looked at the psychological, sociological, historical, and philosophical factors that increase the chances we'll believe things that aren't true. In the example of the Seattle Windshield Epidemic, we can see many of those factors in play. Because we tend to notice things better when we're looking for them, and we aren't as good as we sometimes think at perceiving the world around us, it *appeared* to many as if the chips suddenly showed up at the same time in an unusual manner. The desire to see sinister and deliberate agents behind problems and hardships contributed to the belief that some group (punks, aliens, communists) must have been responsible. Because the incidents happened immediately after the Castle Bravo test, it was easy to make the leap to thinking they must have been caused by it. The news media played a large role in spreading the wild speculations, which in turn led to a shared belief that turned into a mass panic. The route out of that mass panic was the application of the scientific method (including falsification) to rigorously test the speculations and ultimately reject them as groundless.

The subtext for the panic is clear once the context is considered. The Seattle Windshield Epidemic occurred in 1954, at the beginning of the Cold War and the dawn of the H-bomb age. The skies above America were filled with flying saucers, and the halls of government were crawling with communist spies. New technologies were emerging at a breakneck pace, and people were still reeling from the destruction and trauma of World War II. It's hardly a surprise that they were quick to believe that something ominous and threatening was in the literal air when there was so much ominous and threatening in the figurative air.

But while the episode was understandable and very human, it also serves as an important cautionary tale. Ultimately, very little damage was done in the panic that swept across the West Coast in 1954 (and even spread to parts of California, Illinois, Indiana, Kentucky, Michigan, Ohio, Oregon, Wisconsin, and British Columbia), but there were still aspects of the incident that should give us pause. Very early on, there was evidence of scapegoating from the authorities, which historically rarely leads to good outcomes and can prompt discrimination and harassment. That scapegoating was then followed up by an official response in the form of police barricades and car searches. The speculations became wilder and less reasonable as the worry grew. The panic emerged organically and wasn't deliberately encouraged or weaponized by any particular group, but the event does show us how easy it would be to pull off if someone *did* want to manipulate a population into fear and dread.

THE HUMAN ANIMAL

Each human being possesses something incredible: a human brain. It is the most complicated thing we have yet come across. It is capable of processing sensory information taken in from the outside world through our senses and turning that information into a coherent and cohesive worldview that helps us to understand our situation.

And that ability is no small feat, especially as our situation has become more complicated in the last few generations. Our worlds are no longer confined to our immediate surroundings, as the digital networks and devices we've created have allowed us to receive new data constantly and from everywhere. Where we were once in a desert of information, now we're in an ocean. And we need to learn how to swim in that ocean, or we'll drown.

One of the skills that humans use to organize and understand the information they're presented with is the ability to recognize patterns and then discern meaning behind these patterns. This skill allows them to see past the surface level of things into secret intentions and hidden purposes. Early humans sitting around the fire might have recognized that their fellow humans were plotting against them before those plots were realized and taken timely action to interrupt those conspiracies against them.[357]

The problem is, we're not only good at recognizing real hidden plots lurking behind the scenes, we're also good at *inventing* hidden plots where none exist. This can be dangerous to us when we lead ourselves astray and convince ourselves of falsehoods. It's also dangerous because, as we have seen, organizations with an interest in manipulating populations have long recognized this tendency and have weaponized false conspiracy theories to spread through groups of people to change what they think, and in doing so change how they act, and ultimately who they are.

So then what are we to do, as brain owners? We have a responsibility to make ourselves as difficult to manipulate as possible, to prevent ourselves from being talked into believing absurdities and possibly committing atrocities grounded in those absurdities. At the same time, there are genuine conspiracies that surround us, which need to be exposed to public view.

The concepts and theories in this field guide are useful for immunizing us against nonsense. When we understand the psychological factors that make us more likely to be fooled, we are more on guard against being fooled. When we grasp the sociological influences that impact our belief systems, we can recognize more readily when we are getting swept up in a mass panic, organized disinformation campaign, or false belief system. Looking at the underlying assumptions and tropes of conspiracy theories gives us a better understanding of their strengths and weaknesses and allows us to examine them in a more informed manner. If we are more careful with our hypotheses through a familiarity with cause-and-effect relationships and the scientific method, this will act as a filtering mechanism to help us eliminate unfounded and unsupported ideas before they form part of our worldview. Understanding the operations of the media ecosystem (and the information, misinformation, and disinformation organisms that inhabit it) allows us to move through it in a more critical and aware manner.

But protecting ourselves from ridiculousness is only one part of the conspiracy story, since we're impacted not just by our own beliefs but by the beliefs of those around us.

CULTISH BELIEFS AND CONSPIRACISM

Increasingly, people are confronting an uncomfortable reality — it is all too easy for loved ones to become seduced by false conspiracy theories and fall headlong down a rabbit hole into these beliefs. Because of the way social media algorithms work, a brief exploration down a mild conspiratorial avenue can quickly lead to an immersion in far more radical, unsupported, and dangerous beliefs.

What can be done to interrupt this pattern in the early stages, or to bring someone back once they have already been dragged down by the undertow of absurdity? As we have already seen, false conspiracy belief systems often have built-in protective mechanisms in the forms of thought-terminating clichés and baked-in warnings against "elites" who are trying to hide the truth from the true believer. According to one 2013 study, successful conspiracy theory peddlers often try to immunize their followers against being talked out of their beliefs by warning them that such efforts will likely be made, and by preparing their followers with counterarguments.[358] Similar mechanisms are employed by charismatic cult leaders. This is not the only similarity between extreme conspiracy beliefs and cults. Like cults, conspiracy theory peddlers will try to build distrust in their followers and present themselves as the only true and reliable source of knowledge. Like cults, conspiracy belief systems come with a ready-made community of like-minded believers, and the appeal of a community to an isolated or lonely person is a siren call. That community of conspiracy believers itself is a protective mechanism, as people tend to share the beliefs of those around them and reinforce those beliefs for each other. Even when the beliefs are demonstrably false, or the conspiracy predictions fail, there are ways for believers to minimize their cognitive dissonance and maintain their beliefs.

Many studies have tried to come up with best practices to prevent people from falling into false belief systems, and to bring them back once they have been seduced. According to these studies, the cliché that an ounce of prevention beats a pound of cure seems to be accurate; if people can be taught to recognize unreliable sources and disinformation, they are less likely to absorb it and have it become part of their worldview.[359] Teaching critical thinking skills and basic argumentation have been shown to be reasonably effective, as has instruction on recognizing the differences between science and pseudoscience. However, at least one study has noted that conspiracy theories in particular are difficult belief systems to change.[360]

It's therefore important to understand the factors that can make a person — *any* person — susceptible to conspiracism. By recognizing these factors, we can perhaps interrupt the dangerous descents that paranoid spokespeople try to drag us down into. This book has already examined many of the cognitive and social factors that contribute to this, but there is still a missing piece which is vital for our understanding of the situation.

LONELINESS AND ISOLATION

In 2023, U.S. Surgeon General Vivek Murthy wrote an open letter in which he described a dangerous epidemic that was threatening the health outcomes of Americans. This epidemic wasn't a biological virus — it was the scourge of loneliness. Statistics show that North Americans spend more time alone in the 2020s than they did in the 2000s, with a difference of about one day's worth of time per month. People also report having fewer friends now than they did only two decades ago.[361] There are likely several reasons for this phenomenon, including larger historical trends, the shifting nature of the workplace, the effects of years of COVID pandemic lockdowns, and our rapidly changing relationship with information technologies.

Loneliness has a dramatic impact on mortality rates and quality of life. According to the report, loneliness increased the risk of premature death by 26 percent, heart disease by 29 percent, and stroke by 32 percent.[362] In addition to the impact loneliness has on an individual, there are shared risks to a society in which loneliness is common. Trust in institutions and in fellow humans, which is eroded by conspiracism, both affect and are affected by social isolation. When we don't trust the people around us, we become more isolated. When we become more isolated, we trust the people around us less. When we are more isolated and less trusting, we are more prone to being convinced by conspiracism. It gives us a reason to explain our loneliness in a way that protects our ego, by giving us a villain to blame for our situation. It can even make our loneliness seem heroic, as we bravely face a truth that the masses refuse to see. Compounding this, when we are isolated, we receive less corrective feedback from our peers when we start to embrace flawed or hazardous beliefs.[363] Without other people around to provide reality checks and other perspectives, we lose valuable input on our beliefs. When we are lonely, we are both more likely to be seduced by conspiracism and less likely to be talked out of it.

To protect ourselves as individuals and our society as a whole from the manipulative threat of conspiracism and paranoia, we need more than just intellectual solutions. There is a very important emotional component. We don't hold beliefs just because we have been convinced by arguments, we hold them because they serve an important emotional, or even spiritual, need. When we encounter someone who holds a ridiculous untrue conspiracy belief, particularly when it is someone we care about, we need to look past the absurd text of the claim itself to the social and personal context of the person who holds it, to understand the subtext of why they are committed to it. Finding areas of agreement is vital in a situation such as this. Criticizing or mocking a person and attacking a belief that (while false and potentially dangerous) is performing an important psychological function will most likely cause that person to dig in their heels and protect that belief. On the other hand, trying to understand the reasons why the person has embraced that belief is more likely to result in a conversation rather than a confrontation. And it is through conversation that we can bridge the distances between us, reduce isolation, and decrease the feelings of loneliness that can drive us into the arms of the paranoid spokespeople.

NAVIGATING THE CONSPIRACY WORLD

When it comes to trying to navigate our way through to the truth, it can often seem like the ocean of data we're thrown into is too daunting to make it through. We're heavily influenced by our social environment and our own psychology, while the siren calls of skilled manipulators use that knowledge to try to lure us into the rocks.

But things are not nearly as hopeless as they first appear. By practising good mental hygiene and careful thinking, we can help protect ourselves from an increasingly hostile data environment. Just as recognizing the tricks and sleight-of-hand of con artists helps us become harder marks, recognizing the errors and habits of our own brains and understanding how to counteract them strengthens our thinking.

The same social mechanisms that encourage false conspiracy claims to spread through a society can be employed to help prevent that society from falling into manipulative fear and panic. Good ideas, like bad ones, can be contagious; they can be spread through education, both formal and informal. While algorithms and funding strategies can make it a bit of an uphill climb, the same social media platforms in which disinformation thrives can be used by rational influencers, passing on knowledge and skills to their followers, who in turn can pass them on to friends and family. Through this, a kind of herd immunity is possible against malicious falsehoods and dangerous, unsupported claims.

Starting from a place of sympathy and empathy, rather than polarization and ingroup competition, promotes understanding rather than suspicion. This contributes to the reduction of the isolation and loneliness that can drive people away from each other, and from healthy skepticism to paranoia.

We have a responsibility — to ourselves, to our community, to our society, and to our future — to try to see clearly through the noise and the nonsense. We have a responsibility to expose the harms and abuse of power caused by true conspiracies and not become distracted or manipulated by false claims. It is a shared responsibility, as we are all stakeholders in the outcome of our data ecosystem. Ultimately, and regardless of how division-sowing disinformation merchants try to convince us otherwise, we are all in this together.

NOTES

1. For this and other bizarre CIA operations, see: Onlie, Bill, *Secret CIA: 21 Insane CIA Operations You've Probably Never Heard Of* (LAK, 2021).
2. In 2005, the NSA declassified an internal study indicating the attacks were not real. See: Hanyok, Robert J., *Skunks, Bogies, Silent Hounds, and the Flying Fish: The Gulf of Tonkin Mystery, 2–4 August 1964* (National Security Agency, Center for Cryptologic History, 2001), online.
3. See, for example: *MKULTRA Briefing Book: List of Subprojects with Brief Descriptions*, Central Intelligence Agency, c. 1976, online, and Project MK-Ultra Program Review, Central Intelligence Agency, online.
4. See, for example: Henricks, Mark, "The GM Trolley Conspiracy: What Really Happened," CBS News, March 12, 2010.
5. See, for example, the District of Columbia Court ruling *United States v. Philip Morris USA Inc.*, 9F.Supp.2d 1 (D.D.C., 2006).
6. See, for example: Haines, Gerald K., "CIA's Role in the Study of UFOs, 1947–90," *Studies in Intelligence*, 1(1) (1997), 67–84, online.
7. See, for example: Zurcher, Anthony, "The Birth of the Obama 'Birther' Conspiracy," BBC, September 16, 2016.
8. Mueller, Robert S., III, *Report on the Investigation into Russian Interference in the 2016 Presidential Election*, vols. 1–2 (U.S. Department of Justice, March 2019), 1: "Although the investigation established that the Russian government perceived it would benefit

from a Trump presidency and worked to secure that outcome, and that the Campaign expected it would benefit electorally from information stolen and released through Russian efforts, *the investigation did not establish that members of the Trump Campaign conspired or coordinated with the Russian government in its election interference activities*" (emphasis added).

9. "Final Benghazi Report: No 'Smoking Gun' Pointing to Clinton," Associated Press, June 28, 2016, online.
10. *The Pervert's Guide to Cinema*, directed by Sophie Fiennes, written by Slavoj Žižek, Amoeba Film, 2009.
11. "Connecticut Court Upholds $965m Verdict Against Infowars' Alex Jones," Associated Press, December 7, 2024, online.
12. Australian Psychological Society, "Explaining Thought-Terminating Cliches and Why We Should Be Wary of Them," February 8, 2024, online.
13. Reimann, Nicholas, "QAnon Marked Friday as Trump 'Reinstatement' Day — Here Are Other Flop Predictions of Trump's Return," *Forbes*, August 13, 2021, online.
14. "Ray Hyman — How to Tell the Future," July 2012, YouTube, online.
15. Bernstein, William J., *The Delusion of Crowds: Why People Go Mad in Groups* (Grove Press, 2021), 121.
16. Macknik, Stephen L., and Susana Martinez-Conde with Sandra Blakeslee, *Sleights of Mind: What the Neuroscience of Magic Reveals About our Everyday Deceptions* (Henry Holt, 2010), 4.
17. Ibid., 27.
18. Ibid., 143: "Thinking is expensive. It requires brain activity, which takes energy, and energy is a limited resource. More important, thinking takes time and attention away from other tasks like finding food and mates and avoiding cliffs and saber-toothed tigers. The more you can safely file away as established fact, the more you can concentrate on your current goals and interests."
19. Ibid., 9.
20. "McGurk Effect — Auditory Illusion," BBC, November 10, 2010, YouTube, online.
21. "Gondola Wish," Central Intelligence Agency working paper, November 1, 1978, 1, online.

22. Mumford, Michael D., Andrew M. Rose, and David A. Goslin, *An Evaluation of the Remote Viewing Program: Research and Operational Applications* (American Institutes for Research, September 22, 1995), online.

23. Jacobsen, Annie, *Phenomena: The Secret History of the U.S. Government's Investigation into Extrasensory Perception and Psychokinesis* (Little, Brown, 2017), 5. "The real action began in 1972, when a small group of promising young scientists was approached by the Central Intelligence Agency to embark upon a research program involving psychics, or 'sensitives.'"

24. Ibid., 137.

25. Ibid., 118. "At age thirty-five he was a bit of a prodigy, having already coauthored the university physics textbook *Fundamentals of Quantum Electronics*, published twenty-three papers, given fourteen national symposium lectures, and registered two patents, one for a tunable infrared laser." He was also the head of the legendary Stanford Research Institute. Puthoff was a physicist with experience in designing and conducting experiments. With a solid background in the physical sciences and as the head of a major American research institute, he seemed like the perfect choice to test whether psychic abilities were real or mere fakery.

26. Subjects included Ingo Swann, Pat Price, and Hella Hammid.

27. This was not the CIA's first foray into magic. In quite a different context, the CIA employed stage magician John Mulholland to instruct field operatives on sleight-of-hand tricks to help clandestine operations. "For [head of CIA Sydney] Gottlieb and his successors, the techniques of deception used by performing magicians, when added to the 'magic' of technology, presented an intriguing potential to enhance the clandestine delivery of materials and secret communications. Mulholland's principles of magic were consistent with the CIA's doctrine of tradecraft, and in the ensuing decades talented consultants from the world of magic provided the CIA with innovative illusions to mask and obscure clandestine operations." Meton, Keith H., and Robert Wallace, *The Official C.I.A. Manual of Trickery and Deception: Declassified* (Harper, 2009), 19.

28. Randi, James, *The Truth About Uri Geller* (Prometheus, 1975), 105–7.

29. Jacobsen, 143.
30. Targ, Russell, and Harold Puthoff, "Information Transmission Under Conditions of Sensory Shielding" (informally known as the "SRI Report"), *Nature*, October 18, 1974.
31. Targ, Russell, and Harold Puthoff, *Mind-Reach: Scientists Look at Psychic Abilities* (Hampton Roads, 1977), xi. Much of our information on Geller and the Targ-Puthoff experimentation is drawn from this book, notably pages 46, 70, 112, 150–58, 178.
32. While the original article is in *Nature*, the following account came from the same article published in *Communications Society* 13 (1975), 12–19.
33. This and many other examples are recounted in Randi's *The Truth About Uri Geller*.
34. Randi, 61.
35. Ibid., 23.
36. Mumford, Rose, and Goslin, E-4.
37. Macknik and Martinez-Conde, 142.
38. Chabris, Christopher, and Daniel Simons, *The Invisible Gorilla: How Our Intuitions Deceive Us* (Broadway, 2009).
39. Macknik and Martinez-Conde, 8.
40. Ibid., 141.
41. Loftus, Elizabeth F., *Eyewitness Testimony* (Harvard University Press, 1979); Loftus, Elizabeth, "How Reliable Is Your Memory?" TED Talk, September 2003, online.
42. "Lung Cancer Risk Factors," Centers for Disease Control and Prevention, online.
43. Dunbar, David, and Brad Reagan. *Debunking 9/11 Myths: Why Paranoid Conspiracy Theories Can't Stand Up to the Facts* (Hearst, 2006), 37–38.
44. Ibid., 39.
45. Vigen, Tyler, *Spurious Correlations* (Hachette, 2015), 27.
46. Harris, Gardiner, "Vaccine Cleared Again as Autism Culprit," *New York Times*, August 25, 2011.
47. Sprague, Richard E., and Robert Cutler, "The Umbrella System: Prelude to an Assassination," *Gallery*, June 1978.

48. Hallemann, Caroline, "Who Was the Real Life Umbrella Man at the Kennedy Assassination?" *Town and Country*, August 2, 2020.
49. Gleick, James, *Chaos: Making a New Science* (Penguin, 1988), 16.
50. Lorenz, Edward N., *The Essence of Chaos* (University of Washington Press, 2001), 14–15.
51. Lyall, Sarah, "Charles and Diana Agree on Divorce Terms," *New York Times*, July 13, 1996.
52. Lyall, Sarah, "Foul Play Ruled Out in Death of Princess Diana," *New York Times*, December 14, 2006.
53. Ibid.
54. "The Minute-by-Minute Account of Diana's Death," *Daily Mail*, August 19, 2017.
55. Lyall, "Foul Play Ruled Out."
56. "After 11 Years, the Verdict: Diana Killed by a Combination of Henri Paul and Paparazzi," *Guardian*, April 8, 2008.
57. *The Operation Paget Inquiry Report into the Allegation of Conspiracy to Murder*, London Metropolitan Police, 2006, 6.
58. Except where otherwise cited, our account of the history of the Illuminati is drawn from Le Forestier, René, *The Bavarian Illuminati: The Rise and Fall of the World's Most Secret Society* (Inner Traditions, 2022).
59. Wilgus, Neal, *The Illuminoids: Secret Societies and Political Paranoia* (New English Library, 1978), 19.
60. Ibid., 23.
61. Doyle, William, *The French Revolution: A Very Short Introduction* (Oxford University Press, 2001), 37.
62. Wolf, Lucien, *The Myth of the Jewish Menace in World Affairs, or the Truth About the Forged Protocols of the Elders of Zion* (Macmillan, 1921), 19–40.
63. Webster, Nesta, *World Revolution: The Plot Against Civilization* (Small, Maynard, 1921), 164.
64. Carr, William Guy, *Pawns in the Game* (St. George Press, 1967), 25.
65. Carr, William Guy, *Satan, Prince of the World* (IMG, 2019), 93.
66. Hertenstein, Mike, and Jon Trott, *Selling Satan: The Evangelical Media and the Mike Warnke Scandal* (Cornerstone Press, 1993), 104–107.

67. Warnke, Mike, *The Satan Seller* (Logos International, 1972), 26.
68. Walker, Jesse, *The United States of Paranoia* (Harper, 2014), 205.
69. Ibid., 190–91.
70. Ibid., 217–18.
71. United Nations Standard Minimum Rules for the Treatment of Prisoners (the Nelson Mandela Rules), United Nations Office on Drugs and Crime, 2015, online.
72. Ibid.
73. "The Impacts of Solitary Confinement," Vera, April 2021, online.
74. Our account of this study is drawn from Asch, S.E., "Effects of Group Pressure Upon the Modification and Distortion of Judgments," in *Groups, Leadership and Men*, ed. Harold Guetzkow (Carnegie Press, 1951), 177–90.
75. Goodman, Jack, and Flora Carmichael, "Coronavirus: 5G and Microchip Conspiracies Around the World," BBC, June 26, 2020, online.
76. "False claim: 3G, 4G, and 5G Caused SARS, Swine Flu and the New Coronavirus," Reuters, April 7, 2020, online.
77. Larson, Heidi J., *Stuck: How Vaccine Rumors Spread and Why They Don't Go Away*, 62.
78. Ibid., 63.
79. "History of Anti-Vaccination Movements," College of Physicians of Philadelphia, online.
80. Ibid.
81. "Historical Vaccine Concerns," Centers for Disease Control and Prevention, July 31, 2024, online.
82. "Vaccines and Immunization: Vaccine Safety," World Health Organization, September 23, 2025, online: "Vaccination is one of the most effective ways to prevent diseases. Over the past 50 years, essential vaccines . . . saved at least 154 million lives. During the same period, vaccination has contributed to 40% of the drop in infant deaths."
83. Larson, 15, 62.
84. Ibid., 10, 29.
85. "Measles, Mumps, Rubella (MMR) Vaccine Safety," Centers for Disease Control and Prevention, July 31, 2024, online. Also see: Larson, 11.

86. Larson, 10.
87. "Measles, Mumps, Rubella (MMR) Vaccine Safety."
88. "Dr Andrew Jeremy Wakefield: Determination on Serious Professional Misconduct (SPM) and Sanction," General Medical Council, May 24, 2010).
89. Paul Offit, interviewed in "The Origins of 'One of the Biggest Frauds in the World,'" BBC Select, October 21, 2021.
90. Larson, 26–29.
91. Children's Health Defense, online homepage.
92. Baletti, Brenda, "Thimerosal in Vaccines May Contribute to Autism Severity, New Analysis Shows," Children's Health Defense, July 2, 2025, online.
93. Nevradakis, Michael, "'An Encouraging Sign': 60% of Pregnant Women and Young Mothers May Delay or Refuse Routine Vaccines for Kids," Children's Health Defense, July 17, 2025, online.
94. Larson, 24.
95. Ibid., 25.
96. CDC Museum COVID-19 Timeline, Centers for Disease Control and Prevention, online.
97. Ibid.
98. Onyeaka, Helen, Christian K. Anumudu, Zainab T. al-Sharify, Esther Egele-Godswill, and Paul Mbaegbu, "COVID-19 Pandemic: A Review of the Global Lockdown and Its Far-Reaching Effects," *Science Progress* 104, no. 2 (2021), online.
99. Ibid.
100. Tabari, Parinaz, Mitra Amini, Mohsen Moghadami, and Mahsa Moosavi, "International Public Health Responses to COVID-19 Outbreak: A Rapid Review," *Iranian Journal of Medical Sciences* 45, no. 3 (2020): 157–69, online; "COVID-19: Spread, Prevention and Risk," Public Health Canada, modified March 4, 2024, online.
101. Onyeaka et al., "COVID-19 Pandemic."
102. Chris Baraniuk, "Five Years On: The Countries That Never Locked Down for COVID-19," BBC, March 5, 2025, online.
103. "Coronavirus disease (COVID019): Herd Immunity, Lockdowns and COVID-19," World Health Organization, December 31, 2020, online.

104. "Impact of COVID-19 on People's Livelihoods, Their Health and Our Food Systems," joint statement by International Labour Organization, Food and Agriculture Organization, International Fund for Agricultural Development, and World Health Organization, October 13, 2020, online.
105. Larson, 63.
106. In addition to the Children's Health Defense in the U.S., two prominent sites in the U.K. are Stop New Normal (online) and Save Our Rights UK (online).
107. "Masks," TheyLied.ca, online.
108. "Masks and Respiratory Viruses Prevention," Centers for Disease Control and Prevention, August 18, 2025, online.
109. See, for example: "Coronavirus Disease (COVID-19) Advice for the Public: Mythbusters," World Health Organization, January 19, 2022, online.
110. Sandman, Peter M., *Responding to Community Outrage: Strategies for Effective Risk Communication* (AIHA Press, 1993), 2.
111. Ibid., 13.
112. Larson, 28, 54: See the example of the young mother and health-care professionals.
113. Anedda, Jasmine, Caterina Ferreli, Franco Rongioletti, and Laura Atzori, "Changing Gears: Medical Gloves in the Era of Coronavirus Disease 2019 Pandemic," *Clinics in Dermatology* 38, no. 6 (2020): 734–36, online.
114. Woollacott, Emma, "Facebook Shuts Down Russian Campaign That Claimed Vaccine Turns People into Chimpanzees," *Forbes*, August 11, 2021, online.
115. "Freedom of Information Request on What the Chimpanzee Adenovirus Used for in the Oxford/AstraZeneca Vaccine (FOI 21/1174)," Medicines and Healthcare Products Regulatory Agency, May 26, 2022, online.
116. Pannett, Rachel, "Facebook Bans Russian Disinformation Network That Claimed Coronavirus Vaccines Turn People into Chimpanzees," *Washington Post*, August 11, 2021, online.
117. Hewitt, Paul G., "The Evolution of Life," in *Conceptual Integrated Science*, 2nd ed. (Pearson, 2013), 486–510.

118. Vosoughi, Soroush, Deb Roy, and Sinan Aral, "The Spread of True and False News Online," *Science*, March 9, 2018, online.
119. Hewitt.
120. Barkun, Michael, *A Culture of Conspiracy: Apocalyptic Visions in Contemporary America* (University of California Press, 2013), 74.
121. Ibid., 74–75.
122. Kamen, Al, "At FEMA, 'X' Is for Exasperation," *Washington Post*, June 23, 1998, online.
123. Our account of the Georgia Coffins affair draws from Purcell, Kathryn, "Conspiracy or Simply Storage?" *Morgan County Citizen*, August 11, 2008.
124. Editorial Board, "The Ebola Outbreak," *New York Times*, July 29, 2014, online.
125. "The Evidence: Debunking FEMA Camp Myths," *Popular Mechanics*, December 26, 2014, online.
126. Settles, Gabrielle, "Fact-Check: Does a Video Showing Coffins in a Field Prove 'Covid Was Planned'?" *Austin American-Statesman*, September 20, 2021, online.
127. Troianovski, Anton, and Ellen Nakashima, "How Russia's Military Intelligence Agency Became the Covert Muscle in Putin's Duels with the West," *Washington Post*, December 28, 2018, online.
128. McIntyre, Lee, *On Disinformation: How to Fight for Truth and Protect Democracy* (MIT Press, 2023), 8–9.
129. Dickson, Ej, "Why Are so Many Popular Wellness Influencers Red-Pilled?" *Rolling Stone*, June 14, 2023, online.
130. Bowles, Nellie, "Jordan Peterson, Custodian of the Patriarchy," *New York Times*, May 18, 2018, online.
131. Baker-Whitelaw, Gavia, "'Ancient Rome Isn't Real': This TikTok Conspiracy Theory Is Infuriating Historians," *Daily Dot*, November 29, 2021, online.
132. Matamis, Joaquin, "Social Media Mis-/Disinformation and the Risk of Atrocities in the United State," Stimson, October 12, 2023, online.
133. Karter, Erin, "As Newspapers Close, Struggling Communities Are Hit Hardest by the Decline in Local Journalism," *Northwestern Now*, April 5, 2024, online.

134. *Soviet Influence Activities: A Report on Active Measures and Propaganda, 1986–87*, U.S. Department of State, August 1987, online, 45.
135. "AIDS May Invade India: Mystery Disease Caused by US experiments," *Patriot* (New Delhi), July 16, 1983, online.
136. Richard Gillette, "AIDS: A Global Assessment," *Los Angeles Times*, August 9, 1987, online.
137. *Soviet Influence Activities*, 33.
138. "AIDS May Invade India," *Patriot*.
139. *Soviet Influence Activities*, 45.
140. Thompson, Helen "In 1950, the U.S. Released a Bioweapon in San Francisco," *Smithsonian Magazine*, July 6, 2015.
141. "The Untreated Syphilis Study at Tuskegee," Centers for Disease Control and Prevention, September 4, 2024, online.
142. Ogunnaike, Lola, "The Passion of Kanye West," *Rolling Stone*, February 9, 2006, online.
143. *Soviet Influence Activities*, 33–49.
144. "A Report on Active Measures and Propaganda, 1986–87," United States Department of State, August 1987, online.
145. *Soviet Influence Activities*.
146. Ibid., 34.
147. Ibid., 33.
148. Pooley, Jefferson, and Michael J. Socolow, "The Myth of the *War of the Worlds* Panic," *Slate*, October 28, 2013, online.
149. Rid, Thomas, *Active Measures: The Secret History of Disinformation and Political Warfare* (Farrar, Straus and Giroux, 2020), 9.
150. Our account of Field Manual 30-31B, including direct quotes, draws from Rid, *Active Measures*, 233–39.
151. Mueller.
152. "Cambridge Analytica Uncovered: Secret Filming Reveals Election Tricks," Channel 4 News, March 19, 2018.
153. Ibid.
154. Supran, Geoffrey, and Naomi Oreskes, "The Forgotten Oil Ads That Told Us Climate Change Was Nothing," *Guardian*, November 18, 2021.
155. See Climate Files database online.

156. Franta, Benjamin, "On Its 100th Birthday in 1959, Edward Teller Warned the Oil Industry About Global Warming," *Guardian*, January 1, 2018.
157. Cited in Dembicki, Geoff, *The Petroleum Papers: Inside the Far-Right Conspiracy to Cover Up Climate Change* (Greystone, 2022), 43–44.
158. Dembicki, 49.
159. Ibid., 128.
160. "Global Climate Science Communications Action Plan," online.
161. Ibid.
162. Dembicki, 82.
163. Ibid., 85.
164. "Police Suspect 12-Year-Old Girl's Suicide Linked to WhatsApp Terror Game Momo," *Buenos Aires Times*, July 25, 2018, online.
165. Rogers, James, "Sinister 'Momo Suicide Challenge' Sparks Fear as It Spreads on WhatsApp," Fox News, August 21, 2018.
166. Lewis, Sophie, "Kim Kardashian Warns Parents of 'Momo Challenge,' but YouTube Says It Sees No Evidence," CBS News, February 28, 2019, online.
167. Radford, Benjamin, "The 'Momo Challenge' and the 'Blue Whale Game': Online Suicide Game Conspiracies," *Skeptical Inquirer* special report, February 28, 2019, online.
168. Cohen, Stanley, *Folk Devils and Moral Panics* (Routledge, 2002), 23–24. Our account and analysis of this event, including quotes, draws from pp. 16–42 of this book.
169. Our account of the events in Salem draws on Schiff, Stacy, *The Witches: Salem, 1692* (Little, Brown, 2015).
170. See, for example: "How the CIA Missed Stalin's Bomb," *Studies in Intelligence* 49, no. 1 (2005), online.
171. Our account of the Red Scare draws on Tye, Larry, *Demagogue: The Life and Long Shadow of Senator Joe McCarthy* (Houghton Mifflin Harcourt, 2020).
172. Hicks, Robert D., *In Pursuit of Satan: The Police and the Occult* (Prometheus, 1991), 176; Rundle, Lisa Bryn, "What was the Satanic Panic?" CBC News, February 26, 2020.
173. Hicks, 188: "Two years later, Judy Johnson underwent psychiatric treatment and received a diagnosis of acute paranoid schizophrenia."

174. Hicks, 188.
175. "McMartin Preschool: Anatomy of a Panic," *New York Times* Retro Report, March 10, 2014, YouTube, online.
176. Hicks, 185: "There is evidence that the child protection system established to investigate abuse reports is seriously flawed and contributed to the spread of unfounded allegations. The system is geared toward finding abuse — but provides no safeguards for those wrongfully accused. There are few checks and balances on investigators."
177. Rivera, Geraldo, host, "Devil Worship: Exposing Satan's Underground," NBC, October 22, 1988.
178. Hicks.
179. Bernstein, 291.
180. Cohen, 2.
181. Selden, Mark, "A Forgotten Holocaust: US Bombing Strategy, the Destruction of Japanese Cities & the American Way of War from World War II to Iraq," *Asia-Pacific Journal* 5, no. 5 (2007).
182. Unless otherwise cited, our source for information on this experiment is Milgram, Stanley, *Obedience to Authority: An Experimental View* (Harper and Row, 1974), 19–23.
183. Milgram, 6.
184. O'Grady, Joan, *Early Christian Heresies* (Barnes & Noble, 1985), 28–30.
185. Ibid., 65.
186. Hofstadter, Richard, *The Paranoid Style in American Politics* (Knopf, 1965), 29.
187. Ibid., 8–9.
188. "How 'One Nation' Didn't Become 'Under God' Until the 50s Religious Revival," NPR, March 30, 2015, online.
189. Hofstadter, 17.
190. Ibid.
191. Ibid., 31.
192. Oliver, J. Eric, and Thomas J. Wood, "Conspiracy Theories and the Paranoid Style(s) of Mass Opinion," *American Journal of Political Science* 58, no. 4 (2014): 952–66.
193. Barkun, Michael, *A Culture of Conspiracy: Apocalyptic Visions in Contemporary America* (University of California Press, 2003), 3–4.

194. Ibid.
195. Sommer, Will, *Trust the Plan: The Rise of QAnon and the Conspiracy That Unhinged America* (HarperCollins, 2023), 102.
196. Rothschild, Mike, *The Storm Is Upon Us* (First Melville House, 2021), 57.
197. Belluck, Pam, with Jo Thomas, "Wads of Cash, Gossip, Then Fraud Charges," *New York Times*, September 2, 2000.
198. Rothschild, 57.
199. Sommer, *Trust the Plan*, 114.
200. Ibid., 107.
201. Ibid., 108.
202. Robinson, Sean, "Up Against the 'Dark Agenda,'" *News Tribune*, updated July 19, 2004.
203. Sommer, *Trust the Plan*, 109.
204. Q Alerts, online.
205. Ibid.
206. Rothschild, 12–13.
207. Gilbert, David, "Hundreds of QAnon Believers Are Still in Dallas Waiting for JFK to Show Up," *Vice*, November 16, 2021.
208. Ankarloo, Bengt, and Stuart Clark, *Witchcraft and Magic in Europe* vol. 5 (University of Philadelphia Press, 2002), 13.
209. Sommer, *Trust the Plan*, 109.
210. Our account of this ancient Egyptian mythology draws from Cohn, Norman, *Cosmos, Chaos, and the World to Come: The Ancient Roots of Apocalyptic Faith* (Yale University Press, 2003), 9–29.
211. Our account of Zoroastrianism draws from Cohn, *Cosmos*, 77–99.
212. Hamilton, Malcolm B., "Sociological Dimensions of Christian Millenarianism," in *Christian Millenarianism: From the Early Church to Waco*, ed. Stephen Hunt (Indiana University Press, 2001), 12–13.
213. Cohn, Norman, *The Pursuit of the Millennium* (Secker & Warburg, 1957), 4.
214. Porter, Stanley E., "Millenarian Thought in the First Century Church," in Hunt, *Christian Millenarianism*, 63.
215. Cohn, *Cosmos*, 163.
216. Ibid., 215.
217. Ibid., 216.

218. Ibid., 217–218.

219. This section draws from Cohn, *Pursuit*, 14, 38–39, 65, 106–8, 282.

220. Cohn, *Pursuit*, 71.

221. Unless otherwise cited, information in this section is drawn from Cohn, *Pursuit*, 282–307.

222. Barkun, Michael, *Disaster and the Millennium* (Syracuse University Press, 1986), 168–69.

223. McDaniel, Charles A., Jr., "Violent Yearnings for the Kingdom of God: Münster's Militant Anabaptism," in *Belief and Bloodshed: Religion and Violence Across Time and Tradition*, ed. James K. Wellman, Jr. (Rowman & Littlefield, 2007), 68.

224. Sexton, Jared Yates, *The Midnight Kingdom: A History of Power, Paranoia and the Coming Crisis* (Dutton, 2023), 192.

225. Cohn, *Pursuit*, 308.

226. Goldwag, Arthur, *Cults, Conspiracies & Secret Societies* (Vintage, 2009), 206–8.

227. "Hitler Forecasts No Reich Overturn in Next 1,000 Years," *New York Times*, September 6, 1934.

228. Sexton, 202–3.

229. Fukuyama, Francis, *The End of History and the Last Man* (Free Press, 1992).

230. Flandro, Carly, "The Legacy of Elizabeth Clare Prophet," *Bozeman Daily Chronicle*, August 8, 2011, online.

231. Goldwag, 35–37.

232. Vallee, Jacques, *Messengers of Deception: UFO Contacts and Cults* (Daily Grail, 2008).

233. Lalich, Janja, *Bounded Choice: True Believers and Charismatic Cults* (University of California Press, 2004), 92.

234. Ibid., 100

235. Lifton, Robert Jay, *Destroying the World to Save It* (Metropolitan, 1999), 46.

236. Ibid., 59.

237. Juergensmeyer, Mark, *Terror in the Mind of God: The Global Rise of Religious Violence* (University of California Press, 2017), 138–39.

238. Lifton, 118.

239. Ibid., 27.

240. Ibid., 6.
241. Sexton, 287.
242. Landler, Mark, "What Did President Trump Mean by 'Calm Before the Storm'?" *New York Times*, October 6, 2017.
243. Q Alerts, online.
244. FEMA Fact Sheet, online.
245. Rothschild, 236.
246. Sexton, 287.
247. "Why Is MAGA Angry with Trump, Pam Bondi over Epstein Files?" Al Jazeera, July 9, 2025, online.
248. Festinger, Leon, *A Theory of Cognitive Dissonance* (Stanford University Press, 2009), 9–15.
249. Ibid., 3.
250. Sears, Clara Endicott. *Days of Delusion: A Strange Bit of History* (Houghton Mifflin Company, 1924), 244.
251. Festinger, Leon, *When Prophecy Fails* (Harper and Row, 1964), 12–15.
252. Ibid., 17.
253. Ibid., 128.
254. Snow, Samuel, "The True Midnight Cry!" August 22, 1844, 1–4.
255. Loughborough, J.N., *The Great Second Advent Movement: Its Rise and Progress* (Review and Herald, 1909), 166–67.
256. Sears, Clara Endicott, *Days of Delusion: A Strange Bit of History* (Houghton Mifflin, 1924), 172.
257. Ibid., 244–45.
258. Ibid., 245–48.
259. Festinger, *Prophecy*, 4.
260. Ibid., 28.
261. Our account of Dorothy Martin's prophecies is drawn from Festinger, *Prophecy*.
262. Kelly, Thomas, "Debunking 'When Prophecy Fails,'" *The History of the Behavioral Sciences* 62, no. 1 (2025), online.
263. Ibid.
264. For examples, see Aronson, Elliot, and Judson Mills, "The Effect of Severity of Initiation on Liking for a Group," *The Journal of Abnormal and Social Psychology* 59, no. 2 (1959), 177–81; Brehm, Jack W., *A Theory of Psychological Reactance* (Academic Press, 1966); Zanna,

Mark P., and Joel Cooper, "Dissonance and the Pill: An Attribution Approach to Studying the Arousal Properties of Dissonance," *Journal of Personality and Social Psychology* 29, no. 5 (1974): 703–9; Beauvois, Jean-Léon, and Robert-Vincent Joule, "A Radical Point of View on Dissonance Theory," in Eddie Harmon-Jones and Judson Mills (eds.), *Cognitive Dissonance: Progress on a Pivotal Theory in Social Psychology* (American Psychological Association, 1999): 43–70; and Vaidis, David C., Willem W.A. Sleegers, and Florian van Leeuwen et al., "A Multilab Replication of the Induced-Compliance Paradigm of Cognitive Dissonance," *Advances in Methods and Practices in Psychological Science* 7, no. 1 (2024). For an examination of the neurological evidence for the experience of cognitive dissonance, see Colosio, Marco, Anna Shestakova, Vadim V. Nikulin et al., "Neural Mechanisms of Cognitive Dissonance: An EEG Study," *Journal of Neuroscience* 17 (2017): 5074–83.

265. Festinger, Leon, *A Theory of Cognitive Dissonance* (Stanford University Press, 2009), 276.
266. Q Alerts, online.
267. Sommer, Will, "This QAnon Leader Could Control Key Elections in 2024," *Daily Beast*, June 1, 2022, online.
268. Wood, Michael J., Karen M. Douglas, and Robbie M. Sutton, "Dead and Alive: Beliefs in Contradictory Conspiracy Theories," *Social Psychological and Personality Science* 3, no. 6 (2012): 767–73, online.
269. Irwin, Harvey J., Neil Dagnall, and Kenneth Drinkwater, "Belief Inconsistency in Conspiracy Theorists," *Comprehensive Psychology* 4 (2015), online.
270. Rittik, Susmito, "Linking Belief Inconsistency and Religious Commitment with Dogmatism" (2013), retrieved online from Academia.edu.
271. Barron, David, Kevin Morgan, Tony Towell, Boris Altemeyer, and Viren Swami, "Associations Between Schizotypy and Belief in Conspiracist Ideation," *Personality and Individual Differences* 70 (2014), 156–59.
272. Festinger, *Cognitive Dissonance*, 266–77.
273. Ibid., 267–68.

274. Barkun, Michael, "The Occultists and the Spaceman," *Handbook of Spiritualism and Channeling*, ed. Cathy Guttierez (Brill, 2015), 464–79.
275. Ibid.
276. Barkun, *Culture of Conspiracy*, 27–28.
277. For a discussion of Aristotle's theory of telos, see: Bynum, W.F., *A Little History of Science* (Yale University Press, 2012), 30.
278. Crowe, Michael J., *Theories of the World: From Antiquity to the Copernican Revolution* (Dover, 2001).
279. Kuhn, Thomas S., *The Structure of Scientific Revolutions* (University of Chicago Press, 2012), 169.
280. Hoskin, Michael, *The History of Astronomy: A Very Short Introduction* (Oxford University Press, 2003), 1.
281. Crowe, 21.
282. Popper, Karl, *The Logic of Scientific Discovery* (Routledge Classics, 2002), 18.
283. Ibid., 19.
284. Spence, R.B., "Masonic Revolutions in America and France," in *The Real History of Secret Societies* lecture series (The Great Courses, 2019).
285. See, for example: Pearson, E., "5 Ways We Can Prove Earth Is Round, Not Flat" *Sky at Night* (BBC), online.
286. Bynum, 2.
287. A good illustration is provided by Carl Sagan in *How the Ancient Greeks Knew the Earth Is Round* (video), Cornell University, 1980, online.
288. An example of this can be found on a Flat Earth Society homepage online.
289. Our account of the Bedford level experiment draws from Parallax (Samuel Birley Rowbotham), *Zetetic Astronomy: Earth Not a Globe* (Simpkin Marshall, 1865).
290. "The Conspiracy," Flat Earth Society, online.
291. For a good description of the main claims, see: "NASA Moon Landing Hoax," *MythBusters*, season 6, episode 11, hosted by Jamie Hyneman and Adam Savage, Discovery Channel, August 27, 2008.
292. A number of the claims are also debunked at "Moon Landing Conspiracy Theories, Debunked," Royal Museums Greenwich, online.

293. John Uri, "Flag Day — Flying High: The Stars and Stripes in Space," NASA, June 13, 2019, online.
294. "NASA Moon Landing Hoax," *MythBusters*.
295. "Moonlight," NASA, online.
296. Our account of insects used in warfare draws from Lockwood, Jeffrey A., *Six-Legged Soldiers: Using Insects as Weapons of War* (Oxford University Press, 2009).
297. Kristof, Nicholas D., "Unmasking Horror: Japan Confronting Gruesome War Atrocity," *New York Times*, March 17, 1995.
298. Stevens, Shannon, "The Rhetorical Significance of Gojira: Equipment for Living Through Trauma," in *The Atomic Bomb in Japanese Cinema: Critical Essays*, ed. Matthew Edwards (McFarland, 2015), 21.
299. Schaller, Michael, "Godzilla, Present and Past," *New York Times*, May 16, 1998.
300. Stevens, 18.
301. Yam, Kimmy, "'Godzilla' Was a Metaphor for Hiroshima, and Hollywood Whitewashed It," NBC News, August 7, 2020, online.
302. Ibid.
303. Our account of *Invasion of the Body Snatchers* draws from LeGacy, Arthur, "The Invasion of the Body Snatchers: A Metaphor for the Fifties," *Literature/Film Quarterly* 6, no. 3 (1978): 285.
304. Brunvand, Jan Harold, *The Vanishing Hitchhiker: American Urban Legends and Their Meanings* (W.W. Norton, 1981), 4.
305. Morton, Ella, "How a Real Corpse Ended up in a Fun Park Spookhouse," *Slate*, April 11, 2014, online.
306. Brunvand, Jan Harold, *Too Good to Be True: The Colossal Book of Urban Legends* (W.W. Norton, 2014), 96–97.
307. Thompson, Derek, "A Brief History of Teenagers," *Saturday Evening Post*, February 13, 2018.
308. Ibid.
309. Brunvand, *Vanishing Hitchhiker*, 64–65.
310. Ibid., 52–53.
311. In the subsequent six sections, our account of the cattle mutilation epidemic draws from Ellis, Bill, "Cattle Mutilation: Contemporary Legends and Contemporary Mythologies," *Contemporary Legend* 1

(1991): 31–80; Goleman, Michael J., "Wave of Mutilation: The Cattle Mutilation Phenomenon of the 1970s," *Agricultural History* 85, no. 3 (2011): 398–417; Kagan, Daniel, and Ian Summers, *Mute Evidence* (Bantam, 1984), xiv, 142–51; Lebelson, Harry, "Death on the Range," *Omni*, January 1980; Peebles, Curtis, *Watch the Skies! A Chronicle of the Flying Saucer Myth* (Berkeley Books, 1995), 259–67; Root, Chris, "UFOs and a Horse Called Snippy," Denver Public Library History, October 20, 2020, online.

312. Peebles, 264.
313. Lebelson, 28.
314. "Mutilations of Cattle in Texas, Oklahoma Called Work of Cults, *New York Times*, March 2, 1975.
315. Walker, 53.
316. Ankarloo and Clark, 15.
317. Lichtenstein, Grace, "11 States Baffled by Mutilation of Cattle," *New York Times*, October 30, 1975.
318. Lalich, 25–27.
319. "Army Finds Bodies of 26 Wild Horses at Utah Waterhole," *New York Times*, July 7, 1976.
320. Cole, Leonard A., *Clouds of Secrecy: The Army's Germ Warfare Tests Over Populated Areas* (Rowman & Littlefield, 1988), 79–81.
321. *Unidentified Anomalous Phenomena: Independent Study Team Report*, NASA, 2023, online, 40.
322. Ibid., 11.
323. Ibid., 13.
324. Ibid., 20.
325. Ibid., 13.
326. Ibid., 20.
327. Peebles, x.
328. Haines, Gerald K., "CIA's Role in the Study of UFOs, 1947–90," *Intelligence and National Security* 14, no. 2 (1999): 26–48.
329. See, for example: "Roswell," *Unsolved Mysteries*, season 2, episode 1, NBC, September 20, 1989.
330. McAndrew, James, *The Roswell Report: Case Closed* (Headquarters United States Air Force, 1997), 123, online.

331. Davis, Richard, *Results of a Search for Records Concerning the 1947 Crash Near Roswell, New Mexico* (United States General Accounting Office, 1997), online.
332. McAndrew, *Roswell: Case Closed.*
333. Hallion, Richard P., and James McAndrew, *The Roswell Report: Fact vs fiction in the New Mexico Desert* (Headquarters United States Air Force, 1995), online.
334. "Harassed Rancher Who Located 'Saucer' Sorry He Told About It," *Roswell Daily Record*, July 9, 1947.
335. Ibid.
336. Hallion and McAndrew, 30.
337. Ibid., 12–13.
338. McAndrew, *Roswell: Case Closed.*
339. Cahn, J.P., "The Flying Saucer Swindlers," *True*, August 1956, online.
340. See, for example: "Roswell," *Unsolved Mysteries.*
341. Hallion and McAndrew, 15.
342. Sherwood, J.C., "Gray Barker: My Friend, the Myth-Maker," *Skeptical Inquirer* 22, no. 3 (1998), 37–39.
343. Watkins, Leslie, *Alternative 3* (Graham Watkins, 1978), vi.
344. Nichols, Preston B., and Peter Moon, *The Montauk Project: Experiments in Time* (Sky Books, 1992), 96.
345. Haines, "CIA's Role."
346. Hallion and McAndrew, 3.
347. Pilkington, Mark, *Mirage Men: A Journey in Disinformation, Paranoia and UFOs* (Constable Robinson, 2010); Bishop, Greg, *Project Beta* (Paraview, 2005).
348. "Majestic 12" (forged document,) FBI Vault, online.
349. Ibid.
350. Ibid.
351. Klass, Philip J., "The New Bogus Majestic-12 documents," *Skeptical Inquirer* 24, no. 3 (2000), 44, online.
352. Cooper, William, *Behold a Pale Horse* (Light Technology, 1991), 213.
353. Ibid.
354. See: "The UFO Deception," a subseries of *New York Post* video podcast *The Basement Office*, hosted by Steven Greenstreet, especially

his five-episode look at Skinwalker Ranch (the first of those episodes is available online via YouTube).

355. Ibid.

356. Our account of the Seattle Windshield Epidemic draws from: Gardner, James Ross, "What Pitted Seattle's Glass?" *Seattle Met*, April 8, 2020; Medalia, Nahum Z., and Otto N. Larsen, "Diffusion and Belief in a Collective Delusion: The Seattle Windshield Pitting Epidemic," *American Sociological Review* 23, no. 2 (April 1958): 180–86; Stein, A.J., "Windshield Pitting Incidents in Washington Reach Fever Pitch on April 15, 1954" (2003), online; Weeks, Linton, "The Windshield-Pitting Mystery of 1954," NPR, online; "Hundreds See Windshields Pitted," *Vancouver Sun*, April 19, 1954; "Pock-Marked Windshields Baffle Canadian Scientists," *Bellingham Herald*, April 20, 1954.

357. Van Prooijen, Jan-Willem, and Mark van Vugt, "Conspiracy Theories: Evolved Functions and Psychological Mechanisms," *Perspectives on Psychological Science* 13, no. 6 (2018), 772.

358. Banas, John A., and Gregory Miller, "Inducing Resistance to Conspiracy Theory Propaganda: Testing Inoculation and Metainoculation Strategies," *Human Communication Research* 39, no. 2 (2013): 184–207.

359. Pappas, Stephanie, "Conspiracy Theories Can Be Undermined with These Strategies, New Analysis Shows," *Scientific American*, April 5, 2023.

360. Dyer, Kathleen D., and Raymond E. Hall, "Effect of Critical Thinking Education on Epistemically Unwarranted Beliefs in College Students," *Research in Higher Education* 60 (2018): 293–314.

361. Murthy, V.H., *Our Epidemic of Loneliness and Isolation* (Office of the U.S. Surgeon General, 2023), online.

362. Ibid., 8.

363. Bierwiaczonek, Kinga, Sam Fluit, Tilmann von Soest, Matthew J. Hornsey, and Jonas R. Kunst, "Loneliness Trajectories over Three Decades Are Associated with Conspiracist Worldviews in Midlife," *Nature Communications* 15 (2024), article no. 3629.

ACKNOWLEDGEMENTS

This book couldn't have been written without the support of many people. We would like to acknowledge all the children in our families (Cato, Sylvie, Si, Judah, Felix, Agatha, Edith, Iris, Nina, Kailey, and Anthony) for providing inspiration and for being good eggs. We would like to thank our partners, Zoë and Robyn, for being patient and insightful sounding boards. We would also like to thank the people at ECW for all of their efforts on the project.

INDEX

Acoustic Kitty, 2, 3
active measures, 88–89
Adamski, George, 201
Aerial Phenomena Research Organization (APRO), 211
Ahura Mazda, 134
AIDS. *See* HIV/AIDS epidemic
Alberta oil sands, 97
aliens, 195, 200–201, 205. *See also* UFOs
All-domain Anomaly Resolution Office (AARO), 203, 204
Alternative 3 (book by Watkins), 210–12
Alternative 3 (TV show), 209–10, 211
Altshuler, John, 193
Ambitious Card Trick, 15
American Revolution, and Freemasons, 172–73
Anabaptist movement, and millenarian idea, 141–42
Anaximander, 174
Angra Mainyu, 134
Anons, of QAnon, 128–29
Anti-Masons, 123
Anti-Vaccination League, 56
anti-vax community: and community, 55, 65; and COVID, 64–65; experts in, 60; historical overview, 55–58; and loneliness epidemic, 59–60. *See also* vaccination
apocalypse, 137, 141–42
Apophis (evil force), 133
Applewhite, Marshall, 145
Army-McCarthy hearings, 111–12
Arnold, Kenneth, 206, 214
Asahara, Shōkō, 146
Asch, Solomon, 51, 52
asha and druj, 133
AstraZeneca vaccine, and disinformation, 69, 70
astroturfing, 98
attention, lack of, 24
Augustine of Hippo, 139
Aum Shinrikyō, 146
autism, and vaccination, 34–35, 57
"automatic reading," 160
Aztec (New Mexico), UFO crash at, 208

badness and bad acts, 117–19
bandwagon effect, 155
Bankston, Kenneth, 195, 196
Baris magazine, 93
Barker, Gray, 209, 217
Barkun, Michael, 124–25
Bavarian Illuminati, 40–43, 44
beliefs: and changing our minds, 167; conspiratorial beliefs, 55; contradictions in, 164–66; of cults, 227–28; and dissonance, 154–56, 163, 167; doubling down on, 159–60, 161, 166, 167; and group, 54–55, 64, 154–55; not matching up with events, 150, 151, 158–59, 162; and perception, 151–52; social aspect, 49, 52, 54–55, 64–65
Bender, Albert K., 209
Bennewitz, Paul, 212
Berlitz, Charles, 208
Bernard, David, 123
Bible, 45–46, 120–22, 137–39
Biden, Joe, 149, 164
Big Oil, and Climategate, 96–98
Bigelow, Robert, 218
bin Laden, Osama, 165
biological warfare, 84–86, 184
Bittman, Ladislav, 91

black helicopters, 197–200
Blavatsky, Helena, 144
blue jeans and syphilis, 182–86
Blue Whale Challenge, 101
Bockelson, Jan, 142
book of Job, Satan in, 120–21
book of Revelation, and millenarian idea, 137–39, 140, 141
brain of humans, 13–15, 23, 26, 225–26
Brazel, W.W., 206, 207
Brenna, Mario, 40
British royal family, and Princess Diana, 9, 38–40
Broome, Fiona, 3
Buckey, Ray, 113
Buenos Aires Times, 100, 101
Bush, Vannevar, 214
"butterfly effect" (tiny changes, outsized impact), 36–37, 40, 48

Cahn, J.P., 208
Cambridge Analytica, and 2016 election, 94–95
canon, in millenarian movements, 139
Capitol Building, events of January 6, 2020, 149
Car, as planet, 160
Carr, William Guy, 45–46
Castle Bravo hydrogen bomb test, 222–23
Cato Institute, 97–98
cats spying on people, 2, 3
cattle mutilation epidemic: conspiracy hypotheses, 194–201; description, 193–94, 201–2; as extraterrestrial experiment, 195, 200–201; as government secret project, 195, 197–200; as Satanic cult, 195–97
causal reasoning (cause-and-effect): description and use, 29–30, 47–48; mistakes in, 33–36
causality and causation: and chaos, 36–38; as concept, 29–30; and correlation, 33–34; kinds of causes, 30–32; mistakes in, 31, 32, 33–34
Chabris, Christopher, 23–24
chaos: and causality, 36–38; and conspiracy claims, 38–40, 82; Illuminati as case study, 40–47; and order, 47–48
children, in moral panics, 100–101, 107–9, 113–14
Christianity: canon, 139; interpretations of, 121–22; Last Judgment, 138; and millenarian idea, 136–39, 140, 141
Church Universal and Triumphant (CUT), 144–45
CIA (Central Intelligence Agency): fooled by a magician, 15–20; hallucinogenic drugs testing, 3, 4; learning of magic tricks, 233n27; MKUltra project, 86, 181; remote viewing (RV), 17, 22; spying on people, 2, 3
Clarion, as planet, 160, 162
Climategate and climate skepticism, 96–98
Clinton, Hillary Rodham, 6, 95, 147, 163
cognitive dissonance: avoidance and minimization, 155–57; and conspiracies, 154–55, 165–67; description as concept, 151–52, 153, 154, 163; and failed prophecies, 156–57, 159–60, 162, 164–65; how it works, 152–54; of researchers, 166–67; seen as investment, 154
Cohen, Stanley, 101, 102, 103, 105, 106, 115
Cohn, Norman, 135–36, 140
Cold War, Soviets *vs.* U.S., 16, 92–93, 183–85, 188
Columbus, Christopher, 175
common sense and reasoning, 2–4
communism: and millenarianism, 142, 143–44; rise, 109–10; in Soviet Union, 109, 142, 143–44; as threat in U.S., 110–12, 115, 188–89
communist insurgencies, disinformation about, 92–93
Communist Party, membership, 111
community. *See* group
concentration camp conspiracy theories, 74–75
conditioning, as concept, 78–79, 80
confirmation bias, 73, 81, 124, 129
consonance, 153–54, 156
conspiracies and conspiracy theories: aim, 29; amplifiers for, 7; believers in, 224, 228, 229; as conspiracy, 99; contradictions and inconsistencies in, 164–65; counterarguments for followers, 227; definition and use of terms, 4–5; events not matching beliefs, 150, 151, 158–59, 162; impact, 1; ingredients for, 116; online advantage, 73; protection from, 226–28, 229–30; real conspiracies, 85–86, 181; *vs.* real events, 2–4, 5; related concepts, 7–9; reuse of ideas, 55–56; "theory" as term, 4–5; true *vs.* false theories, 5; truth and untruth in, 5–7. *See also* false conspiracy theory; specific topics
conspiracism, description as red flag, 8–9
conspiracists, as saviours, 132
conspiratorial seduction, 14

context: analysis and in conspiracies, 183, 186–87, 188, 192; in cattle mutilation epidemic, 194–97, 198–99, 201; fleas in blue jeans for syphilis, 183, 184–85; in urban legends, 190–91; in windshield epidemic, 224
contributory cause, 31–32
Cooper, William, 216–18, 220
Corbell, Jeremy, 219
correlation, and causality, 33–34
counterculture movement of 1960s, 46
COVID-19 pandemic: and anti-vax community, 64–65; conspiracy theories about, 56, 77; description and impact, 56–57; experts and fact sheets, 60–61; information, misinformation, disinformation, 68–70, 77; lockdowns, 58–59, 64; and loneliness epidemic, 59–61, 228; and loss of community, 55; reactions to, 63, 64–65
Crash at Aztec hoax, 208
critical thinking, as defence, 81–82
cults: beliefs of and conspiracies, 227–28; in cattle mutilation epidemic, 195–98; and millenarianism, 144–46; rise in U.S., 196; thought traps or loops, 173–74
Cutler, Robert, 213–14, 215
Cutler-Twining memo, 213–15
Czechoslovakia, and hidden gold of Nazis, 91

death camp of FEMA conspiracy, 75–77
Deep State, as conspiracy, 216, 218
Dehmlow, Ronald, 85
Dembicki, Geoff, 96, 98
Devil. *See* Satan
Diana (Princess), and royal family, 9, 38–40
digital devices, importance to humans, 66–67
digital information. *See* virtual information
disinformation: on climate, 96–98; and conditioning, 78–79, 80; and conspiracies, 79–80, 87, 99; and COVID, 69–70, 77; defence against, 81–82; definition and example, 68, 69–70, 77–78; and Georgia Coffins photo, 76, 77; historical overview, 88–90; on HIV/AIDS epidemic, 84–86, 87, 89–90; impact, 87–88; motivations and their creators, 78–80, 83; political disinformation, 88–89, 90–92, 94–95, 96–98; and social media, 80–81, 83, 94–95; on UFOs, 212–13; on vaccination, 69–70. *See also* KGB and disinformation
dissonance, 153, 154–56, 163, 167. *See also* cognitive dissonance
dog whistle or dog-whistle conspiracy, 5–6
Donahue, Phil, 114
Doty, Richard, 212–13
dualistic worldviews and battles, 133–34
Dunn, John, 195
Durkheim, Émile, 53, 54
Dzhirkvelov, Ilya, 87

Earth: ancient science of, 171, 174; as sphere, 174–75, 178. *See also* flat Earth
Ebola outbreak scare in U.S., 76–77
Egyptians, and good *vs.* evil, 133
Eisenhower, President, 111, 213, 214
Ekker, Doris, 166
Empedoclese, 174
end of the world (or end of times), 134–35, 141–42, 157–58. *See also* millennialism
Engel, Leopold, 42
Éon de l'Étoile and followers, 140
Epstein, Jeffrey, 149
Eratosthenes, 174
evil: as absolute concept, 117, 119; *vs.* badness, 117–19; and conspiracies, 116, 125, 132–33; definition and understanding of, 119–21; and events of the 20th century, 131; examples, 123; *vs.* good, 122–25, 132, 133–34, 135, 137–39; and "Manichean" as term, 121; in QAnon conspiracy belief, 128–30; and reckoning, 134–35; as relative concept, 116–17, 119
evolution as metaphor, 70–72, 74, 76, 77–78
"extraterrestrial hypothesis," 203–4, 213, 219

Facebook, and political disinformation, 94–95
failed prophecies: and cognitive dissonance, 156–57, 159–60, 162, 164–65; Great Disappointment, 157–60; QAnon movement, 163–64; UFOs not landing or rescuing, 160–63, 166
fake posts and false stories, 73
false conspiracy theory: conclusions about, 26–28; definition, 5; and dissonance, 165–67; study of, 183, 186, 189, 202; truth within, 7
false flags, 3
false positives, in conspiracies, 26–28

"false prophet," 138, 157
falsifiability: and conspiracies, 172–74, 180–81; description and in scientific inquiry, 171–72, 173, 180; and Flat Earth theory, 176–77, 180, 181; in social sciences, 172–74
Fayed, Dodi, 38, 39, 40
al-Fayed, Mohamed, 38
Fazze, memes of, 70
FBI, official records and memos, 213–14
Federal Emergency Management Agency (FEMA), 74–77
Festinger, Leon, 152, 153, 156, 157, 159–60, 161, 164, 165; with colleagues in UFO failed prophecy, 161, 162–63, 166–67
figurative meaning, as red flag, 8
final judgment, 134–35
financial scams, 125–27
Finney, Jack, 188
5G network, and COVID-19, 56
flag in Apollo moon landing, 14, 27, 178, 179
flat Earth and Flat Earth theory: as belief, 174, 175–76, 177–78; as conspiracy, 177, 181; and dissonance, 153, 154–56; and falsifiability, 176–77, 180, 181
fleas, 182–86
Flickinger, Donald, 195, 196
flying saucers. *See* UFOs
folk devil, 106, 108
folk psychology, 15, 23–26
Forrestal, James, 214
Fort Detrick (Maryland) military facility, 84, 85
Frashokereti, description of, 134–35, 138
Fravor, David, 203, 204
Frederick II, 140–41
Freemasons and Masonic lodges, 41, 123, 172–73
French Revolution, 43, 44
Friedman, Stanton, 213, 214
Fugal, Brandon, 218
Fukuyama, Francis, 144
functionalism and functionalist perspective, 53–55

Geller, Uri, 18–21
general knowledge, importance of, 82
Georgia Coffins photo and meme, 74, 75–77
Germany: millenarianism, 141–42, 143; Nazis in after WWII, 90–92
gloves, and COVID, 69
GM, and streetcar industry, 3
Gojira/Godzilla, 186–87
Good, Sarah, 108–9
good *vs.* evil. *See* evil *vs.* good
Goodwin, Shain, 126–28, 130
gorilla suit in video, 23–24
Gottlieb, Sidney, 233n27
Graves, Ryan, 203, 204
Great Britain, resistance to vaccination, 56
Great Disappointment, 157–60
Greeks (ancient Greeks), myths and science, 170–71, 174
group: and beliefs, 54–55, 64, 154–55; conspiracists and self-protection, 227; examples, 53–54; going along with the group, 51–53, 65
group identity, and conspiracies, 6–7
Grusch, David Charles, 203, 219–20
guess, description and *vs.* prophecy, 156, 157
Gunderson, Ted, 114

Haines, Gerald K., 212
hallucinogenic drugs, testing on citizens, 3, 4, 86
Hastings, Leonard, 158–59
hazards, and threat, 62–63
H-bomb tests, 186, 187
Heaven's Gate, and millenarianism, 145–46, 196
hidden plots, 226
"The Hippie Babysitter" urban legend, 192
HIV/AIDS epidemic, disinformation on, 84–86, 87, 89–90
Hoagland, Richard, 211
Hofstadter, Richard, 122, 123–24
Holocaust, 131
Hook, Clyde, 125–27
hook-handed killer, in urban legend, 190–91
horse, mutilated horse story, 193, 200
Howe, Linda Moulton, 200–201
Human Individual Metamorphosis (HIM), 145
humans: brain, 13–15, 23, 26, 225–26; impact of loneliness, 228–29; and inconsistency, 151–53, 165; as social creatures, 49–50, 51
Hyman, Ray, 8

ideas: evolution as metaphor, 71–72, 74, 76, 77–78; spread online, 71, 72–73
ideological groups, and conspiracies, 6–7
Illuminati: as case study of chaos, 40–47; as conspiracy, 6, 43–46; description, 6, 40–41; scams about, 46–47; in U.S., 43–44, 46–47
inconsistency, and humans, 151–53, 165
India, and HIV/AIDS, 84
information: and certainty, 81; and conditioning, 78–79, 80; and COVID, 68–69; definition and example, 68–69; evolution as metaphor, 70–72, 74,

76, 77–78; hidden plots in, 226; as protection from conspiracies, 226–27; quality of, 98–99; and reality, 67–68; spread online, 71, 72–73; and technology, 66–67. *See also* virtual information
infotainment, 99
insects as weapons, 184–85
intelligent people, belief in conspiracies, 13, 16, 21, 23, 27–28
International Flying Saucer Bureau (IFSB), 209
Invasion of the Body Snatchers (film and book), 187–89
isfet and ma'at, 133
Ishii, Shirō, 184
Italy, political disinformation, 93

Jacobsen, Annie, 18
January 6, 2020, events (storming of Capitol Building), 149
Japan, 184, 186, 187
jet fuel, and World Trade Center towers, 32–33
Jews, and conspiracies, 44–45
Jones, Alex and *The Alex Jones Show,* 7
journalism and journalists, 82–83

Kaplan, Raymond, 111
Kelleher, Colm, 218
Kennedy, John F., 35, 129–30
Kennedy, John F., Jr., 129–30
Kenyon, Dorothy, 110–11
Keyhoe, Donald, 201
KGB and disinformation: Field Manual 30-31B of U.S. Army, 92–94; on HIV/AIDS, 87, 88, 89–90; Operation Neptune in Germany, 90–92
"The Killer in the Back Seat" urban legend, 192
Kirkpatrick, Sean, 220
Klass, Philip J., 215
Knapp, George, 216, 218, 219
Koch, Charles, 97
Koch Industries, 97, 98
Kogan, Aleksandr, 94–95
Korean War, 184
Kuhn, Thomas, 169
Kulagina, Nina, 22

Lang, Jacob, 42
Langlie, Arthur, 223
Larson, Heidi J., 56, 57, 58, 60
Laughead, Charles, 161, 162, 166
Lazar, Bob, 216, 217
Lear, John Olsen, 216, 217
L'Europeo weekly, 93
Lifton, Robert, 8
Lindzen, Richard S., 97–98
Loftus, Elizabeth, 25
loneliness, as epidemic, 59–61, 228–29, 230
Lorenz, Edward, 36

Macknik, Stephen L., 14–15, 24–25
MAD (mutually assured destruction), 16, 183, 185
magic tricks and magicians: and attention, 24; belief in, 14–15, 27; fooling of CIA, 15–20; learning by CIA, 233n27
Majestic 12 (MJ-12), operation and documents, 213, 214–15, 216, 220
Mandela Effect conspiracy theory, 3–4
"Manichean," as term, 121, 122, 133
Manichean worldview or Manicheanism: and conspiracies, 125–28, 129; as conspiratorial view, 122–25, 132, 133; example of scheme, 127–28; in Nazism, 143; in QAnon conspiracy belief, 128–30, 147; seductive aspects, 123–25, 129–30
Marcel, Jesse A., 206, 208
Martin, Dorothy, 160–63, 166
Martinez-Conde, Susana, 14–15, 25
The Matrix (film), 7
Matthys, Jan, 141–42
McCarthy, Joseph, 110–12, 115, 188, 189
McIntyre, Lee, 78
McLuhan, Marshall, 66–67
McMartin preschool (California), Satanic Panic in, 112–13, 114
media literacy, and disinformation, 81
memories, changes in, 26
memory, failure of, 25–26
mental hygiene, and disinformation, 81
Michaels, Patrick, 98
Milgram, Stanley, 118, 119
millennialism (or millenarianism) and millenarian idea or movements: belief in action, 139–41; bringing about of the end, 141–42; and canon, 139; in Christianity, 136–39, 140, 141; and communism, 142, 143–44; consequences, 150; and conspiracies, 147–50; description and origin, 135; forcing the end, 146; and NRMs (cults), 144–46; in religion, 135–42, 144–46; in secular movements, 142–44
Miller, William, and Millerites, 157–59
mind control project, 3, 4, 86, 181
misinformation, 68, 69, 70
MKUltra project, 3, 4, 86, 181
MMR vaccine, and autism, 57
Mods and Rockers scare, 102–3, 104, 105, 106
Momo Challenge, 100–101, 104, 105
money wrapped in tinfoil, 125–27
Moon, Peter, 211–12

moon landing, as hoax, 14, 27, 178–80
Moore, William L., 208, 213, 214, 215
moral panics: description and issues in, 101–2, 115; folk devils in, 106, 108; making of, 102–6; Mods and Rockers scare, 102–3, 104, 105, 106; Momo Challenge, 100–101, 104, 105; Red Scare, 109–12, 115; Salem Witch Trials, 107–9; Satanic Panic, 112–14, 115; stages of, 103–6, 107–8
Moro, Aldo, 93
Morse, Jedidiah, 43–44
Mulholland, John, 233n27
Mullis, Kary, 64
Münster (Germany), and millenarian idea, 141–42
Murthy, Vivek, 228
mutually assured destruction (MAD), 16, 183, 185
myths *vs.* science, 170–71

NASA, 177, 211
National Institute for Discovery Science (NIDSci), 218
nature and the natural, and science, 170–71
Nazis and Nazism, 90–92, 142–43
NBC, on Satanism in U.S., 114
necessary cause, 30–31
Negative 48 (Michael Protzman), 129
NESARA (National Economic Stabilization and Recovery Act), 127–28, 147
Nettles, Bonnie, 145
New Religious Movements (NRMs), 144–46, 196. *See also* cults
New Testament Gospels, 121
news, and quality of information, 98–99
newspapers, as source of information, 82–83
Newton, Isaac, 13, 169, 175
Newton, Silas, 208
Nichols, Preston B., 211–12
9/11 events, 32–33
Nixon administration, 85, 198, 199
North Korea, 184
NSA (National Security Agency), and Vietnam War, 2
nuclear weapons: impact of tests, 222–23; as threat, 16, 146, 183, 186, 187, 188

Obama, Barack, 6, 76–77
Offit, Paul, 57
oil and gas companies, disinformation from, 96–98
Old Testament, and event that will "change everything," 135–37
Omega Trust and Trading, 126, 127
omission bias, 61
Operation INFEKTION, 87
Operation Neptune, 90–92
Operation Sea-Spray, 85–86
Osborne, Sarah, 108, 109
outer space, and "automatic reading," 160
outrage, as response, 62, 63

Pabst, William, 74
paranoid spokesmen, as red flag, 7
Parris, Elizabeth, 108
Parris, Samuel, 107, 108
Patriot newspaper, 84, 85, 87
Paul, Henri, 40
Pazder, Lawrence, 112–13
Pearl Harbor attack, 2, 3
Peebles, Curtis, 204
peppered moths, 73–74
perceptual psychology, 23–25
Philippines, political disinformation, 93
philosophy of science, 169–70
phlogiston, theory of, 180
polio vaccine, 56
political disinformation: active measures, 88–89; climate skepticism, 96–98; description and materials for, 88, 89; election of 2016 in U.S., 94–95; Operation Neptune, 90–92
Pomeroy, Allan, 223
Popper, Karl, 171–72, 173
post hoc ergo propter hoc ("after this, therefore because of this"), 34–35, 44, 57
prediction: description, 156, 157; failed predictions, 164
Project Mogul tests, 207
prophecy, 156–57. *See also* failed prophecies
Prophet, Elizabeth Clare, 144–45
prophets, 138, 157
Protzman, Michael (aka Negative 48), 129
psychic abilities (parapsychology), 16–23, 26
Puharich, Andrija (Henry Karl), 18
Puthoff, Harold "Hal," 18–21, 22, 23, 28, 233n25

Q, as poster, 128–29, 147–48, 163–64
QAnon movement/ conspiracy belief: and failed prophecies, 163–64; as Manichean worldview, 128–30, 147; and millenarianism, 147; and the Storm, 147–49; and thought-terminating clichés, 8, 164

Ra (sun god), 133
Ramey, Roger, 207
Randi, James "The Amazing," 18, 21, 28
Rather, Dan, 85
real events *vs.* conspiracies, 2–3
reality, 67–68

reasoning: causal, 29–30, 33–36, 47–48; and common sense, 2–4; scientific, 171–72
red flags, examples of, 7–9
Red Scare, 109–12, 115
religion, function of, 53, 54
remote viewing (RV), 17, 18–19, 22
revealed knowledge, and prophecies, 156–57
rich, collusion from, 6
Rid, Thomas, 88–89, 92, 93
risk, meanings and impact, 62–63
Rittik, Susmito, 165
Rivera, Geraldo, 114
Robison, John, 41–42, 43, 44, 45
Rommel, Ken, 194
Roosevelt government, 2, 3
Roswell Daily Record, on UFO debris found, 206–7
Roswell Incident, 205–9, 214
Rothschild, Mike, 129
Rowbotham, Samuel, 175–77, 178
Russian Revolution, 44–45

Salem Witch Trials, 107–9
Sandman, Peter, 61–63
Sargent, Mark, 176
Satan (Lucifer, the Devil): in Bible, 120–21; and Illuminati, 45, 47; as manifestation of evil, 119–20, 121; in millenarian idea, 137, 138
Satanic cult hypothesis, in cattle mutilation epidemic, 195–97
Satanic Panic, 48, 112–14, 115
Schmitt, Harrison, 194
school shootings, as conspiracy, 7
science: how and why it works, 169–71; wrong theories, 168, 180
scientific inquiry: description as method, 169–70, 180–81; and falsifiability, 171–72, 173, 180
scientific reasoning, pillars of, 171–72
scientific theories, 170–71
"screen," meanings of, 67
Scully, Frank, 208
Seattle windshield epidemic, 221–25
secret groups/societies, 40, 42, 47–48. *See also* Illuminati
seductive claim, 14
Segal, Jakob, 85
Segal, Lilli, 85
self-harm in youth, as hoax, 100–101
Semeter, Josh, 220
September 11, 2001 (9/11), 32–33
Shandera, Jaime, 213, 214
Sherwood, John C., 208
shock machine experiment, 118–19
Shtrang, Shippi, 20
Sibley, Mary, 108
Simons, Daniel, 23–24
Sister Thedra, 166. *See also* Martin, Dorothy
smartphones, importance to humans, 66–67
Snippy the horse, 193, 200
Snow, Samuel, 158
social change, 191–92, 197
social media: and disinformation, 80–81, 83, 94–95; and election of 2016 in U.S., 94–95; as incubator, 71, 81; influencers, 78–80; self-harm in youth hoax, 100–101. *See also* virtual information
social sciences, 53, 172–74
soft disclosure, 211
solitary confinement, impact of, 50
souls, and final judgment, 134–35
Soviets and Soviet Union: blue jeans and syphilis, 182–86; in Cold War *vs.* U.S., 16, 92–93, 183–85, 188; communism in, 109, 142, 143–44; and disinformation in U.S., 86–87, 88, 89–94, 231n8; as threat to U.S., 123
Spain, political disinformation, 93
spying on people, CIA project with cats, 2, 3
Stalin, Joseph, 88, 109
Stevens, John, 39
the Storm of QAnon, 147–49
subtext: in cattle mutilation epidemic, 194–95, 197, 199, 201, 202; fleas in blue jeans for syphilis, 185–86; interpretation and in conspiracies, 183, 187, 188–89, 192; in urban legends, 190, 191, 192; in windshield epidemic, 225
sufficient cause, 31
suicide in teenagers, as hoaxes, 101
sunk cost fallacy, 154–55, 158
superstitions, example of, 34
syphilis: and fleas in blue jeans, 182–86; Tuskegee study, 86

Targ, Russell, 18–21, 22, 23
Taylor, Travis, 218, 219
teenagers, 100–101, 191
Teller, Edward, 96
text: analysis and in conspiracies, 183, 186, 187–88, 189, 192; in cattle mutilation epidemic, 194–95, 196, 197, 200–201; fleas in blue jeans for syphilis, 185; in urban legends, 190–91
theory, as term in conspiracy theory, 4–5
TheyLied.ca, 60
thought traps or loops, 173–74, 180
thought-terminating clichés, 8, 164
Tituba (of Salem, MA), 108, 109
tobacco, disinformation on, 78

Todd, John, 47
Tokyo, firebombing of 1945, 118
true conspiracy theory, 5, 6. *See also* conspiracies and conspiracy theories
Truman, President, 214, 215
Trump, Donald, 6, 95; and QAnon, 128, 147, 149, 164
Turkey, political disinformation, 93
Turnbull, Mark, 95
Tuskegee syphilis study, 86
Twining, Nathan, 213

UFOs (Unidentified Flying Objects): cattle mutilation epidemic, 200–201; as conspiracy, 216–18; as contemporary cultural myth, 204–5, 208–11, 215–16, 218, 220; Crash at Aztec hoax, 208; disinformation about, 212–13; failed prophecies, 160–63, 166; Majestic 12 (MJ-12) documents, 213, 214–15, 216, 220; and mutilated horse story, 193, 200; popular books and shows on, 208–11, 212, 214, 216, 217–18; research by citizens, 212, 218; Roswell Incident, 205–9, 214; sources of myth, 205; terminology, 203; testimony of Pentagon insider, 203, 204, 219–20; theories on phenomenon, 201; U.S. government knowledge of, 203, 204, 205, 209, 212–14, 216, 218; videos of, 220
Umbrella Man (Steven Witt), 35
Unidentified Anomalous Phenomena (UAP), 204
United States: election of 2016, 94–95; "enemies within" speech, 110; government conspiracies, 85–86, 198, 224; Manichean conspiratorial views, 122–23; official records and memos, 213–14; pilgrims, 107; secret programs, 198–99, 224
untruths. *See* disinformation
urban legends, description and examples, 189–92
U.S. Air Force, and UFOs, 205–6, 207, 208, 212
U.S. Army, 74, 85, 92–94, 111–12, 199
USS *Maddox*, attack on, 2, 3

vaccination: and autism spectrum disorder (ASD), 34–35, 57; disinformation about, 69–70; resistance to, 56–57; untruths and omission bias, 61–62. *See also* anti-vax community
Van Tassel, George, 201
Vantage Products Corporation, 76
Vietnam War, 2, 3, 198–99
Viganò, Carlo Maria, 128
virtual information: brevity of information, 72–73; evolution as metaphor, 71, 72–73, 74, 76, 77–78; fake posts, 73; Georgia Coffins photo, 75–76. *See also* social media

Wakefield, Andrew, 56–57
Waldeck, Franz von, 141
Wallace, Alfred Russell, 177
The War of the Worlds (radio drama), 88
Warnke, Mike, 46–47
Watkins, Leslie, 210, 211
weather forecasts, 36
Webster, Nesta, 44–45, 48
Weishaupt, Adam, 41, 42, 43, 44, 45
Welch, Joseph, 112
Welles, Orson, 88
West, Kanye, 86
white hats and black hats, 128–29
Wilcox, George, 206
Williams, Abigail, 107
Williamson, George Hunt, 166
Willott, Wayne, 164
windshield epidemic in Seattle, 221–25
witch hunts, 107–9, 112–14
Witt, Steven (the Umbrella Man), 35
world government, as conspiracy, 216–17
WWII, 2, 118

The X-Files (TV show), 209, 218

Žižek, Slavoj, 7
Zoroastrianism and Zarathustra, 134, 138

ANGELO PRATURLON

NATHAN RADKE has degrees in philosophy and sociology from Trent and Lakehead and is the co-author of *Ethical Perspectives* and several chapters of *Conspiracy Theories in American History.* He is co-host of *The Uncover Up* podcast and teaches historical and contemporary conspiracy theories at the post-secondary level and as a regular guest analyst on television and radio. He lives in Toronto, ON.

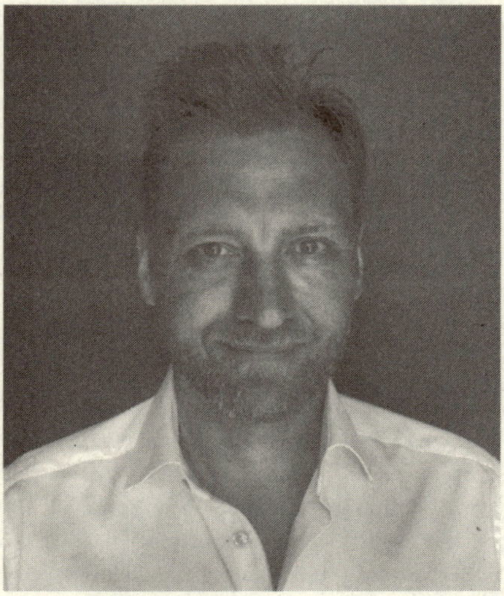

ZOË VON NOSTITZ-TAIT

LEE KUHNLE holds a PhD from York University and teaches on the role of ideology in political society, with a focus on conspiracy theories and the political impact of conspiratorial beliefs. He teaches at Humber Polytechnic and is co-host of *The Uncover Up* podcast and a frequent presenter on television and radio. He lives in Toronto, ON.

Entertainment. Writing. Culture.

ECW is a proudly independent, Canadian-owned book publisher. We know great writing can improve people's lives, and we're passionate about sharing original, exciting, and insightful writing across genres.

Thanks for reading along!

We want our books not just to sustain our imaginations, but to help construct a healthier, more just world, and so we've become a certified B Corporation, meaning we meet a high standard of social and environmental responsibility — and we're going to keep aiming higher. We believe books can drive change, but the way we make them can too.

Certified B Corporation

Being a B Corp means that the act of publishing this book should be a force for good — for the planet, for our communities, and for the people that worked to make this book. For example, everyone who worked on this book was paid at least a living wage. You can learn more at the Ontario Living Wage Network.

eBOUND DIGITAL CERTIFIED

This book is also available as an eBOUND Digital Certification (EDC) ebook. ECW Press's ebooks are screen reader friendly and are built to meet the needs of those who are unable to read standard print due to blindness, low vision, dyslexia, or a physical disability.

This book is printed on FSC®-certified paper. It contains recycled materials, and other controlled sources, is processed chlorine free, and is manufactured using biogas energy.

FSC www.fsc.org MIX Paper | Supporting responsible forestry FSC® C103567

ECW's office is situated on land that was the traditional territory of many nations including the Wendat, the Anishinaabeg, Haudenosaunee, Chippewa, Métis, and current treaty holders the Mississaugas of the Credit. In the 1880s, the land was developed as part of a growing community around St. Matthew's Anglican and other churches. Starting in the 1950s, our neighbourhood was transformed by immigrants fleeing the Vietnam War and Chinese Canadians dispossessed by the building of Nathan Phillips Square and the subsequent rise in real estate value in other Chinatowns. We are grateful to those who cared for the land before us and are proud to be working amidst this mix of cultures.

ecwpress.com